The British
Military Revolution
of the 19th Century

The British Military Revolution of the 19th Century

*"The Great Gun Question"
and the Modernization
of Ordnance and Administration*

DANIEL R. LECLAIR

McFarland & Company, Inc., Publishers
Jefferson, North Carolina

This book has undergone peer review.

ISBN (print) 978-1-4766-7499-5
ISBN (ebook) 978-1-4766-3859-1

LIBRARY OF CONGRESS AND BRITISH LIBRARY
CATALOGUING DATA ARE AVAILABLE

© 2019 Daniel R. LeClair. All rights reserved

No part of this book may be reproduced or transmitted in any form or by any means, electronic or mechanical, including photocopying or recording, or by any information storage and retrieval system, without permission in writing from the publisher.

Front cover: Photograph of Sergeant William Russell, 5th Battalion, Royal Artillery in 1856 by Robert Howlett (Museum of Fine Arts, Boston)

Printed in the United States of America

*McFarland & Company, Inc., Publishers
Box 611, Jefferson, North Carolina 28640
www.mcfarlandpub.com*

To Mrs. Wombat

Table of Contents

Preface	1
Introduction	4
"Pregnant with Disastrous Muddle"	19
"The War Will Not Last a Month"	45
"More Powerful Than the Charge of Cavalry"	71
"Steering Among the Designs of Rival Inventors"	93
"A New Era of Great Guns"	132
An "Epoch of Change and Improvement"?	168
"New Measures Demand New Men"	204
Conclusion: "A Projectile to Be Fired by the Royal Navy"	233
Chapter Notes	237
Bibliography	255
Index	269

Preface

In the second half of the nineteenth century, the British Empire found itself unable to answer what the *Times* termed "the Great Gun Question." Although the phrase originally referred to a dispute between two rival artillery inventors, by the midst of the American Civil War the "question" for many Britons boiled down to an uncomfortable fact: the Empire had fallen behind most major powers in defense technology. Even the rude, backwards United States—disunited and at war with itself—could in 1863 build guns double or even triple the size of the largest possessed by the Royal Navy. The "great gun question," therefore, was less about the size and power of artillery, and much more about the ability of Britain to defend itself against an increasingly more powerful set of opponents.[1]

For six decades—from the Crimean War through the Second Boer War—the Empire struggled to solve this "great gun question": to understand and harness improvements in ordnance and small arms, armor for ship and fortress defense, mechanization of materials production, and the myriad other changes brought about by the ongoing Industrial Revolution. The British public played a surprising but to date unexamined role in these changes, making thousands of suggestions for new weapons and other military material to the civilian-led War Office. In addition, the Victorian era saw a decades-long struggle between that Office and army leaders for control of the country's ground forces, which did not end until reforms of 1904 clearly put all aspects of the military under the Secretary of State for War. An expanding and literate voting population watched this struggle via the press, and put considerable pressure on politicians and the War Office to modernize not only British ordnance but also the military administrative system. The "great gun question," therefore, was as much about weaponry as about who ultimately controlled British military power.

Covering as it does the period between the two great Victorian-era wars, this book fills an important gap in the history of British ordnance development and administration. John Sweetman documented the history of the

Board of Ordnance through its end in 1855, and the story after 1914 is picked up by at least three studies which approach ordnance development from different directions. In 1971, Roy MacCleod and E. Kay Andrews looked at the Board of Invention and Research, appointed to harness scientific efforts for the Royal Navy. Michael Pattison took a similar approach but with army-related weaponry in his 1983 examination of the Munitions Invention Department. Finally, Guy Hartcup expanded such research with his 1988 book, *The War of Invention: Scientific Developments, 1914–18*. As with this project, the picture that emerges from these studies is indeed one of a military procurement and development system that remained unready for the demands that would be made of it in 1915, once the war settled into stalemate and attrition.[2]

Although spanning several decades and many millions of pounds sterling in British weapons expenditure, this project quite literally came to me in a cigar box. In 1992, fellow cartridge-collector Tom Dunn asked what I "specialized" in. Caught a little off guard, I told Tom that at that moment I was really interested in "Boxer" cartridges. Rather than a single piece of drawn metal like modern ammunition, this early cartridge case, adopted by Britain in 1865, used coiled paper and brass foil, an attached metal base, and a multi-piece primer that Boxer is still remembered for here in the United States. Several different military variations existed; I had a few and wanted to "complete the set."

Two years later, Tom handed me a large cigar box *full* of different Boxer-style metal foil cartridges—rifle, pistol, shot shell, and things I had no clue about. Floored, I spent the rest of the day picking out the obviously different (and probably returning several I should have kept, in hindsight!). We later struck a deal, and I returned home with a completely different direction for my collecting interests. But I also had questions. How on earth, I thought, did this easily damaged style of cartridge get so popular in England, when better cases were being made in America? Who was Boxer, and how did he develop his invention? Who else made cartridges like this? Researching such questions in 2010, a weekend visit to the Royal Naval Museum at Portsmouth set me on a different path, as the contrast between HMS *Victory* and HMS *Warrior* suggested a much bigger historical issue. These two warships showcased a true "military revolution" in the nineteenth century, and the longer I studied the documents left by British ordnance committees, the more I became convinced that here was a story worth telling.

Tracking the history of Boxer and the dozens of others that changed British military technology has taken me all over the United States, Great Britain, and via the Internet to many other parts of the world. Along the way I have been privileged to meet some extraordinary people, especially the "three Petes": Peter Davis, Pete de Coux, and Peter Skala, of Australia, Pennsylvania, and South Africa respectively. The first, my business partner and very good friend, died too young in 1997; in 2014, Peter Skala also passed into the ranks of absent companions. Pete de Coux is fortunately still kicking, and I would like to thank both him and his wife Gaye for their many years of friendship and support. Pete gave me some much needed encouragement after Peter Davis's death, without which you might not be reading this today. Charlie Murray, whom I first met when I joined the Texas Cartridge Collectors Association in 1980, has always been very supportive, and I can't thank him and his wife Juanita enough. Another couple that has been of great help is Bill and Beth Woodin. The Woodin Laboratory has been a valuable source of information over the years, and both were always gracious hosts on my occasional visits.[3]

Outside the cartridge collecting community, I must thank Maggie Boxer and her brother Charles, who greatly helped reconstruct the life of the man whose inventions sparked this project. Although most of their contributions must wait for later publication, it was very exciting to meet living relatives of someone whose history I have become so familiar with. Special thanks also go to William S. Curtis of the Crimean War Research Society, who helped steer me into some useful information related to the weapons of that war; Dr. Patrick Marder, for providing a very useful paper on the French ordnance system under Napoleon III; Paul Evans of the Royal Artillery Library, who put up with a barrage of email questions regarding Boxer's career and other items, and Stuart Ivinson at the Royal Armouries Museum Library. Finally, the Murray Miller Foundation provided much-needed financial assistance that allowed me to conduct research in Britain, for which I am very grateful.

There are dozens of other people who deserve thanks for their help along the way, but space—and my faulty memory—prohibits me from naming them all directly. These include cartridge collectors across the globe, as well as many people at the University of Houston, including my graduate school advisor, Karl Ittmann. The staff of the British National Archives in Kew deserves special mention; their professionalism never ceases to amaze me. I also owe a great debt of gratitude to my family for their never-ending love and support during the writing of this. And, finally, to my father, whose foot-square plank of rough pine with glued-on bullets and cartridge cases scrounged as a kid started my fascination with small-arms ammunition. You didn't live long enough to see this get published, Dad, but I hope I've done you proud.

Introduction

In 1854, Britons cheered in droves as their country declared war against Russia in defense of the Ottoman Empire. Allied with France—a deadly enemy only forty years before—Britain scraped together a hastily recruited and armed expeditionary force to fight "the first war in history ... brought about by the pressure of the press and by public opinion." Public opinion, via the press, also followed British forces into battle, confident of a quick and glorious end reminiscent of the Battle of Waterloo in 1815. Within months, however, that same press shocked readers with reports of devastating catastrophe. For a nation that had just recently celebrated England's industrial prowess at the Great Exhibition of 1851, the war showcased a military machine hobbled by technology and leadership decades out of date. While concerned Britons responded with an outpouring of suggestions for improved weaponry, government reformers began overhauling the nation's military administration system. Both efforts combined to see responsibility for weapons research and development pass to an entirely new entity, the "Ordnance Select Committee" (OSC). For the next fifty years, the OSC and its successors acted as the supervising authority over a revolution in military technology, balancing army and navy interests against the efforts of inventors and politicians to influence decisions in the development of modern weaponry.[1]

The story, however, is not one of unqualified success. Driven by crisis as much as scientific inquiry, throttled by a parsimonious financial system yet goaded on by public interest, Britain's nineteenth-century military revolution produced weapons capable of winning the brush-fire colonial wars that the country found itself involved in throughout the second half of the nineteenth century—but usually after the war *du jour* was over. In addition, the army often failed to address issues of logistics, training, and tactics regarding its new weapons to make them truly effective. Finally, despite millions of pounds and hundreds of thousands of man-hours expended in modernization, Britain found itself as unprepared for a major European conflict in 1914 as it did in 1854. This, then, is as much a story of a revolution missed, as of one that took place.

Military Revolutions: Theory and Debate

Michael Roberts introduced the idea of a "military revolution" as a discrete historical time-frame in a lecture presented at Belfast in January 1955. In it, he argued that tactical changes in European military practices from 1560 to 1660 increased the scale of warfare, requiring larger and larger armies to ensure victory. In essence, he claimed that military innovations introduced during this century laid the groundwork for the modern European state system. Roberts's lecture and the half-century of debate that followed are significant for many reasons, two of which are important here. First, his work is an early example of academic or "new" military history. In a move away from the "classic" military history concerned with battles and tactics, Roberts positioned a martial subject in the larger story of the human world, a "contextualization of the history" of military topics. Although the term "new military history" had yet to be coined, Roberts's lecture showed that military historians could link their studies to the broader issues of the impact militaries had on societies other than through combat. As historian Clifford Rogers noted, "the active and wide-ranging debate" ignited by Roberts's theory "brought the explanatory value of military history to the attention of the historical community as a whole."[2]

That debate is the second reason it remains significant, which continues to this day. On one side are historians that clearly accept the notion of a "military revolution" as a distinct period in history, led chiefly by Geoffrey Parker—who, coincidentally, had Roberts as an external examiner for his dissertation. Parker continued to explore and expand the concept, pushing Roberts's original boundaries by two centuries. On the other side are historians such as Jeremy Black, who questioned how anything that occurred over the course of centuries could be called "revolutionary." "Military change arose from the absolutist state rather than causing it," Black wrote, and occurred in a fashion that left relatively little impact on the social structure of European nations. While recognizing that military innovations took place in the late fifteenth through the seventeenth centuries, Black argued that "no military revolution occurred in post-medieval Europe." The same constraints on warfare in the fifteenth century—slow communications, animal-drawn transportation, disease, winter, the short range and massive smoke of black-powder weaponry—remained in force until the nineteenth century.[3]

If short duration, military innovation, social impact and constraint removal are the hallmarks of a "true" military revolution, one certainly occurred during the nineteenth century, as numerous scholars, including Black, have argued.[4] As with any group of historians collected around a central theme, there is considerable dissent, especially over the starting point. A case can be, and has been, made for the French Revolutionary and Napoleonic wars, with mass conscription and the dramatic increase in the scale of battle, as the start of "modern war." All of the four hallmarks noted above may be seen at work between 1792 and 1815, although the area of military innovation is by far the weakest. The French revolutionary armies certainly introduced several advances, refined by Napoleon and gradually copied by other nations. These included more effective infantry tactics, the development of the combined-arms division, and force concentration (particularly artillery) at specific points on the battlefield. The combatants of this age, however, all used technology unchanged for decades. *Ancién regime* weaponry—the bayoneted musket, cavalry sabre, and smooth-bore cannon—had, tactically and technically, been perfected almost as far as they could go. All sides in the Napoleonic Wars fought under the same constraints that had limited combat since the Thirty Years' War.[5]

Weaponry began to change after Waterloo, but what remained stagnant were the military machines of Europe. With the exception of the rifled musket, French, British, and Russian armies fought in the Crimea with essentially the same technology, tactics, and in some instances the same officers that had served in the Napoleonic Wars. This, in turn, imposed the same constraints in 1854 as existed in 1815, and gave no clear advantage to any side. The British Army found itself particularly handicapped. Parliament, intent on reducing government debt incurred after two decades of war, drastically cut military expenditures over the course of forty years of peace, only begrudgingly approving fund increases during war scares. In addition, what actions the British army did find itself in prior to 1854 were small colonial wars, usually against technologically inferior opponents. Although historian Hew Strachan has argued that civilian outsiders and "many half-pay and retired officers ... [turned] their talents" towards military reform, "the Army thought small because it fought small." Reforms occurred at the regimental level, "to meet the demands of imperial garrisoning and home policing." Military administration remained divided between civil and uniformed authorities, a split that "prevented the formulation of a coherent military policy or a school of strategic thought."[6]

The British Military Revolution

Strachan, perhaps more than any other historian, has challenged the notion of a moribund British army devoid of any reform effort before 1854.[7] The Crimean War, however, marks a clear starting point for Britain's military revolution. The war acted as both a catalyst and accelerant, melding public interest in military subjects with the reforming spirit of the ongoing governmental revolution. This in turn combined new mechanical knowledge from the Industrial Revolution and an entrepreneurial spirit eager to tap into the military market to produce an explosion of new ideas for military technology. To this mix must also be added a distinctly British element: an army increasingly focused on colonial defense and dependent on a tight-fisted Parliament for the resources required to perform this mission. As a result, the British experience in the nineteenth century military revolution differed greatly from other Western powers.[8]

The common component for all participants in this time period is the evidence of two of the four hallmarks of a "true" military revolution: innovation and short duration. In less than forty years, the West moved from *ancién regime* to *fin de siècle* technology: smokeless-powder repeating rifles, machine guns, and quick-loading artillery. Coupled with "civilian" technologies, this removed many of the constraints that limited warfare before 1854. The telegraph, and later the telephone, greatly facilitated communications; steam-powered ships and railroads improved transportation and expanded operating areas of military forces. Advances in food preservation, water purification, and medical technologies helped overcome the ravages of disease and the limits imposed by weather. Britain and its imperial competitors could send their armies where they wanted, when they wanted, with a much higher expectation of effectiveness and much lower potential for non-combat casualties than ever before.

Where the British experience diverges from the U.S. and the rest of Europe is in the social aspects of its military revolution. Beginning with the Reform Act of 1832, the British electorate became successively larger over the course of the nineteenth century. By 1885, sixty percent of British males had the right to vote—still far behind France, Germany, and the United States, but a vast improvement for a nation that clung tenaciously to aristocratic tradition. A growing newspaper industry, boosted by changes in printing technology and the repeal of the stamp duty in 1855, helped to inform this expanding voter base. It also gave editors and readers alike a venue for expressing concerns over military issues. Hans Speier has defined public opinion to be "matters of concern to the nation freely and publicly expressed by men outside the government who claim a right that their opinions should influence or determine" government action.[9] Given such a definition and the ongoing digitization of the British Library's newspaper collection, the Victorian press is a rich source of material that illustrates public concerns and opinions regarding military matters in this era. British voters also spent most of the second half of the century perpetually *fearing* a major European war, but not actively *involved* in one. Coupled with ongoing campaigns in various corners of Victoria's expanding empire, this meant that Britons of all stripes took interest in military matters, which the papers avidly fed. Although a lack of scientific polling methods makes measuring the degree of this interest difficult, it is clear from the range of books, periodicals, and newspaper articles related to weapons technology that a strong market existed for such information.

Public interest meant political action, and the dissolution of the old Board of Ordnance represented the first of several attempts to deal with what historian Correlli Barnett termed the "disastrous muddle" in British military administration.[10] The departments that fielded, fed, and financed its land forces had come together haphazardly over the course of decades, if not centuries, and consisted of ill-defined and conflicting spheres of military and civilian control. Like a badly-mixed cocktail, however, the system could not be unmade. Both military and political leaders proved reluctant to throw it out altogether, despite the clamor of the press and the recommendations of several committees appointed to study the matter. Not until the near-disaster of the Second Boer War at the turn of the century did government finally replace the muddle with a modernized military administrative system. Public interest also meant public involvement, as witnessed by the thousands of inventors who attempted to interest the British military in their ideas. Both military and civilian readers kept abreast of technology through popular magazines and newspapers, rather than old channels of patronage and connection. Even British ordnance committees kept track of new technology via the same media, and often used advertisements to make wants known to the public. In short, the social impact of this military revolution out-shadows any previous era by an enormous—and measurable—degree.

This measurability is the unique aspect of the British military revolution. Although France, Germany and the United States proved fertile ground for inventors, Britain's lead in industrialization gave it an edge in technological innovation. This is quantifiable not only in the number of patents issued for military ideas in general, but also in the number of proposals made to the War Office. The committees responsible for evaluating such suggestions compiled their findings into quarterly *Abstracts of Proceedings* with indexed lists of inventors, no matter how ludicrous the idea. Indeed, some of the proposals submitted to the War Office demonstrate a distinctive eccentricity for which Englishmen are popularly known. Regardless of the utility of the suggestion, the evaluating committees went to great lengths to record who brought what to the War Office from 1857 to 1907, along with the disposition of the proposal. Although much of the source documentation was lost to German bombs in World War II, the quarterly *Abstracts* did survive. These records illustrate a pattern of deliberate, methodical consideration of what defined a useful weapons system and the degree to which the British military allowed involvement by outsiders interested in marketing new weapons. Above all, the detail provided allows the compilation of useful statistics by which public participation in the military revolution may be measured.

Studying Society Through Technological Change

Despite the important role played by the public in Britain's military revolution, very little has been written regarding it or the evaluation committees. Although numerous works have been published concerning the hardware—the cannon, small arms, and other equipment made by the Royal Arsenal—most of these have been written by or for the weapons enthusiast. While valuable assets to the military historian, such works do not explore the deeper questions of what influenced Britain to make the technological choices it did, or did not, during this period. The evolution of the War Office as an institution is also a topic that has been overlooked. Only two histories appear to have been written, a 1914 work by Capt. Owen Wheeler, and a 1935 publication by Hampden Gordon as part of the "Whitehall Series" of books on the "great Departments of State." Although John Sweetman produced a good summary of the Board of Ordnance's history before the Crimean War and its expiration "with scarcely a whimper" in 1855, his examination of army administrative reforms mentions very little regarding the Ordnance Department afterwards. Indeed, few secondary sources exist regarding the activities of the Royal Arsenal, the great complex of government factories at Woolwich that produced the majority of British military supplies in this era. Only one history of the Arsenal has been written, a weighty two-volume set by O.F.G. Hogg that is concerned more with the physical buildings (and the occasional cow killed during artillery practice), and less with the activities of the tens of thousands of soldiers and civilians employed there over the course of the Victorian era.[11]

Historians of the British army in the nineteenth century such as Gwyn Harries-Jenkins and Edward Spiers have been very successful in using the "new military history" approach to position their subject within the larger context of Victorian history. Their work, however, concentrates more on army reform efforts in areas such as recruitment, training, and promotion within line units (the infantry and cavalry) as well as the changing relationship between the military and British society.[12] The new technologies that the army struggled with, however, are only mentioned in passing: changes occurred, were important, but seemingly "happened" on their own accord. There are exceptions, of course; the idea of technology as a force multiplier in the colonial wars, in particular, has been the object of several studies.[13] On the whole, however, the technological history of Britain's military revolution is still a subject left unexamined by academics.

"Technology," despite popular conceptions, represents much more than hardware; it is the knowledge used by humans to shape and interpret the world around them. It is also the most visible expression of any given culture; in essence, technology embodies culture.[14] As a subgenre of historical studies, technological history has long been established. As with "new" military historians, technology historians seek to position their subjects in the larger context of human affairs. The works of Merritt Roe Smith, John Ellis, Dennis Showalter and others have taken this "socio-technical" approach in the study of military technology, as will this project.[15] Focusing on the activities of the ordnance committees and their relationship with the government and public, therefore, shows the evolution of military technology and the development processes at work in mid-nineteenth-century Britain.[16] Such an approach stresses the complex and intertwined relationship between people and technology, and illustrates the influence this relationship had on British culture and society.

There are a number of components of socio-technical history visible in the records of British ordnance committees. One is the very cyclical nature of the inventor-adopter relationship, evident in the back-and-forth between the Ordnance Select Committee (OSC) and Sir William Armstrong, an ironmonger turned arms maker and inventor of Britain's first successful breechloading rifled cannon. As the *Abstracts* show, however, the development of any new weapon system required considerable participation by many individuals to work out the details. Few proposals received clearance for testing; for those that did, the ordnance committees oversaw experiments, consulted with the inventor, sought the input of the various heads of Arsenal departments, and occasionally made suggestions themselves, before finally approving an item's adoption into service. Complex systems such as ordnance required changes in a wide variety of materials, such as ammunition, gun carriages, handling equipment, and so forth. Although suggestions for the same did come from Armstrong himself in many cases, hundreds of other individuals brought forward proposals and recommended improvements, all of which the ordnance committees had to consider. Finally, in addition to evaluating such ideas, the committees also monitored the performance of the system in the far corners of Britain's expanding empire, including reports of accidents and even resistance to change from local unit commanders.[17]

Another component of socio-technical history documented in the *Abstracts* is the degree of participation by civilians in the proposal and production of new weaponry. While private inventors had a long history of bringing ideas before the old Board of Ordnance, the Crimean War unleashed a flood of proposals from an inventive and entrepreneurial public. Subsequent conflicts and war scares also prompted submissions of new inventions to solve perceived shortcomings in military gear. Mostly unsolicited, these proposals passed unfiltered to the ordnance committees, who spent considerable effort weeding the absurd from the useful. Statistical analysis of the *Abstracts* shows a pattern that corresponds with British militarization having "accelerated in the 1850s, declined in the 1860s and 1870s, [and] returned with a vengeance in the 1880s." The records also show, however, that public participation tapered off to a trickle in the late 1890s, as weapons systems grew more complex and the British military industrial facilities increased their own research abilities. Regardless, public participation in harnessing the power of the ongoing Industrial Revolution is a key component of British militarization before 1914.[18]

Like civilian technologies, "miltech" (to use the industry buzzword) is open to negotiation between social elements seeking to influence the process of change. Military technology also embodies a society's ability to project force for whatever purpose is deemed important—thus expanding the number of social elements interested in its development. The ordnance committees, as the gatekeepers of British military technology, filled an essential negotiator role between uniformed and civilian elements of British society and the changes made possible by the ongoing Industrial Revolution, and their choices reflect the embodiment of British culture in its military technology. The formation of the OSC in 1855 also signaled the rise of what David Edgerton has termed the "warfare state," a "pioneer of modern, technologically focused warfare ... operated not just by bureaucrats but also by technicians."[19] The creation of a professional committee of technicians that answered to the bureaucrats of the War Office puts the origins of this "warfare state" far earlier than even Edgerton argues.

The ordnance committees also wrestled with increasingly difficult priority-of-invention issues unresolved by the patent laws of the time. Despite an overhaul in 1852, the Patent Office lacked the capability (and funding) to verify originality of patent applications.[20] Numerous inventors came forward claiming infringement of their ideas, and the committees delved, sometimes deeply, into their own archives investigating such issues. Despite an institutionalized desire for a military at the least possible cost, the committees did occasionally, at times even generously, find in favor of the aggrieved inventor (or, to often, his estate). They also judged new materials on their potential worth to the service, balanced against the cost of royalties or potential "embarrassment to Government" in cases of infringement. Lastly, the committees helped develop new rules regarding employees of the Royal Arsenal "manufacturing departments," eventually prohibiting the obtainment of patents and solicitation of reward money for work done in the course of their duties.

British borders did not limit the ideas considered by the ordnance committees, illustrating the growing importance of the international arms industry. Many foreign inventors stepped forward, eager to tap into the British military market and disregarding any issues about trading with a potential enemy. British inventors, in turn, were not hesitant to do the same; many threatened to take their inventions to "other powers" if the War Office declined to purchase them. The committees also showed no favor to British inventors over others, preferring only that a product prove superior to competing designs and could be licensed for manufacture by the Royal Arsenal at a reasonable cost. In addition, the committees kept a close eye on foreign military technology, via news articles, visiting-officer reports, or exchange of recently adopted weapons systems with other nations.

The Victorian Military-Industrial Complex

The *Abstracts* also complement a growing body of study regarding British military and industrial relations in the second half of the nineteenth century, a relationship that had many rough spots both before and well after the Crimean War. Prior to that conflict, the army relied on the "gun trade" for iron ordnance and infantry weapons. The heavy weapons came from large iron works such as Mersey Steel and Iron and the Carron Company, famous for developing the short-barreled carronade used by the British navy in the French Revolutionary and Napoleonic Wars. Small arms and edged weapons were still produced by hundreds of specialty artisanal shops, mostly located

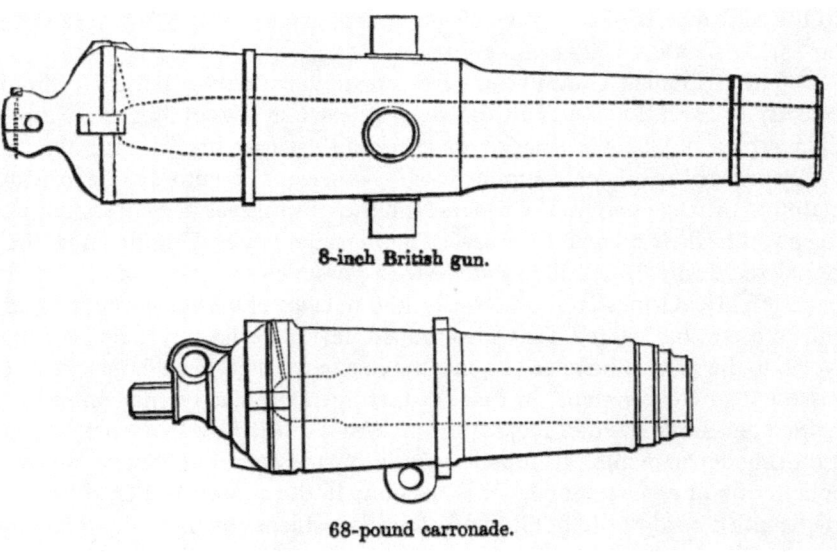

8-inch British gun.

68-pound carronade.

A comparison of British smooth-bore ordnance. The 8-inch gun (top) uses round "trunnions" centered and to either side to mount guns to their carriages, and allow pivot for elevation changes. Below is a short-barreled "carronade," first cast (and named) by the Carron Foundry of Scotland in 1779. Shorter and lighter than guns of similar bore size, they used loops underneath and at the rear for both mounting and elevation (William Greener, *Gunnery in 1858* [London: Smith, Elder and Co., 1858], 114, 116).

in Birmingham. Much as they had done for centuries, these shops produced all of the individual pieces of weapons—stock, barrel, screws, locks, etc.—which were then passed to other shops to be fitted together by hand. This gave the private trade a degree of flexibility that allowed it to cope well in producing weapons for the African, sporting, and military markets. The stress of the Crimean War, however, led to a significant change in the relation between government and the "gun trade." Frustration with slow delivery of the new Enfield rifle, for example, led to the establishment of the Royal Small Arms Factory (RSAF) in 1855. This in turn led several leading Birmingham gun makers to band together to form the Birmingham Small Arms Company (BSA) in 1861, the first private English firm to produce small arms by machine.[21] Public funding helped Armstrong establish Elswick Ordnance in 1859; once the Arsenal reorganized to make iron ordnance on its own, however, Government cut its support for Elswick. Both private companies, therefore, came into being because of government action, which also forced both to go abroad in search of new markets. Despite the launch of these two companies, over the next decades the War Office relied heavily on its own facilities for the manufacture of military hardware. RSAF historians Tim Putnam and Daniel Weinbren wrote that "in establishing a fully mechanized small arms factory, Government had wished to create a supply which could be turned on or off at will." This holds true for the manufacturing departments at Woolwich. Given the military budgetary process, in which monies were voted on a yearly basis and anything not spent returned to the Treasury, having its own manufacturing facilities meant that the War Office could better control arms spending. The factories also gave it the means to estimate costs of production, a useful tool for controlling the costs for materials obtained on contract.[22]

Such information came with a price, however. Royal Arsenal officials succumbed to the same "endemic disease" that plagues modern bureaucrats: "the irresistible urge to expand a department's size, budget and authority by asserting control over more and more key missions and initiatives."[23] The Royal Arsenal continued to grow and expand as it added additional capabilities over the course of the second half of the nineteenth century; its acreage at Woolwich alone doubled while its work force jumped by the thousands.[24] While it acted as an effective development facility and as a check on prices from private industry, the Arsenal also competed with that same industry for skilled workers. Peacetime reliance on these Crown facilities also gave them a near-monopoly on increasingly complex technologies, but also meant that British private industry could not rapidly meet emergency wartime requirements—a capability the War Office long counted on. In addition, the War Office tended to use its various ordnance committees for weapons development, rather than just evaluation. This assumed a high level of technical knowledge on the part of the committee members, but left the body as a whole open to personal prejudices and opinions on technical matters. Rather than simply license the best form of infantry weapon available, for example, small arms committees consistently took a "we-can-do-it-better" approach. This in turn meant every new British rifle took years to go from initial design to adopted weapon. By contrast, a U.S. evaluation board appointed in 1872 to select that nation's first purpose-designed breech-loader had a final decision within a year. Such foot-dragging on the part of the British meant that both the Crimean and Second Boer Wars caught their infantry not only with too few rifles, but also in the midst of a changeover in their primary weapon.[25]

Finally, Parliamentary cheese-paring greatly complicated British weapons programs. Unlike France, Britain required hopeful inventors to self-fund the testing and initial development of any proposal brought before the War Office, due in part to a constant parade of charlatans who occasionally did get the better of the Board of Ordnance. Such a policy kept speculative, immature, or absurd projects from consuming scarce public funds, but it also strangled worthy projects. Much more importantly, it contributed to the termination of Britain's first effort at breech-loading artillery. Had the country persisted in perfecting Armstrong's gun designs, the nation would have been several years ahead of its Continental counterparts in fielding an accurate and fast-firing weapons system. Instead, the Armstrong project suffered from bureaucratic jealousy on the part of the Arsenal, Parliamentary reluctance to spend money on the military, conservative military thinking, and imperfect technology. Britain therefore retained wrought iron rifled muzzle-loaders well beyond when other world powers had moved on to steel breech-loaders.

A Successful—or Failed—Revolution?

Although the *Abstracts of Proceedings* left by the various ordnance committees can provide historians with considerable detail regarding the technology debates of the day, such information must naturally be combined with data from other sources. Extensive use has been made throughout this project of newspaper articles and "letters-to-the-editor," for example, to build the argument for public interest in all aspects of the British military. In addition, the official reports and minutes of testimony recorded by the various committees appointed to study British military administration have also been examined, as have relevant Parliamentary debates. What emerges from this mass of information is a record of mixed success in coping with the rapid changes in military technology by successive Victorian governments, as well as a clear failure to resolve the "disastrous muddle" in military administration before the Second Boer War.

Such mixed results were not experienced by the British alone; all large militaries had to grapple with the problems of rearmament as the Industrial Revolution spawned new technologies. Improved metallurgy and construction techniques allowed gunmakers to build rifled ordnance of immense size, made accurate by improved sighting instruments and recoil-absorbing gun carriages, and forever altering the ship-versus-shore debate on coastal defense. Generals struggled with changes in tactics and logistics brought by the faster-firing breech-loading rifle, and argued over the value of rudimentary forms of machine guns then under development. Decisions regarding armaments, however, were affected by much more than cold, rational choices based on the best available weaponry. Most major European powers as well as the United States adopted some plan for the conversion of their huge stocks of muzzle-loading infantry weapons, for example. Conversions were cheap, expedient, and easy to sell to budget-conscious governments while ordnance officers considered the question of the best form of rifle for the future. Battlefield experience also played a considerable role in technology decisions. The French, satisfied with the performance of their new rifled muzzle-loaders against the Austrians in 1859, chose to retain their bronze field-pieces well past their prime. The Prussians, greatly dismayed by the performance of their field artillery in 1866 in their own war with Austria, chose to completely rearm with Krupp steel breech-loaders firing improved shells.[26] The two different national choices became immediately apparent in the battlefields of 1870, when Prussian guns overwhelmed their French opponents.

Britain, on the other hand, had a different set of decision points at work regarding rearmament, including its own battlefield experiences. Although involved in constant campaigns around the world through the entirety of Victoria's reign, only two wars—the Crimean and Second Boer Wars—proved large enough to seriously strain Britain's military capabilities. In addition, British field artillery decisions were driven more by the need for simple yet strong weapons—a lesson continually reinforced by campaign experiences in India, beginning with the Mutiny of 1857. A long overseas supply line also presented complicated logistics issues for remote outposts, meaning that improvements in the multifarious components of an artillery piece might be weeks or months *en route*. Both were contributing factors to the retention of rifled muzzle-loading guns by the Victorian military well beyond the point when other nations had adopted better weapons.

In addition, the social aspect of British military administration also affected technology decisions in this era as the War Office struggled to transition from an *ancién régime* to a more modern model. The chief obstacle to such a transition remained Prince George, Second Duke of Cambridge and Commander-in-Chief of the British army. Although he served in the Crimean War, on his assumption of the post in 1856 the Duke brought little practical experience to the office. He also felt that the relationship between the Crown and Horse Guards, the headquarters of the army, "could not be too strong or too close."[27] Such a relationship would be directly threatened by the Cardwell reforms of 1870, which made the Commander-in-Chief subordinate to the civilian Secretary of State for War. Coupled with the Duke's thirty-nine year occupation of the post and an increasingly conservative approach to military matters, Cambridge proved an effective damper on reform efforts until his retirement in 1895.

Perhaps the biggest weakness suffered by Britain, and one that gravely affected all aspects of its military, was Government's insistence on running the War Office as a peacetime establishment. As with other departments of the bureaucracy, this put emphasis on efficiency and frugality rather than preparedness for war.[28] Such treatment stemmed from a political reaction to the myriad social, technological and political changes in action from the middle of the century on. As detailed by H.C.G. Matthew, most British politicians felt they could maintain political, and hence social, stability in the nation through the proper balance of direct and indirect taxation, which impacted different strata of society. Although the Conservatives and Liberals approached the question from different angles, both subscribed to the basic tenets of Gladstonian finance. These included a "steady surplus of income over expenditure," "relief of the people" through lower indirect taxes, and a reduction of the income tax. Such goals could only be only accomplished by either redefining the qualifications for paying the income tax, or reducing government spending. The Reform Act of 1867 and the extension of the franchise in Scotland and Ireland in 1868 accomplished the former, but the latter involved reductions in the two major expenditures of public money: defense spending and the national debt. Rather than decrease the latter, Government throughout the nineteenth century concentrated on cutting both military and naval spending. These efforts helped perpetuate the "disastrous muddle" despite the best efforts of British military reformers, and evidence of this continued confusion is shown throughout the *Abstracts* and related documents.[29]

The personal characters of the men involved in decisions about military technology also made a difference. Blessed with the talents of energetic Royal Artillery officers such as Edward M. Boxer and civilians such as Frederick Abel, Britain made tremendous strides in its weaponry in the first decade-and-a-half after the Crimean War. The actions and opinions of others, however, cost Britain its early lead in ordnance technology. Gen. Sir John Adye, appointed Director of Artillery in 1870, was one of a number of artillery and naval officers who argued for the retention of wrought iron rifled muzzle-loading artillery in spite of the French battlefield experiences against Prussian steel breech-loaders. Secretary of State for War Hugh Childers doomed the

Enfield-Martini program with his insistence on retaining the single-shot Martini action, when other countries were investing in repeating rifles. Such demands and opinions retarded the progress of British armaments after the dissolution of the OSC, until a fatal accident aboard HMS *Thunderer* aroused considerable public debate about the state of British weaponry in 1879.

As with the Industrial Revolution, the military revolution of the nineteenth century saw changes in weapons technology grouped in waves. By 1870, "a new period of great guns" had transformed the world's major powers as the first wave crested. Although the rate of proposals put before the ordnance committees dropped during the 1870s, military technological change continued, driven by government research, civilian inventors, and "a state system ... clearly bent toward war and bound to live in constant preparedness for it." Taking off again in the mid–1880s, a second wave saw many of the components of modern warfare adopted or being perfected by British weapons designers. By 1897—the last year of the published *Abstracts* for the Ordnance Committee—the British army had adopted the magazine rifle, the Maxim machine gun, and steel breech-loading artillery, tools that ensured its battlefield supremacy in one of the last of its colonial wars, the 1898 reconquest of the Sudan. It would seem, then, that most if not all the old constraints on warfare had finally been removed.[30]

The British public did not have long to celebrate, however. A scant year later, an expeditionary force sent to pacify the Boers in South Africa ran in to a rude surprise—an enemy not armed with swords and spears, but the latest in European firepower. For the public, it was a scandal reminiscent of 1854, with "almost all aspects of the British military system found wanting in a war against 50,000 farmers." The early stages of the war made clear that the nation's primary restriction on warfare remained an internal one: the "disastrous muddle" that still existed in a "military administration that had never been designed, but which had grown piecemeal, with piecemeal demolitions and re-building, ever since 1660." It also triggered the third wave of the British military revolution, which eventually gave the army quick-firing artillery and a redesigned infantry rifle. More significantly, Government finally threw out the flawed administrative system rather than try to repair it one more time. The reforms that emerged from post-war investigations led to a drastic overhaul in the War Office and army leadership from top to bottom. Changes included the elimination of the antiquated post of Commander-in-Chief (C-in-C), establishment of an Army Council to unify policy decisions and a general staff to assist in battlefield ones, and reorganizations of subordinate departments. Initiated by the Esher Committee of 1904 and furthered by Richard Haldane, who assumed the post of War Secretary in 1906, such reforms produced a peacetime army "gripped with a sense of professional purpose" and designed to take the field in Europe within fifteen days—

a capability unheard of for the Victorian army. Citing Brig. Gen. J.E. Edmonds, historian Edward Spiers wrote that "in every respect the Expeditionary Force in 1914 was incomparably the best trained, best organized, and best equipped British Army which ever went forth to war"—a far cry from the disastrously ill-prepared force sent to the Crimea sixty years earlier.[31]

In terms of technology, administration, and the ability to project power outside of Europe, the British military revolution succeeded. Where it failed, however, was in preparing the British military—indeed the entire country—for the totality of modern warfare, despite what should have been among the lessons taught by the American Civil War. Without conscription and over-reliant on the Royal Arsenal for weaponry, Britain had no means for rapidly assembling an army the size of potential Continental opponents, and could not arm one if it did. Instead, in the case of a large-scale war in Europe, Britain planned to play the naval power, using its small expeditionary force to assist where needed—"the traditional and ever-hopeful view" that a Continental war might be resolved without too much cost to the British taxpayer.[32] It was a plan that nearly produced disastrous results in World War I.

Regardless of how one views the success or failure of the British military revolution, the records of public participation in weapons development during this period offers researchers much to study. For the military and technology historian, they tell a story of incredible change in Britain's ability to project power and influence neighbors, driven in large part by public interest. For the social historian, they document important and incessant negotiations that occurred within a society undergoing a period of radical technological upheaval. For the British historian, the records illustrate a dichotomy of success and failure, inertia and change, which occurred as the Empire found itself wrenched into a new era where the old, understood solutions to technological problems no longer applied, where an island nation could no longer hide behind the wooden walls of its Navy. For historians focused on colonial or imperial history, they showcase the technologies that allowed Britain to control so much of the non–European world. In short, the military revolution launched in 1854 is a critical part of modern British history.

"Pregnant with Disastrous Muddle"

The British army that had developed over the centuries reflected two competing ideologies. Many Britons historically feared a powerful standing army, beholden to the monarch and which might again challenge Parliament. At the same time, the nation needed to defend the home Isles—and a growing overseas empire—against Continental neighbors equipped with such armies. Into the nineteenth century, the British military and its administrative system embodied these fundamentally opposite viewpoints. Indeed, the British "Army" of the Victorian era cannot be referred to in the same sense as the U.S. Army can; no such formal institution existed. Instead, Parliament annually authorized a standing army through the Mutiny Act, which gave permission for whatever size body of troops had been agreed on for the year, but never referred to the "army" as a distinct entity.[1] Any given British expeditionary force sent abroad existed *ad hoc*, built from a collection of independent regiments of infantry and cavalry, with detachments of Royal Artillery and Engineers as needed. Although nominally under one commander when in the field, officers of the independent branches—artillery, engineers, supply and medical—still answered to their service commanders in England.

In the same manner, the military administrative "system" also consisted of a patchwork collection of offices with overlapping—and often competing—duties and priorities. Built and extended as needed, by 1854 it "remained much what it had been under [Queen] Anne": an *ancien régime* bureaucracy that lacked any centralized directing authority and highly resistant to change. What reforms that had taken place occurred to individual parts, never to the system as a whole. Such a situation created a military "pregnant with disastrous muddle" that only worked under strong, experienced, and well-connected generals such as Marlboro and Wellington.[2] Unfortunately for the Crimean expeditionary force, its commander, Lord Raglan, lacked such characteristics. The muddle simply overwhelmed him.

By 1854, an additional factor came into play regarding Britain's military: public opinion and interest in things military. The Reform Act of 1832 expanded the size of the eligible voter pool from 400,000 to 650,000, and the number steadily increased to over a million by 1850. The Act began the dissolution of the old political system that had existed since the reign of George III, moving instead to a modern party-based one that continued to develop into the 1870s.[3] As the franchise expanded, the opinions of the new and mostly middle-class voting public became more important. Driven in large part by an expanding newspaper industry and fueled by tales of battlefield prowess in the Napoleonic Wars, this opinion not only pushed for war with Russia, but also for change in the army on many different levels. Although reluctant to actually put on a uniform, civilians at large enjoyed the spectacle of a well-turned-out military parade, the power displayed by the forges of the Royal Arsenal, and British military industry arrayed at the Great Exhibition of 1851. Mechanically-inclined Britons also sent hundreds of proposals to the Board of Ordnance for improvements in weapons and supplies they were sure would give British forces an edge in battle.

To explore this complicated relationship between the army, the public, and the changes unleashed by the Crimean War, some background is required. This chapter lays out the state of British military administration before the war, as well as the political and military restraints on modernization. It also investigates forms of public participation in military affairs, and in particular how the military responded to the submission of new ideas. Finally, it examines the mechanisms the British military used to examine new technologies for possible adoption into the service. All of these aspects of British military administration would come under close scrutiny as a result of the Crimean War.

Divided Against Itself: British Military Administration Before 1854

In 1849, *Blackwood's Edinburgh Magazine*, in reporting the opening of Parliament for the season, described the civil departments of Britain's armed forces as split between "army, ordnance, and navy."[4] Telling in and of itself, *Blackwood's* description was also far too simplistic. Unlike the Royal Navy, whose administration fell solely to the Navy Board, the British army by 1854 labored under the direction of *six* different entities, divided between those with direct and indirect control. The latter included the Home Office, which had approval authority over many military matters, control of the militia when reformed in 1852, and responsibility for "general military questions relating to Great Britain." It also included the Treasury, who approved military expenditure and controlled transport and provisioning via the Commissariat Department. Finally, the Secretary of State for War and Colonies answered to Parliament, in theory, for the general conduct of the army as well as operations during wartime. The Secretary's office also determined the size of the force to be authorized by the annual Mutiny Act.[5]

The three departments that shared direct administrative control of the army included the civilian Secretary-at-War, the military Commander-in-Chief, and the mixed-breed Ordnance Department. The Secretary-at-War, a Member of the House of Commons, answered to Parliament in order to "control the expenditure of the army in the interests of the public purse." He also dealt with questions related to pay, pensions, interactions between military units and the civilian population, and had financial control of the Medical Department.[6] Both he and the Commander-in-Chief (C-in-C) held offices in the Horse Guards building, then headquarters for the British army. The latter officer, however, answered not to Parliament but directly to the monarch. The C-in-C held responsibility for the military operations of the army at home, as well as promotions and questions of discipline for the infantry, cavalry, and Medical Department. Control of the artillery and engineer branches, however, fell to the Master-General of Ordnance (MGO). Although a political office whose holders changed when new governments came to power, the occupants were usually prominent army officers. Technically the head of the Ordnance Department, the Master-General also had charge of the Royal Military Academy at Woolwich, which trained future officers of Artillery and Engineers. Finally, the Master-General served as Ordnance's representative in Parliament.[7]

Having army administration spread across six different departments provided the main ingredients of the "disastrous muddle" waiting to swallow the Crimean expedition, and the lack of a central command authority kept those ingredients from forming a cohesive whole. Seated at the Colonial Office and concerned more with the expanding empire, the Secretary of State for War and Colonies made major military decisions but paid little actual attention to the business of the army. Those tasks fell to the Secretary-at-War, whose office had financial control over most aspects of the army and the militia but no command authority. The Commander-in-Chief, despite his title, did not have control of army units abroad, looked to the Home Secretary for approval of troop movements in Britain, and had no control over supplies at all. The Master-General, in contrast, retained command of artillery and engineer units wherever deployed. Treasury, through its Commissariat Department, handled supply in the field, but made no decisions regarding the weaponry used by the army. Such decisions came down from the Master-General's office, were implemented by the Ordnance Department, and approved by the Home Office.[8] The lack of a central directing entity, with authorities split between civilian and military departments, meant that the muddle remained just that—a chemical mixture that could not coalesce into solid and effective performance of the Crimean expeditionary force in 1854.

The uniquely British approach to military finance, which enforced the tripartite division of army, navy, and ordnance, further compounded the problem. The three services were separately funded through yearly "estimates" which grouped various budgetary costs together into separate "votes." Each vote had to be approved by Parliament, which provided Radicals such as Joseph Hume multiple opportunities to attack military spending. As a result, a considerable amount of administrative energy had to be expended in preparations of estimates that might—or might not—survive contact with Parliament. In addition, the annual nature of the estimates effectively prevented consideration of long term military needs. Such a financial system let politicians keep a close eye on military spending, but left the country without any form of strategic planning.

"That Most Important Branch of the Public Service"

The Ordnance Department, the other branch of civil administration named by *Blackwood's*, traced its origins to the creation of the "Office of Ordnance" by Henry V in 1414, who assigned to it the provision and maintenance of artillery and ammunition for both army and navy. Termed "that most important branch of the public service" by a 9 September 1833 article in the *Standard*, by 1854 Ordnance had become the second largest government department (Treasury being the first) and straddled most aspects of British power projection. The wide and far-reaching duties of the Department centered on "the provision, custody and supply of every description of warlike stores." This included "ordnance, carriages, small arms, ammunition, pontoons, tents and camp-equipage, entrenching tools; everything, in short which is required to arm a fleet or fortress [or] an army for the field." The Department managed nearly 100 army storage depots at home and abroad (with the exception of India) as well as gun wharves that served the Royal Navy at every British port. Ordnance also supplied non-military government entities, such as small arms for the Irish constabulary and Metropolitan Police, signal devices and rocket-propelled lifelines for the Board of Trade, and even tents to the Board of Health in times of civil emergency. Non-government agencies looked to Ordnance for assistance as well, such as the Honorable East India Company, which bought from the Office what could not be produced by its own Indian arsenals or obtained from the trade. The sprawling Royal Arsenal manufactured much of the "warlike stores" needed by the nation, supervised by Ordnance, which also oversaw inspection, storage, and the handling of contracts with outside suppliers. The Department also held responsibility for the building of barracks and fortifications on the home islands, and carried out cartographic surveys at home and in the Colonies to produce maps for both military and civilian use.[9]

As noted above, the MGO served as the titular head of the Ordnance Department and its chief military officer. This post also traced its origins to 1414, when Henry V appointed Nicholas Merbury as the first "Master of Ordnance." Elizabeth I reorganized the entire Office of Ordnance in 1597, in the wake of widespread fraud and profiteering during England's war with Spain. Her reorganization placed "the whole business of Ordnance for land and sea" under the office of a Great Master of Ordnance, originally to be an appointment for life. The first and only Great Master, Robert, the 2nd Earl of Essex, lost his head for treason in 1601. After the end of Elizabeth I's reign James I reorganized the Office again, replacing the Great Master and his Lieutenant with the Master-General and Lieutenant-General of Ordnance, posts that continued into the nineteenth century. As both military- and cabinet-level positions, the occupants of the Master-General's office often came and went with the rise and fall of governments. Six of the nine men that held the office after Waterloo left in this manner; those who served after the Duke of Wellington's long tenure (1819 to 1827) held the post for an average of only three years.[10]

Much of the day-to-day business of the Ordnance Department fell to the Board of Ordnance, an institution that dated to Elizabeth I's reorganization. After a somewhat confused existence during the Civil War, a Royal Warrant issued on 25 July 1683 by Charles II re-established the Board, which consisted of the top four civilian officials in the Ordnance Department. This included of the Clerk of Ordnance, who purchased materials for the Department; the Principal Storekeeper, responsible for storage of all ordnance supplies; the Surveyor-General, responsible for maintenance and quality control, and the Clerk of Deliveries for the issuance of material. Appointees to the Board were also affected by the fortunes of politics, with the notable exception of Edmund Phipps, who held the office of Clerk of Deliveries from 1812 to its abolition in 1831.[11] Nominally reporting to the Master-General, the Board in fact acted independently in most matters. It dealt with contractors, approved employment matters at Ordnance facilities, oversaw changes in patterns of military stores, and even handled such minutia as the granting of fishing rights on Ordnance properties.[12]

The supervision of the military manufacturing "establishments" or "departments" formed one of the principal duties of the Board of Ordnance. Several Crown facilities produced weapons and munitions for British military forces, most being located at Woolwich, a small town east of London along the Thames and also the site of the Royal Dockyards. Ordnance first built permanent works for the "proof," or test-firing of guns prior to their acceptance into service, near the town in 1651. In 1696 the Crown's "Laboratory," named for its ancient task of mixing the chemicals necessary to produce ammunition, moved from Greenwich to Woolwich. Over the next century, several other ordnance factories grew up in close proximity to the Laboratory. Collectively known as "the Warren," having been built on the site of a rabbit farm, George III declared during an 1805 visit that "the name of one of the tamest of all animals was certainly ill-suited to the nature of the place." He suggested that it be renamed the "Arsenal," which then-MGO Gen. John Pitt agreed to immediately.[13]

As with the army administrative "system," the Arsenal consisted of a sprawling and somewhat chaotic network of facilities responsible for the production and storage of armaments. The oldest, the Royal Laboratory, manufactured "fire-works and cartridges, and [loaded] bombs, carcasses, grenadoes, and such like matters for the public service," and tested supplies of gunpowder received from Royal and private mills. Products expanded during the Napoleonic era to include new inventions, such as the Congreve rocket, Shrapnel shells, and just about anything else that could be fired or flung at an enemy. Laboratory workers also broke down obsolete stores to recover metal and powder for remanufacture. Another long-established department at the Arsenal was the Inspector of Artillery. Although the title implies that this post had no connection with manufacturing, the Inspector of Artillery presided over the Royal Brass Foundry (RBF) as well as the proof of guns obtained by contract. A fatal accident at a private cannon foundry in May of 1716 led the English government to establish its own facility at Woolwich for the casting of bronze field guns and howitzers for the army ("brass" being the term used for bronze gun-metal at the time). The heavier cast-iron guns for the Royal Navy were obtained by contract from a variety of private iron foundries, a situation that did not change until 1856. The Foundry worked occasionally with the other departments, such as a joint project with the Laboratory for the manufacture of small-arm percussion caps in 1842. The third facility located at Woolwich was the Royal Carriage Department (RCD), established in 1803. RCD's primary mission involved the manufacture and repair of land, naval, and transport carriages for artillery pieces of all makes and sizes. The first Arsenal facility to see the introduction of steam power, RCD installed an engine to drive wood planing machinery in 1805.[14] The department made all manner of other wood products as well, but the construction of ammunition boxes and barrels fell to the Laboratory because of its immediate need for such items to pack its products.

Woolwich also served as the headquarters of the Royal Artillery, which along with the Royal Engineers formed the "Scientific Corp," called so for the much higher amount of training required. For many years both regiments operated out of Woolwich, but in 1850 the Royal Engineers moved permanently to Chatham.[15] It is important to note that these units differed greatly from "line units," meaning infantry and cavalry regiments. In addition to being directly under the command of the Master-General, potential officers for both regiments enrolled in the nearby Royal Military Academy. Training for gun crews also occurred at Woolwich, under the aegis of the Royal Military Repository. Unlike line units, the Royal Artillery promoted its officers in peacetime strictly by seniority, rather than by purchase, although brevet ranks—promotions in name and responsibility, without an increase in pay— were very common, especially in the field.[16]

Woolwich did not contain all of the government manufacturing facilities. Waltham Abbey, a few miles north of Woolwich, hosted the Royal Powder Mills, which manufactured the gunpowder (and later explosives) required by the service. This consisted primarily of "black powder," a combination of charcoal, saltpeter, and sulfur that had been in use for centuries. By 1854 the manufacture of black powder had advanced to include various combinations of the base ingredients and finished grain sizes depending on the intended use. The Mills supplied much of the powder necessary during peacetime, but Government supplemented this supply with contracts to private firms such Curtis's and Harvey of London, who also manufactured high-quality powder for sportsmen. The newest manufacturing department, the Royal Armoury Mills, was also built away from Woolwich. Because of quality-control issues with weapons made by outside contractors, the government established a new small-arms factory for the production of parts and construction of muskets, pistols, swords and bayonets at Enfield Lock, north of London, in 1816. Originally created to make musket barrels and gun locks, the factory had a tenuous existence during the "long peace," very nearly being shuttered for a want of work in 1832. Fortunately for the nation the Mills survived, and its long-reigning head, George Lovell, built it into a research and development model for civilian gun makers as well as a weapons assembly, inspection, and repair facility.[17]

The Mills did not produce all the parts required for a finished musket, however, and could not meet the full needs of the military. The government continued to rely heavily on private contractors, centered in Birmingham, for much of its small arms. An 1851 census of workers in the city showed 5,167 men involved in gun manufacture there, divided into nearly fifty different specialties.[18] This army of craftsmen turned out both martial and sporting arms for sale around the world, and would be heavily engaged in the manufacture of weapons during the coming war. Relationships between Ordnance and the "gun trade," however, had become increasingly strained because of Lovell's expansion of the Enfield factory and its role as both a competitor and a check on prices. An 1852 article in the *Birmingham Journal* decried that "Government competition, if carried to any extent, will seriously injure many thousands engaged here," and denounced the Enfield factory as being "carried on at a loss to the country."[19] Such resistance to the new facility and continued reliance on hand-production methods meant that Britain lacked an efficient, modernized and mechanized small arms factory—an anachronism in a country that had otherwise thoroughly embraced industrialization.

The disorder in the top ranks of British military administration extended downward through the Board of Ordnance. Although subordinate to the Board, the manufacturing departments in fact operated as stand-alone institutions. The chief posts of each were considered to be "civilian" although held by a senior Royal Artillery officer. Each department head "had absolute control of the factory under him, and a free hand in its administration provided he did not exceed the financial sum allotted to him." The departments maintained their own books, managed their own stores, had their own clerical staff, set their wages independent of one another, and communicated only on a formal basis. The factory heads ran their facilities as if located in different cities rather than next door to each other at Woolwich, "separately produc[ing] guns, their carriages, and projectiles" in semi-ignorance of what the other facilities did. It also occasionally resulted in the continued manufacture of carriages that no longer fit their intended guns, for instance, or the shipment of obsolete ammunition to the army in the field. Such an enforced separation, bemoaned the *Monthly Review*, resulted in "conflicts of opinion, diversities of system and delays, multiplication of correspondence, and needless formalities."[20]

In addition, promotion by seniority meant that Royal Artillery officers held the same rank for much longer than line officers. A Royal Commission that investigated promotion within the regiment reported in 1854 that "the average age of the officers ... of Ordnance corps is far greater than that of officers" in other arms of the service. The average years in rank of artillery colonels went from thirty-six in 1818 to forty-eight by 1851, and lieutenant-colonels as well as captains could also expect to spend decades without promotion. Not only did this contribute to very lengthy waits for advancement by junior officers, it also meant that senior ones were "senior" in physical terms, with several octogenarians holding high-level posts in the pre-Crimean era. The same held true for selection of officers to head facilities at the Royal Arsenal. As a result, the department heads collectively suffered from a lack of originality and a blind acceptance of traditional manners of doing business.[21]

The late application of steam power to much of the Royal Arsenal illustrates this lack of imagination by ordnance factory heads. Well past the period when steam came into general use in private industry, most of the operations at the Arsenal relied on human or animal power. An 1840 memorandum by MGO Sir Richard Vivian lamented that "in very many instances the work is done in a primitive manner by manual labor, and at a very great expence; in the Carriage Department only is steam power employed as it should be." Indeed, as late as 1841, the Royal Brass Foundry still used horse-drawn machinery to bore out cannon. Although this delayed mechanization may be partially explained by the tightfistedness of Parliament, the 35-year difference between the advent of steam power at RCD in 1805 and the *consideration* of it in 1840 for the other two departments smacked of Luddism on the part of certain department chiefs. Finally, in 1847 the Board contracted with James Nasmyth, an eminent Scottish engineer and inventor of the steam hammer, to inspect its facilities and recommend improvements. Nasmyth later wrote in his memoirs that what machinery the Arsenal did have "was better fitted for a Museum of Technical Antiquity than for practical use.... Everything was certainly very far behind the arrangements which I had observed in foreign arsenals." He made several suggestions, and that year the Laboratory installed its first steam engine, "superintended by Captain [Edward M.] Boxer, an officer of the highest talent and energy." Born in 1822, at age fifteen Boxer enrolled as a "gentleman cadet" in the Royal Artillery and graduated two years later. After a short tour of Malta in 1841, the next year Boxer found himself posted back to Woolwich. Appointed as an instructor on fortifications the same year Nasmyth began his upgrades, clearly Boxer's duties left him time to pursue other interests. And, although the gradual installation of more engines brought some degree of modernization, compared to private industry the Arsenal remained woefully under-mechanized at the outbreak of the Crimean War.[22]

Public Interest in Military Technology

Regardless of its level of mechanization, the concentration of so much military activity into an area close to London made Woolwich a point of interest for anyone visiting the city. British officials regularly granted tours to foreign dignitaries to show off the "vast industrial landscape that explained [British] battlefield glory." Live-fire exercises, such as the bombardment of a mock fort conducted for the Prince of Saxe-Weimar in 1845, demonstrated "the destruction which would be effected in actual warfare" by British gun batteries according to a 21 July article by the *Standard*. An 1841 guidebook touted the cheap fares offered by steam vessels and rail transport and easy access to "the immense number of objects of attraction worthy of being seen in the Royal Arsenal, in the Dock Yard, and in the Royal Repository; and the grand military spectacles often exhibited on Woolwich Common." Such "grand military spectacles" were among the few points of contact that the average Briton had with the army. As historian Gwyn Harries-Jenkins has noted, for "the British public as a whole, the army was ... an unknown institution." Enlisted service remained an option of last resort for most British males, and the officer corps came for the most part from the ranks of the privileged and the aristocracy, especially for line units. Relatively few men had seen service, a number that dropped as the distance from 1815 widened. Many of the officers and men who served did so overseas and therefore out of sight, except for occasional police work at home—a task that hardly endeared soldiers to the general public. The military also had a distinct set of traditions, behaviors, and values that reinforced its sense of identity and separation from the general public. All of these traits combined to make the army, in the words of Wellington, "an exotic in England." Still, military parades held a powerful appeal for Britons of all classes. As Scott Hughes Myerly pointed out in a 1992 article in the *Journal of Social History*, "a gratis public spectacle that involved hundreds or thousands of fancy-dress performers, complete with 'fireworks' was quite a treat for all," even to the point of becoming considered a public right. After discovering that a review supposedly to be held at Wimbledon in 1816 turned out to be a hoax, "the angry, disappointed crowd set Combe Wood heath on fire." Military spectacles "helped to override the traditional dislike most Britons felt" towards their army, which military authorities encouraged. Large-scale maneuvers held at Chobham Camp in 1853 were open to the public, for example; even though this interfered with practice, army commanders hoped that public attendance and enthusiasm might also persuade Parliament to be a little freer with the purse strings.[23]

Technology naturally played a part in the military performances enjoyed by the public, but to get up close to the tools of war they could also visit the "Royal Repository" mentioned in the 1841 guidebook. This actually referred to the Royal Military Repository, a large section of ground used for the training of gun crews but which also hosted a weapons museum. Established in the 1770s by Capt. William Congreve, his first "Repository for Military Machines" (for which he secured Royal patronage) functioned both as a museum and "teaching collection" of specimens and models of artillery, including captured guns. Unfortunately, a fire in 1802 destroyed the original museum as well as adjacent workshops. In 1818, the Prince Regent authorized the movement of an unusual building to Woolwich for the "conservation of trophies ... artillery models, and other military curiosities usually preserved in the Repository." Known as the "Rotunda" for its resemblance to the bell-shaped military tent used by British field commanders, the 110-ft diameter round building had been constructed as a ballroom to celebrate Napoleon's abdication in 1814. Once moved, workmen strengthened the building with a brick exterior, reinforced roofing, and a 50-ft tall central sandstone column. Completed in 1820, the Rotunda re-opened as a permanent exhibit free to the public. The museum's holdings expanded beyond military trophies to include George III's collection of model forts and dockyards, as well as specimens of items proposed by inventors. While a popular destination for visitors, the Rotunda also proved a valuable reference collection for the various committees tasked with evaluating weapons proposals over the next several decades. Visits to the Arsenal itself were more restricted but could easily be arranged for those interested in seeing the great military factories at work. Regulations laid down in 1832 stated that visitors were not to be admitted, except on order of the Commandant's office. The commander of the guard did have the latitude to admit anyone he knew personally or "strangers of respectability from a distance" who might be "ignorant of the necessary forms." Foreigners, however, had to have express permission from the MGO,

"The Rotunda or New Model Room, built in the Royal Military Repository at Woolwich" (Hand-colored etching by R. W. Lucas, 1820. Royal Collection Trust / © Her Majesty Queen Elizabeth II, 2018).

and all visitors had to be escorted by one of the guards on duty. In 1836 the orders were changed to require an entry card; still, a 10 June 1840 article in the *Morning Post* noted that the duty officer usually made such cards available to anyone who wanted one.[24]

Those in search of more information had many options available. The daily newspapers regularly published articles regarding all manner of military-related matters, including activities at the Royal Arsenal. Disasters, such as an explosion that killed seven in 1845, certainly grabbed the most column space.[25] The papers reported just about everything else as well, such as periodic bursts of activities in support of various military operations, results of experiments, or the scheduled adoption of new weaponry. Periodicals, particularly *The Mechanics' Magazine*, carried information regarding advances not only in the weapons themselves but also in their manufacture. *Colburn's United Service Magazine* also regularly examined military technology. While written primarily for the military market, *Colburn's* noted that the magazine is "sold by all booksellers" on its frontispiece, making it available to a much wider audience. Clearly, then, the public had access to much regarding the weapons used by its military. But did it act upon that information?

Interior of the Rotunda at the Royal Military Repository. The building designer patterned it after the bell-shaped tents used by the military (1828 watercolor by George Scharf © The Trustees of the British Museum).

"The Great Mass Are Utterly Worthless"

On 30 October 1841, a fire broke out in the Great Storehouse at the Tower of London. One of the Ordnance Department's major arms depots, the building held the nation's reserve supply of "Brown Bess" flintlock muskets, as well as several thousand arms converted to the new percussion priming system. As described by the *Leeds Times* on 6 November, in a short few hours nearly 200,000 muskets "fit for immediate service [and] tastefully arranged in various forms and directions, present[ing] a most beautiful appearance," became so much smoke, ash, and twisted lumps of metal. Covered extensively by the papers, the loss of so many weapons represented a huge blow to British military capabilities—but also a potential opportunity to those interested in advancing their ideas regarding the right sort of arm for the infantry. Shortly afterwards, such proposals began to filter into the War Office including one submitted anonymously by "RLL." "As I collect from the newspapers," he wrote a scant two weeks after the blaze, "that [as] a quantity of small arms will be required" to replace those lost in the fire, "I take the liberty of submitting ... a little invention of my own ... that [I] propose to call the rifle-musket."[26]

"RLL" represented just one of hundreds of individuals who pitched inventions and ideas to the Ordnance Department before the Crimean War. His reluctance to disclose his true name also suggests a motive common to some of these individuals: patriotism, and concern that British military forces have the best tools that British industry could provide. The range of motives, however, varied almost as widely as did the proposals themselves. Patent holders seeking to profit from their ideas, manufacturers seeking markets for their wares, military officers wanting to make names for themselves, all found ways to put their ideas before the MGO for consideration. A handful of outright charlatans and scam artists also sought the attention of the Board of Ordnance. In a case famous in its day, Samuel Alfred Warner made several public statements in the 1840s claiming that by means of his "invisible shell" and "long range" he could "in a few hours" depopulate the British stronghold of Gibraltar. Pretending to the title of "Captain" because of his supposed service aboard a secret vessel employed "in landing spies" during the Napoleonic Wars, Warner also claimed he had completely destroyed two French privateers with his inventions during the wars. In the months that followed, no trace of either his service, the vessel he supposedly sailed on, or the destroyed French ships ever came to light. Still, Warner found a Parliamentary backer to champion his projects, and managed to get the Board of Ordnance to front £1,300 for a demonstration. Put to the test, his supposed "long range"—not much more than an unpiloted hot-air balloon that carried small bombs—proved to be an utter failure. Warner went to his death in 1854 claiming he was owed thousands of pounds by the British government, as well as having sired seven children out of wedlock.[27] As deluded as he was, Warner at least had an idea in mind; others were much more blatant in their attempts to fleece the Board. Remembering Warner's activities, in 1854 one Guillaume Hole also asked £200,000 for an invention he insisted would "destroy an Enemy at the distance of Twenty Miles on the Sea and an Army on Land at a very long distance," without offering any particulars. Hole also warned that he was seeking buyers from other countries, and included a small French-language newspaper advertisement as proof. The Board declined his services.[28]

On 25 October 1854, Charles Abbott addressed a letter to the MGO, writing that he had been advised by the Duke of Newcastle (Henry Pelham-Clinton, then Secretary of State for War) that "any suggestions which I may have to offer for the improvement in the method of constructing Shot and Shells should be forwarded to the Board of Ordnance." Newcastle's advice to Abbott, however, was only partially correct. Prior to 1805, experimentation with new weaponry in the Ordnance Department fell to the Surveyor-General's office, with assistance as needed by the Master Gunner of England. By 1805, however, the increasing numbers of new proposals, particularly those received from outside the military establishment (such as RLL's "rifle-musket"), led to the formation of a permanent committee for their evaluation: the "Select Committee of Artillery Officers." As the name implied, seven sen-

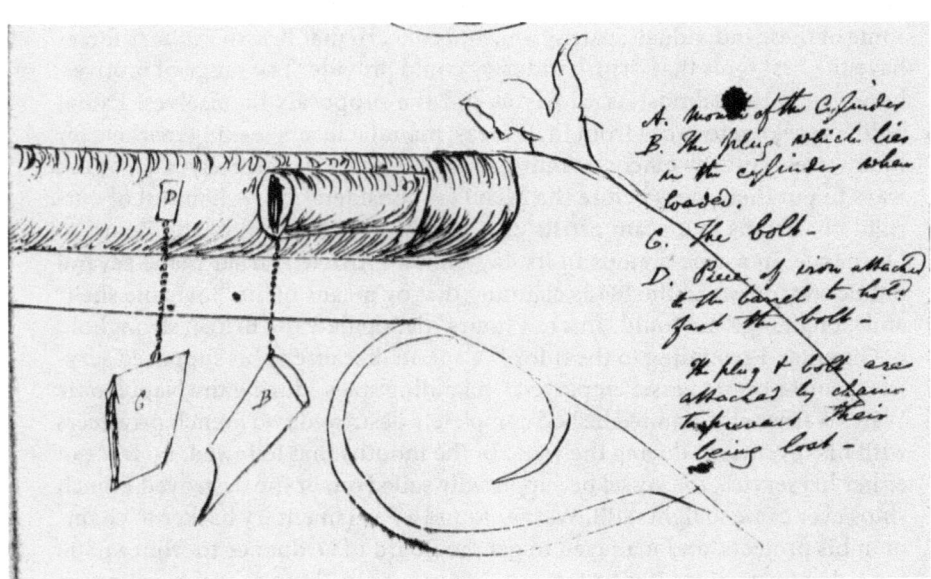

One of the sketches that "RLL" included with his proposal for a "rifle-musket" in 1841 ("RLL" to MGO, 13 Nov. 1841, TNA, WO 44/620, File 15; author's photograph).

ior artillery officers, including some heads of Royal Arsenal factories, sat on the committee, with the Director-General of Artillery serving as president. Although experienced artillerymen, the committee could "whenever necessary ... obtain the assistance and opinion of the most able scientific men in the country." This included civilians, such as the Professor of Mathematics at the Royal Military Academy, Samuel Christie, whose "opinion is always available, if required." The Committee also consulted with Dr. Lyon Playfair, Professor of Chemistry at the recently established School of Mines, "on an important subject, with great advantage."[29]

Once the Master-General forwarded a proposal for review, the Select Committee placed it on the schedule for one of its weekly meetings and invited the submitter to attend, "with drawings or models, or to give any further explanation or information that he may think necessary." After review and discussion with the inventor (if he attended), the Committee drew up a report regarding the proposal and their opinion of it for the Master-General. More often than not, the "projector" (to use the lexicon of the day) left disappointed, the committee having ruled his idea as "inapplicable to the service." Certain topics, such as small arms and coastal defense proposals, could be referred to subject-specific committees "specially appointed whenever the Naval or Military authorities may require their assistance." In the case of RLL's "rifle-musket," however, the Select Committee judged rather harshly that the sketches and attendant descriptions "do not ... merit the attention of the small-arms sub-committee."[30]

In a later memorandum outlining the history and duties of the Select Committee, Maj. Gen. William Cator remarked that of the suggestions brought forward, "very few are new or superior" to current weapons or practices. "Some are ingenious, but impractical," he wrote, but "the great mass are utterly worthless, and it is often painful to witness a vast amount of ingenuity and skill, as well as expense, in the construction of beautifully-executed models and drawings, with minute and laboured descriptions, which are valueless ... from the absence of all practical knowledge [of the subject] on the part of the designer." The list of the impractical included multi-barreled cannon, glass mortar shells, soldiers' caps that doubled as flotation devices, steam-powered flying machines, and Abbott's asphalt artillery projectile. Such ideas, while perhaps making perfect sense to those suggesting them, were useless for the military. The inventor could appeal the Committee's decision, in which case the Master-General returned the proposal for reconsideration along with any further information from the inventor. "Such appeals," wrote Gen. Cator, were "always met in a spirit of fairness and justice ... with a due regard to the good of the service" but generally not to the satisfaction of the inventor.[31]

For those projects judged to have merit, the Select Committee devised

"Sadler's Flying Artillery," circa 1798—an example of one of the many "ingenious, but impractical" ideas brought before the Board of Ordnance (Royal Collection Trust / © Her Majesty Queen Elizabeth II, 2018).

and monitored experimental programs, generally at the expense of the inventor but occasionally paid for out of public funds. An example of the latter is Boxer's 1850 plan of elongated shot for smoothbore cannon, "having the advantages of Rifled Projectiles," such as longer and more accurate range, but "without the defects." Following a limited test of four projectiles, Boxer wrote to the Master-General that the results "[gave] me great hopes of success." After a personal interview, the Select Committee recommended his plan "be put to the test of Experiment." One hundred each of both shot and shell of Boxer's design were obtained by contract, and sent to the experimental artillery range at Shoeburyness for test firing. Unfortunately for Boxer, the new projectiles failed: some broke into pieces on firing, others tumbled in flight, "their Ranges being very uncertain." Boxer, present at the test shoot, finally asked for a halt, "satisfied that no good could be gained from going on with the Experiment." Although the test was a failure, one Committee member noted on the final report that "I only wish that all Projectors were as reasonable as Captain Boxer."[32]

One "projector" not quite as reasonable, or at least more troublesome to the Committee, was Capt. John Norton of the 34th Foot. A long-serving officer fascinated by firearms and explosives, Norton's tinkering with things that blew up would warm the heart of anyone who ever lit off a firework. His 1860 collection of letters and notes included, for example, instructions on "how to make a hash of a wasps' nest" using gunpowder. A prolific inventor, Norton submitted dozens of proposals to the Select Committee. After one particular interview, a Committee member testily remarked to Norton that "you make experiments for your amusement, and then you come before us to know our opinion of them." Norton retorted "I do, and if by amusement I can add power to the arms of England, I shall be proud and happy for it."[33]

Norton's one brush with success illustrates that the Select Committee did, on occasion, reach out to non-artillery officers. In 1842, Norton brought before it a design for a "concussion shell" with a fuze constructed to detonate on impact. Although the Committee rejected the shell for land use, it did report that "the fuze ... is well adapted for the purpose of horizontal fire, and a simple, safe, and efficacious method of exploding shells ... striking solid substances." As such shells were "chiefly calculated for naval warfare," the Committee recommended "that a naval opinion should be obtained of the applicability of the fuze to that branch." Captain Hastings of the training ship *Excellent*, after trying the fuzes, recommended that Norton "be called upon to instruct the operatives in the laboratory at Woolwich" on the manufacture of his fuzes for further tests.[34] Apparently Norton did, as the *Standard* followed up with a 16 November 1844 report of the next round of experiments. "The firing was splendid," the author reported, the shells wreaking havoc on the target ship. "We are decidedly of opinion," the *Standard* continued, "that [Norton's] shell is by far the most deadly and destructive that we have ever seen." Regardless of this successful trial, it appears the Navy did not adopt Norton's fuze or his shell, as no records exist of the manufacture of either.

A shameless self-promoter, Norton did not wait for the November trial to notify the newspapers of his success. An article submitted to the *Times* reported that Norton had gone to Woolwich, repeated the Committee pronouncement of the fuzes as "simple, safe, and efficacious," and claimed that "all batteries for the defence of the seacoast and the protection of asylum harbours (says a correspondent) should be supplied with these shells."[35] That "correspondent" was almost certainly Norton himself. The article also represents one of a long series Norton submitted to any magazine or newspaper he could reach, particularly the *Cork Examiner*. Not all were positive. After the Select Committee rejected yet another of his inventions in 1852, Norton complained in a 13 December letter to the *Examiner* that "my 'suggestions,' as *some* call them, but [which] I call ... trusty and well proved arms, and projectiles" should be considered [instead] by "the British Empire (my Committee) through the British Press, its Secretary." "I write this," he continued, "in the hope that some nobleman or gentleman ... may be induced to incur the expense of two or three pounds" to test his invention, an experimental compound shell. "I should not like that this shot or shell," Norton cautioned, "should be first adopted by a foreign power with whom we may be unfortunately at war." As far as is known, no such benefactor stepped forward.

Failed experiments did not always represent dead ends for inventors, as simply getting a trial by the Committee could be turned into good advertising. In 1828, Joseph Southby, an "Artist in Fireworks," suggested to the Master-General the use of rockets for messaging at night. The primary ingredient in his "Crimson Stars," Southby argued, "is only to be obtained in this country" and therefore "could not ... *be imitated by any other nation.*" The Select Committee, after witnessing a trial, reported that while they found Southby's rockets superior to service signal rockets, "no mode of telegraphing by night (and several have been tried) has hitherto been successful" and declined Southby's proposal. After Lt. John Hughes of the Royal Navy put forward a similar idea in 1832, Southby sent copies of his correspondence with the Committee to the editors of the *United Service Magazine.* "Whatever merit belongs to the *originator* of the idea," Southby wrote, "belongs *to me* and *not* to Lieut. Hughes." Southby also emphasized that the Select Committee found his rockets "to be *excellent* and *very beautiful,*" praise not to be wasted by a fireworks manufacturer.[36]

Although the Committee rejected many projects on the basis of their impracticality or uselessness to the service, it also refused to risk any financial investment in developing new technologies. In 1840, Thomas Beningfield approached the Committee with a plan for a novel "electric gun" dramatically named "Siva, or the destroying power." Beningfield's single-barreled weapon fired five-eighths inch lead balls "calculated to kill at the distance of a statute mile," propelled "not by steam, but by the application of gases exploded by galvanic electricity." Beningfield's printed circular claimed that "many Military and Naval Officers have declared it an engine much more to be feared, either on shore or afloat, than any weapon now in use," and demonstrations seemed to bear out its potential. Firing exhibits for the Duke of Wellington and the Select Committee showed the machine capable of "a swift and effective discharge of a host of bullets," although inaccurate and incapable of penetrating a wood target consistently at ranges over 30 yards. Although Wellington thought the weapon had potential and that "Government should not lose sight of it," Beningfield had not yet patented the device, and proved reluctant to disclose the exact details of how it functioned. This reticence led to a breakdown in negotiations with the Select Committee. Beningfield refused to divulge his "secret" without some guarantee of financial reward, which the Committee would not make before knowing how the machine worked. Had the Committee been willing to risk some financial involvement, Beningfield's "Siva" might have developed into a unique weapon offering a battlefield advantage.[37]

The Failings of the Select Committee

Until the early 1850s, the Select Committee's duties "were comparatively of a routine character," Sir John Adye later wrote, "[as] artillery science had ... been almost dormant for many years." The number of new proposals remained at manageable levels, rarely exceeding three dozen a year. The two years prior to the Crimean War, however, saw a jump that did not recede for decades: forty-one in 1852, sixty-three the following year, and 218 in 1854. William Monsell, the last Clerk of Ordnance before the breakup of the Department, testified before Parliament that by July 1855, "974 projects of inventions in all had been laid before the Committee during the last twelve months, of which 696 had been rejected, and there still remained for trial 123." After the British cabinet dispatched a Royal Navy flotilla to the Dardanelles in June of 1853 with orders to support Constantinople in case of Russian attack, demands on the Royal Arsenal steadily rose as the possibility of war became more likely. The simultaneous increase in proposals overwhelmed the Select Committee, whose members—being the supervising officers of the Arsenal—were "severely taxed to keep pace" with their normal duties, much less deal with a flood of inventions. Consideration of the suggestions "in the usual course was found to be impossible, without serious injury to the service."[38]

The Select Committee had other faults besides being swamped; it also suffered from the inability to devise experimental programs that produced useful results. Lt. Col. John H. Lefroy, then special advisor to the Duke of Newcastle on artillery, wrote a particularly scathing condemnation of past weapons trials. "Unnecessary and futile experiments are tried," wrote Lefroy, "to satisfy or silence a particular inventor," or "stop short at the wrong moment, to grudge a very small outlay of time or money to make a conclusion permanently useful." A proposal for "horse-borne" artillery provides an example of one such experiment. An inventor suggested that "a small gun, strapped broadside across a horse's back and fired from that position, would be useful in mountain campaigns." The Committee considered the idea worth trying, rather heedless of how the horse might react. With the weapon on its back and its head tied to a post, one of the firing party pointed the gun towards the target and lit a slow-burning fuze to set it off. No one thought to secure the horse's tail-end, however. On hearing the burning fuze, the horse danced around the post, pointing the cannon at the Committee instead of the target. As a group, the Committee dived for the ground; the gun went off, the shot flew over the town of Woolwich, and the unfortunate horse ended up on its back several yards away. Uninjured, "the Committee ... gradually recovered their equilibrium, but reported unanimously against any further trial."[39]

In addition to "futile experiments," the responsibility for conducting tests often fell "in blind military rotation, to unsuitable hands," as in the case of English gun maker William Greener's proposal for an expanding musket ball. In 1834, Greener's invention "was referred to the Officer Commanding a Troop of Horse Artillery" who "saw nothing of the real novelty" that a bullet for a rifled musket held. The Select Committee did conduct experiments with Greener's bullet two years later, and Greener re-presented his invention to the Committee in 1842, but nothing came of his efforts. Finally, Lefroy bemoaned the want of "superior military colleges, turning out ... officers well trained in mathematical and physical science." A lack of such officers meant that "many of our experiments, so called, are ridiculously one-sided and inconclusive. No wonder they fail to satisfy the public, command little authority, and yield hardly any solid result for future guidance."[40]

The mostly *ex officio* Select Committee also suffered from the same lack of vision and vigor that affected the Royal Horse Artillery officer excoriated by Lefroy, and which pervaded the Royal Artillery itself. The Committee's first president, Lt. Gen. Sir Anthony Farrington, "was but 66" when he assumed the post, and held it to his death at the age of 83 in 1823. He was, at the time of his passing, "the oldest officer in the British service." Farrington's successor, Lt. Gen. Robert Douglas, also died in harness at 83, as did the third president, Sir John Macleod, who passed away in 1833 at 81. "To put it bluntly," historian Oliver Hogg wrote, "the Select Committee was hidebound, steeped in traditional methods, lacking in imagination and opposed to change."[41] Hogg's charge may be unduly harsh; several of Boxer's inventions were adopted into service, such as his parachute flare, improved artillery fuze and redesigned shrapnel shell. While important, such items represented incremental rather than radical advancements in "artillery science." The Committee never recommended anything truly revolutionary.

In addition, the Select Committee could only pass opinion on the matters forwarded to it by the Master-General. As a body, it could not make proposals, although no prohibition existed against individual committee members doing so, provided they also went through the Master-General. The restriction forbade recommending improvements to materials that showed promise, or could be useful in some way other than the topic under investigation. In the case of Joseph Southby's rockets, despite their proving more effective than the service signal rocket, they could not be considered as a replacement for the latter, his proposal being specifically for the use of rockets to send messages at night.[42] Prohibited from originating ideas, the Committee also lacked any incentive to explore technologies beyond those which its committee members were already familiar. Finally, the Committee operated under a semi-transparent veil of secrecy. Reports often did get passed to the press, and experiments held in the Plumstead Marsh range near the Arsenal were usually open to the public. In general, however, the Committee's closed proceedings meant that inventors could not anticipate what the British military really needed. In effect, its own rules walled the Committee off from the rapid changes in industrial knowledge that would have broken the somnolence of "artillery science" before the Crimean War.

The Board of Ordnance, as the public face of the Ordnance Department, also came under fire for its treatment of inventors. One author, referring to Henry Shrapnel's famous invention, wrote that the Board "had ... shown a degree of negligence disgraceful to themselves ... and that from ignorance or jealousy useful inventions have often been crushed."[43] In a letter to the *Standard* dated 21 February 1840, a "Sailor of Forty Years' Experience" charged that both the Boards of the Admiralty and Ordnance "are utterly unequal to judge of matters brought before them," especially regarding "certain novel inventions he had been appointed to examine." The writer decried having experiments conducted only at Woolwich or Portsmouth, where "it is impossible to preserve any secrecy whatever," and the lengthy delays that occurred in the experiments carried out by the Select Committee. "Had the invention to which I refer been adopted, the saving of money and time would have been enormous," and a fleet then fitting out to fight "a new war ... in a remote quarter of the globe would have already been under way." The author ended by claiming that "the whole matter will shortly come before the public, and then all parties shall be judged." Despite such a dire prediction, however, there is no evidence that the Ordnance Department considered any sort of overhaul of the Select Committee and the general process of weapons evaluation before 1855.

Reform Efforts Before the Crimean War

The Ordnance Department itself also proved resistant to change, symptomatic of the conservatism of the British army as a whole. Much of the latter stemmed from Wellington's long years of influence. The "Iron Duke" had served as MGO from 1819 to 1827, then as Commander-in-Chief in 1827–28 and again from 1842 until his death in 1852. In between years, he very actively participated in politics, and served briefly as Prime Minister from 1828 to 1830 and again for a month in 1834. Even when not in immediate charge of the army, Wellington retained considerable influence over its chief officers, many of whom had served under him and owed their positions to his decisions. The Duke's efforts during these lean years were "less to improve the Army than to save it from destruction" at the hands of a Parliament determined to reduce the burden of military spending on the tax-paying public. He also fought hard against efforts to overhaul a military administrative system that he felt had worked during the Napoleonic Wars, and especially opposed putting more power into the hands of a civilian-led War Office. Such a change, he felt, would strip control of the army from the Crown and hand it to the House of Commons.[44]

Due in large part to the "mutual animosity" between soldiers and politicians, the British military, long a target for a penny-pinching Parliament, had also become very risk averse. Indeed, for many army officers the word "reform" really meant further financial strangulation. Gutted after the close of the Napoleonic Wars, British army ranks shrank from 190,797 in 1815 to 50,856 in 1830—a ruthless seventy-three percent reduction that gravely damaged the army's effectiveness. "Guiding principles were cast to the winds," wrote Royal Artillery historian Lt. Col. Henry Hime, "and we rushed to the demolition of our military ... as if Satan had been bound for a thousand years and there was to be no more war." Satan had not been bound, however; revolution broke out in Canada the year Victoria became Queen, and "there was not a single year in [her] long reign in which somewhere in the world her soldiers were not fighting." France remained one of the nation's primary threats, and Russia rapidly became another as the two countries struggled with each other in their "Great Game" of empire-building in Central Asia. British armies found themselves involved in numerous "little wars" being fought on the fringes of an expanding British Empire. Gradually, over the course of four decades of colonial warfare, Parliament begrudgingly voted the funds that allowed the army to rebuild. By 1853, army strength stood at 102,283—still a smaller force than in 1815, but considered adequate during peacetime.[45]

The forces ranged against military spending varied considerably. Joseph Hume, an ardent Scottish free-trade radical, vigorously opposed profligate spending by any government department but especially the military. In an 1837 speech regarding army estimates, for example, Hume questioned why Britain needed an army larger than the emaciated forces "deemed expedient" in the 1820s. "At a time when the government found it impossible to afford relief to the urgent wants of the people," Hume argued, "it appeared to him to be monstrous" that the public be asked to fund "a standing army nearly doubling in amount" of that in the decade before. The "relief" he sought came in the form of reduced taxation; "seventy per cent of the whole amount," he argued, "fell upon the poorer, the working classes." Given such a burden, Hume felt "it was the duty of the Government to curtail every expense as much as possible."[46]

A vocal "peace movement" also complained about military spending. The movement, which stemmed from pacifist Quaker societies, included many who opposed military spending at all, as illustrated by an article attributed to the *Manchester Times*. After the 1841 fire at the Tower of London, the paper raged that "military taste ought not to be predominant through Christendom" and hoped that the Tower "will never be rebuilt." "The public money that has been spent in ordnance stores since 1815," the paper claimed, "would have sufficed to feed all the poor in the United Kingdom for the next twelve months."[47] The movement included middle-class industrialists such as Richard Cobden and John Bright, both Liberal MP's from Manchester. Such members felt that the nation should only provide what military force would be required for defense. Cobden in particular argued that "savings on wasteful armaments' expenditure and the resultant reduction in taxation would have almost as beneficial an effect on industry and trade as had repeal of the Corn Laws."[48] Others agreed, such as the *Christian News*, who questioned what the military spent its money on. "On looking at the returns to Parliament in the Ordnance department," the paper wrote, "an item of 26,000*l*. sterling appears for salutes. Can this be tolerated by the nation? The idea of blowing away [that much] gunpowder in making a noise is really too irrational and absurd to be much longer submitted to by the taxpayers."[49]

Not every Briton agreed with those clamoring for military austerity. In an anonymous 29 January 1848 letter to the *Yorkshire Gazette*, writer "M." mockingly suggested that "the barrels of all our soldiers' muskets be converted into syringes ... [and filled] with CHLOROFORM." Attacking the enemy in standard formation, "each man will fire (I beg pardon, liquidate,) at about the third button of his opposite antagonist's waistcoat ... in a few seconds the whole of the enemy will be sprawling senseless on the ground." After disarming and looting the enemy of any valuables, "our gallant fellows ... will shave off, in derision" their facial hair, as "nothing can be imagined more galling or insulting to the fine mind of a Frenchman." Such a tactic, the writer claimed, would be extolled by Hume and others attempting to wish away military spending. The plan "will cost but a mere trifle," "M." wrote, "and the quaker disciples of peace need quake no longer ... for no blood will be shed."

In between such extremes stood many individuals who realized that British military administration, especially an Ordnance Department known for its labyrinthine and nearly unfathomable accounting, could be rationalized. The *Daily News* argued on 9 January 1852, for example, that "the Board of Ordnance is full of abuses" and that consolidation of offices and greater centralization might free up enough funds so that "the Artillery could at once be almost doubled." Reform efforts, however, invariably centered on financial, rather than administrative, issues. The Board of Ordnance actually served as a model for a successful reform of the Admiralty Office in 1831, a committee reporting the Board model to be "better for securing an efficient and economical dispatch of business." Ironically, the abolition of two top posts of the Department, recommended in 1828 as a cost-saving measure, served instead to weaken the Board. Membership dropped from five to three with the elimination of a civilian, the Clerk of Deliveries, and the Lieutenant-General, the one serving military officer on the Board and primary technical advisor to the Master-General.[50]

Efforts were made before the Crimean War to clear away the disorder in the administration of both the army and ordnance. Charles Gordon-Lennox, the Duke of Richmond and member of Earl Charles Grey's Whig cabinet, developed a plan in 1833 to break up the Board of Ordnance into its civilian and military components. Richmond passed his plan to Col. Sir Alexander Dickson, then Deputy Adjutant-General of the Royal Artillery, for comment. Known as an outstanding artillery officer, Dickson was also a Wellington partisan, having been brevetted by the Duke from captain to lieutenant-general (a jump of several grades) and appointed overall commander of allied artillery during the Peninsular War. Dickson rejected Richmond's plan as not offering "any advantage that would arise to the public from it, either to expedite the service, or as a savings in expense." Instead, Dickson wrote, the duties of the Board "would be carried on with less efficiency, the progress of improvement would be retarded, and great waste or misapplication of the stores would ensue."[51]

Richmond's plan languished with the dissolution of Grey's cabinet the next year, but in 1835 the question of wholesale reorganization surfaced again during Melbourne's second Whig government. Parliament appointed a commission under Henry George Grey (Lord Howick) and Henry John Temple (Lord Palmerston) to investigate the "Practicability and Expediency of Consolidating the Different Departments connected with the Civil Administration of the Army." *The Monthly Review* used testimony from the commission's report to illustrate the Ordnance Department's role in the British military administrative jumble. "If a supply of arms is wanted for the troops," for example, the requesting officer did not go to a single central authority. Rather, "application is made by the Commander-in-Chief to the Secretary at War, and by him to the Secretary of State, to signify his Majesty's pleasure to the Master-General and Board of Ordnance for the issue of the arms." Since the Board supplied guns and gun carriages for the navy, a ship's captain "must notify his wants to the Admiralty, and the Admiralty to the Board of Ordnance, who transmit their directions thereupon to their officers" for issue, even for something as small as a missing bolt. Finally, the article noted what would become one of the biggest problems Raglan encountered in the Crimea: the lack of an effective logistical command. "Commissaries-general with an army in the field are amenable to two authorities," the magazine explained. "They receive their instructions ... and money from the Lords Commissioners of the Treasury, and, at the same time, they are under the orders of the commander of the army to which they are attached." They also answered to Treasury auditors "for the expenditure of their cash, and to the Board of Ordnance for their stores." The "natural" results of the lack of a central military administrative authority, the article continued, included "conflicts of opinion, diversities of system and delays, involving a multiplication of correspondence, and of needless formalities in the transaction of business." In contrast, the *Monthly Review* pointed out, "every military department [in France] is subordinate to the War Minister," a single authority "responsible for the whole of the military expenditure" as well as the performance and conduct of the army.[52]

The Howick commission ultimately brought forward a modified version of Richmond's plan, but with the added recommendation that the Secretary-at-War become a full-fledged Secretary of State and member of the cabinet. Presumably, the Secretary of War and Colonies, also a Cabinet member, would have given over all duties related to the army, to concentrate on "the civil administration of our numerous Colonies, with all their complicated interests." Such an arrangement would eliminate what the commission felt to be the "chief defect" in British military administration: "the want of some one authority having an efficient control over the whole military expenditure of the country." They also recommended that the military duties exercised by the Master-General remain with him, whereas the civilians in the Board of Ordnance should be made subordinate to the new Secretary's post. Had the commission's recommendations been adopted, they would have effectively dissolved the muddle nearly twenty years before it bogged down Raglan and the Crimean expeditionary force. Instead, the recommendations met with "practical objections of a most forcible nature" from Wellington and other high-ranking army officers such as Sir Henry Hardinge and Charles William Vane, the Marquess of Londonderry. Such a move, the Duke felt, would create a "new Leviathan" in the form of the Secretary of State for War's office, and would "transfer the effective command of the Army from the King to the House of Commons." Faced with such opposition, the recommendations were ignored, victim to "a combination of tolerable success in colonial campaigns, fears about the creation of an over-powerful military authority, bureaucratic inertia, and dedication to cheese-paring."[53]

A "Separate and Irresponsible Existence" Lives On

On 3 November 1849, the *West Kent Guardian* prematurely reported that the "very expensive, very slow, and over-officered establishment, the Board of Ordnance, is no longer to be maintained in its separate and irresponsible existence." Rather wishfully, as things turned out, the *Guardian* wrote that the Department would be broken up "as mere branch departments" attached to Horse Guards and the Admiralty. Instead, Ordnance lumbered on, a major ingredient in a muddied "system" of military administration, production, and procurement practices that remained very much as it was at the close of the Napoleonic Wars. Paradoxically, this antiquated and divided system worked, insofar as it guaranteed a weak army that could not challenge Parliament for supremacy, yet provided just enough for the defense of the empire, a point related to who the "real" enemy was. Britain's wars between 1815 and 1855 were carried out against societies that lacked the resources, training, discipline, and organization of the British army, which made it possible for the British to ignore new weapons technology and serious military reform. In this sense, the imperial focus reinforced the stasis of the military. In addition, the accomplishment of Wellington and his army (not to mention his allies) at Waterloo had convinced the world of the supremacy of British arms for decades after the battle. Had the country not chosen to get involved in the "Eastern Question" brewing between Turkey and Russia, this assumption of supremacy might have gone unchallenged for many more years.

Although the nation in general proved content with the weapons that beat Napoleon, it is clear from newspaper reports and the files of the Select Committee that, while the process was slow, changes were being investigated. It is also clear that many of these changes came into the procurement process from outside the military establishment. The British fascination with things military, the demand for information fed by a willing press, and ideas from the ongoing Industrial Revolution combined to raise questions regarding the technologies in use by the British army and navy. Such questions may have smoldered on for years; instead, the events of the Crimean War fanned the slow burn into a revolutionary change in military technology that continued for the next five decades. To illustrate how dramatic these changes were, it is worth spending some pages to review the state of British arms before the War, and some of the emerging technologies being considered.

"The War Will Not Last a Month"

The latter half of 1853 saw Britain increasingly consumed by war fever. An impending conflict between Turkey and Russia occupied both the headlines and the attention of the Queen's subjects. "The public mind has been greatly agitated," wrote the *Examiner* on 8 October, by the Turkish Grand Council's recent declaration of war against Russia and Britain's potential role in the upcoming conflict. In the view of many, the British cabinet's decision to move the Mediterranean Fleet into the Dardanelles the previous May had "morally committed" Britain to protect Turkey. Not only were British ships "the guarantors of good faith, they could not be withdrawn without a tremendous loss of prestige." Many also felt that Britain had an obligation to stand fast against the predations of a Russia determined "not only to subdue Turkey, but to domineer over all Europe, and extirpate all freedom."[1] "The Russians committed themselves to an overt act of war" by their June occupation of Moldavia and Wallachia, argued the *Worcester Journal* on 22 October, and "if the Turks are unsuccessful in the coming struggle it is impossible to contemplate without dread the disastrous circumstances" to Britain. If, however, "aid is given [to Turkey], as it ought to be, the war will not last a month" argued *Bell's Life* on the 30th. For England and France to not to deliver this aid, the paper continued, "would be treason ... interests and honour alike require that the war should be brought to a speedy and satisfactory termination."

Few in Britain really understood what the nation had committed to, however. Forty years of peace had dulled the public's remembrance of the costs of war, while events such as the Great Exhibition of 1851 and the grand spectacle of the Duke of Wellington's funeral in 1852 sharpened Britons' sense of martial and industrial power. The long peace had also generally stilled military innovation for most of Europe. While some important new technologies, such as steam-powered warships and rifled muskets, had emerged, the basic tools and tactics of warfare in 1854 remained much as they had been at the close of the Napoleonic Wars. Two years of fighting in the Crimea, however, would show the public the great limitations, if not outright obsolescence, of current combat technology. It also cleared the way for a serious reconsideration of that technology in the years following the Peace of Paris in 1856.

To showcase the state of military technology employed during the War, this chapter will concentrate on a few specific engagements: the naval bombardments of Sinope and Odessa, the battle of the Alma, and the siege of Sevastopol Harbor. The picture that emerges is of militaries armed with weaponry decades if not centuries old, but also struggling with new technologies and the appropriate tactics to use them. For Britain, the war began the transition from *ancien regimé* to industrialized warfare, and heavily influenced weapons and tactics development for decades afterward.

The "Massacre at Sinope"

On 21 November 1853—only a month into the conflict—a Russian naval squadron under Vice-Admiral Pavel Nakhimov caught the Turkish Black Sea Fleet at anchor at Sinope. Although three capital ships formed part of his squadron, Nakhimov elected to blockade the Turks while summoning reinforcements from Sevastopol, a scant hundred miles away. Joined in a few days by six additional vessels, Nakhimov took advantage of heavy fog on 30 November to sail his line-of-battle ships into the harbor, leaving two sail and three steam frigates to guard the entrance. As a result of either the fog or Turkish complacency, Nakhimov closed within a mile and a quarter of his intended targets, and the Turks held their fire despite the approach of so many Russian guns.[2]

In addition to the standard cast-iron cannon that armed his ships, Nakhimov brought a weapon relatively new to naval warfare: the shell gun. Although heavy explosive-filled shells capable of damaging ships formed part of coastal defenses, the mortars that fired them did so in high, arcing trajectories. Shooting in such a manner posed considerable fire risk to normal warships crisscrossed with canvas and tarred rope, which limited their use to specially designed bomb vessels. In 1821, however, Col. Henri-Joseph Paixhans proposed arming French ships with purpose-designed shell-firing cannon. He argued that although the thick wooden sides of a then-modern ship of the line could adequately resist solid shot, a shell—lighter in comparison and therefore traveling at higher velocity—would instead punch through. Once inside, the resulting explosion would "scatter death and fire" amidst the decks of the target. Built with a specially shaped powder chamber and reinforced body, tests against the retired 80-gun *Pacificateur* with two prototype Paixhans guns in 1824 demonstrated their effectiveness. The commission overseeing the trials judged that the shells "wrought such havoc ... [that] a similar explosion near the water line might have sunk the vessel." Adopted almost immediately by the French, the Paixhans gun underwent a number of modifications over the next several years. Standardized for naval use in 1842, the smooth-bore *canon-obusier de 80* fired a spherical 60.5-pound shell in its primary role, but could fire 86.5-pound solid shot when necessary. Paixhans, however, also theorized that such a weapon, mounted in steam-powered warships, would initiate a naval revolution and neutralize Britain's command of the seas. Although an effective ship-killer, Paixhans's invention did not prove to be the decisive weapon he predicted. "The only result," historian Walter Millis later wrote, "was that the potential enemy promptly appropriated the idea," and by 1853, Britain, Russia and the United States had adopted their own designs.[3]

Although German coastal batteries used them to destroy two Danish warships at Eckernförde during the First Schleswig War in 1849, the battle at Sinope marked the first major ship-versus-ship action involving shell guns. Either caught napping or deliberately holding fire, the Turkish commander Osman Pasha finally "signaled his fleet to fight bravely ... and at noon a desperate action commenced." For the next hour and a half, Nakhimov's larger warships poured fire into the sides of the smaller Turkish frigates, corvettes, and transports. Solid shot smashed timber and bone; shells pierced hulls and exploded, setting wood, rigging, and clothing aflame. Spreading rapidly, the fires eventually reached powder magazines, blowing ships apart and spreading the inferno to shore. The Russian gunners then turned their attention to the town for several more hours. A later report by HMS *Retribution* put the loss of Turkish life at nearly four thousand dead, wounded, or captured, at a cost to the Russians of thirty-seven men. According to a 5 January 1854 article in the *Sterling Observer*, the attack left the town of Sinope "completely destroyed, either by shells or burning timbers, and the whole coast ... strewn with dead bodies." Only one Turkish vessel, the steamer *Taif*, made it out of the harbor.[4]

Adolphus Slade, British advisor to the Turkish Navy and escapee on the *Taif*, observed that Porte officials "listened, apparently unconcerned" to news of the destruction of the harbor as if "listening to an account ... of a disaster in Chinese waters." Such a lopsided victory for Russia, however, provided considerable grist for the mill of those clamoring for war back home in Britain. The papers quickly named the battle the "Massacre at Sinope," and ignored the possibility the Sublime Porte had deliberately sacrificed the fleet to draw France and England into the conflict. Deliberate or not, the attack reinforced British arguments for intervention as a point of honor. It also

Artist's rendition of the destruction of Sinope, the opening naval battle of the Crimean War (*Battle of Sinop*, oil-on-canvas painting by Alexey Bogolyubov, 1860. http://www.art-catalog.ru/picture.php?id_picture=10118).

prompted George Villiers, the Secretary of State for Foreign Affairs, to write that "the circumstances which have attended this disastrous affair are of the greatest importance." Villiers wanted no misunderstanding between London and St. Petersburg. If the British and French fleets dispatched to protect Constantinople had instead been at Sinope, they "would have protected it, and would have repelled the attack."[5] Sinope would have—or perhaps should have, in Villiers' mind—resulted in bringing France and Britain into the war.

In addition to providing a *casus belli* for the allies, Sinope finally started the naval revolution that Paixhans had predicted. Previous experiments by the British Board of Admiralty from 1846 to 1851 had convinced many navies around the world of the unsuitability of iron for warship construction—experiments conducted with solid or hollow shot, but not shell.[6] The performance of the shell gun in combat, combined with the scope of the disaster at Sinope, proved to both naval authorities and the general public that the wooden warship had finally become obsolete. Only armor could resist the shell gun, only steam could propel an armored vessel, and only larger guns could defeat such ships—the classic cycle of offense versus defense that would drive naval armaments design into the twentieth century.

Odessa: The Revolution's Next Lesson

On 21 February 1854, the Coldstream Guards left England for Malta, part of an expeditionary force the British cabinet authorized two weeks before and placed under the command of FitzRoy James Henry Somerset, then Lord Raglan and the Master-General of Ordnance. The sixty-five-year-old Raglan had won a reputation for bravery during the Napoleonic Wars, famously losing his right arm at Waterloo. Although he never commanded an expedition in the field, Raglan proved an able administrator during the long peace, and many in the army considered him "just the man for the job." The cabinet originally authorized only a force of 10,000 men; Raglan, however, demanded that the number be doubled before he accepted the command. "As an old Peninsular officer of great experience," the *Morning Chronicle* reported on 16 February, "he knew well how rapidly the ranks are thinned in a campaign from fatigue, climate and a host of other diseases"—words that proved all too prophetic.[7]

On 28 March 1854 Britain and France declared war against Russia, two days after their ultimatum requiring the latter's withdrawal from the occupied Ottoman provinces of Moldavia and Wallachia expired. Shortly after the declaration reached the allied fleet at Varna, HMS *Furious* steamed to the Black Sea harbor of Odessa. Once there, the captain dispatched a boat and a lieutenant to collect the British consul. Stonewalled by the Russians, the lieutenant departed empty-handed; travelling back to the *Furious*, the boat took fire from Russian batteries, as did the steamer itself. The British claimed both craft flew white flags, and demanded an explanation for "outraging a flag of truce ... held sacred by all nations pretending to civilization." Such "unheard-of aggression" provided the excuse the Allies needed to open hostilities against the Russians. On 20 April, a combined fleet of nine steamers made their way to the harbor in order to "exact reparation from the authorities" of Odessa. Challenged to explain his actions, the Russian commander claimed he had not ordered fire against the boat, but only against the *Furious*, which he accused of "not heeding customary signals" and of entering the bay to spy on its defenses. Such an answer, which the *Times* labeled "unsatisfactory and untrue," did not mollify the Allied commanders. When a demand for the surrender of the merchant ships in the harbor went without reply, the Allies entered the bay to "punish this outrage on the law of nations."[8]

The bombardment of Odessa that commenced on 22 April represented not just the opening battle between the British, French, and Russians, but one fought with technology centuries apart. Steam power represented the newest of those technologies. One at a time, the Allied warships closed to within a thousand yards of the docks and ships at anchor in the harbor. At that range "each steamer delivered the fire of her enormous guns, then wheeled round in a circle of about half a mile in diameter" before coming back to fire again. "They kept wheeling and twisting about like so many waltzers," the *Times* reported, "without ever touching or getting into scrapes" with each other—a tactic only made possible because of steam power. Firing on the move, however, posed a challenge for the British gunners, and they more often missed their targets, the shore-based Russian gun emplacements, than hit them. A writer for *Blackwood's Edinburgh Magazine* who visited Odessa after the war noted that the British ships had "spread their shot all over an open and harmless city." Such wild shooting, while it did considerable damage, gave the townspeople a much different impression of the battle's outcome than what the British sailed away with. "All the numerous shot-marks," *Blackwood's* reported, were painted with two black circles with "Holy Saturday, 1854" between them, "a memento ... [of] an attack gloriously repulsed."[9]

During the next several hours both sides fired round after round at each other, including heated shot. An old technique shore batteries used against attacking ships, this involved placing a solid iron ball in a special furnace and heating it red-hot before loading and firing. Although gunners used a thick wet wad between powder and ball, such an operation carried the considerable risk of catastrophic accident. A British 32-pounder loaded with heated shot burst at Gibraltar in 1852, and the resulting explosion killed or wounded three officers, ten men, and threw fragments of the gun up to 140 yards away. The effects of the weapon against wooden warships, already vulnerable to fire because of their construction, made taking such a risk worthwhile. One or two strikes could put an attacker out of the fight, and this proved true for the unarmored ships in action at Odessa. Within an hour, the French steamer *Vauban* withdrew from the battle to deal with a fire ignited by such a round. The Russians, however, were not alone in using such a weapon. At least one of the attacking steamers, HMS *Terrible*, had its own furnace, and a lucky strike with a heated round blew up a Russian powder magazine.[10]

The Russians reported "an incessant shower of bombs, rockets, and red-hot balls" fired against them from the attacking British squadron, according to a *Morning Post* article of 9 May. The rockets were launched by a detachment of special "rocket boats" assigned to the fleet. Congreve rockets had seen long service with the Royal Navy, but were too dangerous to use aboard the average warship. Instead, rocket launchers were installed on shallow-draft boats which allowed them to close "within musket shot" of the docks in order to fire their 24 lb. projectiles. Soon, however, they were taken under fire by a Russian horse artillery battery. "Happily nobody was hurt," the *Times* reported, "though a perfect shower of balls fell around" the boats, "knocking the oars about and ploughing up the water around them." The rockets themselves "caused terrible destruction," setting the docks and part of the town aflame.[11]

With the reduction of the dockyards and merchantmen complete, the British finally sailed out of the harbor that evening, but Odessa would have

Congreve rocket boats in action (Major-Gen. Sir William Congreve, *A Treatise on the General Principles, Powers and Facility of Application of the Congreve Rocket System, as Compared with Artillery* [London: Longman, Rees, Orme, Brown, and Green, 1827], Plate 11. Courtesy Special Collections & Archives Department, Nimitz Library, U.S. Naval Academy).

one more lesson to deliver regarding ship-versus-shore combat three weeks later. Early in the morning on 11 May one of the British steamers that participated in the attack, HMS *Tiger*, became grounded during a heavy fog just a few miles away from the harbor. In an attempt to break free, the crew jettisoned all but one of her guns, to no avail. Stuck fast, she became a target for a Russian shore battery equipped with both shell guns and its own portable forge. "The frigate was thoroughly searched by the enemy's fire," *Blackwood's* later reported. "Shell from the howitzers ... passed easily through her sides and decks, bursting and spreading destruction everywhere." Heated shot "lodged in sail-bins, storerooms, and amongst other inflammable matter" and set the ship ablaze. With his ship mortally wounded, the British captain had no option but to surrender.[12] If Sinope was the first lesson of the naval revolution, Odessa was certainly the second; unfortunately for both French and British sailors, it would not be the last.

Infantry Weapons at the Battle of the Alma

The British line units that landed at Calamita Bay on 14 September 1854 arrived with essentially the same weaponry they carried against the

French forty years earlier. Infantry still fought with the bayoneted musket, and cavalry with the sword, lance, and pistol. Guns of all types, from heavy cannon to small arms, were single-shot weapons still loaded at the muzzle, or front of the barrel. For small arms, this required soldiers to reload while standing, which exposed them to the enemy. When fired, the gunpowder produced a tremendous cloud of smoke—quite literally the "fog of war"— and left a heavy deposit of soot in the barrel. Unless cleaned out, the soot built up to the point where loading a weapon became difficult, if not impossible. In addition, the sulfur in the residue combined with moisture in the air to produce sulfuric acid, which quickly corroded metal.

The British service musket had seen two important changes between 1815 and 1854. For nearly two centuries, military small arms used the action of flint striking steel to fire their charge. Although the mechanisms evolved over time, the basic operation remained the same. When the soldier pulled the trigger, a hammer holding a piece of shaped flint scraped against a steel catch. This not only produced sparks, but pushed the catch forward to expose a small pan full of gunpowder on the side of the barrel. The sparks ignited the powder, whose flame passed through a flash hole in the side of the barrel and hopefully ignited the weapon's main charge. Misfires due to weather, improper loading, or poor maintenance were common, as were "hang-fires," delays between the ignition of the priming and the discharge of the weapon. Britain regiments in the 1600s and early 1700s obtained their own weapons, resulting in a confusion of styles with a more-or-less common bore size. In the 1720s the first standardized musket appeared, with colonels ordered to obtain new arms "according to the said Pattern and proved ... by the Proper Officers of Ordnance." The British service flintlock musket, affectionately known as the "Brown Bess," appeared the decade following, and remained in service for nearly a century.[13]

An early-nineteenth-century development finally made the flintlock obsolete, and provides an interesting case study of British weapons evaluation of the period. In 1806, the Rev. Alexander Forsyth brought to London the first working percussion lock, the result of twelve years of experiment to overcome hang-fires in his hunting weapons. Forsyth's lock used the action of the hammer striking a charge of mercury fulminate, an impact-sensitive compound, to detonate the main charge. Faster and more reliable, Forsyth's invention impressed MGO Lord Moira so much that he asked the reverend to adapt his lock to service weapons, particularly cannon, believing "that it may become a matter of great importance to the Military Service." Given a workshop in the Tower of London, Forsyth attempted to do what Moira asked, but met with considerable resistance by "ignorant and prejudiced, if not actively hostile" Tower workmen and chemists "so deeply suspicious of all fulminating compounds" that they refused to mix the chemicals. In fairness to those men, the process required dissolving the toxic metal in nitric acid, a dangerous procedure resulting in an equally dangerous end product. Despite such obstacles, Forsyth soon constructed a lock and improved detonating compound capable of being used on cannon, only to be dismissed from the Tower when John Pitt (Lord Chatham, and a Tory), took office after Moira resigned as MGO on the fall of the Whig government in 1807. Chatham peremptorily ordered Forsyth (a Whig), to submit a final expense report, return all government property, and "immediately to remove his own 'rubbish' from the Tower."[14]

Undeterred, Forsyth patented his percussion lock that same year, and over the next several he and others perfected several designs of percussion systems. In 1818 the first percussion cap—a small copper cup with fulminate deposited inside—appeared, although there is considerable controversy regarding the originator of the idea.[15] The cap proved the key to constructing a simple and effective percussion lock. After loading the weapon, the shooter placed a cap on a hollow nipple on the side of the barrel. When the shooter pulled the trigger, the gun's hammer struck the nipple and detonated the fulminate. As with flintlocks, the flame still had to pass through a flash hole to fire the gun's charge. Unlike flintlocks, however, the percussion lock offered a surer, safer ignition system with much less fire directly in the shooter's face. The percussion lock also made hang-fires exceptional rather than occasional, a definite plus in the minds of many frustrated sportsmen. In a 25 July 1827 article, for example, the *Hereford Journal* reported that "a large Seal ... [which] had been a great annoyance to the salmon-fishing" at the mouth of the Don River for several years had finally been shot and killed. The seal had learned to dive at the moment it saw the flash from a flintlock, "but the cunning animal was at last deceived [by] a gun with a percussion lock ... thus deprived of its usual signal of danger."

The British military, however, hesitated to replace their stocks of the flintlock that defeated Napoleon, despite the entreaties of officers such as famed inventor Col. Frances Maceroni. "A cap is put on much quicker than a flint-lock is primed," Maceroni wrote in an article to the *United Service Magazine*, "and there is no time lost in changing flints" which dulled rapidly after repeated blows against the catch. Service weapons could "be converted into copper-caps, at a trifling expense, and new copper-cap locks will cost less than flint ones," he continued. "The only objection to the change, (and I own it is a very great one indeed), *is the blind prejudice of custom.*" Finally, in 1834, the Ordnance Department organized comparative trials between flintlock and percussion lock muskets. Six weapons of each type fired six thousand rounds in varying types of weather. The results could not be argued with: the percussion locks misfired only thirty-six times, compared to nine hundred and twenty-two for the flintlocks. Still, another five or six years passed before Ordnance launched a conversion effort, which proceeded slowly until the 1841 fire at the Tower of London wiped out the British stockpile of flintlock muskets scheduled for conversion.[16]

Forced to obtain new weapons, the "Pattern 1842" percussion musket retained many of the flaws Col. John Mitchell pointed out in a letter printed by the *Standard* on 18 October 1841. British muskets, the former infantry officer wrote, were supplied by the private gun trade, constructed by workmen "who can hardly know much of musket practice" and who produced "a heavy, clumsy, unhandy weapon; but good, strong, and substantial of its kind, without knowing that it is a bad kind." Mitchell pointed out that the standard infantry musket had only one sight, which made accurate aim impossible. The "Light Infantry" weapon had two, but so badly placed that the soldier tended to "fire high above the heads of the tallest sons of earth that ever sported Grenadier caps." "Our skill in the manufacturing of small arms is confined to the making of fowling pieces," Mitchell charged, "for gentlemen take an interest in the goodness of the implements intended for the destruction of hares and pheasants" but not in those "intended for the protection of national honour and interest."

The smooth-bore barrel, however, remained chief among the weaknesses of the Pattern 1842 musket, still referred to as the "Brown Bess" even with the new lock. Accuracy was poor; even in the hands of well-drilled troops, hit rates dropped significantly after 100 yards. At longer ranges, "few shots found their marks, and not only was ammunition wasted ... the enemy were encouraged by the fire's ineffectiveness, and one's own men were disheartened and became 'unsteady in the ranks.'"[17] Accuracy could be improved by rifling the barrel, which involved cutting grooves inside that spiraled down its length. Rifling imparted spin to the projectile and stabilized it in flight, but required a much tighter fit between the bullet and the barrel wall. Rifle shooters of this era wrapped the round lead ball in a greased cloth patch, which engaged the rifling to get the spin desired and also partially cleaned the rifle bore of powder residue. Loading a rifle required additional motions, however, as well as considerable effort by the rifleman to force the ball down the barrel; this not only slowed the soldier down but could affect his aim. British riflemen fought in the wars with France, but by and large they were in specialized units. The average infantry regiment in all armies of the time carried smooth-bore muskets, with much more emphasis on close-order drill and firing by volley than shooting accurately.

A number of inventors in Europe devised alternative means of loading rifles in the early 1800s, but Captain Claude-Etienne Minié of the French Army developed the most effective solution for muzzle-loaders. Instead of the traditional round ball, Minié used a cylindrically-shaped bullet with a conical nose and a hollow base lined with a thin iron cup. On firing, the exploding gunpowder forced the cup into the base of the bullet, which flared out the side walls to engage the rifling. The bullet had a much flatter trajectory and considerably longer range than a round ball, extending the effective reach of infantry fire out to 600 yards. Since the bullet diameter was smaller than the rifle bore diameter, it required no lubrication for loading. Grease on the outside of the projectile, however, helped prevent the build-up of gunpowder residue in the rifling grooves and so improved accuracy.[18]

Prussia took a different and much more revolutionary path with the 1841 adoption of the Dreyse needle-fire rifle, the first breech-loading weapon fielded in large numbers by any European power. Named after its inventor, Johann Nicolaus von Dreyse, the weapon used a combustible cartridge containing the charge, bullet and primer in one unit. On firing, a long needle perforated the cartridge to strike the fulminate at the base of the bullet. Loading at the breech meant not only could the soldier load and fire from any position, but the single-piece cartridge made recharging the weapon much quicker. Prussia went to great lengths to keep its new weapon secret, to the point of misnaming it the "*Leichte Perscussions-Gewehr M1841*," or "Light Percussion Rifle Model of 1841." Use in the 1848 revolution, however, brought the rifle to the attention of the rest of Europe. A fairly detailed description of the weapon appeared in the 18 August 1849 edition of the *Morning Post*; three months later, the Duke of Arundel brought a sample to England, with the *Dublin Evening Mail* reporting on 15 October that "authorities have graciously given orders for [its] admission, duty free."[19]

With so many changes offering to put an effective rifle in the hands of every infantryman, Britain took a hard look at its military small arms in 1850. After testing the Dreyse and other weapons, the Small Arms Committee chose the Minié "system" which paired his bullet with a four-groove rifled barrel. Despite its potential, the needle-gun proved "too complicated and delicate an arm for general service" in the opinion of the Committee. In addition, the rifle suffered from an ineffective breech-seal that allowed fire to flash into the face of the shooter, a problem that only grew worse with wear. The Committee found the Minié to be simpler, more accurate at longer ranges than the Dreyse, and much more reliable. In 1851, Britain licensed Minié's invention for £10,000 and placed an initial order for 28,000 "Pattern 1851" rifled muskets with Birmingham gunmakers.[20]

Not all military authorities were happy with the decision. Sir Charles Napier, the army's Commander-in-Chief in India and famed veteran of the Napoleonic Wars, published a pamphlet entitled *A Letter on the Defence of England* decrying the new rifle. In it, he wrote that he was "much disposed to doubt the '*minié rifle*,' as a weapon of war, though it may suit the deer stalker.... We do not want fire-arms, in the infantry, for individual combat, but for combat in masses, where the *nice aim* of the deerstalker is not *wanted*."

Raging that the Minié rifle "is not yet *proved*," Napier declared that "I would by no means 'be off with my old love'" the Brown Bess, "till the new one's temper has been better tried!" Napier may or may not have been representative of the general attitude of army officers, as a period historian noted that once adopted on the Continent, "there was a strong popular *furor* created for [the Minié rifle] in England."[21] Still, Wellington himself had "an almost superstitious admiration for Brown Bess," according to biographer Sir Herbert Maxwell, and it took a personal demonstration of the weapon's accuracy to convince the Iron Duke to sanction its adoption. Even so, he insisted that the Pattern 1851 retain the same .702" bore as the Brown Bess, for the dubious purpose of firing smooth-bore musket ammunition in an emergency.[22]

There were a few issues with the new weapon, chief among them the tendency of the iron expansion cup to be forced all the way through the bullet, which left its perforated carcass blocking the barrel. The original sight also proved faulty in both construction and graduation. Such problems could be easily fixed; the iron cup proved unnecessary in later trials, and subsequent muskets had a redesigned sight. The large size of the cartridge with its heavy bullet, however, meant soldiers could only carry fifty rounds in their ammunition pouch instead of the regulation sixty. This could not be fixed, but MGO Henry Paget (Lord Anglesey) understood that the Pattern 1851 represented a temporary solution based on the state of the technology, and pressed ahead with his decision to arm the entire infantry force with the rifle. The bottleneck proved to be the Birmingham gun trade, still very much a cottage industry; problems in the manufacture of the rifle delayed the completion of the first order until November of 1853.[23]

Hardinge, who replaced Anglesey as MGO with the 1852 change of government, also recognized the temporary nature of the weapon, and in April of that year advertised to "our most eminent Gunsmiths" for a lighter weapon of smaller caliber. Such a move "was undoubtedly due to the persistent outcry made by the gun-makers and the sporting public that a better rifle was possible." The Small Arms Committee found faults with all of the samples submitted, including one designed by George Lovell of the Royal Armoury Mills at Enfield. Setting a precedent followed by every small arms committee for the rest of the century, the Committee therefore decided to design its own rifle. The new design had a bore size of .577-inch, which retained the weight of the old Brown Bess bullet (480 grains, or just over an ounce of lead) but not its diameter. Specifications were passed to Enfield for refinement, and what emerged would be "arguably one of the finest muzzle loading rifles ever to be put into the hands of a soldier." The "Pattern 1853 Enfield Rifle" proved extremely reliable over its lifetime of service. Its lighter weight and lessened recoil meant that a far greater percentage of British infantrymen handled the weapon effectively; thirty-three percent of the force qualified as first-class shots, as opposed to only ten percent armed with the earlier rifle.[24] Finally, the smaller diameter bullet meant a lighter and equivalently smaller cartridge, which brought the amount of ammunition that could be carried back to the regulation sixty rounds per man.

In twelve years, Britain had gone through three changes in its primary infantry weapon before finally arriving at what Hardinge described as "the most deadly weapon ever invented." The Enfield shot farther than the 600-yard standard effective range of smooth-bored field artillery, and could fire twelve rounds in the time it took cavalry to cover 800 yards. Both Master-Generals recognized, however, that the physical weapon represented only one element of a larger system. Prior to the adoption of the new rifle, small-arms training had been indifferently conducted at the regimental level. In February of 1852, Ordnance began building a systematic approach to musketry training with the Minié rifle, resulting in the foundation of the School of Musketry at Hythe, Kent, in 1853. The next year, the School published the army's first official *Instruction of Musketry*, and the first detachment of trainees arrived in April. The army was at a loss as to how best to harness the powers of the new rifled musket, however; the adoption of the Pattern 1842 smooth-bore did not require a change in tactics, only a change in the loading drill. The long range of the rifled musket, on the other hand, offered "a complete revolution in the art of war," but 1854 found British military authorities "only just beginning to digest the killing power of the Minié, without fully appreciating its tactical consequences."[25]

Unfortunately for the Crimean expedition, events in 1854 also caught its units transitioning between these three different types of muskets. Although Pattern 1851 Minié rifles were to be issued for the first wave of infantry units departing for the Crimea, the low initial production order meant most reinforcements went out with the older Brown Bess. Those first-wave units that did receive the Pattern 1851 underwent hurried training at Gallipoli before shipping out to the front. Continued problems with the Birmingham gun makers, including a strike at the outbreak of the war, meant that very few soldiers were equipped with the Pattern 1853 Enfield. Most regiments at the front would not exchange their larger Pattern 1851 muskets until early in 1855—with the curious exception of Royal Artillery gun crews, armed with the carbine version of the .577 Enfield. This mix of three different weapons made the supply of proper ammunition a challenge. The Royal Navy, which retained many of its older muskets, had worse issues; the *Morning Post* of 29 August reported that the Admiralty issued a special circular to denote "the proper denominations of ball cartridges for each description" for the five different weapons in use in the Royal Navy.[26]

Napier, who so condescendingly dismissed the Minié as a deerstalker's rifle, did not live to see it proved in combat. Despite the problems caused by a major weapons transition, the infantry wielded their rifles with deadly effect in their first contest with the Russians at the Battle of the Alma. The British, firing as they advanced up Kourgané Hill, inflicted heavy casualties amongst the defenders, many of whom were struck in the head. The large Pattern 1851 bullet traveled at higher velocity than the smooth-bore round ball and "tore and broke all before it." "The common musket ball at such a range would have done no great damage," the *Leicester Chronicle* reported on 14 October, "but here the balls had come out through the top of the skull, rending the bone as if done by a hatchet. The wounds were awful." In a letter reproduced in the *Cork Examiner* on the 18th, however, a Russian infantry officer admitted that "the fire of the Minie rifles, with their long range, did us a good deal of mischief," but tellingly added that they "would have done us much worse if more of the enemy had had better shots among them."[27]

As a piece of infantry equipment, the Minié rifle represented a significant advance over the old smooth-bore musket. But as the Russian officer's opinion indicates, a weapon system is composed of more than just equipment. The new rifle required changes in logistical support, soldier training, and tactical thinking to truly be effective—areas that the British army either did not have time to address, or failed to consider completely, before marching off to war in 1854. In addition, although infantry played a major role in getting the allied army to the gates of Sevastopol, reducing that harbor's formidable defenses rested with a weapon the British army was most deficient in: artillery.

British Guns Before Sevastopol

Having cleared the Alma heights on 20 September 1854, the allies approached the harbor fortress of Sevastopol at the end of the month. Defenses were far from complete, and Raglan suggested an immediate assault. His chief engineer, Sir John Burgoyne, insisted on reducing the fortress's artillery before the infantry attacked, and the French commanders agreed. For the next eighteen days, the French and British dug assault trenches and struggled to emplace their siege cannon. The Russians, given a tremendous gift of time, reinforced their defenses, shelled the entrenching allies, and prepared for the coming battle.[28]

The Royal Artillery siege train that landed at Balaklava included 24- and 32-pounder long guns for direct fire against the fortress walls, 10-inch mortars for dropping shells into the forts, and 8-inch shell guns, also for direct engagement but with shell instead of solid shot. Unlike the French Paixhans gun, the British Millar shell gun was too light at 52cwt to withstand the powder charge required to fire solid shot for battering down earth and stone defenses. Instead, the army borrowed several 68-pounder broadside guns from the Navy.[29] Weighing 9,500 pounds each, these monsters required back-breaking effort—under fire—to haul into place. The guns had "to be taken all to pieces," wrote one artillery officer, as the small wheels designed for use onboard ship meant the carriages could not "be moved along by themselves." With a maximum charge of sixteen pounds of gunpowder, however, the guns could throw either a sixty-eight pound solid shot or fifty-one pound explosive shell over four thousand yards distance. Designed to smash through the thick timber sides of line-of-battle ships, such cannon were expected to wreak havoc on the walls of Sevastopol. Their use, the same officer optimistically predicted, "will tell more than any battery ever heard of at a siege before."[30]

Size notwithstanding, the guns "were in all essential particulars much of the same type as those of the days of Queen Elizabeth": cast-iron, smooth-bored, muzzle-loading pieces which required considerable engineering work to bring to bear against the fortress. The complex process of loading the weapon required the construction of protective embrasures for the besieging gun crews to shield them from Russian retaliatory fire. Artillery of this era also lacked any means of controlling recoil; after firing, the crew had to roll the piece back into position and re-aim for the next shot. Wooden firing platforms had been sent from Britain, "of a new and ingenious structure, which ... [served their ends] admirably when tried upon a perfect level at Woolwich." On the rocky ground around Sevastopol, however, the new design proved unworkable, and engineers pillaged timber from local houses to build new

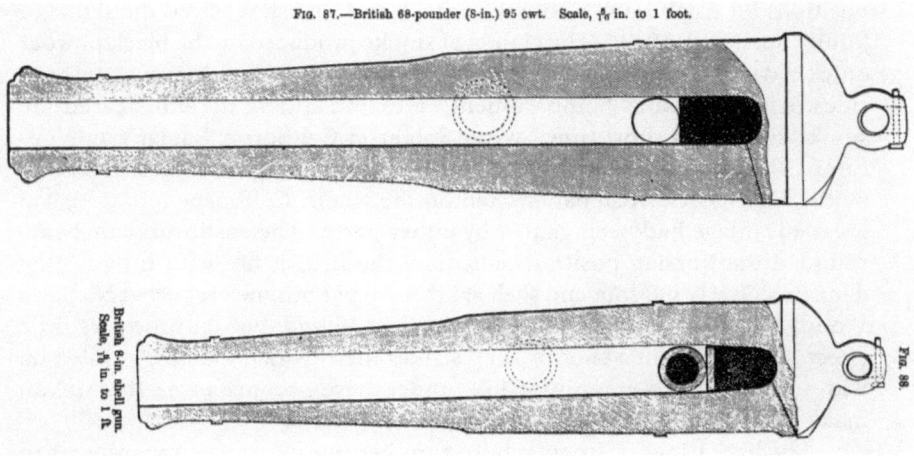

British cast-iron guns in use at the siege of Sevastopol included (upper) the naval 68-pounder and (lower) the Millar 8-inch shell gun (Alexander Lyman Holley, *A Treatise on Ordnance and Armor* [New York: D. Van Mostrand, 1865], 122).

platforms. Finally, the lack of mechanical means for moving equipment meant that the "heavy guns, great stores of ammunition, and the loads and loads of material required for the business of siege work" had to be hauled seven miles inland by the very limited number of horse and bullock carts available.[31]

The lack of rifling combined with the spherical shape of their projectiles meant that the shot and shell fired by smooth-bore guns rapidly lost velocity, which reduced their striking power at long ranges. To open a suitably wide enough gap in the walls to allow for an infantry assault, the British had to get in close and pound the Russian fortifications hard. A pre-war experiment by the Royal Engineers calculated that to open a one-hundred-foot breach took over ten thousand rounds of 24-pounder solid shot, fired at full charge from 500 yards. Unfortunately for the attackers, chief engineer Burgoyne "saw insuperable difficulties in carrying on his Engineer works within breaching distance ... [given] the heavy fire which could be brought upon them" by the Russians, and placed the British batteries out further than their most effective range. Burgoyne's conservative approach meant that the British had to "consider their position as principally one of bombardment" in support of the French on their left. Despite this, *Times* correspondent William Russell hopefully reported that "the superior weight of our siege guns will more than compensate for the difference in distance."[32]

By the morning of 17 October, over one hundred and twenty allied guns, howitzers, and mortars stood ready to bombard Sevastopol, opposed by about the same number of Russian pieces.[33] The Russian gunners, seeing the enemy embrasures cleared for action, fired first, and hammered away at the allied positions for a half hour before the French and British received the signal to jointly open fire at 0630. The clouds of smoke produced by the black powder quickly darkened the air over the battlefield and obscured targets on both sides. After an hour's bombardment, "a breeze sprang up and cleared the smoke away for a short time," wrote Somerset Calthorpe, Raglan's aide-de-camp. The top portion of the Malakov Tower had been "knocked to pieces" by the rightmost British battery, but on the whole, Calthorpe reported, "no great advantage had been gained by either party." The earthworks that surrounded the Russian positions absorbed the British fire with little lasting damage. "Nearly 100 shot and shell are thrown per minute," reported Nicholas Woods, the correspondent for the *Morning Herald*, but "it produces little effect.... The instant a shot or shell strikes their works, the hole is filled up with sandbags—It seems impossible, under these circumstances, that we can make any impression on our foes."[34]

The limitations of smooth-bore guns became ever more apparent when the Royal Navy joined the fray later that day, in what *Blackwood's Edinburgh Magazine* later termed "the final experiment of wooden ships against granite and earthen walls." Prevented from getting in close to the harbor by a line of sunken Russian ships, the allied fleet took position an average of twelve hundred yards from the Russian coastal bastions and opened fire. Over the next six hours, their 1,240 guns fired over 50,000 rounds against the 150 Russian shore batteries, both sides producing so much smoke that Russian gunners took to "firing at the gun flashes of the invisible ships while shells crashed around their heads." For all their fury, however, the British and French warships caused very little damage. As at Odessa, the long range combined with the motion of the sea served to greatly lessen the effectiveness of the allied guns. The Russians, firing from land, could do so much more accurately; when the allies broke off the engagement they sailed away with five badly damaged ships, thirty dead, and over five hundred wounded. The true lesson of the "massacre at Sinope" was now made crystal clear to both British and French naval leaders. The age of the smooth-bore-armed, shot-firing wooden warship was over.[35]

Another technological problem was the lack of a truly effective shell fuze. As with the Minié rifle, the Crimean War caught the British military transitioning between two different time fuze designs, both intended to be ignited by "windage." The difference between the cannon bore diameter and the slightly smaller diameter of the shell, windage allowed the gunpowder flame to wrap around the ball and ignite the fuze, which would burn down to the projectile's internal bursting charge. The older "common" fuze consisted of a wooden plug bored through, filled with compacted gunpowder. Depending on the amount of burn time required, several different lengths of fuze were available. For finer adjustments, however, the gunner either cut the fuze or bored out the bottom. Either action left the central column of powder unsupported, often resulting in

An American Civil War–era 10-second time fuze. To adjust the length of the burn, a gunner would cut the fuze along one of the graduated lines. On the right is a view of the fuze bottom, showing the exposed powder column.

"blinds" (shells that did not burst), late bursts, or premature explosions in the gun—the latter being particularly hazardous to the crew.[36]

The problem of the fuze was solved by the inestimable Captain Boxer, who in 1849 proposed a new type of time fuze. Also made of wood, his design had holes drilled into the side at specific intervals along its outer length; the artilleryman simply punched the hole desired to set the burn time. This left the internal powder column supported at the bottom, resulting in far fewer failures. Brought before the Select Committee in 1850, Boxer's fuzes "passed with such flying colors that the ... Committee recommended their adoption for all gun and howitzer shell." Approved 2 September 1850, the new pattern required a few more years of experimentation to perfect, and it is very possible that some of the earlier and more unreliable versions were sent to the Crimea. An 1852 modification added a head that projected above the shell surface, making the fuze vulnerable to damage and prone to dislodgement on ricochet, a tactic commonly used with shell guns. Some fuzes made before the summer of 1854 also suffered misfires because of grease seeping into the wood during manufacture. Boxer continued to refine the fuze to overcome these deficiencies, however, and by the time of the first bombardment of Sevastopol, "England possessed probably the best fuze in Europe."[37]

Unfortunately for British gun crews, the batteries that participated in the initial bombardment had been sent out with the old common fuze, and the mortars in particular experienced an alarming number of premature bursts. As a stop-gap measure, London telegraphed an order for gunners to bore, rather than cut the fuzes, in an effort to at least decrease the problem until a supply of new fuzes could be sent out. Once Boxer's invention reached the theatre of operations, Royal Artillery historian Col. Julian Jocelyn laconically wrote, "there was no more trouble." Gen. Sir Richard Dacres, who rose to command all the British artillery in the war, called Boxer's fuze one of the "greatest improvements in artillery stores that ... appeared during the war."[38]

Boxer's fuze, while efficient and reliable, detonated the shell strictly by time of the internal burn; it did not detonate the shell on impact with the target. Two different types of impact fuzes were then in service. In 1846 the army adopted a wooden fuze designed by Quartermaster Freeburn of the Royal Artillery. As with the Boxer time fuze, this "simple and ingenious" device ignited by windage; the sudden stop on impact with the target drove the burning material into the body of the fuze, which in turn detonated the shell. Its use in the Crimea is unknown, but likely. The navy, on the other hand, used a metal fuze designed by Lt. William Moorsom. Adopted in 1851, this fuze had a complex, multi-chambered internal design. On impact, one or more of the hammers struck a percussion detonating compound, which then set off the main charge in the shell. Noted by an 1862 author as being "liable to accidents," the Moorsom fuze worked well when impacting solid

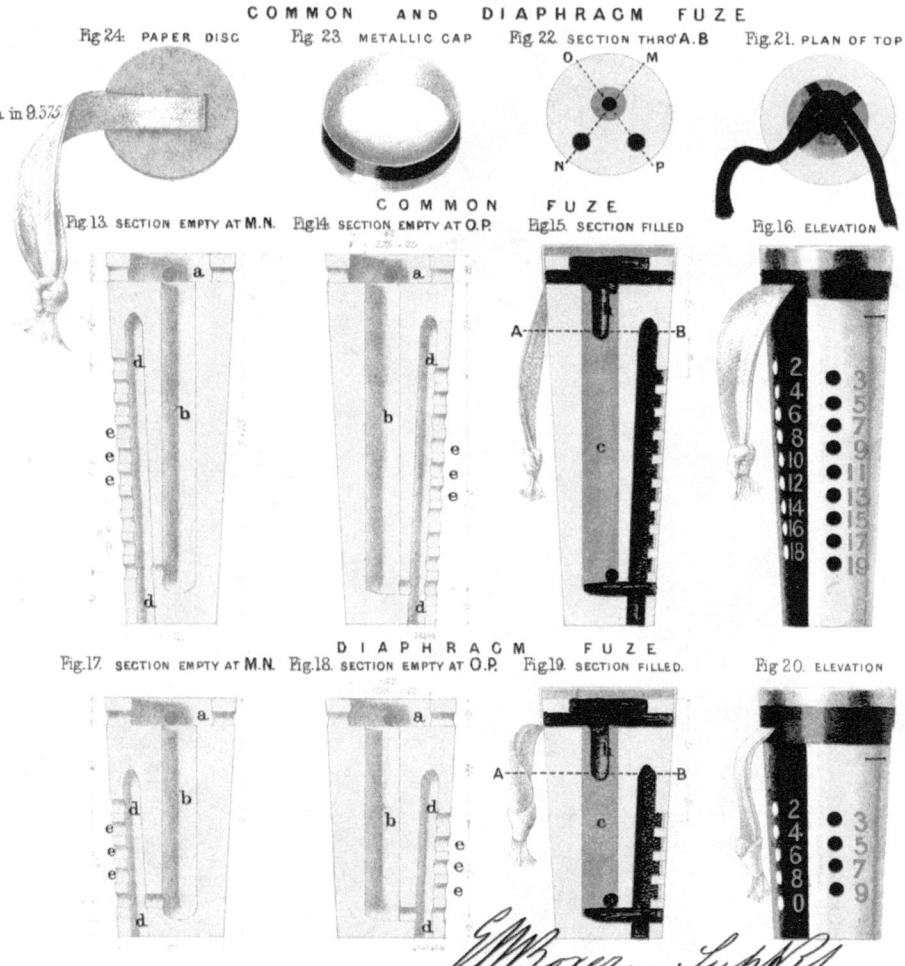

Boxer's wooden time fuzes for muzzle-loading common and diaphragm shells (Capt. Vivian Dering Majendie, RA. *Ammunition: A Desricptive Treatise...* [London: HMPO, 1865; rep. Gettysburg, PA: Thomas Publications] Plate 2).

objects—such as ships' sides.[39] Fitted to both the 68-pounder and Lancaster shells, the fuze often failed to detonate when impacting the packed earth surrounding the Russian defenses at Sevastopol.

Regardless of the type, a malfunctioning fuze turned an explosive shell into nothing more than a lighter and less effective shot round. Both the British and Russians suffered fuze misfires, littering the battlefield with unexploded ordnance, a particular hazard to the drunk or ignorant. One party of inebri-

64   The British Military Revolution of the 19th Century

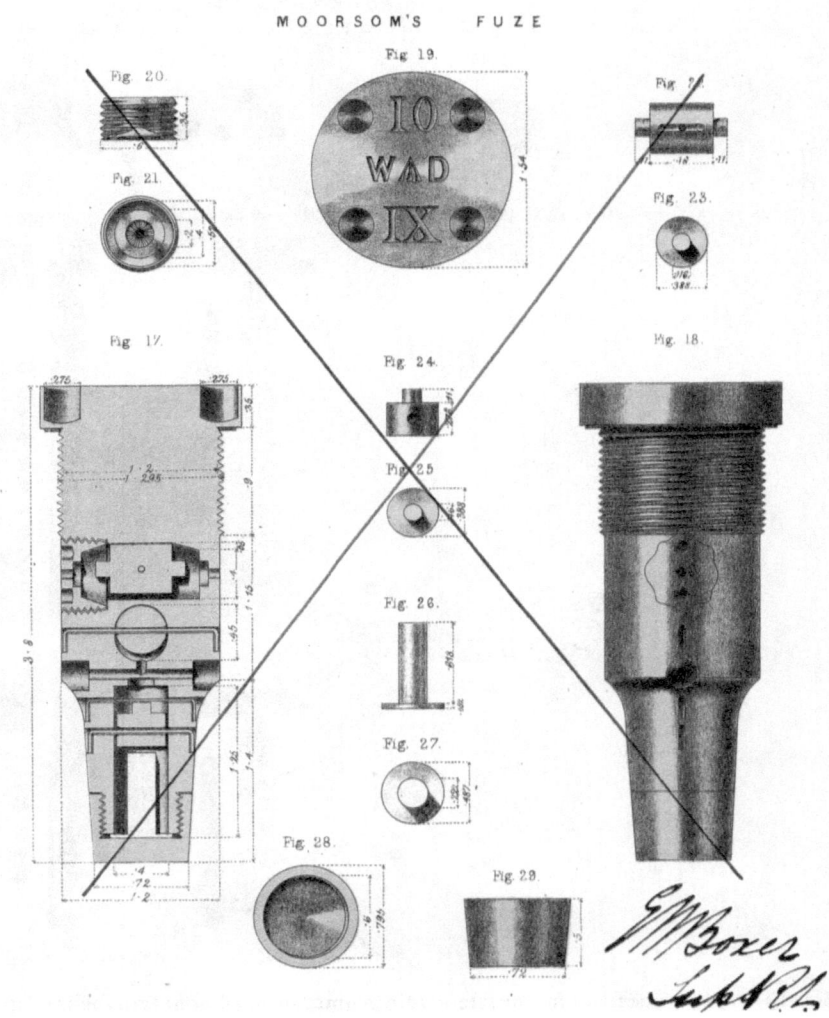

The Moorsom naval time fuze. The large "X" indicates that the fuze had become obsolete by 1865, replaced by a metal version of Boxer's fuze (Majendie, Plate 3).

ated British soldiers lit a fire and put an unexploded shell into it, "then seated themselves around the fire, eagerly watching the result: the shell exploded, and every man was killed or fearfully mangled." Another soldier of the 47th Regiment "had the foolhardiness to jerk the ashes of the tobacco in his pipe, which he had just finished smoking, into the fuze-hole" of a large shell whose fuze fell out during flight. "Both his legs were shattered" when it exploded, "and he was frightfully scorched about the head and face"; five other men were also wounded, according to a 10 August 1854 report from the *Dublin Evening Mail*. Such behavior required "the greatest watchfulness on the part of the officers to make [the men] sufficiently thoughtful of their own safety, and that of others around them."[40]

Although smooth-bore cannon formed the vast majority of the artillery deployed by the British, the Royal Navy included four experimental 68-pounder "Lancaster" rifled guns in the equipment loaned to the siege effort. A recent invention of famed gun maker Charles W. Lancaster, these muzzle loaders used an oval-shaped bore rotated along the axis of the barrel to impart spin to their specially-shaped projectiles. Originally developed as a rifled small arm, Lancaster designed a full-sized 68-pounder artillery piece to display his rifling principle at the Great Exhibition of 1851. Instead, Government persuaded Lancaster to keep his new cannon under wraps and send it to Shoeburyness for trial. Impressed with the long range and accuracy of the weapon, the Royal Navy purchased several for use aboard its *Arrow*-class gunboats, which arrived in time to lend the guns to the siege efforts.[41]

Despite impressing naval and ordnance authorities, the new gun did not live up to its promise. Reports from its use in the field were mixed. On the

"A quiet day in the Diamond Battery—Portrait of a Lancaster 68 pounder, 15th Decr. 1854." The artist mistakenly added a regular round 68-pdr shot (lower right corner) rather than the elliptical Lancaster shot (lithograph by Day & Sons, London, 1855).

one hand is Woods's rather breathless description of its effects as published by the *Preston Chronicle* of 11 November 1854. He claimed that Lancaster rounds "rushed through the air with a noise and regular beat like the passage of a rapid express train." The peculiarity of the noise "excited shouts of laughter among our men, who instantly nicknamed it the express train." "The effect of the shot seemed most terrible," Woods continued. "A battery of twenty or thirty such guns would destroy Sebastopol in a week," but the short supply of ammunition meant the two guns "are only fired once in eight minutes." Still, "the delicate attentions of the Lancaster gun ... effected a most unfavourable change" on Malakov Tower, he wrote. "Huge holes were visible on its side, where masses of the solid masonry were dislodged." Once the smoke cleared, "the Lancaster gun on our right redoubled its fire.... I never saw such firing. Every shot told full upon the building, and the officers of all ranks ... were speculating on how long the tower could stand." Against the Russian earthworks, however, the Lancaster shells proved much less effective. Captain Stephen Lushington, commander of the brigade of borrowed Naval artillery, observed that the light Lancaster shells burrowed into the earth with little impact. "I fear the Lancaster is a failure," he reported, "and we might as well fire into a pudding as at these earthworks." William Russell of the *Times* was much more succinct. "The Lancaster guns made bad practice," he reported, "and one burst." The latter unhappy trait, combined with the requirement for special ammunition, meant that the Lancasters played only a minor role during the siege. Of the seven eventually deployed, three were rendered "unserviceable from use," and in total, fired only 1,542 shells—not even one percent of the total thrown against the Russians.[42]

Curiously, the British did not make use of what might have been a game-changing weapon during the siege, one that they themselves invented: the diaphragm shrapnel shell. Into the Napoleonic Wars, British field artillery used two types of cannon: the gun and the howitzer. The longer-barreled field gun formed the bulk of traditional European artillery batteries, and fired a solid iron ball along a relatively flat trajectory. Also known as round shot, if accurately pitched the ball carved its way through the close-ordered ranks of infantry and remained deadly as long as it kept rolling. During the American Civil War, there are numerous recorded instances of soldiers having their lower leg taken off when trying to stop moving round shot with their foot. The other form of cannon, the howitzer, formed a much smaller portion of many artillery batteries. These weapons, with shorter but generally larger-diameter barrels, were designed to fire gunpowder-filled "common" shells in a higher trajectory to drop down onto targets. Very useful for destroying enemy artillery, howitzer shells could also be ricocheted into opposing troop formations where, even if it did not explode, the shell could be as deadly as round shot. Once attacking troops started closing in, gun crews serving either weapon switched to firing canister (also called case shot), consisting of a brass or tin case filled with iron balls. This effectively turned the cannon into an enormous shotgun—devastating against troops at close range, but only effective to about 400 yards or so, depending on the size ball in the case.[43]

Although deadly under ideal circumstances, all three projectiles had limits to their effectiveness. A well-placed solid shot could shred an enemy column; once the men deployed into line, however, that same ball might only take out one or two soldiers unless fired obliquely. Field guns, due to their flat trajectories, could not fire over the heads of friendly forces; howitzers could, although their numbers in European artillery batteries were much lower than standard field guns and varied by country. They could also fire either solid shot or explosive shell, and the latter often proved disturbing on the battlefield. General Cavalié Mercer, a British artillery officer, noted in his Waterloo memoir that French howitzer shells fitted with long-burning fuzes "lay spitting and sputtering several seconds before they exploded, to the no small annoyance of man and horse." Shells were unreliable, however; fuzes often fell out in flight or on ricochet, and crew error could lead to premature explosions. When a shell did properly function, the outer iron case tended to break into several large fragments. Although a much better choice for close-in work, canister rounds did not always separate; when they did, as many as three-quarters of the balls struck earth rather than the intended target. The much-smaller balls also lost kinetic energy quickly, which at longer ranges took out attacking front-rankers but left those behind intact. The two- to three-hundred-yard difference between canister's maximum range and the minimum range generally accepted for round shot also left an enormous gap on the battlefield.[44]

In 1784, then Lieutenant Henry Shrapnel proposed a remedy, what he called "spherical case shot." This consisted of a thin iron shell filled with lead musket balls, with gunpowder poured into the gaps. The powder charge burst the shell open when detonated by a time fuze, gauged to fire before reaching the target. The bullets then continued forward at the same velocity and direction as the previously unbroken shell. This delivered a hail of lead at a considerably farther distance than case or grape shot, allowing the artillery to hit exposed troops harder and earlier than before and break up attacks before they became a threat. In spite of its potential, Shrapnel's proposed projectile did not appear before the Select Committee for evaluation until 1792, and another eleven years passed before the Committee finally approved it for service. This may have been in part to Shrapnel's importune description of his invention "as of equal importance with the introduction of gunpowder, which would hardly sit well with tradition-bound artillery officers."[45]

First used against the Dutch at the battle of Fort Amsterdam, Surinam, in 1804, "shrapnel had so excellent an effect as to cause the garrison ... to

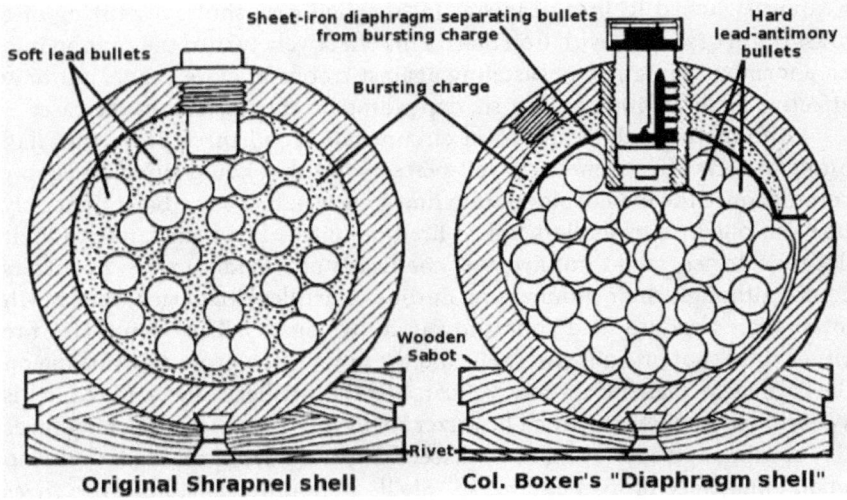

Original Shrapnel shell **Col. Boxer's "Diaphragm shell"**

The original Shrapnel shell design (left) v. Boxer's redesigned "diaphragm" shell (Douglas T. Hamilton, *Shrapnel Shell Manufacture* [New York: The Industrial Press, 1915], 4).

surrender after receiving the second shell" according to Major Wilson, the commander of the British artillery. At the battle of Vimeira (Portugal, August 1808), British 9-pounders firing spherical case shot routed the French infantry, who complained that "devils were in the British shells."[46] The shell in its original form suffered from a number of defects, however, made plain in testing after the close of the Napoleonic Wars. Experiments carried out in 1819 with the final pattern resulted in a twenty-three percent failure rate. Boxer developed his improved time fuze in large part to correct this problem, but muzzle bursts remained common. In 1849, therefore, the inventive captain began experimenting with the means of separating the bursting charge from the bullets. After testing several different methods, he settled on a shell having a curved iron plate over the lead balls, with the bursting charge between the plate and the shell wall; grooves cast on the inside of the iron casing facilitated fracture when the bursting charge detonated. Tests demonstrated the efficacy of his "diaphragm shrapnel shell"; when coupled with his new pattern of fuze, only six percent of the shells failed, a significant decrease compared to the 1819 tests. After further refinements, MGO Hardinge approved adoption of the diaphragm shell in 1853.[47]

In combination, the improved fuze and diaphragm shrapnel shell represented a significant advancement in artillery ammunition, "the beginnings of a whole new era" rather than an evolutionary step in smooth-bore equipment. New tactics, such as overhead fire in support of advancing troops and

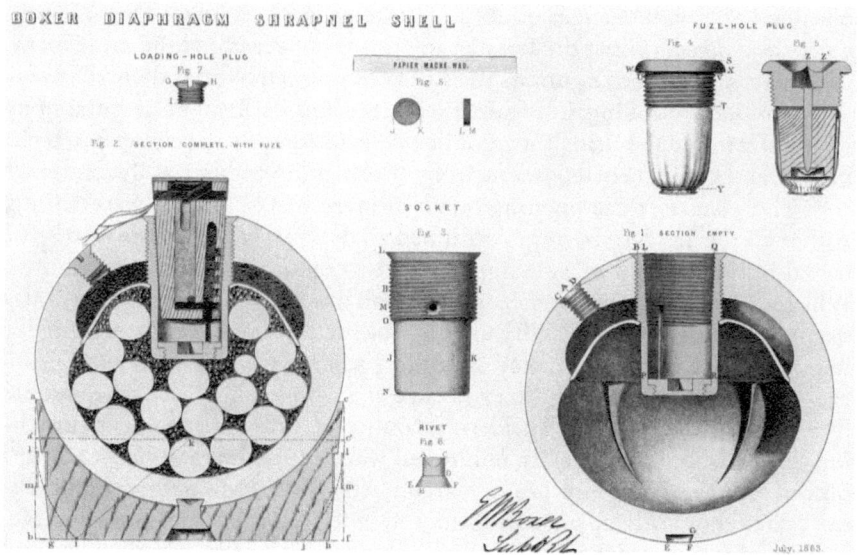

Detail of the Boxer "diaphragm" shrapnel shell for smooth-bored muzzle-loading guns (Majendie, Plate 24).

counter-battery fire against opposing artillery evolved—post–Crimea—to take advantage of the greatly increased effectiveness of the weapon. Within ten years, the shrapnel shell would be referred to as "the most important part of [British] armaments at the present day," ultimately becoming the primary artillery shell of choice in the First World War. The Royal Laboratory, however, lacked the ability to manufacture Boxer's improved shell—which in turn meant that the Royal Artillery sailed off to the Crimea in 1854 without it. Spherical case shot—the older and much more unreliable pattern—did see service during the bombardment of Sevastopol, but the amount fired equates to around one and a half percent of the total rounds of shot and shell expended in the siege. In addition, shrapnel shells were only available for the 24-, 32- and 68-pounder guns used; none of the howitzers or mortars fired shrapnel. Clearly, British tactical thinking had not fully embraced the potential of what author Nick Lipscombe argued had been a "force multiplier" in the Napoleonic Wars.[48]

The British expeditionary force that marched off to do battle with the Russians did so with a combination of weapons systems almost as antiquated as the military administration such arms operated under. Although some improvements had been made, such the Pattern 1853 rifled musket, reliance on outmoded manufacturing practices kept the army from rapidly fielding the new weapon. The nation's artillery in particular suffered from near-obsolescence; with changes in only a few items, such as Boxer's fuze, British gunners arrayed against the Russian fortresses of Sevastopol the same forms of cast-iron and bronze guns as the Russians pointed back at them. Conservative military thinking, bureaucratic inertia, and Parliamentary parsimony effectively mired the British army at its 1815 peak, despite the changes in technology and civilian society wrought by the ongoing Industrial Revolution.

The results of the opening bombardment of 17 October were telling. Although the artillery barrage continued all day—in fact, into the next—the initial bombardment of Sevastopol failed to reduce the Russian defenses. While a chance hit on a French ammunition magazine early on significantly decreased their partner's ability to fight, the ineffectiveness of British fire lay in large part with the dormancy of artillery science between 1815 and 1854—if not with that of British military science as a whole. The Minié rifle, despite its performance on the battlefield, could only play a supporting role in breaching the well-built and heavily reinforced walls of the Russian harbor. Manpower could not emplace heavy enough artillery, and horse- and bullock-carts could not bring up enough ammunition to feed what guns were in place. The sacrificial use of the Russian fleet to blockade their own harbor negated the massive broadside weight of the allied navy, which could not get close enough to do any real damage. There were technologies that might have tilted the balance for the British, but the Lancaster gun failed in its first combat test, and under-mechanization at the Royal Laboratory meant Boxer's diaphragm shell could not be put into production in time. By November, the prediction of *Bell's Life* proved true. The war did not last a month. It lasted, to the great consternation of the public, much longer.

"More Powerful Than the Charge of Cavalry"

As events in the Crimea unfolded before the eyes of the public, the disorganization confounding British military administration became all too apparent. The papers reported everything, from the numbers felled by cholera, to troubles with the medical and supply systems, to the failure of the first bombardment of Sevastopol. Then, disaster struck. On 14 November 1854, following three days and nights of freezing rain, a fearsome winter storm sprang up and hammered the exposed allied forces. "In the memory of men," *Times* correspondent William Russell wrote, "such a hurricane has not desolated the Crimean shores." In his dispatch printed by the *Sussex Advertiser* on 19 December, Russell reported winds so great that the soldiers on the cliffs over Balaklava "lost tents, clothes—everything! the storm tore them away over the rocks and hurled them across the bay, and the men had to cling to the earth with all their might to avoid the same fate." Russell later estimated the loss of men "cannot be less than a thousand." The storm also caused tremendous damage to the fleet, with "forty-six transports and other vessels being destroyed, and many more injured."[1] The greatest calamity, however, was the loss of the *Prince*, a new British screw steamer carrying "forty thousand suits of clothing, with under-garments, socks, gloves, and a multitude of other articles of the kind ... the whole of the winter clothing for the British army." It also carried provisions, hospital stores, and "a vast quantity of shot and shell." The latter, along with 900 tons of gunpowder, formed the cargo of the *Resolute*, also sent to the bottom by the storm. The loss of the two ships, the *Times* wrote on 5 December, meant that "all the materials for carrying on the siege and providing against the severity of the winter have been carried off at one fell swoop ... we are not in a condition to stand our worst foe, the coming winter."

Despite the implications of such a disaster, the *Leeds Intelligencer* gamely reminded its readers on 2 December that "we cannot expect to carry on war without loss.... It must be submitted to with patience, and produce a greater exertion on our part." Ships must be replaced or repaired, the efforts of the army, navy, and civilian society redoubled. "In sounding the heroic deeds of our veterans abroad," the paper explained, "we at home must earn for ourselves the consolation that we have left no effort untried to bring them success." Such a message reflected the mood of the British public: the country must stand behind their military forces and provide them all possible assistance. This translated into a much greater and more active level of participation in war efforts since the close of the Napoleonic Wars. Although the average British subject still disdained wearing a uniform, many volunteered to organize fund-raising campaigns for supplies or donations to the *Times* and Royal Patriotic Funds. Others travelled to the Crimea to donate their time and expertise. This included Florence Nightingale, famous for reorganizing the hospital at Scutari, and Chef Alexis Soyer, who overhauled the kitchens of the Balaklava Hospital and introduced several important improvements in British army culinary practices.[2] Concerned Britons also bombarded their favorite newspapers with letters regarding all aspects of the war, while writers with a more inventive streak—or a product to market—pelted the Board of Ordnance with their suggestions.

What the *Intelligencer* editorial did not imply, however, was uncritical support for a government seemingly incapable of handling the war effort. Public opinion, which Palmerston had once declared "more powerful than the charge of cavalry or the thunder of artillery," rapidly turned against the Aberdeen ministry, which had led the country to war at the behest of the public to begin with. The loss of support, coupled with the strain of a war Britain was clearly unprepared for, led not only to a change in government; it also led to the elimination of the antique Board of Ordnance, a process started under Aberdeen and completed by subsequent administrations. As part of this shakeup, the old "Select Committee of Artillery Officers" gave way to a new "Ordnance Select Committee" (OSC), also responsible for weapons evaluation but with a longer reach and more flexible mandate. Although little noticed by the greater public, the creation of the OSC was a crucial step in the professionalization of British military research and development, and critical to the nation's transition into the era of modern weaponry.[3]

"*The Board of Ordnance Ceased to Exist*"

Both the public and government were confident of a short, triumphant war in April of 1854, and the latter took few steps to deal with the military administration muddle. Raglan, despite being dispatched to the front to coordinate with the French, retained his post of MGO. Surveyor-General Lauderdale Maule traveled with him, only to die of cholera at Varna later that year. This effectively left only two experienced members of the Board of Ordnance to coordinate war supply in London. On Raglan's recommendation, the seventy-five-year-old Lt. Gen. Sir Hew Ross took over the recently resurrected post of Lieutenant-General. Ross considered his duties limited to military affairs, however, and concentrated on getting the Royal Artillery ready for war. Without effective supervision, the remaining two members—William Monsell, the Clerk of Ordnance, and Principal Storekeeper Sir Thomas Hastings—quarreled constantly. "For all intents and purposes," wrote Arsenal historian Oliver Hogg, "the Board of Ordnance ceased to exist" before England fired its first shot in anger.[4]

In June of 1854 the Aberdeen government took an important first step in overhauling British military administration by splitting the overburdened Secretary of State for War and Colonies post in two. It made a crucial error in the creation of the new office, however, as it prepared no "Order in Council, Minute, or other document ... defining the special duties" of the new Secretary and his subordinate officials, except an estimate for funding the post. Aberdeen's cabinet felt the change to be "initiatory to [others] ... which would necessarily follow," but never further considered the issue. On 17 July Lord John Russell, minister-without-portfolio in the cabinet, presented the estimate for the new office and an explanation for its creation. He hinted at changes to come, such as an overhaul of the Board of Ordnance, and stated that the Commissariat would transfer from Treasury to the War Office. Otherwise, Russell left the definition of the new office hanging. After some debate, backbencher George Butt sarcastically summed up the government's position. Russell, Butt claimed, "says 'appoint the new officer, and from time to time he will consider what duties it will be convenient for him to undertake,'" whereas Sir Sidney Herbert, then Secretary-at-War, "said 'we cannot tell what duties are to be assigned to this new officer, but give us time and we will find him something to do.'" Butt wrapped up with the hope that the new office "should be intrusted with the superintendence of all our preparations for the conduct of the war."[5]

Despite the amorphous definition of power, Henry Pelham Clinton, the Duke of Newcastle and Secretary of State for War and Colonies since 1852, became the new Secretary of State for War; Sir George Grey took over that of Colonies. The Parliamentary Under-Secretary post also split, with a Permanent Under-Secretary—an apolitical accounting and managerial position—created to assist the new Secretary. Newcastle, a career politician with a reputation for hard work built over a long history of public service, must have been aware of the confusion in the office that awaited him. Still, he took the post, and defined it along the lines that Butt had hoped for. Considering himself "officially responsible for the all the departments under his control"—the War Office, the Board of Ordnance and their subordinate departments, and now the Commissariat—Newcastle "issue[d] such orders as he though fit for their guidance" as well as those to supply the army in the field over the next several months.[6]

As with the rest of the British military, the Royal Laboratory proved woefully unprepared to meet wartime demands. As Boxer later wrote, "nothing could have been more unsatisfactory than the state of the Ordnance Department as regards ... war *matériel*, or the means for their production." In particular, "it was found impossible to procure, by the ordinary means, a due supply of efficient Shrapnel shells" for the field artillery units bound for the Crimea. Early in 1854 Boxer, still only an instructor at the Royal Military Academy, "undertook [on his own accord] to supply the deficiency, a service of no ordinary difficulty." By refurbishing old-style shells with his improvements, Boxer made ten thousand "efficient" shrapnel shells available in less than a month.[7] Boxer's success led to his formal transfer to the Royal Laboratory as Assistant Firemaster on 13 April. That same month, Monsell "saw clearly that in the event of any large expenditure of shell in any military or naval operations, [the Laboratory] should have been entirely unable to supply the wants of the service." A "man of action" who knew Boxer to be the same, Monsell sent for the energetic young officer and explained the situation to him. "If there is any one in the world who can get us out of our difficulties," he later testified saying, "I am sure you can." Boxer "pledged himself to place the department in five weeks in a position to supply any number of shells that would be required."[8]

Boxer drew up a list of £7,150 worth of machinery and supplies needed to establish a temporary factory in a storehouse. Approved on 2 May, Boxer used the money to install the necessary equipment and took over production of Congreve rockets as well. By the end of the month he received further funds for fuze-making machinery. "Such was the energy and determination displayed," wrote Hogg, "that within the scheduled time [the shell] manufactory was in operation with two steam engines, many hundreds of feet of shafting, machines, tools, etc. producing a large increase in ammunition." In addition, the finished products cost £200 per day less than shells manufactured using older methods, a reduction that allowed the new factory to recoup the initial outlay within six months' time.[9]

Such a heroic effort led to Boxer's June promotion to Firemaster, second in command and responsible for ammunition and rocket production. In that post, he continued his drive to increase mechanization and efficiency at the Laboratory, and his efforts led the Board of Ordnance to direct him to establish an experimental shell foundry. The Board had long done business with foundries such as Low Moor Ironworks, but the increasingly specialized

The Shell Factory, Woolwich Arsenal, 1856 (photograph by Robert Howlett; Royal Collection Trust / © Her Majesty Queen Elizabeth II, 2018).

nature of ordnance materials (such as the shrapnel shell) and a lack of familiarity with producing the same meant that private industry could not rapidly meet wartime needs, as in previous wars. Building its own foundry would allow the Arsenal to determine "the best mode of manufacturing ... to meet sudden emergencies, and to control the prices" of shells supplied by contractors. For help with the project, Boxer approached John Anderson, the Inspector of Machinery at Woolwich and who had already constructed a factory for the manufacture of shells for Lancaster guns "at great personal sacrifice, [and] in the space of only two months." Given a budget of £10,000, the pair set out to construct a model factory, "in which the great manufacturers of this country can learn ... the best mode of overcoming the difficulties which now exist in adapting establishments and machinery to the production of shells."[10]

Boxer and Anderson threw themselves into the effort, but building the foundry very nearly cost Boxer his job. Col. Julian Jocelyn, in his *History of the Royal Artillery*, described the young captain as a "mechanical genius endowed with a nervous energy ... fully impressed with the vital importance of his work and grimly determined to trample on everything and everybody that interfered." Such spirit led Boxer to dismiss workers he felt were not giving their all to the project, usurping the power of hiring and firing that rested with the Master-General and Board of Ordnance for himself. The commanding officer of the Royal Laboratory, Col. J. A. Wilson—"an old and courteous gentleman thoroughly versed in routine"—charged Boxer with insubordination. In his own defense, Boxer wrote to Wilson on 16 January 1855 that as there was "yet much, very much, to be done in the department ... my endeavours will be of little avail" without the power to discipline his own work force. Sir Hew Ross, the only member of the Board in London at the time of the incident, felt that Boxer's demand for such authority was "dictated more in the spirit of a foreman of mechanics ... than ... of an officer holding the rank of Captain in the Royal Artillery." Furthermore, Ross felt the tone of Boxer's letter disrespectful to Wilson, regardless of Boxer having made a formal apology. Ross warned Boxer that "a repetition of such disrespect will involve the necessity of return to the ordinary duties of his regiment, that he may learn what is due to discipline and to the rules of Her Majesty's service."[11]

On 24 January 1855, Boxer, "without any previous notice, or without having had any opportunity of saying one word in his own defence, received ... a most severe reprimand" from Ross in the presence of Wilson and other Arsenal officers, "simply for writing the letter" of 16 January. The censure included Ross's comparison of Boxer's actions to a "foreman of mechanics," an imputation against Boxer "as an officer and a gentleman" that Monsell felt would almost certainly lead to the young captain's resignation. While not "denying that, in the excitement and hurry of business, Captain Boxer has ... paid too little attention to the rules of official routine," Monsell held that the services of the creative officer were of vital importance. "Captain Boxer is the officer most distinguished for inventive skill and scientific knowledge that we have had for many years," Monsell wrote in his defense. Boxer had "saved the department from disgrace, and the country from imminent danger" with his shell foundry, projected to save the country £40,000 over the first year's operation. Monsell "earnestly" called for his "colleagues to reconsider the whole matter, and to concur with me in withdrawing the Minute of censure." When they did not, Monsell threatened to take the matter before Fox Maule (Lord Panmure), the newly installed Secretary of State for War and brother to Lauderdale, the late Surveyor-General of the Board of Ordnance. Such a threat prompted Ross to reword the censure so as to remove any character references; Boxer retained his post, and eventually replaced Wilson as head of the Laboratory when the ordnance factories were reorganized later that year.[12]

Boxer's struggle over his continued employment at the Laboratory highlights the dysfunctional nature of the Board of Ordnance. Where Monsell saw talent and potential, the established military authorities, Ross and Wilson, saw an unwillingness to defer to the accepted order of things. A serving officer, Boxer also found himself caught between two competing chains of command. The military side rightly required obedience to orders, but the civilian side, under intense emergency pressure, required only the efficient production of materials needed for the prosecution of war. The split personality of the Board could not resolve such a dilemma, and the "disastrous muddle" very nearly consumed one of Britain's rising technological talents. Finally, despite the rewording Monsell still forwarded the papers to Panmure at the latter's request, and the incident most likely reinforced the Secretary's determination to do away with the Board of Ordnance.[13]

"We Erred in Our Confidence in Common with the Public at Large"

The efforts of energetic young officers such as Boxer, while contributing to the overall war effort and the foundation of a new post-war administrative system, could not rescue the British expeditionary force from disaster over the winter of 1854–1855. Newcastle, despite his great efforts, was handicapped by the occupation of a new department with no separate office, ill-defined powers and responsibilities, and a working staff of himself and two Under-Secretaries.[14] Neither he nor Raglan could overcome the perfect storm of "disastrous muddle" and disastrous weather. The failure of the first bombardment of Sevastopol, the losses inflicted by the November gale, and the scenes of a frozen and forlorn British army painted by William Russell and his fellow correspondents proved too much for Britons at home. A 20 January 1855 editorial in the *Hereford Times* summed up the mood of the public. "The history of this country," the paper wrote, presented no "parallel where a war has been so thoroughly popular, where the Government was so thoroughly supported in every relation, and where the results, as a whole, have been so thoroughly unsatisfactory."

Calls for the resignation of the Aberdeen government began shortly after news of the November storm reached London. In a particularly sarcastic editorial, on 2 December 1854 the *Worcester Journal* reminded its readers that "the siege of Sebastopol does *not* continue. That Russian stronghold, taken by the *Times* on the 25th of September and securely held by our contemporary for several days, now remains in the hands of the enemy. The place is not likely to be *re*-taken this winter." "Is the Aberdeen Administration to continue its baneful existence?," the *Journal* continued. "We are indebted for our disasters to the policy and subsequent blunders of the Aberdeen Ministry. We have lost men, we have lost treasure, we have lost influence.... Let it not be supposed that our present position and condition are due to any other cause than the conduct of the Government." The *Herts Guardian* went even further, with an accusation on 9 December that Aberdeen and his cabinet had been "anxious to harm Russia as little as possible," apparent through the "conduct of the war, and in the bungling attempts at treaties which preceded it." "It is the first time in the history of this country that England has been engaged in a war," the *Guardian* charged, "with the heads of the Ministry sympathizing with our foes. It is a most disgraceful and shocking fact but it is so."

On 12 December, Queen Victoria called for a special joint session of Parliament "in order that by your Assistance I may take such Measures as will enable Me to prosecute the great War in which we are engaged with the utmost Vigour and Effect." During the following debate, Conservative party leader Edward Smith-Stanley (Lord Derby) charged that "from the very first to the very last, there has been apparent in the course pursued by Her Majesty's Government a want of previous preparation—a total want of prescience ... [which] appeared to live from day to day providing for each successive exigency after it arose, and not before." In addressing Derby's accusations, Newcastle admitted that the siege of Sevastopol "was likely to be more protracted than I readily admit the Government at first expected." He also suggested that "if we were over-confident—I believe that we erred in common with many men of great experience in war, and men whose opinions were well worth having—and we erred in our confidence in common with the public at large." *Blackwood's Edinburgh Magazine* pounced on Newcastle for this remark. "Good heavens! has it come to this, that a British minister ... excuses himself and his colleagues for a hideous error in the conduct of a campaign, on the ground that 'the public at large' shared in that same delusion?" Government, before sending the army to "die before the fortress or carry it by breach and assault," should have known more about the intended target than "the best informed of the public." If not, the ministers "are answerable before God and man for every life that has been lost in the attempt."[15]

Applying What "Scientific Discovery and Invention Have Supplied" to the War Effort

While the papers were calling for the heads of Aberdeen and his ministers, reports from the Crimea moved many British subjects to find some way to assist in the war effort. For most, this meant a contribution of money or time to one of two relief funds set up during the war. The month before the storm, the *Times* established its "Crimean Fund for the Relief of the Sick and Wounded" after receiving an outpouring of letters and donations as a result of Russell's report of hospital conditions at Scutari. The paper eventually gave control of the money to Florence Nightingale, which helped fund her efforts to overhaul British army hospitals. That same month, Queen Victoria established the Royal Patriotic Fund to assist the families of fallen servicemen. The Queen appealed to the public for support, and the response was tremendous. "Meetings are being held throughout the length and breadth of England, and of Scotland and Ireland too," wrote the *Chelmsford Chronicle* on 3 November 1854, "in aid of the funds for the support ... of the widows and orphans of those who have perished" from cholera or "the shot of the Russians before the stronghold of the Crimea." Such meetings raised enough money to allow the fund to establish two new schools for orphans of the war, as well as provide assistance to families left destitute by the loss of their soldier-fathers.[16]

Those with a more military or technical bent peppered their local papers with observations or suggestions regarding the conduct of the war, including the shortcomings of Britain's military technology. The failure of the bombardments of Sevastopol proved particularly fertile ground for those with opinions to offer. A lengthy analysis by "A Prussian Engineer" to the *Daily News* that appeared on 11 April 1855, for example, took apart the mistakes of the French and British besiegers piece by piece. After critiquing the entrenchments, transport issues, and tactics of the allies, the writer came to the technology. "A large proportion of the French artillery," he wrote, consisted of undersized and underpowered cannon. "The English guns were more powerful," he continued, but were "placed at such distances from the Russian works that correct aim and precise and effective firing were quite unattainable" because of "questionable notions" regarding the utility of long range fire. "The 'long range' idea has proved a bane throughout the siege ... and never was powder and ball spent to less real purpose." The writer blamed the rise of such notions on the illusory abilities of the Lancaster gun. Any of its faults—"excessively short barrel, a windage, a weak charge of powder, and a bullet of very questionable shape, wanting a correct centre of gravity"—would have been enough to prevent accurate long range fire. "But," he concluded, "this is not the first instance in military matters that the very best results have been expected from the greatest accumulation of defects."

The Lancaster gun's predilection for bursting—and the measures the government took to cover up such a flaw—threatened what Newcastle later described as "embarrassment to the Government." Even before news arrived of the cannon's performance at the opening bombardment, the *Daily News* published a scathing report that questioned both the gun's worth and the behavior of Government as regards the weapon. Their 21 October article revealed that a Lancaster that burst at Shoeburyness in September of 1854 had killed three sergeants, but the fact had not been made public. When questioned, an unidentified workman confirmed the men had been killed, but remarked that "they tries to keep them kind of accidents out of the papers." The very thin and oft-pierced veil of such secrecy surrounding the manufacture and trials of the weapon put the *Daily News* on the offensive.

"We claim and shall exercise," the paper wrote, "the right of questioning whether a siege, a campaign, or the grand problem of the whole war, is to be put to the hazard of such crude and unsafe instruments as the Lancaster gun."[17]

The exposé prompted a spirited debate in the *Daily News* between readers as to the exact cause of such bursting. Samuel Haughton, a professor of geology at Trinity College in Dublin, felt the fault lay in the use of too heavy a projectile. In a 25 October letter, he suggested lengthening the barrel, as "the guns which I saw at Woolwich did not appear to have the requisite length for the very great diameter of the bore and great weight of the ball." Other writers had differing theories, but in the habit of many who wrote to their favorite editor, declined to give a real name. "Conjecture" felt that "the oval shape of the bore, cut into a gun cast in a circular form, resulted in uneven thickness in the barrel." His 27 October letter suggested that "the defect [might] be obviated by giving an elliptical form to the outside as well as the inside of the gun." In that same edition, "Papin" thought that "the least shifting of position by the explosive force of the powder must tend to fix the ball in the gun," a flaw which could be corrected using lead on the outside of the projectile, more giving than bare iron—but which already was a feature of the Lancaster shell. "A. Landman" agreed, but thought such a proposal would be too expensive. Instead, he suggested on 28 November the use of "patent felt, vulcanised India rubber, leather, or gutta percha" in a manner used by "many of the best riflemen, both here and in America."

"Papin," however, had not stopped with a contemplation of the cause of the Lancaster gun's bursting problem; in the same letter he castigated British military authorities for not harnessing "all the appliances at command which scientific discovery and invention had supplied since the last European war." The operations at Sevastopol suffered from a blind adherence to "war conventionalities" on the part of allied commanders, "rules prescribed before the invention of rockets, of the Minie rifle, and the large pieces of ordnance now used for battering" fortress walls. For example, he recommended a scheme of simultaneously discharging several cannon at one target, something "accomplished with great ease by means of voltaic electricity." Vauban, the great seventeenth-century French authority on fortress warfare, "would gladly have availed himself of the means of accomplishing what he deemed so essential"—such as the speedy reduction of the defenses around Sevastopol with new technologies. "His disciples in the art of war hesitate to take advantage of the power conferred by science," "Papin" continued, "because it is not so set down." "If a novel invention be bound with red tape it may have a chance of being received with favour," "Papin" complained, but otherwise "it then becomes too visionary and impracticable a matter for serious consideration by the devotees of routine."

Such letters, and the dozens—if not hundreds—of others like them show a segment of the British public not only interested but actively participating in discussions regarding military technology. They also show that writers such as "Papin" were aware of the institutional wall constructed by the "devotees of routine"—the Master-General and the Select Committee—aimed at keeping out inventors and proposals that didn't conform to commonly accepted military thinking. It would take a revolution in military administration to bring down such a wall—a revolution very much on the horizon when "Papin" penned his letter to the *Daily News* in October of 1854.

From the "Select Committee of Artillery Officers" to the "Ordnance Select Committee"

With the War Department under siege by the press and public, Newcastle sought professional advice on military matters from Col. John Henry Lefroy, then secretary of the Royal Patriotic Fund. Early in his military career Lefroy had exhibited a keen interest in advancing the "science of artillery." In 1838, he and another young artillery officer, Frederick Eardley-Wilmot, helped establish the Royal Artillery Institution at Woolwich. After spending several years abroad conducting magnetic and meteorological observations for the British government, Lefroy returned to Woolwich in 1853 and helped re-animate a moribund Institute as well as outfit its laboratory. With war on the horizon, in 1854 Lefroy compiled the *Handbook of Field Artillery for the Use of Officers*, a textbook published by the Institute for use in theatre. The first three hundred copies were sent to the Crimea in July, and the book remained a staple of officer instruction for the next thirty years. Newcastle appointed Lefroy his confidential technological adviser in December 1854, and tasked him with examining military inventions at home and abroad, to include a review of the procedures by which the Ordnance Department handled unsolicited proposals. Lefroy, concerned with the weaknesses of the Select Committee, persuaded Newcastle to reorganize the whole system. In one of his last acts before resigning over the conduct of the war, therefore, Newcastle proposed replacing the "Select Committee of Artillery Officers" with a new "Ordnance Select Committee" (OSC). This decision, shepherded by Lefroy and supported by Panmure, proved of immense significance to the history of British military technology.

In an 8 January 1855 letter to Sir Hew Ross, Newcastle explained his primary reason behind the change. "Appeals from the decisions" of the old Committee and "complaints against its mode of dealing with subjects brought before it," wrote Newcastle, were "of frequent occurrence, so much so as to threaten embarrassment to the Government." Both Ross and Cator, however, objected to such a condemnation. The latter, in his defensive summary of the Select Committee's activities, wrote that "if complaints have been made, they have not reached the Committee in tangible form"—hardly surprising, since no mechanism existed for handling such complaints. Anecdotal evidence, however, existed aplenty, which Cator and other Ordnance officers seemed willfully ignorant of. A 27 October 1854 letter to the editor of the *Daily News*, written by Alexander Melville and prompted by "Papin's" correspondence two days before, provides one such example. In August of 1850, Melville and Edward Callow received Pat. No. 13,215 for "improvements in cannon and small arms." "Our invention in several forms was submitted to the Board of Ordnance," Melville complained to the paper, but "you know too well the fate of most matters submitted to official notice, unless by some of the 'favoured few,'" most likely referring to Lancaster. Melville and his partner resubmitted their plan in 1852, but after attending the meeting of the Select Committee, "we saw in a moment how little chance we had" of overcoming the evident prejudice against inventors "being [neither] military men [nor] members of the government gun trade." "Our plans and proposals," Melville wrote, "were laid quietly on the shelf alongside of many others, and we were politely bowed from the room." With the Baltic Fleet poised to set sail in 1854, Melville tried one last time to bring the proposals before "the 'old gentlemen' at Woolwich," but with the same results. "Not having time ... to throw away on dancing attendance at the 'front' door of the Ordnance, and being unacquainted with the keeper of the 'back' entrance," Melville "despaired of ever [getting] my plans properly considered."[18]

Blaming such complaints on the small size, limited scope, and strictly military makeup of the Select Committee, Newcastle proposed nearly doubling its membership from nine to over sixteen members made up of both military and civilian authorities. Such a construction would endow the OSC with "the special knowledge and talents of individuals holding scientific and professional offices" in and outside the Royal Arsenal. As with the original Select Committee, *ex officio* military officers formed the bulk of the first OSC, such as the Director-General of Artillery and the heads of the manufacturing establishments. Civilian officials such as the Professor of Mathematics at the Royal Military Academy, the Chemist to the War Department, and the resident Civil Engineer of the Royal Arsenal, also were assigned. Newcastle, however, proposed adding one or more "Associate Members, selected by the Government from the scientific professions." Such an expansion, he felt, would make participation on the committee "a less burdensome duty" for the various departments chiefs. At the same time, civilian members would give "the advantage of obtaining other than strictly military opinions upon questions of a mixed scientific and practical character." Newcastle also suggested that "the admission of officers, selected for their scientific attainments," would be "a measure which cannot but open a most honourable distinction to the junior members of the Corps of Artillery and Engineers." This latter appears to have been of particular importance, as Newcastle repeated it in a subsequent letter.[19] Finally, the OSC would report its findings directly to the Secretary of State for War, unlike the older Select Committee which reported to the MGO.

Newcastle directed the OSC to assemble forthwith, their first duty being to frame procedural rules and determine the meeting schedule. He also asked that they "report ... the powers they may desire ... and the arrangements that may seem ... most suitable for considering, for testing if necessary, and for reporting upon the various matters that may be brought before them." After several meetings, the OSC reported back on 26 January 1855 with suggestions that underscored the transition to a more permanent and professional organization. The OSC asked, for example, that the assistant secretary be "permanently employed as such," rather than having a junior member tasked with that duty, and that their clerks receive a raise and housing. "Increased accommodation" for the expanded committee should also "be immediately afforded." The OSC also requested the Director-General of Artillery be given authority "to obtain ... such assistance, ammunition, and stores, as may be necessary for the purpose of carrying on the experiments and practice that may be required." In an effort to impose some limit on their workload, the OSC suggested that "no subjects should be entertained ... except as are referred to them" by the Secretary of State for War. Such a restriction would have made the OSC merely an evaluation committee along the lines of its predecessor. Newcastle replied that a similar proviso restricted the old Select Committee from originating proposals, which "must deprive the public service of one of the greatest advantages than can be derived from the great military experience and scientific knowledge of the officers and gentlemen composing the Committee." The OSC, therefore, would be "empowered to originate, and recommend for adoption, any improvements it may deem important," subject to final approval. The OSC then requested that some process be constructed to weed out the "vast proportion of inventions submitted for consideration ... totally inapplicable to military service" in order to relieve the committee "from the useless expenditure of their time, which must otherwise be bestowed on the consideration of such subjects." Newcastle agreed, and suggested that a screening sub-committee could handle the task, "provided that a register be kept, by number, of all the subjects considered, so that they can be at all times referred to." This suggestion does not appear to have been put into action, as the records of the Committee's investigations contain numerous complaints regarding the useless expenditure of time and money on proposals of questionable value. Finally, Newcastle emphatically dismissed Gen. Cator's hope that "the power of referring

Artillery questions [be left] to officers of Artillery." None of "the most eminent English writers on gunnery, were Artillery officers," Newcastle pointed out, nor were many "inventors of important improvements in Artillery." "I am of opinion," he continued, "that many questions must arise upon which all the light that can be shed by general mechanical knowledge or high mathematical skill, [which] will be of national importance." By removing such a straitjacket, Newcastle ensured that the new committee could make the most of the intellectual resources available both in and outside the military establishment. Such a decision remains one of Newcastle's most important contributions to the advancement of British military technology.[20]

One request made by the OSC that the War Department did grant was expansion of the artillery test range at Shoeburyness. In the 1840s, weapons practice on the Plumstead Marsh next to the Arsenal became problematic, as inaccurate or accidental shooting posed a grave threat to shipping on the Thames. In 1849, the Board purchased land near the town of Shoeburyness at the mouth of the river. An isolated coastal site, the grounds provided a safe impact area for experiments and practice shooting regardless of tide, coupled with easy access to the Arsenal by boat or barge. Named after the nearby town, the new range saw five years of summer use before the threat of war led to more permanent development beginning in 1854. The OSC requested not only that the facility be extended, but that the officer commanding, "having very great responsibility and important duties to perform," be provided an assistant officer and "experienced" sergeants, "in order to insure that accuracy which is requisite in conducting, as well as in ascertaining and recording the results of, important experimental practice."[21] The establishment of a permanent test facility, with a professional staff, represented a significant maturation of the "science of artillery" in Britain.

Replacing the "Slow, Jarring, and Cumbrous Machine"

Newcastle did not remain in office long enough to see his plans for reorganization bear fruit. On 29 January 1855, the House of Commons passed a motion for a special committee "to inquire into the condition of our Army before Sebastopol, and into the conduct of those Departments of the Government whose duty it has been to minister to the wants of that Army." The motion had been introduced by John A. Roebuck, who would eventually head the committee. It also led the Aberdeen government to resign the next day.[22] The first attempt to form a government under Derby failed, which prompted a gloomy comparison between the military and the political battlefield by the *Burnley Advertiser* on 3 February. "Our prospects in the Crimea, that great Golgotha in which so great a portion of the flower of the British army have left their bones, are not a whit better than when last we wrote," moaned the *Advertiser*. "We are now rapidly approaching to as lamentable a state of disorganization and anarchy at home as still continues, and we fear will continue to prevail in the Crimea, minus only the starvation, diseases, misery and death." Fortunately the state of political anarchy proved short-lived; three days after the *Advertiser* article, Palmerston—"for whom press and public were clamouring"—became prime minister.[23] Panmure, former Secretary at War under Russell, succeeded Newcastle as Secretary of State for War.

The press, as may be expected, had not been unanimous in calling for the heads of the Aberdeen ministry. The *Elgin Courier*, for example, defended the outgoing government in a 9 February editorial, and reminded its readers that the *Times* had only the year before "denounced Lord Palmerston as the greatest quack of modern times" for his opposition to the war. More importantly, however, the *Courier* pointed out that "the late Cabinet have been made the victims of a vicious military system—a system that had been long sanctioned and supported by the House of Commons." Such a system had to be fixed, and in an article the day before the *Daily News* predicted Panmure the man for the job. "To carry into effect the radical and sweeping reforms called for in the British army," it wrote, "a Minister is required who can, when necessary, do unpleasant things; and Lord Panmure has shown that he not only can do unpleasant things, but takes pleasure in doing them."

Palmerston and Panmure came into office determined to finally deal with that most unpleasant of things, the "disastrous muddle" of military administration. Without waiting for the Roebuck committee's first report, Palmerston "signed [the] death warrant" of the antiquated and often antagonistic post of Secretary-at-War "on half a sheet of note-paper" in early February. What duties the post had passed to the Permanent Under-Secretary of State for War under Panmure. In addition, plans were announced to divorce the military from the civil branches of the Ordnance Department. Hardinge, now the Commander-in-Chief, assumed control of the Royal Artillery and Engineers, whereas the manufacturing departments and other non-military functions passed directly to the Secretary of State for War. The Secretary-at-War post continued to exist, but remained vacant until its final abolition by an act of Parliament in May of 1863.[24]

An unsigned memo dated 17 February emphasized that the heads of the Arsenal manufacturing departments were to remain serving Royal Artillery officers. "It is necessary that the person who is responsible for the work has a sound scientific knowledge of … the different articles manufactured," the memo argued, "and at the same time [have] an experimental acquaintance with their use." Placing such officers under a civil rather than military head eliminated the "evils that at present exist," such as the interference in manufacturing by a higher-ranking officer, or chain-of-command issues that nearly cost Boxer his future at the Royal Laboratory. It would also encourage professional scientific education among the officer corps. The latter particularly vexed the author of the memo. "Although there is a considerable amount of talent among the officers of Artillery," the memo noted, few ever pursued such education, and none saw it as a means of advancement. "It has been by the sheer obstinacy of some able officers," such as Boxer, "that the authorities have been forced to undertake works which were required for the safety of the country." A second confidential memo, also unsigned but most likely written by Panmure, laid out the future chain of command for ordnance development. At the head would be the Director-General of Artillery (DGA), then General Sir William Cator. Charged with supplying "a professional opinion on all subjects connected with the *matériel* of the Artillery Department," the DGA would now decide the "nature of all armaments": their size, intended use, construction, types of projectiles, and so forth. Panmure also tasked the DGA with gathering statistics regarding the "number, nature and condition of all guns, mounted or unmounted, in charge of the Artillery all over the world." Finally, the DGA would preside over the Ordnance Select Committee in his supervisory role regarding changes of ordnance equipment and supplies.[25]

The transition in government both stalled Newcastle's reorganization of the OSC and opened a door for those wishing to keep civilians out of military matters. In March, Panmure heard from an inventor who "declined submitting an invention on discovering that no mathematician was present" at the review of his proposal. Col. Lefroy, on behalf of the War Department, wrote to Sir Hew Ross regarding the status of the committee in March 1855. In the letter he pointedly remarked that "it was the intention of the Duke of Newcastle to guard against the want of mathematical skill on the Committee" by the inclusion of a civilian authority. Ross responded with a memorandum "showing what will be necessary ... to carry out fully the instructions conveyed in [Newcastle's] letter of 6th February last," largely a request for additional funding. After review, Col. Lefroy passed the request on to Panmure, along with a recommendation that travel expenses for the civilian associate members be reimbursed. The lack of authority to pay such expenses may have been the tool that Ross used to keep the civilian gentlemen out of committee business.[26]

Panmure, however, had another battle to fight before giving final approval to the OSC's organization. Having been some weeks in office and dealing with the warring factions of the Ordnance Department—such as the fight he inherited over Boxer's future—Panmure had enough. His decision may have been helped by the release of a preliminary report of evidence gathered by the Roebuck Committee on 30 March 1855.[27] In a confidential Cabinet memo dated 2 May, Panmure wrote that "all experience in the administration of the War Dept. has convinced me of the necessity of getting rid of the Board of Ordnance altogether." A "slow, jarring, and cumbrous machine" with an ill-defined set of duties and responsibilities for its members, Panmure felt that the "constant system of compromises" required to keep the machine functioning "[made] it difficult for any one mind to make itself felt throughout the numberless ramifications of a Department which extends half round the world." By way of illustration, Panmure pointed to the continued problems with the supply of small arms. Despite placing large contracts both at home and with Belgian gunmakers, to whom the Board often turned when needing additional weapons, the army could not arm all of the regiments destined for the Crimea with the new Minié rifle, a fact made painfully clear by a 25 April news article in the *Dundee Courier*. That paper reported reinforcements shipping out armed with the old "Brown Bess," with one unit reportedly told "they 'must take their chance of picking up stray muskets'" on the battlefield. Panmure also noted that the officers responsible for small arms procurement disagreed on the basic question of how fast the weapons could be obtained. One, "the officer who has charge of the store branch has always believed that our prospects of obtaining arms were good." The other "always felt [such prospects] to be alarming in the highest degree, and yet it was only by constantly interfering beyond his province, that, backed by the Minister of War, we have been able to make even the slight progress that has been made."[28]

Panmure detailed other "evils" as well. Considerable problems resulted from the internal conflicts within Ordnance, for example, where "the slightest delay may paralyse great undertakings. Three months have been lost in even taking the first step to supply an important article, and the country suffered a heavy pecuniary loss by its hasty preparation, consequent upon this delay." Patronage also weighed down the Department, with "many inefficient old men ... kept in offices for which they are altogether unfit, by the traditions of the department, and by the memory of their former services." Finally, "in scientific acquirements our Artillery is much inferior to the French," owing to many factors, but especially "to a want of appreciation on the part of those that govern, of scientific as compared with military proficiency."[29]

Panmure's solution to these problems mirrored the ideas detailed in the memo of 17 February: dissolution of the Board of Ordnance, placement of the military duties into the hands of the Commander-in-Chief, and assignment of civil administration to Panmure's own office. The plan removed all the functions of the Master-General's office, which made that post redundant. On 18 May 1855, Queen Victoria, by Royal Letters Patent, eliminated the Board, all posts but the Clerk of Ordnance, and "under the Great Seal [vested] the Civil Administration of the Army and Ordnance in the hands" of Panmure. An Order in Council, issued 6 June, further defined the offices responsible "for carrying on the duties hitherto performed by the Master-general and Board of Ordnance." This included a new Naval Director of Artillery, charged with "advising on all matters related to the material of ordnance intended for naval service."[30] Made an *ex officio* member of the OSC, the new post gave the Admiralty some input, but the War Office now held considerable control over naval gun development. This proved a source of contention between itself and the Admiralty over the next several decades.

Although applauded by the *United Service Gazette* as having ended a department "extravagant in its outlay of public money and ... not altogether free in doing so from the influence of nepotism and partiality," not everyone welcomed the change. Raglan himself criticized it as the "reverse of beneficial to the public" and an "imperfect measure" that put military officers in "the disagreeable position of having two masters." Ross felt "astounded ... that any gentleman new to a great office should consider himself [capable of] discharging the duties of Master-General, Minister of War, Minister for War, and Commanding in Chief.... There never was such folly." Storekeeper Hastings, whose position the Patent eliminated, predicted that placing "the great manufacturing military departments in the hands of a civilian ignorant of military and naval requirements cannot work well." Such grousing, however, did not turn into influential opposition to Panmure's plan and in the end the Ordnance Department "expired with scarcely a whimper." Because of the war and the need to amalgamate the Department's staff and duties with the War Department, the Board limped along for another year and a half handling routine business. Ingloriously, the last action of the centuries-old Board regarded "tenders accepted for emptying privies in Ireland" on 31 December 1856.[31]

"Hope That Inventions Will Be Received with Due Respect"

The OSC had to hit the ground running, as "Papin's" wish that the application of the nation's capabilities of "scientific discovery and invention" came true in 1855. Gen. Cator noted that between the 10th and 26th of January, while the OSC struggled with defining its rules and desired powers, "upwards of 160 new inventions have been referred to the Committee for consideration and report."[32] And, although Britons generally remained unaware of Newcastle's reorganization, the *Times* took notice in a blistering article that appeared on 13 July, the same month Panmure approved the final rule changes regarding the OSC. The paper charged that "the extent to which the Russians have matched us in their munitions of war" had not shown "ingenuity and progress" on their part, but Britain's "perverse backwardness and neglect of the material facilities which we have so abundantly at command." The *Times* put the blame squarely on the outgoing "select committee of the Board of Ordnance, a piece of machinery carefully devised to shut out inventors." Their actions, the *Times* wrote, had kept the British army "dependent for its success upon deadly bayonet conflicts" and preserved "in the ranges of a small and costly service the traditions of war in its most barbarous and unskillful forms."

The *Times* assured their readers, however, that "the mechanical resources of the country are every day being brought nearer to a practical bearing upon the prosecution of the war" through the efforts of the "eminent machinist," Joseph Whitworth. A mechanical engineer of considerable renown, Whitworth had been a member of the special commission dispatched to the United States in 1853 to report on that country's small-arms industry, and whose report led to the outfitting of the fledgling Royal Small Arms Factory with American machinery. Aided by a government-sponsored shooting range constructed near his home, Whitworth undertook numerous experiments to determine the best size bore and shape of rifling for small arms. The paper spent several column inches describing Whitworth's careful ballistics studies, his hexagonally-bored small arms, and plans for scaling that design up for artillery. Such efforts had resulted in "several patents" regarding weaponry, the *Times* reported, which Whitworth had "placed freely at the disposal of Government." The paper suggested that "now that the Select Ordnance Committee has been enlarged there is some ground for hope that the inventions ... will be received with due respect, and fairly tested." This included not only the inventions of Whitworth, but several other "eminent machinists ... actively engaged in bringing the resources of their art to bear on the improvement of our present munitions of war." The *Times* also noted that "the obstinacy of the Birmingham manufacturers in resisting" mechanization had led to a rapid transfer of business to Manchester, where "bayonets and rifle sights and shells are being made ... upon a great scale." "To those who know what the industry of this country is capable of," the paper regretted that "so much valuable time has been lost" harnessing the abilities of British inventors. Such men "alone had it in their power to back up with the requisite superiority in *matériel* the invincible courage of our troops."

Along with the press, inventors themselves formed another group of parties interested in the creation of the OSC. As before, many used notices in the papers to generate public interest in their proposals. On 31 October 1855, for example, Bashley Britten "[took] the liberty of sending" the editor of the *Times* "a few particulars" regarding his long-range artillery shell and rifled cannon, hoping to pressure the OSC into further action. Britten wrote that Monsell, in testimony before the House of Commons, noted "in July last my shells acquired an effective range of more than 1,000 yards beyond the service solid shot, with little more than half the usual quantity of powder." Since those experiments, however, little more had been done with his inventions, and Britten claimed the reason to be "very curious." On recovery, the fired shells "had not received the impression of the rifled grooves, as was naturally expected." Based solely on that evidence, the OSC ruled "that the principle of my invention had not been proved," attributing the long range to other reasons. Britten protested their decision, and defended his inventions in the letter. He also noted that although the shells cost "about 15 per cent. per ton [more] than ordinary shells, this would be compensated for by the saving of nearly 50 per cent. of the powder" as well as giving the army an effective rifled cannon without the defects exhibited by the Lancaster gun. "Such is a brief but true description," Britten claimed, of his "extremely simple invention, but which will within a few weeks have now been 12 months under official consideration."

Some inventors used the papers to simply crow about their success before the Committee. Gunmaker William Greener took advantage of the change in military administration to appeal to Panmure for some form of reward for his expanding musket ball. Panmure turned to the OSC for their recommendation regarding Greener's claim. After reviewing the evidence, the committee ruled that "although the principle which [Greener] advocated ... is considered to be substantially the same as that upon which" the Minié bullet acted, the latter's "adoption is not considered to have been due to [Greener's] communication." Panmure, however, "desirous of rewarding the ingenuity displayed" by Greener's "first suggestion of the principle of expansion," approved a rare £1,000 award "as a public recognition of [his] priority in bringing this invention before the War Department." Greener "respectfully submitted" Panmure's letter, with copies of the OSC's judgment, to the *Newcastle Journal*, which published the correspondence on 27 December 1856.

Greener's reward, Britten's appeal, and Whitworth's activities all point to two other parties interested in the launch of the OSC: the British public, and because of it, the British government itself. Newcastle's concern over potential "embarrassment to Government" led to the creation of the OSC, but Panmure took one final step in assuring the new entity's accountability. On 30 July 1855, he approved the budget and rules regarding the committee's operation. Rather than a single annual report of proceedings, however, Panmure requested quarterly reports, as well as the construction of "a register of all inventions ... showing the date of their reference, the time consumed in their examination, how eventually disposed of, and the name of the inventor."[33] This change meant greater—and more timely—civilian oversight of the Committee's activities, but also introduced the potential for political and financial interference in its operations. With the end of the war in late 1856, and the subsequent closing of the public purse, such interference would become a point of contention between the OSC and the parties interested in its operations.

"Restoring Circulation to That Military Mass Which Is Stagnant in the Crimea"

While the press lambasted the government over the war and pundits pronounced judgment on British tactics and technology, the siege of Sevastopol ground on. On 28 December 1854, the *Morning Post* announced in great detail the preparation of nine ships bearing construction crews, materials, tools, and even "two railway missionaries" to build a railway at Balaklava, in order to clear the backlog of supplies and ammunition at the harbor. Work began on 8 February, and although the crews laid a mile of track per week over the next seven weeks, the railway could not bring up enough materials to ensure the success of the bombardment that opened on 9 April—nor the two that took place in June. The second June cannonade opened on the 17th in support of an assault planned for the next day, the fortieth anniversary of the Battle of Waterloo. Raglan, in a misplaced effort to symbolize the new spirit of cooperation with the French, "thought that it was essential for the British to storm *something*, even at the cost of unnecessary losses." The Roebuck Committee also thought the date significant, and scheduled the 18th for the release of their final report. It proved a day of futile gestures; the attack consumed over 5,000 allied soldiers with nothing gained. Meanwhile, the committee ineffectually blamed the conduct of the expired Aberdeen administration as "the first and chief cause of the calamities which befell our army" without making any recommendations for avoiding such fiascoes in the future. Ill with dysentery, demoralized by the deaths of so many British soldiers, and depressed by criticism of his handling of the war, Raglan died on 28 June 1855.[34]

Raglan's position as commander of the expedition was unenthusiastically taken up by Major-General Sir James Simpson, Raglan's chief of staff and senior British officer on the spot. Simpson, who supposedly said that "they must indeed be hard up when they appointed an old man like me," despaired over his own health and found working with his allies "irksome and embarrassing." Newcastle, who visited the front in July of 1855, harshly described the despondent Simpson as a "raving lunatic" without any real plan for prosecuting the siege. The Russians changed the situation with their 16 August attack on the combined French, Sardinian, and Turkish positions along the Chernaya River, on the outskirts of Sevastopol. Hoping to break the coalition, the attack instead resulted in disaster for the Russians, shattering their field army and ending any hopes of lifting the siege. With the external threat eliminated, the allies opened their fifth bombardment on the defenses the very next day. Although officially ending on the 21st, with the "sixth" bombardment starting on 5 September, improvements in inland transportation meant the gunners kept up fire "with more or less intensity," unlike previous efforts.[35]

On 8 September, the allies launched their final assault at noon, which caught the Russians by surprise. The French, able to bring their trenches to within a few paces of their main target, the Malakov Tower, penetrated the defenses and took their objective after ten minutes of hard hand-to-hand fighting. The British effort against the Greater Redan, however, ended in panic and disorder, with men refusing to press home the attack. Despite this, the Russian commander recognized that the fall of the Malakov meant the eventual fall of Sevastopol itself, and ordered the evacuation of his forces across a prebuilt pontoon bridge during the night. Although operations continued in other areas, the fall of Sevastopol pushed the combatants to the discussion table, and on 28 February 1856 the two sides signed an armistice that brought fighting to an end. Another month's negotiation ensued before a final peace treaty was signed on 30 March; a further month passed before the allies started evacuating the Crimea. The British departed last, with their final contingent leaving in July. "Not for the last time in the country's history," author Trevor Royle wrote, "British troops [left] a foreign shore, uncertain whether all their courage and sacrifices had been worth the effort."[36]

Despite the ambiguous end of the war, the "courage and sacrifices" resulted in two important and far-reaching changes in British military administration: the replacement of the Board of Ordnance, and the construction of the Ordnance Select Committee. Although another fifty years passed before the civilian War Office finally emerged superior in the battle over control of the military, the dissolution of the antique Board represented a crucial first step in dissolving the "disastrous muddle" that had so long consumed the efforts of British political and military officials. Likewise, the creation of the OSC represented a significant step in the modernization of British military technology. For the next fifty years, the OSC and its successors functioned as an important gatekeeper between the British military and the ongoing industrial revolution. What remained to be seen, however, was if what the OSC let through the gate would allow the nation to stay technologically competitive with rival powers on the Continent and across the Atlantic.

"Steering Among the Designs of Rival Inventors"

The conclusion of the Crimean War in 1856 did not bring peace to the British Empire. On 30 December, the *Liverpool Daily Post* opined that "England has quite enough on her hands just now": war with China, the East India Company's involvement with Persia, and "affairs all over Europe demanding the fulfillment of promised intervention." Then, in the summer of 1857, telegraph reports from India contained "disastrous news." "The mutinous spirit ... in our Bengal native army has broken out into a formidable and extensive insurrection," reported the *Liverpool Mercury* on 29 July, "accompanied by a fearful destruction of British life." For the next eleven years—over the entire life of the Ordnance Select Committee—Britain would be actively engaged in warfare over much of the globe.

This same period also saw an expansion and deepening of the ongoing Industrial Revolution. Many historians have argued that a mid-century quiescence in industrial development splits the Revolution into two phases. As the records of the OSC show, however, military technology underwent astounding change during this time. *All* of the weapons deployed against the Russians at Sevastopol in 1854—some having served the Empire in good stead for five decades—were obsolete by 1868. The British public played a considerable role in this transformation, not just as passive consumers of technological news, but actively contributing their ideas or, in the case of several entrepreneurs, their money.

Joel Mokyr has described the First Industrial Revolution as having "created a chemical industry without chemistry, an iron industry without metallurgy, and power machinery without thermodynamics"—in other words, without industry fully understanding the science behind the advances.[1] This was equally true of military technology, witnessed by the public guessing-game as to why the Lancaster gun burst. Although mathematics had long played a role in fortress design and trajectory calculation, much of the "science of artillery" remained based on received wisdom and tradition. The Industrial Revolution made new technologies available for the study of the action of guns when fired, for example, and the minutes of the OSC document the increased understanding of artillery that velocity- and pressure-measuring devices made available.

OSC records also illustrate the numerous and occasionally conflicting factors that could influence the weapons development process. The Committee itself was not a static organization, and its makeup mirrored the ongoing reorganization of the British military administrative system. The topics brought to the OSC's attention reflected new opportunities presented by industrial advances, but also more esoteric factors such as current affairs, overseas developments, and the desire for fame and fortune. And, while largely an apolitical organization, the subordinance of the OSC to the Secretary of War meant that those with access to the latter could occasionally get their proposals before the Committee, whether the military was really interested in the project or not. This subservience ultimately gave control of technology decisions to civilians, a situation that many military authorities resented—and may have also laid the seeds for the OSC's later dissolution.

The *Abstracts of Proceedings* also show that British ordnance authorities took an active interest in military developments around the world, as one of the major Committee functions included gathering reports on the rifled ordnance, breech-loading small arms, and rudimentary machine guns in use by most major powers. As a result of its investigations, the arms of the Empire in this era were equal to, if not better than, what other nations had in their arsenals. What is also evident, however, is that in many cases the British were followers, not leaders, in arms innovation. Given the fast pace of change, events abroad continually caught the nation with a stockpile of suddenly obsolete equipment. Although the country invariably caught up during this era, it is a pattern that would repeat itself over and over in the decades to come. Finally, the trail of evidence left by the OSC makes painfully clear the dilatory effect that War Office micro-management had on British military improvements. Promising developments went underfunded or were terminated because of interference by Secretaries of State, while in the case of one famous program, the nation spent thousands of pounds for a spectacular failure due to such interference. Inventors had to absorb the costs of bringing their projects forward—not an unwise policy in an era plagued by cranks and charlatans, but one which certainly discouraged a few otherwise useful ideas. In the end, government parsimony also led to the dissolution of the OSC itself, a move that probably cost the nation more than it saved in the decade to follow.

The Evolution of the Ordnance Select Committee

As with any reorganization effort, the operations of the OSC in its first years of existence required some tinkering, beginning with the manner in which the Committee documented its activities. In addition to quarterly reports and the "register of all inventions" requested in his 30 July 1855 approval of the OCS's rules of operation, Panmure also directed that the first report be "a resumé of [OSC] proceedings since the re-organization." What the Committee delivered for 1855—four bound volumes of hand-written minutes and correspondence—was "far from satisfying," according to a 16 February 1856 memo. While Panmure viewed "with interest ... the systematic prosecution of the important labours of the Committee," he found what the OSC submitted "a mere diary of subjects considered" without "any distinction between trivial proposals dismissed at once, and those which have appeared to merit fuller consideration." It also lacked any form of project classification or index.[2] Panmure also raised the question of greater dissemination of information regarding the Committee's activities. In a 6 June 1857 memo, Under-Secretary Sir J. Ramsden passed to the OSC Panmure's concern that newspaper reports of ongoing experiments could "lead to erroneous conclusions, and very false impressions" of the object being tested. Such reports, he felt, were "prejudicial to the public service" and tended "to create a spirit of partizanship for or against any particular invention or improvement" that might affect the impartiality of the OSC. Panmure made several suggestions, including "a system of publication ... as will satisfy the natural desire of the public for information, and guide persons who are occupying themselves with improvements in Artillery." The OSC balked at this, however. Such publication, Gen. Cator replied, would cause much controversy between the Committee and certain hopeful inventors, "many of whom would require to be taught the whole art of artillery before they could be convinced of the inutility of their projects." Six years would pass before the OSC finally began publishing an official summary of changes recommended for adoption into the service.[3]

To help satisfy the War Office's demand for organized information and an effective summary of the Committee's activities, Gen. Cator ended his reply by stating the OSC "have lately commenced the preparation of a Synopsis of Reports and Experiments" to "give some information on each subject that has passed before them." Compilation and printing took some time, but 1859 saw publication of the first *Abstracts of Proceedings of the Ordnance Select Committee*. This first edition contained issues discussed by the Committee from 1857 to 1859; subsequent volumes were year-specific. As per Panmure's instructions, inventions were grouped into four classes: adopted, under consideration, rejected after trial, or dismissed altogether. It also contained a clear index of inventors by name, as well as inventions by subject. With some variations, successors to the OSC continued this practice until 1897, an extraordinary compilation of the progress of British military technology during the nineteenth century.[4]

Panmure also recommended an expansion of the Committee's reports for subjects that required mathematical explanations. On 5 March 1857, the OSC asked a special subcommittee composed of Boxer and the two civilian associate members, Professors Wheatstone and Sylvester, to review a theory on the trajectory of shells proposed by Col. Philip Anstruther of the Madras Artillery. The sub-committee, after review, decided not to recommend any experiments to test the theory, "considering the scheme unsound in principle." While Panmure "accept[ed] with perfect confidence the conclusions" of Anstruther's theory as "unfounded and erroneous," the Secretary thought it important that the OSC "should briefly show his fallacies by mathematical or physical reasoning" and asked for the sub-committee's report as well. In addition, he recommended that "when the subject is susceptible of it," such information be attached as appendices to the main OSC report. By doing so, "it would both strengthen the decisions of the [OSC]" through demonstrable logic rather than suspected bias against new theories by the military, "and place valuable information on record for the use of its junior members."[5]

February of 1858 saw the finalization of the OSC's operational rules, as well as its composition. Although the twenty-man committee included five civilians, one naval captain, and two Royal Engineers, Royal Artillery officers predominated. This came under attack almost immediately from Sir John Burgoyne, the Inspector-General of Fortifications and primary advocate of the deliberate siege of Sevastopol. Burgoyne complained of the "inconvenience of referring all inventions and suggestions … to one Committee, composed chiefly of officers of … the Royal Artillery." Whether Burgoyne felt the OSC encroached on his own territory is unknown, but as a remedy he pitched having a separate engineers committee "analogous to the [OSC] … for the sake of the instruction which will be afforded in the prosecution of experiments." Panmure agreed, and on 8 May 1858 divested the OSC of questions regarding the "improvement of the materials, processes, or engines" of fortress warfare, as well as troop housing, tools, and other articles used exclusively by the Royal Engineers.[6] Presumably, this removed one person from the lengthy Committee roster, although Panmure's memo did not explicitly state so. Regardless, the OSC remained a collection of individuals whose occupations already demanded much of their attention. In addition, several of the superintendents of the Ordnance factories served as chairs of standing topic-specific sub-committees related to their departmental products. The time spent by OSC members on their full-time jobs and the burdens of duty on a Committee whose membership carried "no additional emolument" led to the

OSC itself recommending a wholesale change. In May of 1859, therefore, the War Office authorized the dissolution of the *ex officio* Committee, and replaced it with what the *Daily News* on the 13th termed "a small body of officers, who are to dedicate their time and attention exclusively" to questions of improvements in weaponry—and "salaried accordingly."

The changeover to the smaller, professional Committee approved by then Secretary of War Maj. Gen. Jonathan Peel (who replaced Panmure earlier that year), pared the OSC down to six officers: two from the Royal Artillery, one each from the Royal Navy, Engineers, and an infantry regiment, plus the permanent Secretary. All of the standing sub-committees were eliminated, and their duties given to the revised OSC.[7] The reduction in size proved too drastic, however, and over the next several years the Committee's membership crept back up to thirteen by 1868. In addition, the 1859 change eliminated all civilian associate members from the OSC. On its face, the decision seemed a partial victory for Gen. Cator—the officer who entreated Newcastle to leave "Artillery questions to officers of Artillery" in 1855—insofar as weapons decisions were to be left to military officers, and excluded outside technical experts. Civilian authorities continued to play critical roles in the evaluation of military technology, however, such as Frederick Abel, the Chemist to the War Department. A native of Woolwich, Abel had returned there in 1852 to become an instructor in chemistry to the Royal Military Academy. A talented individual with a published textbook already to his credit, Abel became the chemist to the Royal Arsenal in 1854, then to the War Department in January of 1856 as well as becoming a member of the original *ex officio* Committee. The post–1859 OSC frequently requested his opinion on subjects related to chemistry, and in 1865 complimented "his careful inquiries and his clear and practical report[s]" which helped in "furthering their view" on many subjects. In 1867, the War Office approved Abel's reattachment to the OSC as Associate Member. In addition a non-commissioned officer, Quarter-Master H. Behenna, came on board in 1860 as "Acting Commissary of Stores," presumably to facilitate the acquisition of materials needed for experiments. Behenna occupied this "temporary" position for at least eight years, and presented several proposals of his own before the OSC; he also made the very rare jump from the enlisted ranks into the officer corps as a result of his service and inventions.[8]

The Committee in Operation

Regardless of its makeup, the OSC's process for evaluating a new invention remained consistent, and began when the Secretary's office forwarded a new proposal. It also sent to the inventor (or his agent) a copy of the regulations regarding inventions and any request from the Committee for drawings, models, or other explanations of the idea and its benefits to the service. The OSC then scheduled the proposal to be reviewed at one of its weekly meetings. The proposer would be notified of the review date, and informed that he was "at liberty to attend ... to give any explanation [he] may consider it necessary to afford." OSC rules, however, forbade payment of any expenses related to "assisting the individual to bring forward his invention, unless expressly authorized." Any request for advance funding, such as W.W. Hubbell's petition for £1,000 to travel from the U.S. to explain his inventions, practically guaranteed rejection of the proposal.[9]

More often than not, new proposals—like so many before 1855—did not survive initial review. Some were simply impractical given the limitations of technology of the day, such as B. Byerley's 1859 suggestion for "iron tungsten shot," hampered by "the metal in question [not being] manufactured at all upon a practical scale." Others were dismissed as inferior to existing service items, such as H.K. Jackson's "patent vertical lever jack." While described by the OSC as "very ingenious," the jack offered "no advantages for military purposes over that now in service." Others were dismissed because, in the view of the Committee, they simply could not be put into practice. The OSC judged, for example, that "no advantage would be gained" from William Fletcher's proposal to prevent the report and recoil of small arms, "even if it could be practically carried out (which appears very doubtful)."[10]

Shielded from the inventor by the Secretary of State's office, the OSC had no qualms about identifying foolish projects for what they were. In reply to a continued effort by Col. Anstruther to promote his plan of calculating shell trajectories, for example, the OSC noted in 1862 that his theories "involve a contradiction of the simplest principles of mechanics, which have been admitted as axiomatic from the time of Galileo and Newton downwards, in all countries where mathematical evidence is cultivated." J. Woodcock Graves' 1864 plan for a star-shaped "projectile for penetrating iron plates" prompted the OSC to declare that "the whole proposal is based on complete ignorance of everything which should be known to gentlemen who pretend to make improvements in artillery." Occasionally, however, their comments had to be more circumspect, as in the case of General Sir J.G. Woodford, who insisted over several letters that spiraled barrel rifling was a "needless complication." After rejecting yet another of his proposals, the OSC reported that they "feel seriously that their time is too valuable to be taken up by refuting views which if not held by a General Officer they should characterize as ignorant and absurd."[11]

Although removing the manufacturing department heads from the OSC trimmed its membership, and undoubtedly simplified the superintendents' lives, it did mean that the OSC had to formally request their input. In 1859, for example, the Committee passed a proposal for construction of small-arms ammunition to Boxer for comment, who replied that he found the plan "quite unsuited to the making of a firm and serviceable cartridge," without explaining why. Recalling Panmure's 1857 directive, the OSC requested further clarification—but received the same reply from Boxer, who apparently did not like his professional opinion questioned. The Committee testily reminded the officer that "the directions of the Secretary of State for War ... entitle them to receive more full and explicit information from the Head of a Department, than that afforded in this instance." Boxer finally sent a subordinate to visit OSC in person, who satisfactorily explained his rejection of the plan.[12]

In general, the OSC adhered to the recommendation of Arsenal superintendents, but this was not a hard-and-fast rule. Despite his request for an exorbitant amount of travel money, Hubbell's plan for an impact-detonating artillery fuze seemed promising, and the Committee passed it to Boxer for comment. Despite the latter stating that "in his opinion, no advantage would be derived from the arrangement proposed," the OSC requested the Royal Laboratory "prepare fifty fuzes for experiments, at a cost of 26*l*., 5*s*., 0*d*.," which the War Office sanctioned. Unfortunately for Hubbell, the fuze did not perform well in testing, and the inventor never got the travel money he hoped for.[13]

By and large, the OSC simply noted that "no encouragement" should be given to inventors of rejected proposals. On occasion, however, the Committee took more active steps. One gentleman presented a number of proposals before the OSC, until finally the Committee stated that all "appear to be equally ridiculous and impractical ... [and] recommend that he should be discouraged from making any further communications on the subject of artillery and small arms, the elements of which he appears to be profoundly ignorant." The OSC also complained that a particular Royal Artillery sergeant consumed too much of their time with "worthless proposals," and recommended "that a decided discouragement be to give to the ill-directed ingenuity of this Non-commissioned Officer."[14] In the case of several troublesome persons, the Secretary of War eventually declined to receive any further letters from them.

Rejected proposals were not always dismissed negatively. In 1859, a Sergeant Hunter submitted a recommendation for improvements in shrapnel shells; although his suggestions were not adopted, the OSC reported that the man deserved "much credit for having paid such attention to the subject." Although it dismissed Colour-Sergeant G. Knapton's "instrument for measuring distances" without testing, the OSC recognized the "zeal and intelligence [displayed] in his endeavours" with a rare recommendation that he be allowed travel expenses which would "probably amount to 3*l*." And, in the case of Sir W. Hamilton's "proposed system of recoil," the Committee congratulated him on submitting a proposal "with a clearness and completeness ... highly creditable to him, and that they have perused and considered his memoir with interest" (but, ultimately, decided not to test his suggestion).[15]

As illustrated by Hubbell's fuze, proposals the OSC thought worthy of trial then moved on to the experimentation phase. Private inventors would be requested to submit materials for testing, but at their own expense. Only if the proposal showed exceptional promise, or in the case of an in-house development, would the Committee request funding.[16] In such instances, OSC had to "state distinctly why that trial should be made at the public cost, and not at the risk of the inventor"; in Hubbell's case, the small public outlay greatly offset the cost of his requested travel expenses. Department heads of the factories supplying materials would then be asked to provide cost estimates, which the Committee forwarded, along with the proposed experimental program, to the War Office—and which the latter audited with care. Such micro-management is evident throughout the records of the OSC. After reviewing an 1859 test of a new mortar carriage, for example, the Office noted a £57 difference between what it calculated the costs of ammunition to be, compared to what the OSC estimated. Embarrassed, the Committee requested from the manufacturing departments revised price lists "of all articles manufactured by them for issue" so as to "prevent the recurrence of such discrepancies."[17]

Once approved by the War Office, the OSC then instituted and monitored the success of experiments, and reported the results back to the Secretary of War. Such experimentation contained no small degree of risk for the gun crews, as accidents did happen. The *Birmingham Daily Post*, reporting a series of ongoing experiments at Shoeburyness on 5 March 1863, noted the rather spectacular end to a 7-inch gun designed by Lynall Thomas. On firing, the gun exploded, shattering the breech and tossing a one-ton section nearly 140 yards away. Fortunately, the crew had cover underneath nearby "splinter proofs" and had fired the gun via an electrical fuze, the latter a normal albeit relatively new safeguard; no injuries were recorded. In another incident that did produce a minor casualty, Earl Spencer, a member of the Small Arms Committee, test-fired a breech-loading infantry rifle submitted by "Mr. Wilson, of Birmingham." The *Royal Cornwall Gazette* reported on 1 October 1868 that "the piece exploded, and several small fragments flew in his lordship's face." Spencer's injuries "were confined to a few cuts on both cheeks," but illustrate the risks that committee members themselves took when conducting experiments.[18]

If an invention proved itself in testing, the OSC would recommend adoption, and once approved, "seal the pattern" as a model to govern future manufacture. In general, the Secretary concurred, but this was not automatic. In 1857, Boxer proposed a new form of grape shot, which the OSC at first rejected as possessing no advantage over the service pattern, even though more accurate at longer ranges. Undeterred, Boxer pointed out that his design better withstood careless handling, as might occur in the field, and which the Committee proved by dropping samples "from a height of about 15 feet, on to some rough stones." Boxer's survived undamaged, but the "service pattern ... went to pieces." After further tests, the OSC recommended adoption, but Sir Sidney Herbert, the reigning Secretary of War, vetoed the plan. "After a full consideration ... on the comparative merits" of Boxer's versus the service pattern, the War Office reported that Herbert was "unable to perceive that the new pattern (Boxer's) promises sufficient advantages to warrant the expense and inconvenience of a change."[19]

Aside from cost objections, there are few cases of political pressure on the Committee to reconsider its decisions. Backing a failed proposal carried considerable risk, as demonstrated by the case of Robert Mallet's "monster mortar." Mallet, a civil engineer and Fellow of the Royal Society, first approached the Board of Ordnance in December of 1854 with a plan for an enormous 36-inch mortar made in sections for ease of transport. The OSC tabled his improved design in January of 1855, after which Mallet appealed directly to Palmerston. Impressed with Mallet's credentials and the weapon's potential, Palmerston took upon himself, "as First Minister of the Crown, the full responsibility of carrying [the proposal] into execution" and ordered the Board of Ordnance to arrange the construction of two mortars "without the slightest delay." Although the Board complied and had a signed tender by 7 May, design complications and the bankruptcy of the original contractor led to a two year delay. The completed mortars were not delivered until May of 1857, too late to assist in the war effort for which they were proposed. The OSC arranged for trials anyway, and "Palmerston's Mortar," as the newspapers labeled it, fired its first round on 19 October. A crack in one of the external sections suspended practice after only seven rounds, and after costly repairs, the OSC resumed firing again on 18 December. After six rounds another component failed. The *Times*, in reporting the results three days later, pointedly noted that Palmerston had, "without the previous sanction of the War Department and the Woolwich authorities," ordered the building of the mortar. "The latter," it continued, "are probably anxious to have it clearly understood that they have had no share in recommending the construction for so useless a piece of ordnance." The OSC had the mortar repaired one more time in July of 1858, but a third component failed. Although Mallet urged repairs, the Committee judged that no "practical advantage will accrue to the public service" by furthering the program. In total, the two guns cost £14,000 to build, with a further £675 spent for the nineteen shells fired, with little to show for the money but future museum displays.[20]

Despite the OSC's screening process, unusual proposals did make it to the testing ground, such as an "infernal machine" proposed by Spanish officer Col. M. Yturriaga in 1862. The OSC report described the machine as "an oblong iron box curved so as to fit to a man's waist [and consisting] of five compartments, each ... having 12 chambers, arranged so that the operator is able to fire one compartment at a time." To demonstrate the machine, Colonel Yturriaga's son wore it around his waist and aimed at targets some yards distant. Although he intended to set off one chamber at a time, "at the word 'fire' 30 chambers accidentally went off, blowing away a part of the iron case, which took a backward direction, with considerable danger to the operators as well as the spectators.... The Committee are of opinion that this machine is extremely dangerous, and do not recommend any further trial."[21]

The unfortunate experience of Col. Yturriaga's son illustrates another aspect of the OSC's work. National borders did not limit the proposals considered, and demonstrate the growing importance of the international arms industry during this period. Armstrong's Elswick Ordnance took a leading role in this trade, as it sought new markets for its famously effective wrought iron muzzle-loaders after British government orders dried up in late 1862. The American Civil War proved a boon to the English gun trade, but in turn brought American engineers, particularly small arms developers, into great

An Armstrong rifled muzzle-loader in place at Ft. Fisher, North Carolina, 1865. Note the numerous "coils" used to build up the exterior of the gun (T.H. O'Sullivan, photographer. Photographed 1865, printed between 1880 and 1889. Courtesy Library of Congress).

prominence around the world. France successfully marketed the "la Hitte" system of rifled muzzle-loaders to Spain and Italy, and "it has been closely imitated by Austria, by Russia, by Holland, and ... by Sweden and Denmark." The Prussian firm of Krupp also began to make its mark in foreign sales, and tried repeatedly to get the English interested in their cast-steel guns, even offering to sell to the War Office the several models displayed at the 1862 London International Exhibition.[22]

The growing ranks of foreign inventors were eager to get their proposals before the OSC and hopefully into the English military market. They also seemed heedless of any issues about trading with a potential enemy—such as the German nationals perfectly willing to sell details of the supposedly secret Prussian breech-loading rifle. The OSC, in turn, showed no favor to British inventors over others, preferring simply that a product prove superior to competing designs and could be licensed for manufacture by the Royal Arsenal at a reasonable rate. In addition, the OSC kept a close eye on foreign military technology, through news articles, visiting-officer reports, or exchange of recently adopted weapons systems with other nations. The *Northern Whig* reported on 20 November 1858, for example, that a howitzer gifted by Napoleon III to the Queen had been forwarded to Woolwich, "where the gun is now being much admired."[23] The Committee even went so far as to

A fifteen-inch smoothbore Rodman gun at Battery Rodgers, Alexandria, VA, 18 May 1864. Britain purchased one of these in 1866 for comparison against its own heavy guns (A.J. Russell, photographer [1864]. Courtesy Library of Congress).

recommend the purchase of an American 15-inch Rodman smooth-bore in 1866 for comparison against Britain's own heavy guns. This very rare suggestion came with the proviso that the Ordnance Department's budget for the year "will cover the expenses of the proposed experiments" (which, fortunately, it did).[24]

Financing a Revolution on a Shoestring

Budgetary concerns regarding the purchase of the Rodman gun is but one example of many that demonstrate the fiscal tension between the military and Parliament; the question of who should bear the costs of invention development is another. Unlike in France, where all experiments were conducted at the public expense, private inventors in England were expected to bear the cost of any trials made. Such a restriction meant a person attempting to bring a proposal forward could find himself "unexpectedly thwarted and embarrassed by heavy expenses," complained Thomas Cattell in a letter printed in the *Daily News* on 14 July 1855. "I ask, sir, is it fair that one member of the community should suffer in his endeavours to benefit the whole?" he continued. "Is it right that any discovery embracing the general good should fail of successful development, owing to a circumstance which is altogether an accident of the social economy?"[25]

Panmure answered Cattell's question with an emphatic "yes," as illustrated by a 20 February 1857 memo regarding experimental programs. In mid-January of that year, the OSC had recommended the construction of a portable furnace for heating shot, proposed by Major Arthur Vandeleur of the Royal Artillery and to be built at the Royal Gun Factory at an estimated cost of £10. Panmure refused to authorize the expense for two reasons. First, he strongly objected to the "use of the public factories for experimental purposes not directly connected with the objects for which they are maintained," preferring instead that experimental items be procured by contract. Second, he reminded the Committee that "before recommending the trial of any invention, either of a Military Officer or of a civilian, the [OSC] should state distinctly why that trial is to be made at the public cost, and not at the risk of the inventor." Ironically, Panmure later argued that "facility should be given to an inventor who has already been the means of introducing a valuable invention in the public service," and approved, without the OSC's prior recommendation, a £37 advance to a Captain Addison, also for a shot furnace. The OSC rejected Addison's more expensive design after testing, whereas Vandeleur's cheaper one proved efficient enough to be recommended for further experiments. Despite this, the War Office reinforced its stance against the public funding of experiments in a further memo. On 8 January 1858,

Under-Secretary Sir Benjamin Hawes stated that "the War Office cannot charge itself with any expense which may be incurred, either for travelling or any other purpose, with a view of assisting the individual to bring forward his invention, unless expressly authorized."[26]

Parliament kept such a close eye on War Office finances that it is difficult to determine how much was spent for weapons development in the first several years of the OSC's existence. In the estimates prior to 1863–1864, the budget for the Committee explicitly stated fixed costs only, such as officer and clerk salaries. Except for 1858, when £2,000 was set aside for "Contingent Charges incidental upon Experiments conducted by the Select and Small Arms Committees," the OSC had no allotment of monies under its control for weapons testing. Rewards to inventors, such as the £5,000 granted to Boxer for his wartime exertions, were carefully tucked into the budget. Boxer's award appeared in the 1857 vote under the line item for the United Service Institution, to give the appearance of the money as coming from that organization. Palmerston's Liberal government made the question of weapons development costs much more transparent with an 1863 restructuring of the estimates. Categories for "effective services," which formed thirteen votes on the amalgamation of the army and ordnance estimates in 1855, were reorganized into eighteen categories, to include Vote 17 for "Miscellaneous Services." The budget of the OSC formed a great part of that vote, which now included estimates for "experimental services." These included the "purchase of Stores for Experimental purposes generally, and for incidental Expenses connected with Experiments" as well as rewards to inventors. Estimates for 1862–63 were £31,220; for the OSC's final year, they had risen to £69,472.[27]

On the whole, Victorian governments preferred to spend as little as possible on military equipment, and there are numerous instances in the *Abstracts* where projects were put on hold for lack of money. The conversion of Navy cap-and-ball revolvers to breech-loaders in 1868 forms one such example. The OSC found the converted revolvers to be "superior ... in accuracy, rapidity of fire, facility in working, and penetration" than the unconverted, and recommended the 7,000 pistols in Naval stores be altered. Sir John Pakington, then Secretary of State for War, approved of the recommendation, but not the timing, stating that "there are no funds available this year for carrying out this conversion." When presented with a cost estimate of £7,700 plus replacement ammunition, Pakington refused to make a special request to Parliament "for so large a sum as the conversion of these pistols would involve." Considering the £25,500,000 actually voted for the military that year, the needed funds represented a mere fraction—but also a political fight that Pakington wanted to avoid. Not until the Director of Stores pointed out that there had been "a saving of £5,000 on the vote for the conversion of the 1853 pattern rifles" did the Secretary authorize a limited alteration of 700 firearms.[28]

Despite the reality of a tight-fisted government, many inventors thought the War Department a source of considerable potential wealth, regardless of its warning that "no expectation of reward can be held out" except for inventions actually adopted. Even then, "the amount of reward ... must be left to the decision of the Secretary of State for War." The British military represented a huge market for products ranging from horseshoe nails to heavy guns. Many proposals—particularly from patent holders—came with a stated price tag, often in the thousands of pounds. One plan for turning muzzle-loading rifles into breech-loaders carried a £1,000,000 cost for "assignment of the invention or patent to the Secretary of State." The OSC, however, found "the terms named ... as absurd as [the] proposal." Others approached the War Department with claims for reward based on previous proposals they saw being put into practice by Government. While dismissing most claims, occasionally the OSC did recommend rewards, but could be very stingy in doing so. John Kellow, a Royal Carriage Department workman, pressed a claim in 1862 for "small expenses necessarily incurred in the construction of models, &c." for two proposals adopted into service. The OSC responded by recommending a paltry £20 as "a gratuity," on the grounds that "a higher motive than the hope of ... reward should induce" every employee "to bring forward improvements that suggest themselves to him."[29]

Any reward—or even reimbursement for expenses—suggested by the OSC still had to be approved by the Secretary of War. More often than not, the latter denied or modified the payment, as in the case of Lt. Francis Bolton and his patent "rifle stopper and sight protector" for the Pattern 1853 rifle. Sanctioned for adoption into the service in 1864, the conversion of Enfield muzzle-loaders into breech-loaders in 1865 made the stopper obsolete nearly overnight. Bolton appealed to the OSC in 1867 for some degree of financial relief, in light of his "having expended a large sum of money in machinery, in making experiments, and in taking out patents" over the course of five years. The OSC recommended the payment of his expenses, less that for "taking out patent, and the value of old machinery and material at hand ... and that he receive such further gratuity as the Secretary of State may see fit to award." The War Department, claiming that his invention had "not been sufficiently tested" and that no provision had been made for such in the year's budget, not only declined to make an award, but authorized only half the amount of expenses recommended.[30]

Bolton's case also highlights the complicated dealings of the OSC with patents and patentees. Although his stopper combined some characteristics of other such devices, Bolton possessed a viable patent on it. In ruling on his appeal for financial aid, the OSC stated that "the question now for consideration appears ... to be the extent to which the government have involved themselves in patent rights" and recommended that Bolton should be dealt with "liberally." In other cases the OSC took a harder stance so as to stay out of patent disputes. In 1861, Boxer suggested that combustible cartridges for revolvers could be made without infringing on the 1856 patent of Capt. J.M. Hayes. The OSC ruled, however, that "although the validity of Captain Hayes' patent is questionable ... it is not considered advisable to render the War Department liable to legal proceedings by adopting a cartridge so nearly resembling that of Captain Hayes."[31] The OSC also wrestled with increasingly difficult priority-of-invention issues unresolved by the patent laws of the time. Numerous inventors came forward claiming infringement of their ideas, and the OSC delved (sometimes deeply) into its own archives investigating such issues. Despite the institutionalized desire for a military at the least possible cost, the OSC did occasionally—and sometimes generously, in the case of Greener and his expanding bullet—find in favor of the aggrieved inventor or his estate.

The Rise and Fall of the Armstrong Gun

The 21 December 1857 *Times* article that bemoaned the failure of the Mallet mortar also raised alarm about the general state of British artillery. "The [Crimean] war clearly enough demonstrated that the British army has not, as it ought to have, any conspicuous or decisive superiority over those of other countries in the artillery arm," the paper charged. The Royal Artillery and Navy were still armed, as were many other European militaries, with cast-iron or bronze smooth-bore cannon, a situation that the *Times* felt clearly uncomfortable with. "Do our unrivalled mechanical resources offer us no escape from a position which the backward state of artillery science throughout Europe only renders the more humiliating?" it asked. William Greener also lamented that "all great improvements in Gunnery in England have been forced upon the authorities by absolute necessity." "By the time our officials have discovered the best cast-iron for heavy guns," he continued, "French batteries on sea and land will be bristling with RIFLED STEEL CANNON of tremendous range and endless endurance. Woe betide this country if at the commencement of a war we should find ourselves just where we are."[32]

Greener's charge bore more than a little truth. With the apparent failure of British guns before Sevastopol, one of the most pressing questions for the British military should have been the future direction of artillery. Post-Crimea retrenchment and preoccupation with events in India, however, left the question simmering on the back burner until Gen. Jonathan Peel took over as Secretary of State for War in 1858, the only military officer to hold that post. For him and others, salvation seemed to lie with William Armstrong's rifled breech-loading cannon. Constructed of concentric "hoops" or "coils" of metal, built up around a central tube, the Armstrong gun and the shell designed for it seemed to be the total package. According to the *Times* of 28 February 1859, the construction of the gun lowered its comparative weight to a quarter of service pieces of similar bore size, decreasing the number of gunners required to handle the weapon. Rifling made it phenomenally accurate compared to smooth-bore guns, and loading from the breech gave the weapon a much higher rate of fire. The multi-purpose "segment shell," fitted with percussion fuze, could act as solid shot, shell, or canister as needed. Declared by Panmure to be "a most valuable contribution to our Army," in November of 1858 a special committee recommended the "immediate introduction of guns tried on Mr. Armstrong's principle, for special service in the field." In return for assigning his patents to the War Office, in 1859 Armstrong received an appointment as "Engineer to the War Department for Rifled Ordnance" along with a £2,000 annual salary and a knighthood. He also received public capital to finance the privately held Elswick Ordnance Company, which would produce his guns until Woolwich could manufacture them as well. To assist in that effort, Armstrong took over as Superintendent of the Royal Gun Factory (formerly the Royal Brass Foundry) while it geared up to for its new mission of the manufacture of iron ordnance in addition to bronze guns.[33]

That same year—and one of the principal reasons for government's generosity to Armstrong—France deployed new rifled artillery against the Austrians with devastating effect. Developed in great secrecy by the French *Comité d'Artillerie* (the equivalent of the OSC) and named after that body's President, the new "la Hitte" system used studded shells that matched up with the rifling in the bore of steel guns. While still a muzzle-loader, the new gun could be fired without the necessity of sponging between rounds, greatly shortening its reload time. French government ordnance factories produced enough of the new la Hitte guns to equip all of its field batteries deployed to Italy, including a few large 30-pounders. At the Battle of Solferino on 24 June, the guns proved their great worth; "the extraordinary rapidity of the fire [of the French guns] ... arrested the Austrian advance at a range which then appeared incredibly great," *Blackwood's* later reported. Nearly overnight, the question of guns for the British army suddenly became of prime importance. As British army historian J. H. Stocqueler later wrote, "a perfect panic was aroused in England by the manifestation of the new power which her ancient foe had acquired."[34]

The next several years saw a frenzy of activity by the OSC related to "Subject No. 1671": the perfection and fielding of the Armstrong gun. Any piece of artillery requires a host of supporting material to make it a successful weapons system, and this was no less true for nineteenth-century ordnance than it is today. Depending on the size of the gun—and the 1859 recommendation suggested thirteen different calibers—the Committee had to seal patterns of carriages, ammunition, loading and cleaning equipment, and so forth, as well as the guns themselves.[35] Three hundred and forty different proposals, requests, and questions required consideration and judgment by the OSC over the course of the Armstrong breech-loader program. While the majority came from Armstrong himself, superintendents of the Arsenal factories dealt with or made suggestions regarding changes to materials provided by their departments, as did officers involved with testing the weapons.[36] The War Office, Admiralty, and Horse Guards also initiated discussion over many components of the program. Armstrong rightly deserves credit for this ingenious piece of ordnance, but it took the efforts of many individuals to bring it to perfection.

As field artillery, the new guns seemed without equal, and were used with great effect during Gen. James Hope Grant's 1860 invasion of China. Impressed with its performance, Cambridge believed the demonstration of the Armstrong's power to be "even more important than the whole expedition." By 1864, then Secretary of State for War Spencer Cavendish (Lord Hartington), reported to the House of Commons that "the whole of [the British] field batteries [were] armed with the Armstrong gun," which were "now almost universally approved and liked by the troops who possessed them.... They were a most excellent gun, and very far superior to those they had supplanted." The *Times*, in reporting Hartington's comments on 5 March, added that "our field artillery is as well armed and provided as we could wish it to be, nor do we know of any foreign models superior to our own."[37]

As a naval gun, however, Armstrong's invention fell short. The war scare with France in 1859 had been triggered not only by the performance of its artillery against Austria but also by the construction of *La Glorie*, France's first ironclad line-of-battle ship. Faced with its imminent launch, the Board of Admiralty requested "in the strongest manner" that the War Office "supply them with as little delay as possible with a large number" of heavier Armstrong guns. By October, Armstrong had scaled his design up to produce a 7-inch, 110-pounder gun, although he personally had doubts about the breech mechanism's ability to withstand the pressures produced by large charges of gunpowder. Rushed into production before the design could be properly tested, the gun experienced numerous failures during the short 1862 action against Japan. In addition, tests by the Board of Admiralty showed the striking power of the 7-inch shot to be less than that of the 68-pounder smooth-bore. In an era when naval tactics still dictated fighting at close quarters, the Admiralty determined the 110-pounder Armstrong insufficient to serve as a broadside gun. Although the Armstrong shell may have been destructive against wooden ships, "the old 68-pounder," they determined, remained "the most effective gun in the service against iron plates."[38]

With the increasing amount of armor being added to both ships and

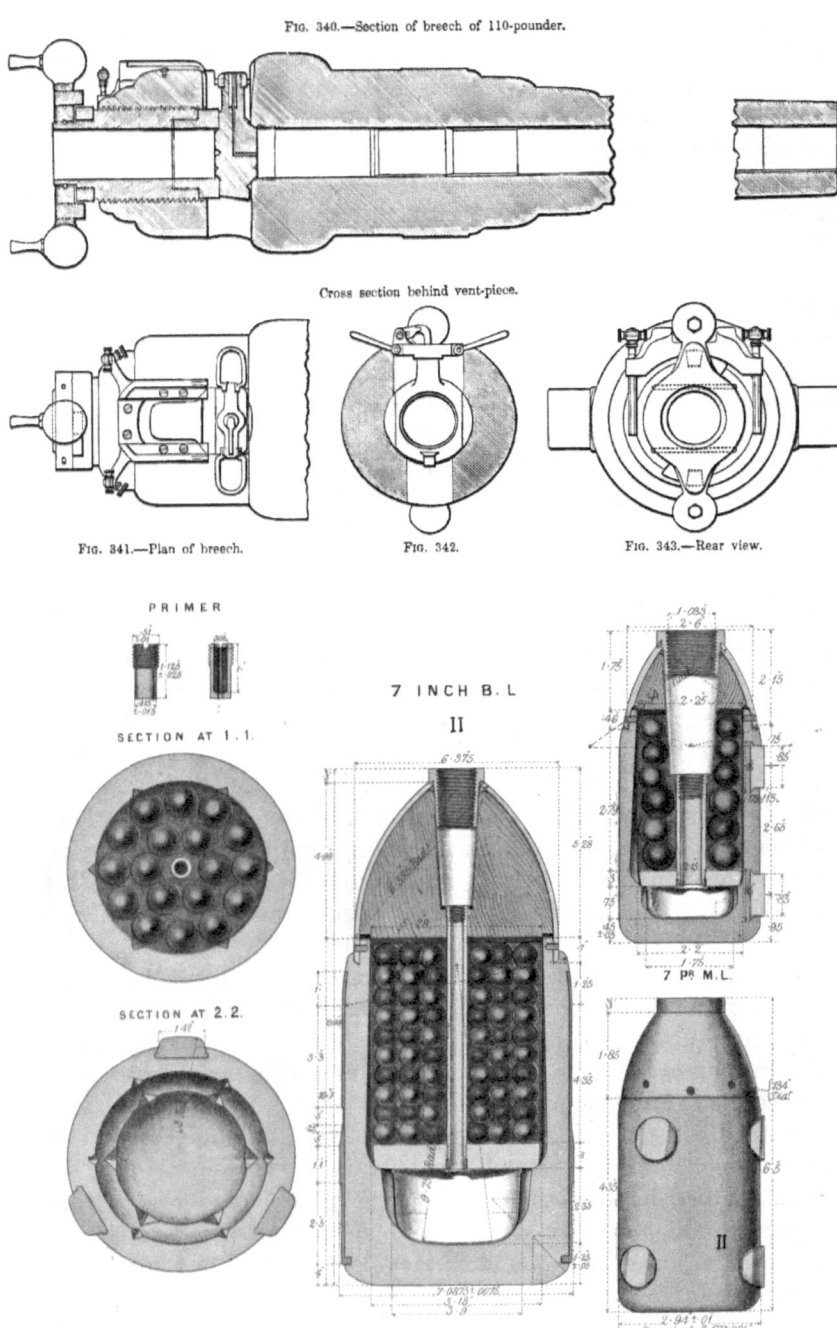

Fig. 340.—Section of breech of 110-pounder.

Cross section behind vent-piece.

Fig. 341.—Plan of breech.   Fig. 342.   Fig. 343.—Rear view.

PRIMER

SECTION AT 1.1.

SECTION AT 2.2.

7 INCH B.L

7 Pr M.L.

Powder charge with lubricator for the Armstrong breech-loader. A Boxer invention, the lubricator consisted of two copper disks welded together, containing a tallow and oil mixture. On firing the discs compressed, ejecting the lubricant. This allowed the gun to be fired repeatedly without lead from projectile sheaths building up inside the barrel (Holley, 456; for description, see TNA, Abstracts 1861, 659).

coastal forts, however, Armstrong knew that a gun heavier than the 110-pounder would be needed. In 1860, Armstrong started developing rifled muzzle-loaders using his built-up method in ever increasing sizes, and by 1863 had constructed a massive 22-ton, 13½-inch gun that could throw a 600-pound projectile to a distance of over four miles. Wrought iron guns were costly, however, so when Captain (later Sir) William Palliser of the 18th Hussars passed to the War Office a plan for lining the bore of the existing stock of cast-iron guns with a wrought iron reinforcement tube, the young captain found a willing audience. At first a plan simply for strengthening the older weapons, Palliser soon realized this could also turn them into rifled guns. Although it took some years to perfect, by 1868 the OSC recommended the conversion of "our present cast-iron smooth-bored guns into rifled guns ... for secondary purposes of defence."[39] Such a plan greatly appealed to those who sought to solve the problem of rearming the British military with heavy rifled cannon at the lowest possible cost.

The battle over the future of British artillery was exacerbated by the battle between Armstrong and his competitors. Armstrong borrowed the idea

Opposite top: Cross-section of Armstrong 110-pounder rifled breechloader, and views of the breech mechanism (Holley, 596). *Opposite bottom:* The Boxer shrapnel shell for a 7-inch Armstrong breechloader (center) and for a 7-pdr muzzle-loading gun (right) (Majendie, Plate 56).

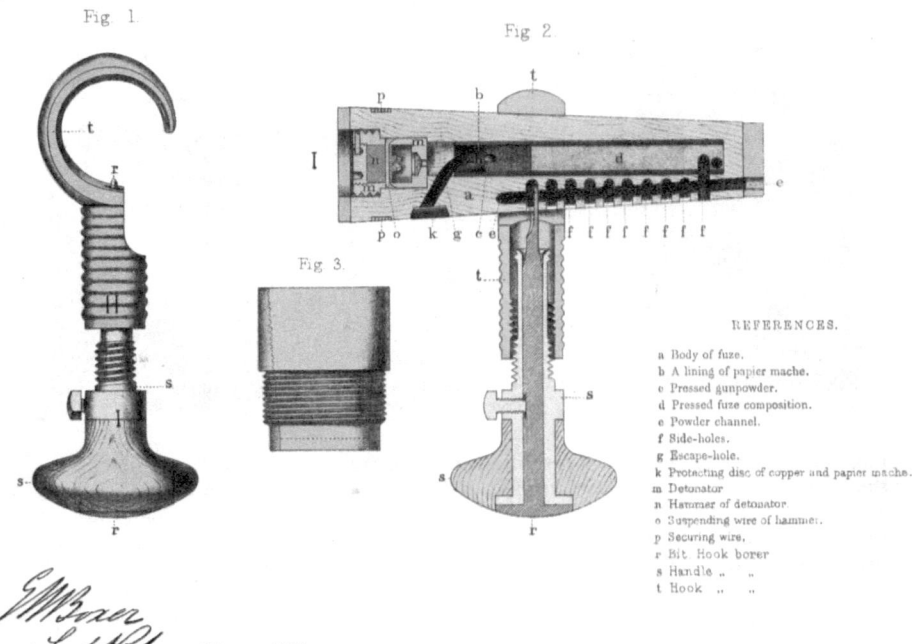

A Boxer wooden time fuze for rifled ordnance, probably for an Armstrong 12-pound breech-loader, shown with the gunner's boring tool. Boxer's design also served as a percussion fuze, detonating on impact (Majendie, Plate 36).

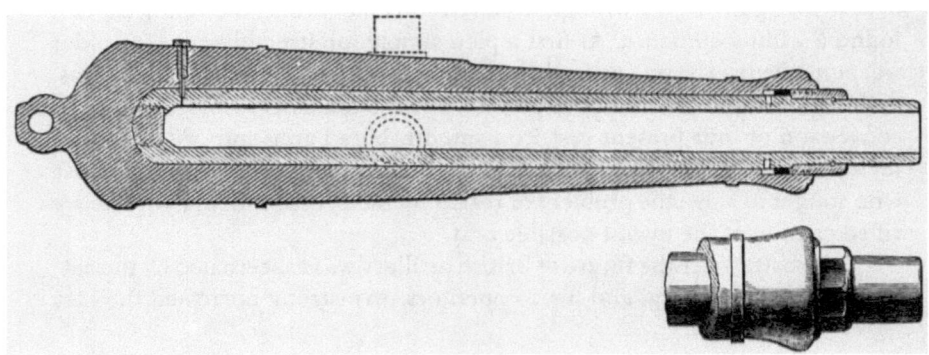

A cast-iron 68-pdr strengthened and converted into a rifled muzzle-loader with a Palliser steel tube. The lower drawing shows the enormous "screw washer" that locks the tube in place (Holley, 277).

"Steering Among the Designs of Rival Inventors" 113

Capt. T. A. Blakely's 8⁹⁄₁₆" muzzle-loader at the Great Exhibition of 1862. Blakely originated the idea of using concentric "hoops" or "coils" to build guns (Holley, 38).

of building-up guns from Capt. T. A. Blakely, who in 1854 had submitted to the Board of Ordnance an experimental 9-pounder. The next year, Blakely received Pat. No. 431 for the design, and licensed it to James Longridge, who in turn commissioned Elswick to construct a gun—the most likely route for the idea to come to Armstrong. By 1863, the Blakely Ordnance Company had sold over 400 guns to both sides in the American Civil War, Russia, and other European powers. That year he offered to lend a 12-inch 700-pounder to the OSC, but then withdrew the offer when told Armstrong would be on the examining committee. Armstrong's main rival, however, was Joseph Whitworth, who in 1857 had put his 0.450" hexagonally-bored rifle against the Pattern 1853 Enfield in public trials. Whitworth claimed the results "established the superiority of my weapon," and by the late 1850s had scaled it up for artillery. Armstrong's design used la Hitte–style studded projectiles matched to deep grooves in the barrel wall for his rifled muzzle-loaders. Tests supervised by the OSC over the next several years pitted both Whitworth and Armstrong systems against each other. As the guns fired their respective shells against ever-thickening armor at ever-longer ranges, partisans for both sides argued their cases in the papers and occasionally leveled charges of malfeasance against each other.[40]

To settle the increasingly acrimonious debate, in 1863 the War Office appointed—over the protestations of the OSC "that they are considered unfit to be intrusted with the proposed inquiry"—a special committee to investigate not only the merits of the Armstrong and Whitworth systems, but the

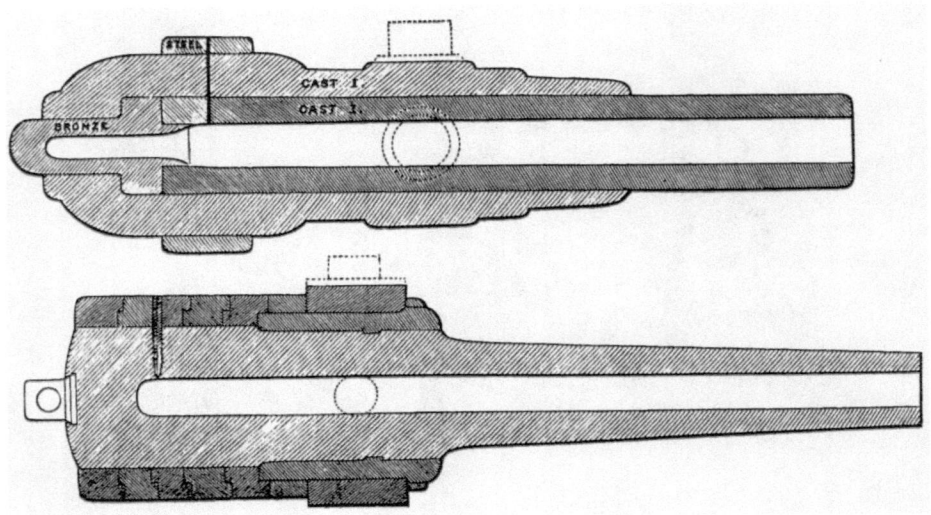

Two different large-bore Blakely rifled muzzle-loaders: (upper) a 900-pdr (12¾") gun sold to the Confederacy, and (lower) an 11-inch gun sent to Russia (Holley, 44).

general question of breech- vs. muzzle-loading artillery. For three years the special committee gathered evidence, not only of the performance of the guns in testing, but of the Armstrong breech-loader's performance in the field. The results showed what many opponents to the Armstrong gun argued: that the simpler rifled muzzle-loaders outranged, outshot, and were easier to work than the breech-loader, although the latter did have an advantage in rate of fire. In addition, the Armstrong breech-loader had more accidents, wore out more quickly, and cost more to manufacture. In 1866 the War Office appointed a second committee to reconsider the use of Armstrong field guns, headed by the reactionary chief of the Royal Horse Artillery, Gen. Sir Richard Dacres. That officer not only disliked breech-loaders, but had previously testified in favor of the "beneficial inaccuracies" of smooth-bores as unpredictably useful on the battlefield. Unsurprisingly, the Dacres committee declared that "the balance of advantages is in favour of M.L. field guns, and that they should be manufactured hereafter."[41] The decision to return to muzzle-loading ordnance thus put Britain back on par with most of its potential rivals. Only Prussia—then not a threat to British power—elected to continue development of breech-loading guns, due to the close relationship between its military and the Krupp steel company that built that nation's ordnance.

Despite such a decision, Armstrong breech-loaders remained in service for a number of years, and were not immediately withdrawn.[42] While the

Top: A captured CSA Whitworth 12-pounder on a wharf in Richmond, VA, awaiting shipment to the North, April 1865. Made of steel, this rifled breechloader is considerably smaller and lighter than cast-iron guns of similar size (retrieved from the Library of Congress, www.loc.gov/item/2018671130/). *Bottom:* General (later Field Marshall) Sir Richard James Dacres (1799–1886) circa 1856. Dacres commanded British artillery during the Crimean War, and championed the return to rifled muzzle-loaders for field artillery in 1866 (Royal Collection Trust / © Her Majesty Queen Elizabeth II, 2018).

special committees deliberated, the OSC supervised numerous experiments designed to improve both the guns and their ammunition, and closely monitored quarterly reports regarding naval practice with the guns. By 1866, the Committee reported that "the absence of complaint from so many vessels [was] evidence that with the improvements that have been introduced ... since the Armstrong guns were first issued to the navy, the equipment generally is satisfactory." The next year, the Superintendent of the Royal Gun Factories suggested dispensing with such quarterly reports, as accidents "are now extremely rare, and when one does happen, there is almost invariably a *special* report of the circumstance," to which the OSC agreed.[43]

The success of the Armstrong rifled breech-loader required the inventiveness of Sir William Armstrong for its birth, the efforts of the Ordnance Select Committee to live through a difficult infancy, and public support to survive beyond that point. Through a number of technical issues and reactionary opinions, the gun lost—or never had—the backing of some powerful military authorities. An 1863 investigation into the costs of the Armstrong gun had alarmed Parliament; when coupled with the quick-fix offered by the Palliser converted gun, this frayed what political support the Armstrong breech-loader had. Finally, the very public battle between Armstrong and Whitworth polarized debate over the two systems and sharpened the awareness of the failures—real or illusory—of the breech-loader when compared to muzzle-loading ordnance. Britain made the fateful decision to give up perfecting a gun which offered considerable advantage over foreign designs (Krupp being the exception), a decision not rescinded for well over a decade.

Hale's "Stickless Rocket"

Another type of ordnance that saw considerable change during the OSC's existence was the British war rocket. William Congreve, son of Maj. Gen. William Congreve (Controller of the Royal Laboratory), used captured Indian rockets as a pattern for a redeveloped weapon he brought before the Board of Ordnance in 1805. His first design used a 25-foot-long wood "guide stick" for balance and stability, mounted on the side of the rocket. Although used to set fire to Copenhagen in 1807 and in the bombardment of Fort McHenry at Baltimore in 1814, the notoriously inaccurate rocket left much to be desired. Originally fired from a tray resembling a ladder, launching early rockets must have been harrowing to the crew exposed to their exhaust. Over time Congreve continued to refine the weapon, shortening the guide stick by ten feet and mounting it centrally along the rocket's axis to improve reliability and accuracy, and work continued during the post–Waterloo era. In 1842, the then 20-year-old Lieutenant Boxer had his first proposal approved for adoption, an improved frame and launching tube very much resembling the tubes used by many modern-day military rockets. Boxer's launcher offered better accuracy, and marginally better crew protection, than the earlier open tray.[44]

By the Crimean War, Congreve's weapon had a challenger: a rocket designed by William Hale. Born in Essex, England in 1797, Hale had a long interest in mechanics. He received his first patent, for "improvements in propelling vessels" using an internal screw at the age of thirty. In 1832, he presented a paper on the invention to the Royal Society in London, later winning a gold medal from the Royal Society of Arts in Paris. Afterward, he submitted the invention for consideration to the Admiralty, but "by his own admission ... lost interest in the project" and moved on to investigate "ordnance matters." Hale relocated near Woolwich and began experimenting with improvements to Congreve's rockets. In September of 1843 he had made sufficient progress to put a design before the Select Committee. Interested, the Committee approved trials at Hale's expense, setting a pattern that bedeviled him for many years and through many improvements.[45]

Although the Committee declined the weapon, Hale received his first

William Hale at Shoeburyness for a test of his rockets. In front of him is his stickless rocket on its launching tray. Hanging above from a triangular gyn is a Congreve rocket, presumably of similar weight, in its far larger launch tube. To the right of the device is an iron shelter for crewmen working experimental guns (reproduced by permission of the Royal Engineers Museum, Library & Archive).

patent for his "stickless rocket" on 11 January 1844. As the name implies, Hale's weapon required no guidance pole, relying instead on directed exhaust ports for spin and stability. Although more complicated to manufacture, the Hale rocket required much less room to stow and handle and a much shorter launch platform, either a tube or an open tray. A period photograph shows Hale standing next to his weapon on its four to five foot launch tray. Suspended well above him, from a high triangular support, is a Congreve rocket of the same weight with its long guide stick. The entire assembly occupies considerably more square feet than the visibly smaller Hale rocket—a factor that would have weighed heavily in his favor. Another advantage came from the method of manufacture that Hale used. The Royal Laboratory employed a manually operated "monkey press"—in effect, a small pile-driver—to pack the propellant into the metal case of Congreve rockets. Inefficient and labor-intensive, manual pressing did not produce a uniformly-shaped charge that resulted in early burn-outs, inaccurate flight, or even premature explosions. Hale, on the other hand, loaded his rockets using a hydraulic press which produced a much more uniform yet denser charge, increasing both reliability and range. A 31 May 1850 report in the *Chelmsford Chronicle* comparing service rockets to Hale's noted that with such a press, "[Hale] is able to put 4lb. weight of [powder] in the same space as 3½lb. can be put by the 'monkey' used at the Royal Arsenal." Although his role in the development of the hydraulic rocket press is unknown—Congreve himself having recommended it many years before—Hale used the hydraulic press to load all of his rockets.[46]

Hale made his first overseas sale to the United States in 1846, which bought the manufacturing license for use in the war with Mexico. At home, however, a British committee appointed to consider his rockets rejected them after three different trials. Hale's business suffered, but despite a flirtation with bankruptcy between 1849 and 1850 he continued to market his rockets overseas as well as in Britain.[47] Prince Albert, who witnessed a demonstration in 1850, "was much pleased ... both in a military and scientific point of view" according to the *Yorkshire Gazette* of 29 June. Perhaps because of the Prince's opinion, Hale optimistically wrote to the Board of Ordnance requesting that "a public trial of [his rockets] might be made preparatory to their being introduced into the service." The June letter also noted that he had "invented a machine for firing them in salvos," a concept ninety years ahead of its time. Then MGO Anglesey, however, shortsightedly declined a trial of the machine as it did not fire "the sort of rocket used in the service."[48]

Then, in 1853, disaster struck. Acting on a tip from an undercover informant, London police raided Hale's Rotherhithe factory and seized his stocks of powder, shells, and rockets. Accused of manufacturing them for the Hungarian revolutionary Lajos Kossuth, Hale's arrest—derisively termed "the

New Gunpowder Plot" by the *Daily News* on 18 April—came at a critical time. Instead of selling weapons to the allies preparing for the coming war with Russia, Hale had to fight his country in court. Eventually cleared of any collusion with revolutionaries, Hale pled guilty to the improper storage of explosives near London, resulting in the forfeiture of gunpowder in excess of 57 pounds and a fine of 2 shillings for each pound lost. Hale later appealed directly to Palmerston, then Home Office Secretary, "to relieve him from the proceedings" and "humbly [submitted] that the law has been sufficiently vindicated" by his guilty plea. In large part because of war preparations, Palmerston accepted his plea and "intimated that [Hale] will not be called up for judgment." Hale later asked for the release of the confiscated material, and wrote that "an opportunity now presents itself for bringing my Inventions into operation in Turkey," to which Palmerston also agreed. Hale joined the Allied fleet at Varna in December 1853, and although his rockets were not used at Odessa, he held several demonstrations in 1854. Raglan, impressed with the weapon's potential, bought what materials Hale brought with him for £500 and the inventor returned home to construct more. By the end of the year Ordnance finally relented, and the Royal Laboratory began small-scale manufacture.[49]

With the end of the Crimean War the future of the Hale rocket stalled; the first entry regarding Hale's products before the OSC appears in the 1861 *Abstracts*, which notes the failure of a "comet shell" brought before a special committee, but no further details are available. His next batch of rockets failed in 1862, with several bursting shortly after launch; Hale withdrew the lot, and declared to the Committee that "he will never bring forward another rocket if they burst any more." The OCS had its doubts, as their "experience of Mr. Hale hardly warrants implicit confidence in this pledge." True to his word, however, a new design brought forward the next year showed "so much promise ... that further experiments are very desirable." The Committee recommended the immediate purchase of a hundred 24-lb. rockets, with launcher, for further tests, and inquired about the possibility of smaller rockets as well.[50]

Buoyed by his success, Hale proposed that the he be provided with space at the Royal Arsenal for the construction of his weapons. At first, the OSC declined under the questionable justification that it was "undesirable to allow so dangerous a manufacture under other than official superintendence." After more negotiations, the Committee forwarded to the War Office the recommendation not only of a site for rocket construction, but also the supply of necessary materials, and the retention of his and several employees' services at an estimated £650 for six months. "Such an arrangement," they felt, would "not only materially expedite the enquiry, but will be found to be far more economical." It would also have reinforced the precedent, set with Armstrong, of hiring a talented outsider who could improve the nation's military technology. Instead, the War Office demurred; it did offer the use of government property, but chose to buy another hundred 24-lb rockets outright at £1,000—a gamble that Hale might need more than six months to perfect his design. In the short run, the gamble paid off; experiments with Hale's rockets did go longer than six months, and the first pattern would not be sealed until 1866. Hale continued to try to tempt the War Office into a longer-term relationship; in 1865 he again offered a salvo launcher "on which he is currently engaged" and other improvements "provided his services are retained ... at a fair remuneration." When asked if such an offer would be of value, however, Boxer complained that he had "received no assistance from Mr. Hale beyond being supplied with his specification for the 24-pr. rocket, and ... does not consider that any advantage would be gained" from such an arrangement.[51] Hale ultimately received a lump-sum payment of £8,000 the next year for his invention, but with manufacture and improvements now under the direction of the Royal Laboratory, the inventor found himself cut out of the future of a weapon he had labored so long to bring to perfection.

The "General Question of the Best Arm for the Infantry"

Although Greener and the *Times* feared that the nation was falling behind Continental powers in artillery in 1857, no similar apprehension surfaced regarding its infantry weapons. The Pattern 1853 Enfield rifle had proven itself in battle, and with small modifications to the cartridge to ease loading, British military authorities were content with the weapon's performance. In addition, the Royal Small Arms Factory (RSAF) in Enfield served as a model factory that attracted considerable attention in and out of Europe. The Birmingham gun trade itself used the RSAF as a pattern when fourteen of its leading gunmakers decided to launch the Birmingham Small Arms Company (BSA) in 1861. Their efforts to build a mechanized small arms factory paid off two years later, when the company won a contract to supply Turkey with 20,000 infantry rifles.[52]

Given the relatively crude state of breech-loading rifles at this point, decisions by most powers to retain muzzle-loaders are unsurprising. British tests of the Dreyse needle-gun showed that the weapon had serious flaws, as did practically every other plan of breech-loading small arm. Greener himself—no minor authority on firearms technology—declared in 1858 that "breech-loaders do not shoot nearly so well, and are not half so safe, as muzzle-loading guns" because of the lack of an effective breech seal. Still, the potential of the weapon was not lost on the OSC, and select cavalry and volunteer units in the 1860s carried breech-loaders supplied by noted gun-maker Westley Richards.[53] In 1861, however, the Committee stated that "no present intention exists of providing the army generally with breech-loaders." Hartington reiterated that position in 1863, when American William Mont Storm approached the War Office with a request to convert a handful of Enfield rifles to his system of breech-loading. The Secretary approved, but only "on the distinct understanding that this step is not to be regarded as expressing any opinion in favour of the adoption of breech-loaders as an infantry arm."[54]

As with rifled cannon, war brought the issue of breech-loading infantry weapons into very sharp focus in 1864. Tension between Denmark and the German Confederation turned into armed conflict on 1 February, when Austrian and Prussian forces crossed into Schleswig-Holstein. The Prussians, the *Dundee Advertiser* noted on the 5th, carried with them "the famous needle-gun, the qualities of which will now probably be put to the test for the first time on a large scale." By all accounts, the Dreyse served the Prussians very well, allowing their infantry to deliver higher rates of fire and reload from any position, in weather that reduced the Danish Minié to uselessness. Newspaper reports prompted at least one reader to suggest to the *Times* on 27 April that "the proved excellence of the Prussian needle rifle should, and doubtless will, draw the attention of our own military authorities ... to place some weapon on the same principle in the hands of our own soldiers."

Now headed by George F.S. Robinson (Earl de Grey and Ripon), the War Office did indeed have its attention drawn to the Danish battlefields and the success of the breech-loader. On 13 June, de Grey authorized the appointment of "a Committee of Practicable Officers to report whether it would be advisable to arm the Infantry, either in whole or in part, with breech-loading arms." In particular, he directed the committee to take into consideration the long-standing objection that "troops thus armed might fire away their ammunition too rapidly," which could lead to supply problems in an era of animal-powered logistics. The committee met four times over two weeks, beginning on 27 June 1864, and gathered testimony from a number of sources. Lt. Col. T.L. Gallwey and Capt. H.I. Alderson had recently returned from a tour in America with "favourable reports" from Union officers of the breech-loaders in use, particularly the Spencer repeating rifle. James H. Burton, an American engineer then in England to purchase machines for a new Confederate arsenal, stated that breech-loaders "are the favourite weapon in the Federal cavalry," and predicted that "the system will be universally adopted" in the U.S. Reports from Col. Beauchamp Walker, a member of the committee who toured the Danish front in 1864, confirmed the needle-gun's superiority over the Minié rifle, especially in wet and snowy weather. At the last meeting, the British military attaché in Paris informed the committee "that the question ... has been under consideration in the French army" and that "some distinguished officers have been pressing the question upon the Emperor" in spite of "the usual objection, of a too-rapid expenditure of ammunition." Given that three of the four potential powers Britain might have to engage in the next years—France, Prussia, and the United States—were either armed with or contemplating such weapons, the committee "[begged] to report their opinion in favour of arming the Infantry wholly with breech-loading arms."[55] This was a quick about-face on the issue, from a military that had only recently rejected the wholesale adoption of such rifles.

Report in hand, de Grey added two associate members to the OSC "to assist in ascertaining the speediest and cheapest mode of placing a breech-loading rifle in the hands of the troops" via the conversion of the Pattern 1853 rifle. Although a stop-gap measure, conversion made sense in view of the large stock of serviceable muzzle-loaders on hand, and could be done inexpensively and quickly. Given the "urgent nature of the question," de Grey instructed the OSC to "lose no time" in contacting anyone whose arms or plans for conversion might be worth a try, including proposals previously brought before them such as Mont Storm's. To do so, the OSC adopted a suggestion made by Maj. Gen. Hutchinson of the Small Arms Committee in 1859: a direct appeal to interested gun-makers by newspaper advertisement. The notice, scheduled for printing over 24–25 August, stated that plans were due by 20 September, should cost no more than £1 per arm, with accuracy on par with the existing rifle. Six Pattern 1853 rifles would be provided to anyone whose plans were judged worthy of trial, with altered arms and a thousand rounds of ammunition "ignited in such a manner as the competitors think suitable" to be delivered within five weeks.[56]

The 1864 "Call for Proposals" elicited considerable interest among the British press. The *Sheffield Daily Telegraph* wrote on 27 August that "some of your Sheffield mechanicians and inventors ... have a chance of making a fortune if they can only hit on the best way of converting the Enfield rifle into a breech-loader." The paper went on to recommend that "if any local genius in Steelopolis has a notion that he can do what is wanted" he should get his plans into the War Office promptly. It did warn, however, of "a shabby remuneration" of £20 for "time, thought, labour, and outlay" for any plans rejected after trial. The paper also congratulated de Grey "for his energy in providing British soldiers with some rifle that will cope with the Prussian needle gun, and for his resolution to resort to open competition." The *Times* also praised de Grey, since "the facts brought out in the Schleswig campaign prompted him to instant action." "There can be no doubt," the *Times* continued, that through "the ingenuity of our gunsmiths ... we may soon hope to see the infantry armed with a weapon which will put them on equal terms with any enemies they may have to encounter."[57]

In all, the OSC received forty-seven different schemes for converting the Enfield, out of which thirty were summarily rejected. Of the remaining seventeen, eight were selected for trial in October of 1864. The cartridges, however, varied as widely as the conversion plans, and herein arose one of the great hurdles: determining the best type of ammunition for breech-loaders. This question separated itself from the problem of converting the Enfield almost immediately, as one of the major advantages of the Dreyse needle-gun lay with the self-contained ignition of its cartridge. Such a system meant that the soldier did not need to fumble around with a small copper cap—easily lost in the heat of combat—in order to fire his weapon. Just three months before, the OSC had rejected the American Spencer repeater because Cambridge judged "the circumstances of the arm requiring a cartridge containing its own ignition ... sufficient to preclude its adoption for military purposes." Of the eight finalist systems, three used self-primed cartridges, which forced the OSC to concede that, perhaps, this was an idea worth considering. When asked, Boxer replied that "it is quite possible to make a safe metallic or strong paper cartridge" containing its own ignition. The key, according to Boxer, lay with keeping the detonating pin separate from the cap, "but so arranged as to be readily applied at pressure."[58] Boxer's remarks foreshadowed the invention by which he is remembered today.

The OSC commenced its experiments with the altered rifles on 9 January 1865. Three of the competing designs could not be tested; one was delayed in New York because of the U.S. government's refusal to grant an export permit, one because of flaws in the gun and the third due to the "dangerous nature of the cartridges." In tests that were as much about the ammunition as they were about the rifles themselves, the Committee compared the converted arms for rapidity of fire, accuracy, durability, velocity and penetration. All of the systems had flaws of one type or another, but two of the remaining five stood out, both designed by Americans. The OSC judged Mont Storm's "on the whole, superior to the others," but had the disadvantage of requiring an external percussion cap. Jacob Snider's system, on the other hand, used a self-contained cartridge that, although imperfect, the Committee found "encouraging." Confident Snider could correct problems with both the altered rifle and the cartridge, the OSC recommended conversion of a further thousand Enfields. The Committee hedged its bet, however, and continued trials of the Mont Storm rifle, under the dubious advantage that, in an emergency, it could be loaded from the muzzle using the Pattern 1853 cartridge. The War Office placed an order for 3,000 rifles converted to the Mont Storm system in July of 1865, and the OSC sealed a pattern rifle in September. Then, a month later, Col. Boxer reported that in response to a request from the Assistant Secretary of the OSC, "he has succeeded in making a cartridge for the Snider ... which gives even better results as regards accuracy" than the original, or even the Pattern 1853 cartridge itself.

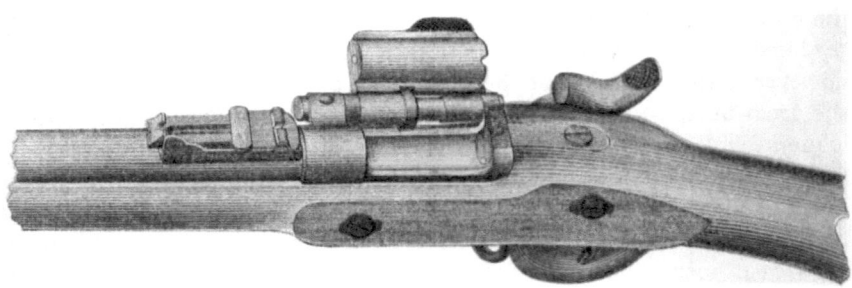

The action of the Snider-converted Enfield. The cartridge had the primer at the base, and was made of rolled brass foil and paper. The case required manual extraction after firing but gave a better gas seal and was more weather-proof than both the original Snider and the older Enfield paper cartridge ("The Needle Gun," *Nature and Art*, Francis Beckford Ward, ed. [London: Day & Son, Ltd., 1866], 92–93).

Boxer's cartridge, fired from an improved Snider conversion, did indeed give excellent results. Impressed, the OSC ruled that "pending the approval of a more efficient small-bore breech-loading rifle ... they recommend the trial of the Snider ... be resumed, with a view to an extensive conversion." They also recommended that RSAF prepare to carry out the conversion, discontinue manufacture of the Pattern 1853 Enfield, and plan for production of newly made Sniders "as may be necessary" to meet the needs of the military once the conversion was completed.[59]

Research into a completely new rifle had begun shortly after de Grey's order for conversion of the Enfield. Maj. Gen. Sir John St. George, then the Director of Ordnance, requested in December of 1864 that the OSC open investigations into the "general question of the most perfect military weapon with which to arm the infantry." St. George laid down several conditions for the new weapon, the major requirements being a breech-loader using a self-primed cartridge, and a smaller bore than the service muzzle-loader. The OSC used the same advertising tactic to invite proposals as it did with the issue of converting the Enfield, but noted that the breech-loading system, rifling, and cartridge type would be considered separately. The response, however, was disappointing; although the OSC sub-committee chose four rifles for further examination, it "point[ed] out the inferiority of the whole collection" and asked "whether it may not be desirable to postpone the inquiry, and at present to go more largely into the conversion of the Enfield rifle on the Snider system." The OSC concurred, "to allow more time for the development of the many rival plans of this nature which are now engaging the attention of gunmakers at home and abroad." The improvements made to the Snider, coupled with Boxer "having designed an ammunition which has enhanced the shooting of the ... converted Enfield to an extent which makes it positively superior to the unconverted arm" helped support the decision.[60] Over six years would pass before the successor to the OSC finally approved a new small-bore rifle for its infantry.

Although never tested in combat against its European counterparts, the Snider-Enfield rifle, coupled with the Boxer cartridge, offered the British infantryman a number of advantages. Unlike the Prussian and later French "Chassepôt" cartridge, the Boxer was impervious to all but direct submersion in water, and even then could resist a prolonged dunking. Relatively simple and soldier-proof, the Snider action did not suffer from the blow-back of gas into the shooter's face as did the Dreyse needle-fire, which forced many Prussian soldiers to fire inaccurately from the hip. Britain, therefore, ended the 1860s with an infantry weapon in many respects better than any other in the field. The search for "the most perfect military weapon with which to arm the infantry," however, would prove to be much more difficult in the years beyond.

Furthering the "Science of Artillery"

In 1855, when the OSC came into being, the empirical tools available to evaluate new technology were limited to manual observation and measurement. The thirteen-year career of the Committee, however, saw a considerable improvement in such tools, leading to new understandings of the actions that took place when a gun fired. One of the first occurred in devices used to determine projectile velocity. British mathematician Benjamin Robins had made measurement possible with the invention of the ballistic pendulum in 1740, which allowed the proper calculation of a gun's range. Robins's device measured the arc of a wooden pendulum when struck by a bullet fired from a stationary gun, from which the velocity at the point of impact could be determined. A slightly different mechanism, called a gun pendulum, measured the speed of the projectile as it exited the barrel, known as "initial muzzle velocity." In this device the gun itself formed the pendulum; hung from a frame and fired, the backward recoil equaled the initial velocity of the projectile leaving the muzzle. Scaled up, the ballistic and gun pendulums were used to measure the velocity of artillery projectiles as well as small arms. A 10 February 1816 article in the *Royal Cornwall Gazette* described the pendulum at the Arsenal as "about 7400 pounds" capable of withstanding the impact of a 24-pound shot. With such an immense device, the *Gazette* crowed, "the velocities with which balls move propelled from the heavier artillery will no longer remain a matter of mere induction, but a fair result of actual experiment."

Boxer, in his 1854 textbook on artillery, credited the data developed via the ballistic pendulum as forming "the basis of the whole science of artillery." Robins's ingenious device, still used today, had many limitations when scaled up for artillery. As the *Gazette's* report indicates, big guns required a heavy and expensive device for measuring their performance; the one built at Shoeburyness in 1859 weighed nine tons. The wooden pendulum had to be repaired and rebalanced after every shot, and could only absorb so many projectiles before needing to be rebuilt. This greatly limited the number of tests that could be conducted in any experimental program. The inaccuracy of smoothbore cannon also limited the distance at which velocity could be calculated to a hundred yards, far shorter than the increasing range of big guns. In addition, such a heavy piece of gear could hardly be moved, unless laboriously taken to pieces and reassembled.[61]

In 1840, Prof. Wheatstone suggested that electricity might be used to determine velocities, and over the next few years he and others made several experimental devices. Finally, in 1849, Belgian Army Capt. A.J.A. Navez developed an "electro-ballistic apparatus" that used magnets to release and trap a pendulum at the moment a projectile crossed two tripwires. On the recommendation of Wheatstone, the OSC requested the purchase of an improved version of Navez's apparatus in November of 1857, priced at £25. For unknown reasons, Panmure delayed the purchase until April 1858. In a minor comedy of errors, the device arrived at Woolwich in January of the next year, but without instructions for assembly or use. It took a further fifteen months to obtain a translated manual and arrange for copies to be printed. Finally, on 30 March 1860 the OSC "directed[ed] that the necessary arrangements be made for commencing experiments."[62]

The OSC assigned the task of conducting the first round of velocity measurements to an exceptional young lieutenant, William H. Noble. The twenty-two-year old Noble graduated with honors from the Trinity College in Dublin in 1856, where he studied experimental science. Just before graduating, Noble received a direct commission into the Royal Artillery, one of a small group of men offered a chance to do so because of the dire need for officers during the Crimean War. Appointed an associate member of the OSC in 1861 specifically to supervise ballistic and other scientific experiments, Noble remained in that role for the duration of the OSC's existence. In September and October 1861, Noble measured velocities for several guns and howitzers, including the Armstrong 110-pounder, and in December reported the velocities from experimental rifled cannon at both the muzzle and at thirty yards. Impressed with the results, the War Office approved £200 so "that the wires of the Navez apparatus may be extended" two days after receiving Noble's report—an exceptionally quick disbursement of funds for that age.[63]

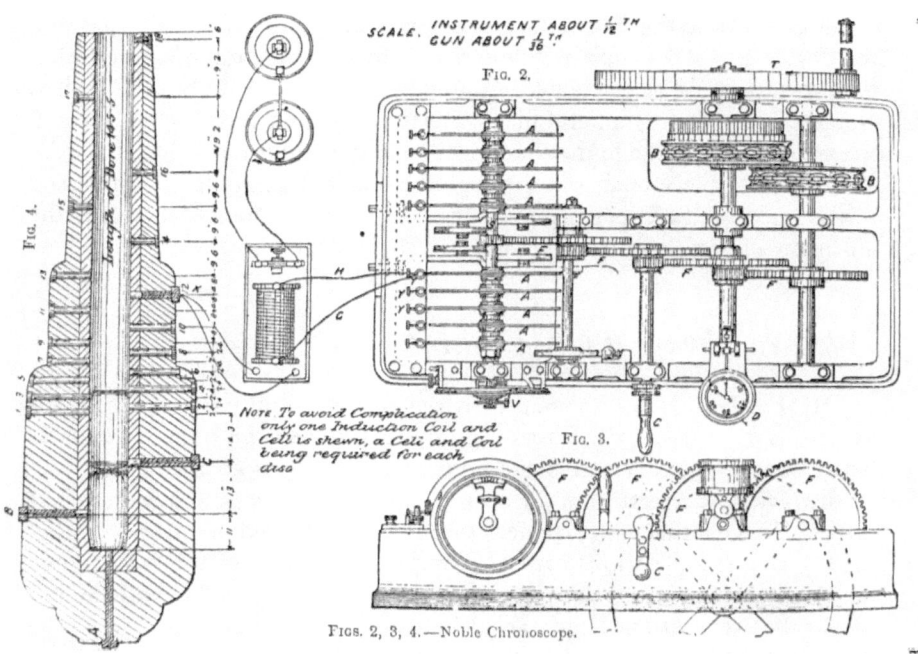

FIGS. 2, 3, 4.—Noble Chronoscope.

The Noble chronoscope. Holes drilled into the side of a gun allowed hot gases to escape into special gauges that crushed a copper disk; the amount of deformation would be used to mathematically calculate the force delivered, and therefore the velocity of the expanding powder gas within the gun itself. This system remained in use until the 1960s, when electrical sensors began to replace crusher gauges ("Gunnery." In *The Encyclopaedia Britannica* [New York: Charles Scribner's Sons, 1880], 298–9).

A different Noble, Capt. Andrew Noble, contributed much to demystifying the actions that occurred inside of guns at the moment of firing, an important question in an era when larger and larger guns required more control of gunpowder burn speed. Capt. Noble, who attended Edinburgh Academy before joining the Royal Artillery at the age of sixteen, exhibited a keen interest in mathematics and science even after being posted to Canada on his graduation from the Royal Military Academy. After eleven years' service abroad, Noble returned to Woolwich in 1858 and became secretary to the Royal Artillery Institute. A few months later he joined the special committee formed to test the Armstrong gun. Impressed with his mathematical skills and knowledge of artillery, Armstrong lured the young captain out of the Royal Artillery with a partnership in Elswick Ordnance in 1860. That same year Noble constructed his first pressure measuring device, called a "crusher gauge," although it took several years to perfect. Noble's gauge screwed into a hole drilled into the side of the gun barrel; the pressure of escaping gas into the device crushed a copper cylinder, and from the amount of deformation the pressure could be calculated. Aware of his work, in 1866 the OSC invited Noble, "a mathematician and mechanician of the first class," to assist them in experiments related to the changing nature of gunpowder. Joined by Frederick Abel, Noble agreed, and although the final report would be some years in the making, the experiments by the pair greatly enhanced not only the efficiency of, but the science behind British artillery.[64]

"We Are Always a Little Behind"

If the plethora of newspaper articles related to military technology is any indication, the British reading public followed the ongoing debates between arms manufacturers and before the OSC with great interest. Both Whitworth and Armstrong, for example, wrote the *Times* to advance their position in what that paper labeled "the Great Gun Question" on 1 September 1863. A report on "various natures of improved ordnance," the *Times* noted on 30 July, "is suggestive of furious encounters, not only on the battlefield ... but in the arena of Parliamentary debate and scientific controversy.... The partisans of Sir W. ARMSTRONG and Mr. WHITWORTH," the paper continued, "have plied each other to such good purpose with destructive projectiles as to leave the public in doubt which is the greater master in the production and use of them." A search of the *British Newspaper Archive* website for the words "Armstrong" and "Whitworth" between 1855 and 1868 garnered over 15,000 articles, but interest did not confine itself just to that topic. A search on the phrase "Ordnance Select Committee" resulted in over 5,800 articles, and for "Snider Rifle," nearly 3,500.[65] Although these numbers must be tempered with the understanding that many regional newspapers simply reprinted articles from the major dailies or notices from the War Office verbatim, it still indicates a strong interest in the changing nature of military technology in that era.

The number of books and pamphlets, while much harder to count, also point to great public interest in military technology, as these were popular tools for persons interested in promoting their position or invention. George Daw, who worked with Snider in developing the original cartridge for the latter's converted Enfield and who felt Boxer usurped his invention, used such a tactic to put his case before the public. Gun-maker Westley Richards published an 1863 plea for "a fair and impartial trial for Breech-loading Ordnance of a large caliber ... conducted in public previous to the adoption of any new system," as was not done with the Armstrong gun.[66] Sir James Emerson Tennent's 1864 *The Story of the Guns*, although sympathetic to Whitworth, reminded his readers that, in addition to the inventors and the military, "there is *a third party* interested in the investigation;—the nation at large, who look to acquire an effective armament in return for the expenditure incurred." Patrick Barry, in his muckraking volume *Shoeburyness and the Guns*, took a similar line, but treated Whitworth much more harshly. "The public money has been spent on him—positively squandered on him—and, as far as I am aware, to no purpose" while "other inventors have been repelled, trifled with, injured," Barry wrote. In addition, Barry charged that certain officers, most notably Boxer, were not the impartial participants they should be. Boxer, by then a full colonel, "should henceforth cease to divide his time between the public and [Whitworth's] Manchester Ordnance Company, and either throw the public or the Manchester Ordnance Company overboard."[67] Whitworth retaliated in 1866 by publishing the proceedings of the "Armstrong & Whitworth Committee" prefaced by a letter to Earl de Grey, "as a means of proving to my friends and the public that, while the competition has ended in a substantial victory to me, it has yielded results of great importance to our artillery service."[68] Although a very small sampling, these works show the wide range of subjects that writers interested in military technology brought before the reading public during the reign of the Ordnance Select Committee.

Perhaps no better measurement of the level of public involvement in military technology exists than the records of the Committee itself. Over the first eleven years for which the *Abstracts* were published, the OSC minutes discussed 26,577 items, and the committee issued 5,173 reports of findings to the War Office. Additionally, 3,425 new proposals, questions, and requests for opinions appeared before the OSC; of those, 974 came from military officers, primarily British, and 699 originated with the War Office or some other government entity. The remainder—1,752, or just over half—came from civilians, most unconnected with the military or the Royal manufacturing departments, with a very small handful from enlisted army or navy personnel. Granted, most individuals approached the War Office with pounds-sterling in their eyes, but an exceptional few—Armstrong among them—did so out of a sense of duty to their country. Regardless, such participation, for whatever reason, disproves any notion of these two decades serving as the start of the decline in British inventiveness.

If there was a lack of inventiveness or originality in British military technology in this era, the problem lay elsewhere, as illustrated by a 1 September 1864 article in the *Standard*. "How is it," the paper asked, "that with all our mechanical genius as a people we are content to take the leading improvements in our army and navy at second hand from other nations?" "The result is inevitable," the *Standard* continued. "We are always a little behind, and sometimes more than a little." The article went on to list several British reactionary responses to overseas military development, beginning with the launch of *La Glorie* five years before, but more recently to news coming out of America. "When Federal and Confederate ships spit great shells at each other we conclude that solid shot is not the right sort of thing," for example. "We hear of torpedoes," but only when "the Confederates blow up an ironclad bodily with one of these submarine contrivances ... [do] we rub our eyes, and begin to think there is something in it." The same situation had arisen with British military small arms. "The American evidence is striking," the paper claimed, "as showing the value of the breech-loader to an army which is numerically weak in comparison with its opponents" such as the British when compared to the massive conscription armies of Europe. "Most decisive evidence comes from some of [the American] generals in favour of the breech-loader, and the only lingering objections appear to be those which arise rather from prejudice than from experience." The paper's complaint would become all the more apparent in the following decade, as Britain stubbornly retained muzzle-loading artillery beyond when other nations had adopted breech-loaders.

The changes in British military weaponry shepherded by OSC, on the other hand, are nothing short of remarkable. Heated iron shot had been replaced by J. Martin's shells filled with liquid iron in 1857; William Hale's stickless rocket finally supplanted the unwieldy and less accurate Congreve; the Pattern 1853 Enfield muzzle-loader gave way to the Snider breech-loader in 1866, and rifled cannon—on whatever system would be finally selected—were now permanent fixtures in British artillery. A scant four years after moaning about British arms, the *Standard* now wrote about the "wonderful" advancements being made. A 29 May 1868 article remarked that "chemistry has largely called in to the aid of our manufacturing departments," resulting in improvements in gunpowder, and "the manufacture of carriages ... is going forward with wonderful strides." "It is impossible," the *Standard* wrote, "for any honest man to read [the minutes of the OSC] without acknowledging how difficult must be the tasks of steering among the designs of rival inventors ... [and] the thousands of applicants for trials at the public expense." Rather breathlessly, the *Standard* went on to claim "how great a thing it is for the nation that so far beyond question is the honour of [the OSC] that no dissatisfied inventor, however much he may impugn their judgment, has ever ventured to breathe one syllable against the purity of their motives."[69]

Such a glowing endorsement of the Committee, however, could not prevent its fall by the basest of Victorian political motives: parsimony. On 3 December 1868, Lefroy, then President of the OSC, informed the attendant officers that the Secretary of War had decided to replace the Committee with "other arrangements" in order to eliminate its dedicated operating costs. Lefroy received a promotion to "Director General of Ordnance, with full powers for the conduct of immediate and necessary business pending the reorganization of the Department," while the rest of the Committee members went their separate ways. What remained to be seen, however, was if such business could in fact be accomplished—a question perhaps not fully considered when Pakington decided upon the elimination of the Ordnance Select Committee.[70]

"A New Era of Great Guns"

Although it saved a few thousand pounds a year in operating expenses, Pakington's decision to shelve the OSC cost the nation the services of a competent and generally well-regarded supervisory body that had successfully kept British arms on par with other European militaries. What replaced the Committee was, in effect, a miniature version of the muddle that crippled British military administration during the Crimean War. While not nearly as disastrous, the new "Experimental Branch" consisted of a much smaller committee under the Director of Artillery, who also oversaw the actions of a number of subject-specific committees. Operating independently of one another, these bodies often duplicated the efforts of each other and occasionally issued conflicting opinions on similar subjects. In addition, the Secretary of State had a separate "Ordnance Council" to which he could refer subjects related to military technology—or simply duck responsibility for making such decisions himself. Such a profusion of committees created a relatively chaotic system that, coupled with reactionary military opinions, put the nation at an increasing technological disadvantage compared to the rest of Europe in the 1870s.

The eleven-year duration of this smaller muddle remained a source of continued tension between competing interests over the future directions of British military technology. A number of important investigations passed from the OSC to the Experimental Branch, including the question of the British infantry's future rifle, new forms of gunpowder, and the best way to defend—and defeat—armored warships. Such topics continued to stimulate public debate, as did emerging technologies. In addition, because of a growing number of public complaints, the War Office created a formal board of investigation into claims for reward and priority of invention, and generated new rules regarding inventions by public servants such as Boxer.

The creation of the Experimental Branch ultimately concentrated considerable power into the hands of the Royal Artillery, and the experiences and training of those officers drove ordnance development for the next several years. Britain's involvement in small-scale colonial wars, for example, kept it wedded to muzzle-loading field guns because of their simplicity and ruggedness in the field, despite the battlefield experiences of a potential enemy: the newly unified German Empire. The Royal Navy shares equal blame in Britain's retention of outdated artillery. The Admiralty's preference for familiar technology meant that their ships carried increasingly large and heavy rifled muzzle-loaders longer than France or Germany, even after Elswick Ordnance perfected Armstrong breech-loaders. It took the fatal explosion of a 12-inch gun on board HMS *Thunderer* in 1879 to convince authorities that the future of naval artillery lay with steel breech-loaders, rather than wrought iron muzzle-loading guns. In addition, the accident's investigation finally led to the dissolution of the weapons development system introduced by Pakington, and the resurrection of a single oversight committee responsible for artillery questions—a throwback to the earlier OSC.

A "Small Economy ... Utterly Misplaced"

In June of 1868 Gen. Sir Robert Napier wrapped up "the most astonishing feat of modern days": the expedition into Abyssinia against its Emperor Theodore. As with all British military actions, after congratulations came calls for retrenchment. The expedition costs had doubled beyond the original estimate and been partially funded by a tax increase. On 1 October 1868, the *Times* reported that "the authorities at the War-office, in conjunction with those at the Horse Guards, have determined on making a considerable reduction in the army" for the following year. Originally rumored to involve the elimination of battalions stationed at home depots and withdrawal of troops from Canada and Australia, on 2 September the *Morning Post* reported that reforms included "the immediate abolition" of the OSC. The *Pall Mall Gazette* confirmed the Committee's impending demise on 12 November, stating that "all new inventions, changes in war matériel, and the like will be referred to special committees appointed from time to time ... as the occasions may rise."[1] The quote also illustrates a built-in flaw of the new technical-committee system: an assumption that technological change would slow down, rather than remain at the brisk pace of the previous fifteen years.

The papers reacted to the news with considerable misgivings. The *Gazette* reminded its readers that, although not free from defects, "on the whole the work of the committee has been well done" and that "the existence of some such body is indispensable." "Never," the paper continued, "has any one ventured to suggest that its judgments have been formed upon any unworthy motives. Its reports have been official documents of a high character, eagerly sought after by foreign Governments." Certainly the OSC "has had too much to do," the *Gazette* continued, but "how is the work to be done without any committee at all?" The paper also wondered what person or body would decide which inventions should move forward, and who would decide what special committees were needed. "We trust these things have been well considered, and that in a search for economy efficiency will not be abandoned." The *Morning Post* of the same date questioned "if it is desirable to entirely suppress a body which has adequately performed very arduous and important duties at a time of transition." In addition, the *Post* blamed the House of Commons "which encourages the system of inventors and contractors and other interested persons pushing their views in that assembly" and pointed to the "the case of the wearisome and absurd ARMSTRONG and WHITWORTH competition" as an example. With Prime Minister Benjamin Disraeli's cabinet in political danger, the *Post* also cautioned that "governments ... on the very eve of extinction should not undertake in a hasty manner any business to which objections can be raised, and which is not of an urgent and irrepressible character."

Despite such a warning, Pakington ordered the dissolution of the OSC on 3 December. In the letter announcing the change, he claimed that "he has not resorted to this step on the ground of any dissatisfaction with the Committee," but in favor of "other arrangements, by which it is hoped that the business heretofore referred to them will be conducted with greater economy and despatch." If there were other reasons behind the decision besides economy, they were not stated overtly. It is very possible, for example, that the OSC fell victim to the ongoing turf war between the political and military branches of the War Office. Pakington may have also been influenced by frustration on the part of military authorities, such as Cambridge, with the continuing dispute between Armstrong and Whitworth. In addition, Pakington had formed at least one special committee to reconsider the OSC's experiments regarding iron armor shields being installed at Gibraltar and Malta. This pattern of specialty committee may be the "other arrangements" that Pakington had in mind.[2]

In place of the OSC, Pakington created an "Experimental Branch," headquartered at Woolwich and under the control of Lefroy, the incoming Director-General of Ordnance. Composed of four Royal Artillery officers, this new entity included then–Captain William H. Noble, who had previously served as an associate member of the OSC. Responsible for initial screening of inventions, the much smaller committee received proposals from the War Office, and passed those worthy of consideration to topic-specific sub-committees in a manner sometimes used by the OSC. On paper at least, this allowed Pakington to claim £6,271 in savings by eliminating the operational costs of the Committee. Under the new arrangement, however, the number of sub-committees expanded rapidly, as did the costs associated with the

Experimental Branch. By the end of 1870, thirty separate committees had been formed to consider questions involving all manner of ordnance materials and the efforts of dozens of officers, primarily from the Royal Artillery. Over the next ten years, the budget of the new Branch crept to £4,462 annually, still less than the OSC, but with the added confusion of so many different committees.[3]

Pakington's announcement met with some skepticism. The 7 December 1868 issue of the *Dublin Evening Mail* "supposed that there will be increased economy and efficiency" in the new arrangements, but reminded its readers that the OSC "has done a great deal of very honest work." The *Standard*, on 27 January 1869, echoed the original rationale behind the creation of the OSC by pointedly mentioning that the new "committee on inventions, or whatever it may be called" consisted of artillery officers only, with no representation from the navy or other branches of the army. In addition, the paper doubted "whether, considering the immense importance of the questions submitted," it would not be best to make the salaries of committee members good enough to draw "the highest talent and experience from all branches of the service. This is not at present the case," as one of the former OSC members (most probably Capt. Noble) transferred to the new committee at a reduced salary, and the department heads received no additional pay for their service whatsoever. Finally, the *Standard* warned that "we cannot conceive any department of the army where any small economy could be more utterly misplaced. We doubt if the present constitution of the committee will give complete satisfaction to the public."

Because of the gains made in Parliament by the Liberal Party in the general elections earlier in the year, Disraeli's cabinet gave way to the Gladstone government on 3 December 1868. As Chancellor of the Exchequer under Palmerston, Gladstone had fought the prime minister over military spending, preferring to limit Britain to a defensive strategy reinforced with diplomacy, rather than build up the nation's offensive capabilities. Such a policy would allow greater reductions in government spending and the final elimination of the income tax, long one of Gladstone's chief political goals. Now premier himself, Gladstone felt he could finally make that goal a reality, and to assist in the effort installed Edward Cardwell as Secretary of State for War on 9 December. Cardwell had a head for finance that Gladstone appreciated, having served as president of the Board of Trade in Aberdeen's government. In 1855 he had been tapped to succeed Gladstone at the Exchequer, but declined to serve in Palmerston's government, as had Gladstone. Charged by the new prime minster to find reductions in military spending, Cardwell appointed a special committee under Thomas George Baring (Lord Northbrook) to do a complete review of the systems of financial supervision in place in the War Office. Cardwell, however, recognized the need for some form of advisory body to assist with changes in military technology. In March of 1869, therefore, he appointed a new "Council of Ordnance, whose duty it will be to advise him on such questions connected with Arms, Armaments, and Experiments, as he may refer to them." Similar to the *ex officio* OSC, the Ordnance Council consisted of designated heads of departments in the War Office as well as chief ordnance, engineer, and naval officers. Unlike the OSC, however, the Council was not a permanent standing body. Although charged with the consideration of "any question ... which involves consequences of serious importance" suggested by either the Director-General of Ordnance or the Lords of the Admiralty, the Council only met when specifically called by the Secretary of State.[4]

With the release of the second report from the Northbrook committee in May 1869, on the 27th the *Pall Mall Gazette* jumped to the conclusion that the OSC would "be revived on a somewhat improved and extended footing." The paper congratulated Cardwell for having "avoided the dangerous path" set by Pakington before leaving office. "We have always been puzzled to know how the duty of deciding upon the merits of different inventions would be carried out with the assistance of some such body," the paper continued. "Without a Select Committee of some sort our experiments must assume an intermittent, unscientific character, highly prejudicial to the interests of the service." The *Gazette's* congratulations proved premature; Cardwell did not resurrect the OSC, and a close reading of the report shows no such recommendation. Such a proposal would also have met with considerable resistance on the part of Cambridge. In an appearance before the Northbrook commission, the Duke testified that he "approved highly of the abolition" of the OSC, a body "interested in multiplying experiments, many of which were useless," or costly even if successful. "We were," he claimed, "experimenting for the benefit of the world."[5]

Ultimately, what the final Northbrook report recommended and what Cardwell presented in his "War Office Act" of 1870 was the division of that office into three distinct departments: Military, Finance, and Supply. The Commander-in-Chief would head the first, and serve as principal military adviser to the Secretary of State. Finance and Supply would be headed by the new posts of Financial Secretary and the Surveyor-General of Ordnance, respectively. The former would be responsible for preparing the annual army estimates, maintaining army financial books, and auditing accounts. The Surveyor-General would be in charge of logistics, clothing supply, fortification construction, and the procurement of ordnance and military stores, both through the Royal Arsenal and by contract. Holders of both offices could, if elected, occupy voting seats in the House of Commons, which served to extend representation of the War Office in Parliament.[6]

Cardwell also abolished the Director-General of Ordnance position created by Pakington and replaced it with the "Director of Artillery and Stores," responsible for the manufacture and supply of all ordnance materials for the British military. This included oversight of the manufacturing departments of the Royal Arsenal, as well as supervision of experiments. Similar directorships, also answerable to the Surveyor-General, were appointed for Supplies and Transport, Clothing, and Contracts. When announced, at least one writer questioned the decision. "By clubbing all manner of different services together under one head," "Mus Urbanus" noted in his 16 April 1870 letter to the *Grantham Journal*, "we are assured that there is not only a reduction of expenses but an increase of efficiency. It may be so, but to insure success it may be as well to keep as long as possible on peaceable terms with other nations."

The first man selected to fill the new post of Director of Artillery and Stores, Maj. Gen. Sir John Adye, had served with distinction in the Crimean War and spent many years in India. Adye testified before the Northbrook committee that "some such machinery" like the OSC "is indispensable" and predicted that "its re-organization is only a matter of time." Adye put that opinion into practice soon after his appointment to the new post. Concerned over the possible "diverging decisions and ultimate confusion" the mushrooming subcommittees might produce, in April 1870 Adye proposed the resurrection of the *ex officio* OSC of 1855 in all but name. Noting that "the best advisers the Government can have are the Heads of the Manufacturing and Store departments," he proposed that he "should personally confer, once a week, or oftener if necessary" with such officials. "Points of manufacturing detail and minor changes could be decided at once," Adye wrote, "whilst others

General Sir John Miller Adye (1819–1900) c. 1882 (Royal Collection Trust / © Her Majesty Queen Elizabeth II, 2018).

involving experiments and larger issues would be discussed, and Subcommittees, if necessary, named to carry them out." He also pointed out that "the scheme in its general working will involve no addition to present establishments, and therefore no additional expense"—an important consideration in the penny-pinching atmosphere of the War Office.[7]

Adye's reorganization put considerable power and responsibility into the hands of the Director of Artillery and Stores, a position only held by himself and Maj. Gen. Sir Frederick Campbell over the next decade. Adye's years of campaigning, especially in India, convinced him of the need for simplicity and reliability in military hardware. He also had strong views on the importance of commonality in equipment. "We are a great naval, military, Indian, and colonial empire," he later wrote, "with fleets, troops, fortresses, and reserves of munitions to maintain in every quarter of the world." "It is essential," he continued, that the armaments of the army and navy "be identical in pattern, and that the reserves at home and abroad be available for both." By contrast, Campbell brought technical expertise to the post. Sent overseas only once (to Canada, from 1838 to 1846), Campbell sat on the OSC from 1860 to 1863, then as served as Superintendent of the Royal Gun Factory at Woolwich until 1875, when he took over the Directorship. While the long tenures of these officers brought a degree of stability to their post, it also contributed to the stagnation of thinking in British military technology during this period, illustrated by Adye's own hand. His April 1870 reorganization memo claimed that "the great changes which commenced about 12 years ago, by the introduction of rifled ordnance, may be considered for the most part at an end."[8] Such an opinion suggests Adye brought a relatively closed mind to his post along with his military experience.

Finally, Adye helped cement the control that the War Office had over ordnance development, even for the Royal Navy. With the elimination of the Board of Ordnance in 1855, the Navy lost its own Bureau of Ordnance, which had up to that point designed the guns required by the service. Responsibility for naval ordnance fell to the OSC, which included a naval officer but was firmly under the control of the War Office. With Adye's expansion of the Experimental Branch, the Ordnance Council—which also had naval representation—stopped consideration of all but questions of remuneration to inventors. By relying on Arsenal department heads for opinion, Adye eliminated any voice the Navy had in the consideration of new proposals brought before the War Office. Only when specifically requested by the Director of Artillery could the Director of Naval Ordnance contribute an opinion. Then, in June of 1870 Adye complained of "the inconvenience likely to arise from two departments communicating with gentlemen on the subject of their inventions" in response to the Admiralty's discussions with Whitworth regarding the trial of a 9-inch gun of his design. Despite protestations that the adoption of a single-communication rule "would lead to delay and serious inconvenience," the Admiralty agreed to the new restriction, ceding to the War Office—and Adye—oversight of its ordnance for the foreseeable future.[9] The Admiralty may have felt that it had no option in the matter, as the monies for naval guns and stores were included in the yearly army estimates, rather than the Navy's. That curious anomaly in military financing would not be changed for nearly two more decades.

The Experimental Branch in Action

As with the OSC, the path for a hopeful inventor began with getting his proposal to the War Office. Individuals and companies alike did this by direct communication or through an agent or third-party representative, a common occurrence for persons outside of England. Military officers also approached the War Office directly; enlisted men generally went through their chain of command. Occasionally, the route was not so direct, as in the case of "a young German" whose tale of woe appeared in *The Star* on 13 July 1880. According to the paper, the man took the drastic step of enlisting in the army "for the purpose of bringing his invention into notice." Apparently unable to get any assistance, he then joined a different regiment whose commander "he heard spoken of as a man who would help him"—only to end up in prison for deserting the first regiment. There were also the occasional anonymous submissions. In what would be a headline-making incident today, Cambridge turned over to the Experimental Branch an incendiary grenade "with rather a dangerous detonator" for examination. Col. T.W. Millward, then superintendent of the Royal Laboratory, defused the device, and speculated it to be "one of the numerous inventions proposed during the Ashantee war." When asked its origin, the Duke "[could not] recollect who gave it to him."[10]

Adye's reorganization added a step between the War Office and the consideration of new projects by any of its special committees. Once received, the Director of Artillery turned the proposal over to a new "Secretary of Experiments." That officer searched the Ordnance archives for anything similar; if found, the matter would be returned to the Director with remarks on any previous judgment. The archives were deep; the dismissal of R. J. Watson's plan for a fifty-barrel "rifle battery" noted that "a very similar [proposal] may be found in 'The Gunner,' published [in] 1628." For those judged to be original and which "seem[ed] to present some prospect of advantage to the service," the Secretary then forwarded the item to the relevant head of an Arsenal manufacturing department. Together the two officers would furnish a short report. If deemed to be a trivial matter, the Director of Artillery could handle it at once; otherwise, the question would be discussed at the weekly meeting with department heads.[11]

As with many propositions that came before the OSC, inventors were motivated by a wide range of factors. War scares, particularly the threat of French invasion stemming from their war with Prussia in 1870, drove many to bring ideas before the War Office. Mr. J. Macintosh used the war to press for reconsideration of his "plan for the use of incendiary materials in warfare," rejected by the OSC in 1859. Macintosh fretted that "knowing the terrible power of his system," made him "anxious ... that [Britain] become the sole possessor of his invention." Mr. T. Smith resubmitted his 1862 plan for a "locomotive battery," essentially a steam-powered armored car, "in consequence of the uncertain and alarming state of the country" in 1870. Continued unrest in India also led Major F. Hinton, late of the 1st Dorset Artillery Volunteers, to submit a plan for a form of incendiary shrapnel shell. Hinton claimed that it would "be most valuable in the *coming* rebellion in India"; his prediction of another uprising, however, never came to pass.[12]

The possibility of reward continued to motivate inventors, and as before, some of the demands were extravagant. Americans I. and J. A. Joseph demanded "one million dollars in gold" for a secret composition that they promised "will destroy anything it touches" but that "only exploded when lighted or fired from a gun." Carl Deutsch asked "for a fee of £500,000, or less if a title be conferred on him" for details of a cartridge he had invented, along with "information on the latest mode of construction of the Prussian breech-loading guns." Both proposals were rejected, but not all requests for funds were dismissed outright. Samuel Goddard, whose competing proposal for breech-loading cannon lost out to Armstrong's in the late 1850s, wrote to the War Office in 1877 "begging government to purchase his 6-pr rifled breech-loading gun, submitted for trial ... in 1854, and still at Woolwich Arsenal." Perhaps partly in sympathy for Goddard, who had claimed a loss of £5,000 in developing his cannon, the Director of Artillery (then Maj. Gen. Campbell) "consider[ed] the gun an interesting relic of past experiments," and recommended £100 for its purchase, which the War Office approved.[13]

Although many potentially useful suggestions came before the Experimental Branch, cranks and dreamers continued to plague the War Office. Lt. Col. Heyman, the Secretary of Experiments, found a plan for cannon by a Mr. Neilsjen of Denmark, "most absurd, and thoroughly impractical." Heyman also judged Swiss Artillery Lt. H. Studer's proposal for disc-firing artillery "one of the wildest [proposals] ever brought to notice," and wrote that Mr. A. Ciofti's plan for cannon "only exists in the proposer's head." Col. H. H. Lloyd, formerly of the Bengal Army, forwarded drawings and specifications for a steam-powered "cycloidal field gun" whose "deadly and exterminating fire will greatly contribute to, if not entirely, produce the extinction of war." That fanciful claim, plus the £10,000 requested to develop the gun, led to the shelving of Lloyd's plan. Once determined to be impractical or of no use to the service, the proposal then went back to the inventor, usually with a simple statement that it was "not required for the service." Occasionally, however, the Director of Artillery weighed in on the subject, as in the case of a system of breech-loading "for guns of all calibers" by Lt. W. Sedgwick of the Royal Engineers. Heyman noted that it was the third such plan received from the lieutenant, and after conferring with the head of the Royal Gun Factory, judged it to have major defects. When Sedgwick requested further information to allow him to remedy the issues, Adye rather harshly replied that "his system is so faulty in principle, and open to such grave objections, that no modifications would render it applicable to the service, and that the Secretary of State decline[d] to enter upon any discussion." The rebuke was enough to keep Sedgwick from troubling the War Office for the next decade.[14]

The unfortunate lieutenant's proposal illustrates one of the principal flaws in the Experimental Branch system of weapons evaluation: the degree of control that a single member of one branch of military service had over the weapons development process. Both Adye and Campbell were conservative in their opinions, and the lack of vision retarded British military technological progress. Despite American experience in the Civil War, for example, Adye saw no need for improving British hand grenades, and thought the weapon "almost out of date for European warfare" although possibly useful in colonial conflicts. Campbell felt the same way, and dismissed an 1879 proposal with the remark that he found "the notion of a soldier laying aside his rifle in order to light a hand grenade … and of light cavalry riding about with bags of bomb shells … curiously absurd." Given the millions used during the Great War, such a statement proved anti-prophetic, and also illustrates a mindset towards technology that extended throughout the Experimental Branch system. When Lt. E. Donnithorne, a cavalry officer with the Royal Scots Greys, proposed a combination time and percussion artillery fuze in 1871, the Special Committee on Fuzes replied that "they are satisfied that the [Boxer] wood time fuze is the best in the world." They also felt that a separate percussion fuze "already proposed for adoption [appeared] likely to answer satisfactorily." By not investigating the potential of Donnithorne's or similar combination fuzes, the Committee missed the opportunity to reduce the number of fuzes British artillery units had to carry into the field.[15]

Adye's interference did not limit itself to weapons. In 1872, the commander of the 42nd Highlanders submitted a sample cooking stove designed by Armourer-Sergeant Warry, a member of his regiment. Trials of the smallest design, capable of cooking for twenty-five men, showed the stove to be "light, compact, simple, efficient, and consuming very little fuel," and Cambridge suggested its partial adoption. Adye, however, complained that "Warry's stove, though very well adapted to peace maneuvers or for picnics, [was] too complicated for war purposes." Overall, he felt it "inferior to the ordinary camp kettles" which the army had in considerable numbers. Using the latter as justification, Maj. Gen. Sir Henry Knight-Storks, then the Surveyor-General of Ordnance, "decided that no new description of cooking apparatus could be entertained at that time."[16]

Proposals that managed to get the approval of both the appropriate special committee and Director of Artillery, however, were not assured of survival. A steam cooking wagon, designed by a Mr. Fraise, had been recommended for adoption after trial in July of 1873. Knight-Storks, however, "decided that none could be purchased as there were no funds" provided for it in the army estimates for that year. The War Office also quashed projects, such as one for a "reflecting pocket level" brought forward by Lt. W. de W. Abney of the Royal Engineers and approved in 1870. When Abney brought an improved version forward along with an appeal for a reward, Northbrook, then the Under-Secretary of State, took a closer look at the matter. Although the Royal Engineer Committee thought the improved version "superior in many points to the original," Northbrook felt that "instruments of the kind are only rarely required ... and the best article should be obtained in the market" as needed. Not only did Northbrook deny Abney's request for reward, but also ruled that "the pattern already sealed should be cancelled."[17]

The reluctance to spend money coupled with an insistent reliance on in-house industry contributed to the financial strangulation of at least one business: Hale's Rocket Co. The company had passed to William Hale, Jr., on the death of his father in early 1870, and in August he approached the War Office looking for orders. Hale offered improved 12- and 24-pounder rockets with "greater range, velocity and accuracy of flight" than those of his father's pattern then being manufactured at the Laboratory. He also "[submitted] for inspection an 8-inch shell rocket, which, when filled, will weigh nearly 250lbs...." and "asked for an order for 100 prepared for firing, at a price of £1,850, which included the stand with all fittings complete." No such orders were forthcoming, however; Col. Millward of the Royal Laboratory tersely told the War Office that "rockets of any size which may be required can be manufactured ... without any assistance" from outside the Arsenal. Hale's Rocket Co. struggled on, but finally shut down in 1876.[18]

Another problem with the Experimental Branch system lay in the proliferation of special committees. Adye, in his proposal for weekly meetings with department heads, noted that the first year of the Branch's existence saw the creation of "a series of independent Sub-committees, about 13 of which [were] now sitting" by June of 1870.[19] This did not end with Adye's reorganization; between 1869 and 1880, the two Directors of Artillery saw fit to create forty-six different sub-committees, excluding those related to small arms, engineer equipment, and other topics outside the scope of the Director's office. The Committee on Explosive Substances, for example, remained in existence beyond 1880; its work greatly improved the efficiency of British gun powder, and kept Britain abreast with new forms of chemical- rather than charcoal-based explosives. Despite this success, the creation of so many committees greatly complicated weapons development in this era.

A Horse Designed by Committee: The Camel That Was the Martini-Henry Rifle

No other project illustrates the War Office's predilection for special committees than the development of the Martini-Henry rifle, a completely new weapon rather than a converted muzzle-loader like the Snider. In 1866 Secretary of War Gen. Jonathan Peel authorized the creation of a "Special Sub-Committee on Breech-Loading Arms," attached to the OSC, to head the effort to rearm the military with a modern rifle. Unlike the committee that selected the Snider action to marry to the Enfield rifled barrel, the "Fletcher Committee," named after its president Lieut. Col. H.C. Fletcher of the Scots Fusilier Guards, had a much more complex task. All the components of the weapon—the breech action, the form of rifling, and the cartridge—were thrown open for consideration. As with the competition for the Enfield conversion, the Fletcher committee released an advertisement offering a reward for the best design, and listed the criteria desired. These included all the usual requirements for a military arm: sturdiness in the field, bayonet and sling attachments, designated weight and length limits, and so forth. Inventors could submit guns of any caliber and form of cartridge, as long as the latter carried its own ignition and "be as little liable to injury by rough usage, damp, and exposure in all climates as the Boxer cartridge." The committee also specified mean figures of accuracy, trajectory, and penetration better than those of the Enfield, but an increase in recoil of no more than ten percent.[20]

The rewards offered by the War Office were substantial, and divided into several categories. Each competitor whose weapon survived initial screening would receive £300 to provide six rifles and a thousand rounds of ammunition for further evaluation. The arm which the Committee judged to best meet all the requirements would receive an award of £1,000; the best breech mechanism would receive £600. Cartridge designs were to be judged separately, with the winner in that category receiving £400. Repeating arms designs were also welcome in their own category, with a first-place purse of £300, but none were submitted for competition. Finally, the advertisement noted that "the Secretary of State will take care that no ingenious novelty produced in answer ... shall be adopted in the service without proper acknowledgement" and promised that the inventor's name would be associated with it.[21]

Of the 120 rifles submitted, sixty-seven were eliminated outright as not in compliance with the terms of the advertisement; a number of gunmakers, however, elected only to compete for the breech action prize, as they could adapt their design "to any barrel which may be approved." Of the remaining thirty-seven rifles, only nine were judged worthy of further trial, which after numerous delays finally took place in February of 1868. Using the Snider for comparison, the Fletcher Committee fired the different rifles against each other for accuracy, trajectory, and penetration, and ran them through tests to determine susceptibility to jamming by sand or exposure to weather. None of the weapons met all the specifications laid down by the War Office, which "proved by experiment to have been very high, and in some particulars far beyond the attainment of the [Snider]." The Committee therefore did not recommend anyone receive the grand prize; Scottish gunsmith Alexander Henry received that for the best breech action. London gunmaker George Daw received the prize for the best cartridge even though the Committee considered "the [improved Boxer] ammunition at present in use in the service [to be] ... superior to that submitted by Mr. Daw."[22]

Even before the trials finished, however, the War Office extended the purview of the Fletcher Committee to consider all the characteristics necessary for an efficient and accurate breech-loader. The Committee spent much of early 1868 taking testimony from "distinguished gunmakers" in the British private arms trade, as well as "others who had studied the subject of military arms" such as Boxer. "All," the Committee reported, "were of opinion that the principal qualifications were ... strength, lightness and safety, flatness of trajectory, and accuracy." It also re-examined the many forms of breech mechanisms brought before it in 1866, as well as those received afterwards, and tested several types of rifle barrels adapted to fire Boxer cartridges of various bullet diameters and powder charges.[23] Work on all of these components of Britain's future rifle continued during the transition of the OSC to the Experimental Branch; the "Special Sub-Committee" became one of several "special committees" loosely connected to the Branch, with membership that remained intact but now answering directly to the Secretary of State.

On 11 February 1869, Fletcher presented the committee's decision: Henry's barrel of .45-inch bore would be married to the breech mechanism of Swiss gun designer Friedrich von Martini, whose rifle had recently been adopted by that nation. The cartridge would remain the composite centerfire case then in service, loaded with a Henry-designed 480-grain solid lead bullet. In keeping with Peel's original directive that inventor names be associated with the finished product, the new arm would be called the "Martini-Henry," and ammunition to be known as "Boxer-Henry." The Committee also requested that both Martini and Henry receive awards for their contributions. The British insistence on producing a completely new weapon, rather than license an existing design, was in keeping with most—but not all—major militaries of the era. Remington successfully sold rifle systems to several nations, as did the Providence Tool Company of Rhode Island, who held the patent for Henry O. Peabody's action that Martini based his design on.[24] In every case, however, the selected weapons system required adaptation to local requirements. As far as can be determined, however, England was the only nation that took such a "mix-and-match" approach, pairing a barrel from one inventor with the action of another.

Consideration of the question then went before a special conference of the Ordnance Council, one of the few topics that body reviewed that did not center on questions of priority of invention or reward. Satisfied with the Fletcher committee's work, the Council recommended further experiments with the new weapon by both the army and navy. It also recommended that "no other expenditure of public money be made for the trial of any other arm" in the meantime, closing the door on any alternatives that the rapidly changing world of small arms might develop. The Council also recommended manufacture of two hundred arms by hand for the experiments, while the Royal Small Arms Factory at Enfield underwent modification of its machinery for full-scale production, at a cost of £4,500, with an expectation of new machine-made arms by the end of the year. The Council finally recommended that "minor questions referring to the Martini-Henry arm ... be settled by the [standing] Committee on Small-Arms," which should have put that body in the loop regarding the nation's new rifle.[25]

The two hundred hand-made weapons went out for troop trials with one known and major flaw: the cartridge. In an effort to match the long range of the Chassepôt, the design committee specified a powder charge nearly equal to that of the French rifle. Standard English military small-arms powder, however, was coarser-grained than that used in the Chassepôt cartridge; the Henry bullet was heavier and longer as well. The result was a cartridge of excessive length: 3.25" for the Martini-Henry, as opposed to only two inches for the Snider. Such a long case proved easy to bend out of shape, and the edge of the rifle's chamber often tore the outer paper wrapper of the cartridge; either could prevent proper loading of the ammunition. Aware of such a problem even before the first batch of rifles went into production, the Committee sought a remedy, which came from William T. Eley of the Eley Brothers firm, the nation's largest private ammunition company. Instead of the paper-and-foil design originally proposed by Boxer, Eley used plain wrapped foil, and shortened the overall length by forming the cartridge with an enlarged lower portion to hold the same size powder charge. This "bottle-necked" design resulted in a shorter yet stronger cartridge that, while still damageable, resisted deformation better than the original design.[26]

Tests of both the original "long chamber" rifle and the newer "short chamber" continued into 1871, overseen by yet another committee: the "Special Committee on Martini-Henry Breech-Loading Rifles." This group published its first report summarizing feedback from field testing on 12 July 1870. Another seven months passed, however, before any further report surfaced. In the meantime, the public and the press became increasingly agitated by both the delay in the adoption of the rifle and rumors of fatal flaws, spread by disgruntled inventors or others whose opinions weren't matched by the Martini-Henry's design. A 23 March 1871 article in the *Standard* summarized much of the public clamor surrounding the rifle, especially the delay of its adoption. "The public," the paper wrote, "ignorant of the occult processes of reasoning in the Liberal Circumlocution Office," had become suspicious of a supposed "improvement in the national armament which demanded such extraordinary efforts to become of use." "The press has teemed with arguments" that the Martini action "ought to and *must* break down," although the

Some of the military rifle cartridges in use when the Franco-Prussian War began in 1870. From left to right: (1) 15.43mm Dreyse needle-fire, Prussia; (2) 11mm Chassepôt, France; (3) .50–70 Springfield, USA; (4) .577 Snider, (5) .45 Martini-Henry, Long Chamber, and (6) Short Chamber, Britain.

reports of the Committee showed that it did not. Finally, "noble lords wrote to the Times to press this or that pet system on the attention of the public, and to war it against the Martini's incurable defects." While this went on, the *Standard* charged, "we have added some 300,000 to our store of Sniders, and are still turning out a virtually discarded weapon at the rate of about 1,000 a week."

The *Standard* article raised a very valid charge of foot-dragging on the part of Gladstone's government, something even the Special Committee recognized. In its final report of 8 February 1871, the committee, still headed by Fletcher, took pains to note that "the various trials ... since the issue of the report which first recommended [the rifle's] adoption, have now extended over a period of more than 18 months," with only minor alterations to the final form of the rifle. "After full consideration of the whole question," the Committee reported that they were "of the opinion that the short-actioned Martini-Henry rifle is admirably adapted for a military arm" and recommended its adoption. The War Office, rather than rely on such a judgment, punted the question once more to the Ordnance Council, who on 30 March concurred with the Committee's decision "that the short-actioned Martini-Henry Rifle ... with Short-chambered Boxer-Henry Ammunition, be adopted" for both army and naval use. A final pattern of the rifle and its accoutrements were sealed to govern manufacture on 3 June 1871.[27]

The acceptance of the Martini-Henry rifle into the service did not silence its critics, however. The month after the Ordnance Council decision, Sir Walter Barttelot rose in the House of Commons to propose that yet another "Select Committee be appointed to inquire into the merits of the Martini-Henry Rifle." Barttelot, a Conservative MP and former infantry officer, clearly had doubts "whether it is the most suitable rifle as compared with others now manufactured to arm our troops with." His motion, after much debate, went down in defeat. A July article in *The Field* magazine, republished by several newspapers, noted that "the celebrated, or perhaps we should rather say the notorious, Martini-Henry rifle" had shown a number of problems at the National Rifle Association match at Wimbledon. "Unfortunately for the country," the writer said, "our fears as to the demerits of its [breech action] have been confirmed," although it did not state exactly what those fears were, except for an overly sensitive trigger. Regardless, *The Field* urged reconsideration of the rifle, "even at this eleventh hour." These supposed defects led Ralph Osborne, then MP for Waterford, to press Cardwell in Parliament to "consent to an independent inquiry into the cause of the defects." Cardwell, however, stated that no such adverse opinions regarding the weapon had reached him. "I am of opinion," he replied, "and this opinion the House after full debate has confirmed, that there is no ground for disturbing the decision of the [Fletcher] Committee in favour of the Martini-Henry rifle."[28]

Full-scale production of the service pattern rifle began in 1872 at RSAF Enfield, once the factory retooled—no small process, and one that idled a considerable portion of its workforce. Initial manufacture rates were low, no more than five hundred rifles per week, many of which failed inspection. Still, enough trickled out to begin arming infantry units on an experimental basis. By November, production had increased to 1,200 rifles per week, and Enfield closed out its fiscal year in March of 1873 with over 60,000 rifles manufactured.[29] Alterations ordered by a yet another committee slowed production the next year, especially regarding a controversial "locking bolt" or safety, added by the original Special Committee to prevent accidental discharge of the firearm when loaded, but dismissed by the Superintendent of RSAF as "difficult, and consequently costly to make, and ... liable to get out of order." A "conference" called by the War Office to consider field reports on the Martini-Henry eliminated the bolt in October of 1873. It also recommended lengthening the rifle stock to help lessen what some soldiers found to be excessive recoil.[30]

The October 1873 conference was the first of seven called over the next three years to guide the future of the Martini-Henry, rather than turn the program over to the Committee on Small Arms as the Ordnance Council had recommended. The decisions made by these conferences generally improved the weapon, but as in the case of the "locking bolt," delayed production and often required previously-manufactured rifles to be recalled for alteration. The *United Service Gazette* was not happy with the delays. "It appears somewhat strange," the magazine wrote in October of 1874 that "after 150,000 stand of the arm having been made, and after these having been distributed nearly over the whole Service, we should still be merely in the experimental stage as to its utility." Questions remained over problems with sighting, barrel heating, and especially recoil, according to a *Star* article of 20 October 1874. "Seeing that we have it admitted that the recoil ... is so great as to bruise and cut the face and hands of the men who use it, and that it becomes so hot after the firing of ten rounds," the paper wrote, "we have hit two blots which ought to be seriously looked at."

In the end, neither the recoil nor the barrel heating issues were corrected. In December of 1874 a committee headed by Adye proposed reducing the recoil with ammunition using a lighter bullet and powder charge; five months later another committee, also headed by Adye, judged such a change unnecessary. A leather guard shield for the barrel had been tested and a pattern sealed in early 1874, but with the caveat that, at 1 shilling each, no supply should be ordered unless "found absolutely necessary." Two years later a committee headed by Maj. Gen. J. W. Armstrong decided that such shields were not required. The rifle, however, had yet another defect, potentially fatal on the battlefield: a weak extractor that, when combined with the composite construction of the Boxer-Henry cartridge, could result in a jammed cartridge case. An 1875 report noted that if a soldier left a fired cartridge in the chamber for any length of time, the barrel cooled to the point that the case could not be removed. The extractor tended to rip the head of the case off, leaving the body in the chamber and requiring the soldier to ram it out with the cleaning rod. Both Fraser and his successor, Col. T. W. Milward, felt that this was simply a matter of training and experience with the arm—as perhaps was learning to handle the recoil and to keep one's hands off a hot barrel. Unfortunately for British infantrymen fighting in the sands of Egypt and the Sudan in the next decade, the problems with the composite case—and the British military's stubborn insistence in retaining it well beyond when other nations had adopted solid-cased ammunition—proved much more than a simple training issue.[31]

In April of 1877, the "Rifle, Martini-Henry, Mark II"—actually the fourth pattern of the weapon to be adopted—became approved for manufacture, after having passed through the hands of a dozen committees and nearly ten years of development. The lengthy delay in getting just the first pattern Martini-Henry into the hands of its soldiers put Britain behind most other powers in Europe. This included Russia, which in 1868 chose simply to license both the rifle and the solid-case cartridge designed by American Gen. Hiram Berdan and manufactured by Remington Arms. When offered, free of charge, a hundred similar rifles—already adopted by Spain and other countries—for comparison against the nascent Martini-Henry in 1870, Lefroy cited "defects of ammunition" noted in the now four-year-old original evaluation of that arm. Such a rejection illustrates both a willful ignorance of the speed of change in military technology, and a dogged determination by the British military establishment to perfect its own chosen weapon. Britain's committee system, tasked with producing the "best rifle in Europe," did indeed end up with a hard-hitting and accurate weapon that saw service until the end of the black powder era. The weapon, however, had intrinsic flaws and was technically only on par, not superior, to weapons being adopted in the rest of Europe.[32]

From the Battle of the Sedan to the Battle of Dorking

While British ordnance officers debated the future of their infantry arm, the question of the best form of artillery arose again with the outbreak of hostilities between France and Prussia in 1870. As they had with Prussia's two previous wars in the 1860s, Britons watched events on the Continent from the sidelines via their newspapers. Crimean War correspondent William

Russell returned to the field for the *Times*, for example, embedded with Prussian Crown Prince Friedrich's 3rd Army. In addition to covering the movements and clashes of armies, the papers also discussed at length the various technologies employed. Comparisons between the French Chassepot and Prussian Dreyse rifles generally concluded that the former had considerable advantages, including a much more effective breech seal and longer range, although the *Manchester Evening News* took pains in a 1 August article to remind its readers that in recent tests "the accuracy of the Martini-Henry far excelled the Chassepot." The *Pall Mall Gazette*, in a 9 November column, quoted a correspondent "who has studied abroad the character and performance of the Chassepôt" and who declared the long range of the rifle to actually be a liability. French infantry "[fire] away rapidly from twelve hundred to a thousand yards' distance, and by the time their enemies have closed in upon them" had heated the barrels of their rifles so "as to prove no longer serviceable." Still, the Prussian Crown Prince decreed that the French weapons "should be seized at every opportunity, [as they] may be advantageously used by good marksmen."[33]

Despite their advantage in infantry weapons, however, French artillery proved woefully inadequate, and by reflection reopened debate within the British press regarding the right form of ordnance for the Royal Artillery. After their war with Austria in 1866, Prussia and the other major German states rearmed with Krupp-manufactured steel breech-loaders, which could fire faster, farther, and much more accurately than the nearly obsolescent la Hitte bronze muzzle-loaders. Coupled with new, massed-weapon tactics—the Germans fielded hundreds of guns against the fortress city of Sedan on the first of September—such weapons gave their artillery arm a crushing advantage. Russell toured the battlefield at Sedan after the fall of the city, and described the "prevailing expression" on the faces of the dead as "one of terror and of agony unutterable." He mused that "there must have been a hell of torture raging within that semicircle" of unseen German ordnance pounding the city, "in which the earth was torn asunder from all sides with a real tempest of iron hissing, and screeching, and bursting into the heavy masses" of French soldiers. "I cannot," he continued, "imagine anything so trying to the bravest man as to meet death almost ingloriously … nothing so maddening to soldiers as to be annihilated without a chance of vengeance—nothing so awful to the fugitive as to see his comrades blown to fragments all around him."[34] Unbeknownst to Russell, he had described a scene that would become a common aspect of industrialized warfare in the future.

Russell also had a warning for "our soldiers and statesmen at home." Sedan "was decided solely and entirely by artillery fire … [and] won at a comparatively small expense" by the German armies, he charged. "I know the able director of our artillery at home is bent on making a radical change in our system of ordnance," Russell wrote, but if "Adye had seen the battlefield of Sedan ... I think he would have been shaken in his strong conviction" to return the British army to muzzle-loaders. "I speak of him with the greatest respect, but I entreat him to stop and inquire before he carries a vital change," Russell continued. "It is quite clear that any attempt to adopt the French muzzle-loading system, or anything like it, ought to be resisted strenuously until a careful inquiry has established its superiority."[35] On 10 September the *Examiner and London Review* agreed with Russell. "It is, perhaps, no secret that many artillery officers in this country, disgusted with the complicated manipulation and eccentric performance of the Armstrong cannon, entertain a serious prejudice to breech-loading artillery," the paper wrote. Just because that gun was "a pig in a poke," however, "it does not follow that good breech-loading artillery cannot be obtained." "We have no wish to see the Martini-Henry business repeated ... on a larger scale," the paper opined. "If the War Department have nothing worthy of trial among the things locked up" at the Rotunda Museum or in their archives, "let them invite plans and specifications, and let two or three practical soldiers, *with two or three practical mechanics* (for we have no faith with one without the other) decide which, if any, is the best."

Others disagreed with Russell's conclusion. The *Morning Post*, in a 4 October 1870 report of comparative tests between the new 9-pounder bronze muzzle-loading gun designed for India and the service breech-loading Armstrong gun, noted that "if the great bulk of our artillery officers have been urgent in condemning the breech-loading as compared with the muzzle-loading field guns, there must be good practical reasons at the bottom of their opinion." The *Pall Mall Gazette* of the 15th went further, reminding its readers that "the essence of the argument against the breech-loading Armstrong guns [is] that their equipment will not continue good and serviceable under the trying conditions of service" in the field. "Even the *Times* correspondent with the Prussian army would ... have found it hard to defend" the service gun in such a case, the *Gazette* wrote. The defects of the system "have been fully recognized by at least three independent committees, and have been repeatedly pointed out in these columns," which the *Gazette* then went at length to repeat again on 5 December. The paper did remind its readers, however, not to assume that "the science of artillery has stood still since 1859." "Many minds have been engaged upon the question [of the best form of artillery for England] for many years," it continued, "and the natural consequence is that other guns have been designed which present all the advantages of the breechloader without its attendant complications and difficulties." Even as Prussian artillery pounded French fighting men into hamburger at Sedan, however, the British army remained at least two months away from fielding such an improved gun. Not until December of 1870 could the *Gazette* announce that "a beginning has at last been made" of switching the Royal Artillery from the older Armstrong breech-loaders to new pattern rifled muzzle-loaders "made of steel, with coiled iron exteriors instead of bronze."

While the papers argued the merits of rifled breech- versus muzzle-loaders, France continued what was becoming a rather one-sided struggle with Prussia. German forces crushed one French army after another; Paris fell after a prolonged siege on 28 January 1871, and Napoleon III, who had been captured at Sedan, left for exile in England in March. The end of an active war, however, did not diminish public interest in military events, as witnessed by the reaction to an imaginary conflict. In May, *Blackwood's Edinburgh Magazine* electrified its readers with "The Battle of Dorking: Reminiscences of a Volunteer," a fictitious and anonymously written narrative of an England invaded and defeated by a newly unified Germany. An article in the *Morning Post* on 4 May 1871 gave a brief sketch of the story. "One morning war was declared against Germany," the paper wrote, but with both the Royal Navy and regular army engaged around the world, defense of the home isles fell to what ships and volunteer infantry units could be scraped together. A sudden torpedo attack took out the British fleet in the Channel; the Germans landed at Portsmouth, and shattered the volunteers armed with too few rifles or even antiquated "Brown Bess" muskets. "Overrun by the enemy, the whole country was laid waste," the *Post* continued. "The battle of Dorking was the death-warrant of England's supremacy as a nation."[36]

The *Post* concluded with the warning that "the [*Blackwood*] article should be read and re-read by everyone; for a stronger argument in favour of being always prepared against the enemy could not be put into words." "Everyone" seemed to agree; *Blackwood's* May edition went through six printings; by 18 July, when the *Pall Mall Gazette* finally identified Col. George Chesney of the Royal Engineers as the author, a separate sixpenny pamphlet had been published, which sold over two hundred thousand copies by August. On 29 June the *Morning Post* attributed the story's "extraordinary circulation and popularity" to its having "[given] expression to a wide-spread feeling of insecurity and trust" in Britain, aroused by the unexpected fall of France and rise of a unified German Empire. Translated into several different languages, the Chesney article spurred numerous alternative versions in English, including the *Times'* own "Second Armada" story, appearing in the 22 June edition, in which the German invasion fleet "shared the fate of the first." *Punch* tried to reassure the public in a 20 May satirical poem that "*this* Dorking bird seems to be a cross between a Dung-hill Cock and *Canard*," and "if the British Lion's asleep, 'twill prove no joke to wake him." One British company even devised a board game based on the story.[37]

Concerns raised by press coverage of the Franco-Prussian War and the publication of "The Battle of Dorking" translated into suggestions for improvements in England's weaponry. The year before the outbreak of the war, 154 proposals came before the new Experimental Branch; this jumped to 273 in 1870, and fell slightly the year that "The Battle of Dorking" came out, down to 214. Between 1872 and 1877, the numbers averaged 143 per year; in 1878 they started to climb again, peaking at 234 in 1879 during the midst of the 2nd Afghan and Zulu Wars. Other influences also brought inventors to the War Office beyond active or imaginary combat, however, especially advances in technology. Torpedoes and sea mines—the "deadly engines" that destroyed the British fleet in Chesney's story—account for forty-four separate proposals; dynamite and other new explosives, forty-one. The problem of accurately measuring distances to targets netted sixty-seven suggestions, and various plans for improving gunpowder and guncotton (a primitive form of nitrocellulose, used in modern smokeless powders) amounted to thirty-six. All totaled, the eleven years of weapons development shepherded by the Director of Artillery saw 2,031 separate proposals or inventions, with thousands more recorded minutes of investigations and decisions connected to long-running programs. Gen. Adye's opinion that the "great changes" in ordnance "may be considered for the most part at an end" was clearly off the mark.[38]

One of the weapons that *really* exercised the imagination of the British reading public was the *mitrailleuse*, a multi-barrel predecessor to the modern

A Krupp-manufactured "new pattern" 6-inch naval gun and carriage, circa 1880. Although improved, this is similar to the guns used against the French ten years earlier (Sir Thomas Brassey, *The British Navy: Its Strength, Resources, and Administration*, Volume 2 [London: Longmans, Green, and Co., 1882], 64).

machine gun that the French had put great faith in. Invented in Belgium and perfected by gunsmiths Louis Christophe and Joseph Montigny, the weapon consisted of a number of rifle barrels grouped together in a single tube, operated by a hand crank. The original version had fifty barrels; Christophe and Montigny's improved version had thirty-seven, and the gun fielded by the French decreased that number to twenty-five barrels of 13 mm diameter each. The size of a small field artillery piece, the gun had a crew of four that could load and fire five full volleys in under a minute and send the bullets out to a considerable range; a stray shot accidentally killed a peasant 3,000 yards away during testing. The French had developed their version in great secret, but Christophe and Montigny shopped their weapon around the world; an 1867 report by the OSC noted that "specimens have been purchased by the Russian, Prussian, and Austrian Governments."[39]

If used properly, the *mitrailleuse*, or *Höllenmaschine* ("hell machine") in German, could be a fearsome weapon. British correspondent Archibald Forbes, covering the opening battle near Saarbrücken, reported the first German contact with the machine when the French used it to clear a bridge. The sound of its firing, he wrote, "was very curious and distinctive ... [and] gave one a lively sensation of his coat being torn down the back." The weapon "swept the bridge thoroughly; nothing could live where its hail fell." The *mitrailleuse* had two distinct flaws, however. Mechanically, the gun carriage lacked any sort of traversing mechanism. As historian Geoffrey Wawro graphically noted, fire from the weapon "tended to fix on a single man and pump thirty balls into him, leaving nothing behind but two shoes and stumps." In addition, such secrecy surrounded its development that the French had no time to develop proper tactics. The army tended to use it in place of the weapon it most closely resembled: a field artillery gun, but with a shorter effective range of 1,200 yards. This left the crews exposed, and its large size prevented quick reposition of the gun. German forces rapidly learned that their Krupp cannon outranged the *mitrailleuse* and often smothered the guns with artillery fire before the French could bring them into action.[40]

Although a battlefield failure, the concept of the *mitrailleuse* appealed to seasoned gun designers and amateurs alike. The War Office received seventy proposals related to various forms of the weapon in the next ten years; two dozen came in 1870 alone, and ranged from the practical to the fantastic. Noted gunmaker Joseph Needham, for example, submitted a photograph of his thirteen-barrel, swivel-mounted gun, although the Special Committee already investigating such weapons felt his design "far inferior to others under consideration." Mr. H.R. Addison claimed to be "the original inventor of the weapon termed the 'Mitrailleur,'" and submitted a description of a lightweight weapon that "can be worked and transported in pieces from place to place by four men," but without much further detail. Mr. J. Black forwarded

Top and bottom: A sketch of the de Reyffe "mitrailleuse." The French Army put considerable stock in the weapon, but it proved a battlefield failure in their 1870 war with Prussia (Edmund Ollier, *Cassell's History of the War between France and Germany, 1870–1871* [London: Cassell, Petter & Galpin, 1870], 42–43).

"sketches of a revolving field piece of his invention" with an improbable "600 to 1,000 barrels," whereas A. Bryant's design required ten men to operate—but had the added bonus of "elements of a war chariot."[41]

Unfortunately for these hopeful arms inventors, the Experimental Branch already had the Montigny *mitrailleuse* and its closest rival, the American Gatling gun, under consideration for some time. Experiments with the two systems began in August of 1870, leading the *Pall Mall Gazette* to remark on the 12th that "it is not often that the quiet, dispassionate inquiries of the practice ground are carried on contemporaneously with the ruder trials of actual warfare." Comparative shooting took place between the Montigny gun, Gatlings of four different calibers, case shot and shrapnel from 9- and 12-pounder rifled breech- and muzzle-loading guns, and rapidly-fired infantry rifles at various ranges against both dummies and wooden targets. "Of the two systems of machine guns," the Special Committee reported, "the Gatling has proved to be far superior" despite a report from two years earlier in favor of the Montigny. The Committee therefore recommended the "immediate introduction of the small Gatling gun for employment in the field," with the understanding "that they do not for a moment contemplate [machine guns] supplanting or displacing a single field gun."[42]

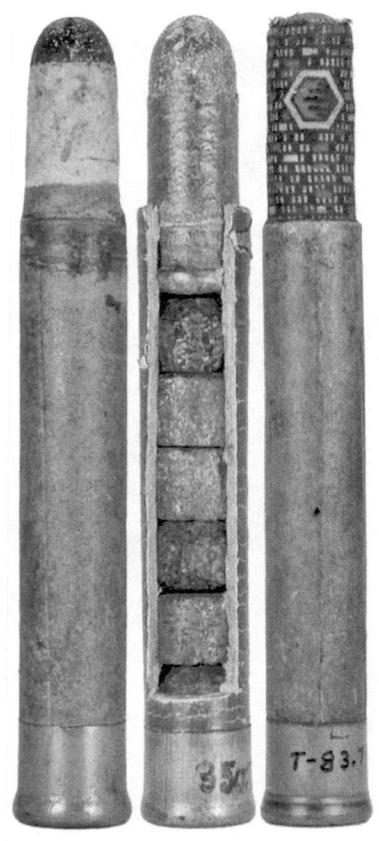

Cartridges for the de Reyffe gun. Left is the solid, or "ball" cartridge; right is a multi-ball load. The latter may be found with a variety of cloth coverings, as any available fabric would be used.

Refinement of Britain's first machine gun continued into 1871. Elswick Ordnance, which represented American Richard Gatling's interests in Britain, worked with the "Special Committee on Mitrailleurs" to reduce the overall weight of the gun and produce appropriate carriages. What should have been an off-the-shelf purchase, however, was needlessly complicated by the Committee's decision to use the Boxer-Henry cartridge in the small Gatling, in an effort to have a common type of ammunition for both rifle and machine gun. The brass foil case and the great difference between the diameters of the neck and body made the service Martini-Henry cartridge extremely prone to jamming inside the gun's drum magazine. Eley approached the War Office in April, "prepared to submit suitable cartridges for the Gatling gun, which will be found to fulfill every condition required." When asked if they wanted samples, however, the presiding officer of the Gatling committee replied that "the Royal Laboratory is capable of doing all that is necessary." In fact, the Laboratory failed to develop a satisfactory Gatling cartridge, and the Committee elected to adopt a special solid-cased cartridge, one *not* interchangeable with the Martini-Henry rifle.[43]

A rather fanciful "Camel Corps" Gatling. This pattern of gun, with its vertical-feed drum magazine, would eventually be adopted by Britain in .45" caliber for land use and .65" for naval use (Charles B. Norton, *American Inventions and Improvements in Breech-Loading Small Arms, Heavy Ordnance, Machine Guns, Magazine Arms, Fixed Ammunition, Pistols, Projectiles, Explosives, and Other Munitions of War*, 2nd ed. [Boston: James R. Osgood and Company, 1882], 240).

"A Frightful Accident"

Although Britain had elected to revert to muzzle-loading ordnance for the Royal Navy, breech-loaders continued to serve alongside the new guns in the Royal Artillery. Adye used the opening of hostilities between France and Prussia to press for replacement of the heavier siege train and coastal defense Armstrong guns with muzzle-loaders. In November of 1870, however, he also authorized the preparation of a number of six-gun batteries of 12- and 20-pounder Armstrong breech-loaders as well as the new 9-pounder rifled muzzle-loading bronze guns recently adopted for service in India. Despite such a move, Adye and the Royal Artillery clearly preferred to return to muzzle-loaders for all their ordnance. In 1871 the Germans arranged to exchange an example of their 4-pounder cast steel Krupp breech-loading gun "with carriage and equipment of latest pattern" in return for the new British 9-pounder. The German field piece arrived at Woolwich in early June. Although judged "an efficient weapon," in firing trials the "Special Committee on Shell Guns" found the Krupp weapon "complicated in construction and inferior in power" when compared to the new British muzzle-loader via velocity tests by electric chronograph.[44]

The development of a less-expensive method of constructing wrought iron ordnance contributed to the military's reluctance to part with their front-loading cannon. Designed in 1865 by R.S. Fraser, the principal executive officer at the Royal Gun Factory, this system simplified the Armstrong principle of building up a gun with successive iron tubes around an inner steel barrel. Unlike Armstrong's, the Fraser plan used cheaper iron and fewer but longer

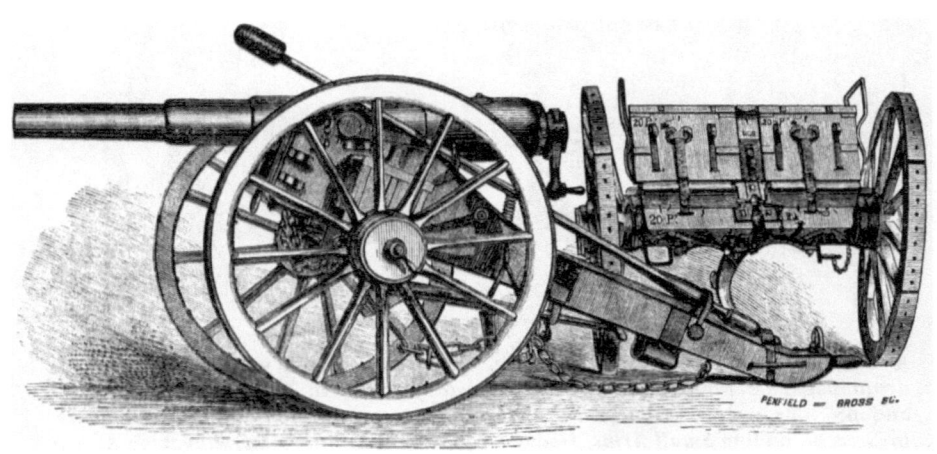

The Armstrong 20-pdr field gun with limber, circa 1865 (Holley, xviii).

tubes. Such a design allowed the Royal Arsenal to manufacture muzzle-loaders of extraordinary size and strength at £70 per ton of weight, as opposed to £100 for the Armstrong version. For an empire with an inventory of thousands of heavy guns, the cost of ordnance upgrades played a large role in making arms-related decisions, especially with a Parliament that scrutinized every farthing spent on the military. Fraser's design allowed Britain to scale up its naval ordnance at a pace that made everyone happy; in 1871, for example, the Navy adopted a 35-ton gun with a 12-inch bore, and from there the guns became larger and larger as shipboard armor increased. The largest actually produced was a monster 17.72-inch, 100-ton cannon, although designs of 160-, 190-, and 220-ton weapons were drawn up in 1878 on the Navy's request for a gun capable of defeating yard-thick armor.[45]

Even as the Arsenal underwent development of the "Woolwich Infant," as the press later nicknamed the new 35-tonner, Krupp tried to "call attention to the principal advantages that his system of breech-loading for heavy ordnance" had over muzzle-loaders. In 1870 he suggested that Britain order "an 11-inch gun, such as he has supplied to Russia and other countries" for comparison against the service RML gun "as to ease in working, range, accuracy, and power against an iron shield." Lefroy, then Director-General of Ordnance, noted that "the mistrust of breech-loading guns in the Naval Service is very strong," and felt it "needless to open the question" at that time. Krupp repeated the suggestion in 1872, offering to supply one of his 12-inch, 34-ton breech-loaders "such as he is at present making for several continental governments" for tests "against any other class of gun." Adye also saw "no reason at present for re-opening this question," although he did think "it would be desirable at all events to obtain full details of the gun referred to."[46]

By 1874, Germany had taken advantage of improvements in gunpowder and gun construction to upgrade their 4- and 6-pounder field guns, mostly worn out from the war with France, to a more advanced 88mm design. With nearly twice the effective range of their older weapons and firing redesigned ammunition, the new "C-73" gun could outrange and outfight the field artillery of any other European power. Britain, in the midst of updating its own field guns, discovered that its new 13-pounder muzzle-loader, intended to supplant the lighter 9-pounders, were now "inferior in ballistic effects to that of some continental nations," again through chronographic velocity tests. The following year, Col. Frederick Campbell (then the Superintendent, Royal Gun Factory) proposed to adapt the French-designed "interrupted-screw" breech to a 12-pounder gun, but no action seems to have been taken on the idea for the next four years.[47]

British recalcitrance in the face of the new French and German guns can only be explained by its reluctance to take risks in weapons programs unless absolutely required to, driven in part by a Parliament reluctant to ade-

"The Infant School at Woolwich Arsenal, as seen by the Czar" (*The Illustrated London News*, 27 June 1874, 5).

quately fund its military. Concerned about the nation's increasing artillery backwardness, on 5 April 1875 Royal Navy Capt. Philip Nolan rose before the House of Commons to "call attention to the present exceptional position of the country as regarded the manufacture of muzzle-loading ordnance, a system abandoned by the Continental Powers of Europe." Lord Eustace Cecil, the Assistant Secretary of War, rose in rebuttal, and his answer illustrates the unwillingness to risk anything but the tried-and-true. Cecil defended the government's decision to retain muzzle-loaders by reciting a list of previous judgments on the matter. He also claimed that "the Artillery opinion of Woolwich was quiescent upon the subject at this moment ... [without] any very strong opinion one way or the other." "The Government," Cecil added, had "committed itself entirely to the muzzle-loading system; the plant at Woolwich was adapted to the sole manufacture of that system of gun, and it would now require an immense superiority in the breech-loader to induce them to adopt that system."[48]

Krupp tried once more to interest Britain in his heavy breech-loaders that same year. During June debate over the reconstitution of the OSC, a

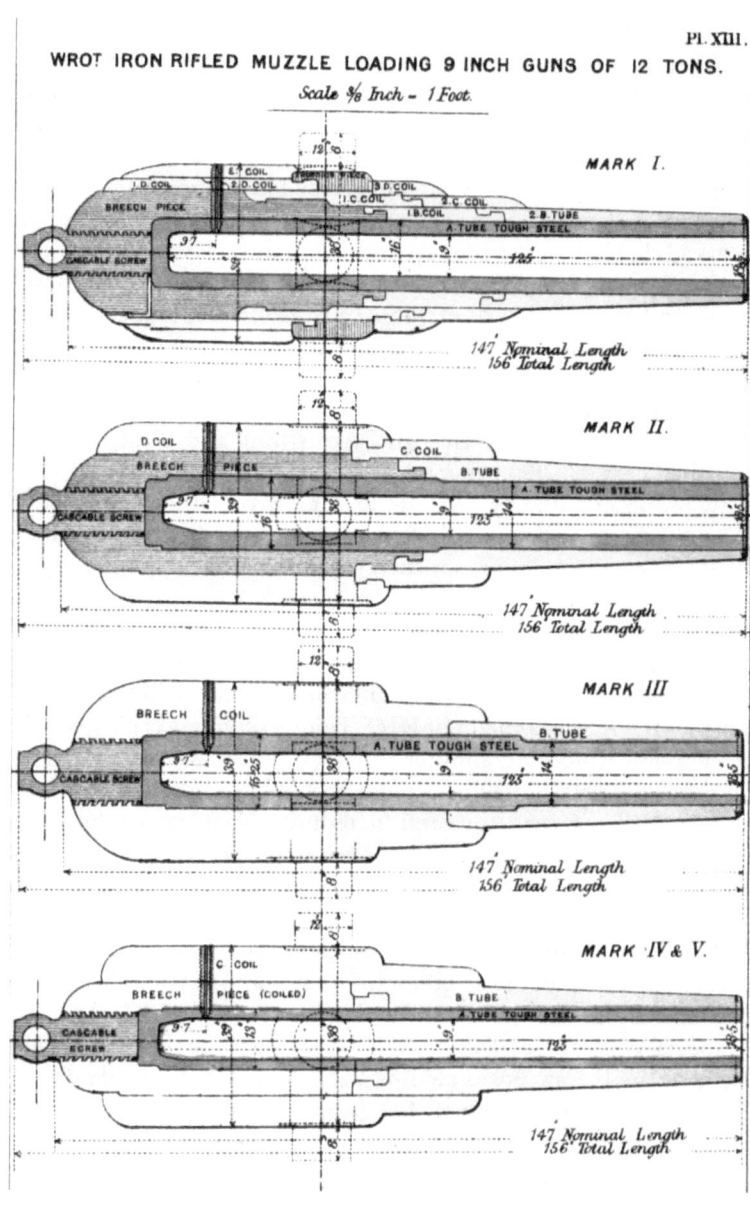

The evolution of wrought-iron RML 9-inch 12-ton guns by 1879. The Mark I used the complex and expensive Armstrong design; the others are variations of the Fraser plan using fewer external coils (John Fletcher Owen, *Treatise on the Construction and Manufacture of Ordnance in the British Service Prepared in the Royal Gun Factory* [London: HMSO, 1879], Plate XIII).

member of the House of Commons charged that the German gun-maker had never offered to sell an example of his guns to Government, perhaps out of "fear of the severity of the test to which it would be put." In response, Krupp essentially demanded an ordnance shoot-off. He stated that on order of the Government he would make "a breech-loading steel gun of any desired calibre, and to weigh up to 150 tons, with all the latest improvements ... to be tested in any reasonable manner" against an English gun of similar size. Krupp asked, however, that the test take place at his own practice grounds in Germany "on account of the inexperience of the Woolwich Staff in working such guns, and also because of prejudice against breech-loaders." The Assistant Director of Artillery responded by noting that, although he had seen the Krupp guns exercised and recommended obtaining one for testing, a thorough comparison "of different systems of guns is not so simple a matter." The three-year trial of the "relatively light" Armstrong and Whitworth guns in the 1860s had cost £32,000, "much less than would be the case in trying the guns now proposed." Finally, "muzzle-loading wrought iron guns have been introduced [into British service] after exhaustive trials, and both the Navy and the Royal Artillery appear satisfied with them."[49] Krupp's challenge went unanswered.

On 3 January 1879, a "frightful accident" aboard one of the ships armed with "Woolwich Infants" forced the British nation to reconsider the issue. During a live-fire exercise in the Mediterranean, one of the two 38-ton 12-inch guns in the forward turret of HMS *Thunderer* burst explosively, killing eleven men and wounding another thirty-six. The "Woolwich Correspondent" for the *Standard* wrote the next day that officials at the Arsenal received the news "[with] consternation and incredulity. That one of the Woolwich guns ... should burst passed comprehension and belief." "It had become a fundamental principle in the Royal Gun Factories," the author continued, "that, by fair means, it was not possible to burst one of its guns." Yet the impossible had happened, and "the authorities at Woolwich refuse to attribute the accident to any fault of the gun itself ... it may be stated that any gun in existence may be destroyed by careless loading."

A special committee investigating the accident reported on 13 February that, in fact, the theory postulated by the "Woolwich Correspondent" was correct. The gun had unknowingly been double-loaded, a situation that arose from the unfortunate combination of several factors: a misfire that left the previous charge in the barrel, the crew drill used to work the gun, and hydraulic loading equipment without a barrel obstruction indicator of any sort. Ultimately, all of these factors traced back to the Navy's insistence on retaining muzzle-loading ordnance. To confirm the committee's findings, the Admiralty returned the surviving gun to Woolwich, which was then turned over to the "Special Committee on the Construction of Ordnance" appointed in May for further tests. Housing the gun in a specially-built "bursting cell" constructed at the cost of £2,100, the committee drew up plans to test the alternate theories of why the weapon burst, including that of being double-loaded. One by one, all were proved wrong except for the latter. Loaded with a duplicate double charge, the other gun finally burst in a manner nearly identical to that aboard the ship.[50]

The *Thunderer* accident followed hard on the heels of a war scare with Russia the year before, which had worried Parliament into purchasing three partially-completed ironclad warships originally commissioned by Turkey in 1876. Fortunately for Britain, Elswick Ordnance had pressed forward with the development of breech-loading artillery, and had designs for new guns at hand. In August of 1879, the Admiralty forwarded to Gen. Campbell an offer from Armstrong of a new 8-inch breech-loading gun. Armstrong had "kept on hand for many months the particular gun, in the hope of its being tried by the Government," but without orders prior to the accident had decided to sell the original. Armstrong, however, had "in progress, a considerable contract for these guns" with various foreign governments, and stated if an "early trial" could be arranged, one could be made available—to which the president of the Special Committee readily agreed. By the end of the year, the Navy evinced interest in Elswick's 12- and 10-inch guns as well, along with a 20-pounder for boat service.[51]

Breech-loading guns also returned to the Royal Artillery. In September 1879, as work neared completion on the new 13-pounder muzzle-loading field

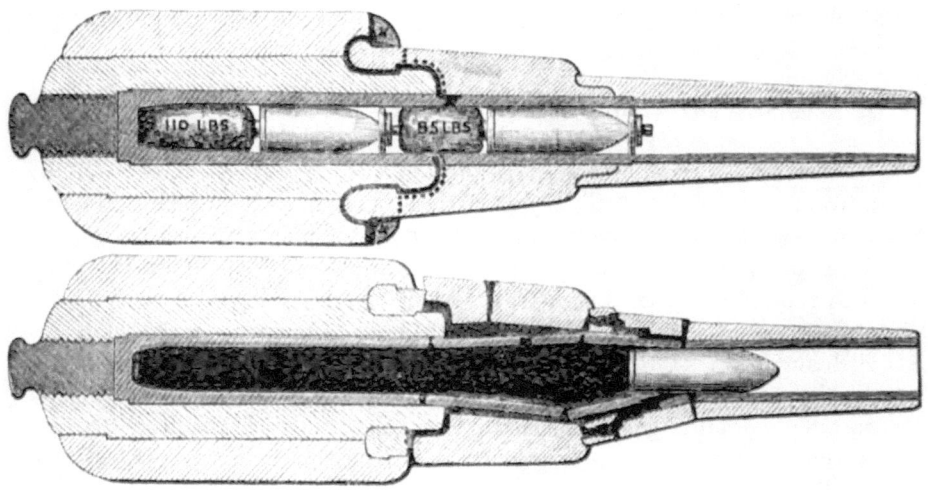

Sketches showing sectioned guns from HMS *Thunderer*. Above shows the double-loaded gun before firing; below is the probable mode of bursting (Brassey, 84).

piece, the heads of the manufacturing departments sat down for their weekly meeting. In light of the *Thunderer* accident and the Admiralty's newfound interest in breech-loaders, the Arsenal's chief officers decided that "before the manufacture of any larger number of [muzzle-loading] guns is undertaken," the forgotten 1875 breech-loading design needed to be put to trial. A crash development program ensued, with as many of the main features of the new gun made to match the muzzle-loader as far as possible, including a common bore size to allow it to fire the same ammunition.[52] By 1880 the first six-gun battery was ready; on 6 September the *Western Daily Press* reported that the Royal Horse Artillery took possession of Britain's new breech-loading field guns "to ascertain [their] suitability ... for the knocking about amidst dust and mud and bad weather which they must expect on active service."

Although Woolwich had perfected wrought iron muzzle-loading guns as far as possible, such weapons were a technological dead end. By 1879 the Committee on Explosives had several years of research into different shapes and compositions of black powder based on a better understanding of its action on detonation. Krupp's all-steel guns also pointed the way towards the future of ordnance, especially as British metallurgical methods improved. Rifled muzzle-loaders remained in service for nearly two more decades, but the *Thunderer* accident had finally broken the fascination that British ordnance authorities had with a centuries-old method of loading cannon.[53] Although unfortunate that it cost the lives of eleven sailors, had the British met the Germans in battle beforehand—or the Russians, or any other of Krupp's major customers—the cost of the lesson would have been much, much worse.

A Dysfunctional Military-Industrial Complex?

Dwight D. Eisenhower, in his farewell speech to the American public, introduced the phrase "military-industrial complex" to describe the relationship between government, the military, and private industry. Tracing weapons development through the *Abstracts of Proceedings* in this era makes clear that such a complex was developing in Victorian Britain. While most—but not all—of the proposals brought before the War Office came from outside of Woolwich and Elswick Ordnance, several other firms participated in the weapons development process. Generally, the work done by such companies formed part of long-running programs under the supervision of the appropriate special committee. The engineering firm of Easton and Anderson worked with the Royal Arsenal in developing the Moncrieff disappearing carriage and other projects, and steelmakers such as Vickers, Sons & Co. and John Brown & Co. supplied a variety of products such as shot, shell, and artillery targets.

Such contracts, however, were for things either outside the expertise of the Arsenal (such as casting steel), or for small numbers of items needed on an occasional basis.

A nascent "military-industrial complex" therefore existed in Britain during this period, resting primarily in the relationship between the Arsenal and Elswick but with the participation of other companies. The lack of a central controlling committee to oversee weapons development, however, made the relationship unstable. The *Abstracts* demonstrate that the War Office had no conscious desire to foster military industrial growth at home, as witnessed by its refusal to give orders to Hale's Rocket Company, Eley Brothers, and others. Indeed, the Office's preference for developing weapons in-house grates against a professed policy of "free trade" by Government, to the point of handicapping its armed forces. The prolonged birth and perfection of the Martini-Henry rifle serves as a good example; by laboring so long to construct the best possible weapon, Britain barely kept pace with its potential rivals. This coupled with a refusal to admit it had fallen behind in some areas—as in the case of the composite cartridge case—meant that British infantrymen went into battle with a weapons system that could, and sometimes did, fail.

The committee "system" also contributed to the muddle constraining British military technology in this era. Although work continued through the 1870s on all manner of projects, unless actively supervised by a special committee things occasionally fell by the wayside, such as the 1875 design for a breech-loader to match the German "C-73." Even when directed, decisions on weapons were not timely, as in the case of the Martini-Henry rifle, which also suffered from the introduction of conflicting ideas and prejudices into the refinement phase of the program. Cambridge's lack of practical experience and position as the nation's highest military authority (as Commander-in-Chief) also led to questionable decisions, such as the elimination of the rifle's safety mechanism in 1873.[54] It also led to continued resistance to the introduction of repeating rifles into the service, proven in battle in the American Civil War, by the Turks at the siege of Plevna in 1877, and under serious consideration by other European nations. When offered an example of the new magazine arm being fielded by Austria, Campbell commented that "we do not contemplate introducing repeating arms into the service, and do not ... think we should ask the Austrian Government to give us a specimen."[55]

Another area of dysfunctionality lay with the money that Parliament made available. The British military services, charged with defending an increasing empire, lived in feast-or-famine mode during the 1870s, as shown by the emergency acquisition of half-finished Turkish ironclads during the war scare of 1878. Gladstone slashed over £3 million from army and ordnance expenditure between 1868 and 1870, reducing spending to £12.1 million—the lowest amount since 1854. Although spending increased in 1872, expenditure remained relatively flat until the war scare of 1878. The Navy's budget was squeezed even harder, with Parliament only begrudgingly increasing it from a paltry £9 million in 1871 to a high of £11.8 million in 1879. Such an existence, coupled with the sheer size of the Empire, made the appeal of cheap solutions—such as the Fraser wrought iron muzzle-loading gun and the Boxer cartridge—irresistible in an era still dominated by tight-fisted politicians. In addition, demands for materials routed through the Director of Artillery's office, whether for experiment or otherwise, were routinely scrutinized and occasionally reduced. The Special Committee on Ordnance, in drawing up a program to test Armstrong's 8-in. RBL gun in 1879, suggested a firing program of "at least 500 rounds," but Campbell replied that "only 200 rounds were to be obtained at Government expense." In the case of a request from Malta for special railroad trolleys used for moving artillery shells from the island's magazine to its heavy gun emplacements, Campbell approved only four out of the two dozen originally requested.[56]

Parliament and the War Office complicated matters through an ill-defined system of awards, which caused no end of friction between Government and inventors. Palliser received £22,500 for his system of converting cast-iron smoothbores into rifled guns, for example, which made two different inventors jealous. Perceval M. Parsons, who had approached the OSC with a similar proposal in 1860, badgered the War Office incessantly, finally being awarded £1,000 after arbitration. Boxer also appealed for further rewards, only to have a financial deal between himself and Eley for his cartridge patent uncovered in the process. Cardwell requested his resignation after Boxer refused to disclose details of the arrangement.[57] Boxer at least had been allowed to apply for patents; not so Fraser, whose request to patent his method of gun construction "was refused, on the grounds that [he] was to be adequately rewarded." Fraser put a claim forward for reward before the OSC in 1867, and although it judged that "all the risks of failure" in the development of his system "have been borne by the Government," recommended a flat sum reward of £6,000 and a raise. Although he received the raise, Pakington lowered the flat sum by £1,000. Both Fraser and then–Col. Campbell, who worked together on the project, felt the money to be inadequate, and Fraser brought the subject up again in 1876 during Campbell's tenure as Director of Artillery, who passed the matter to the Ordnance Council with a strong recommendation for "the most favourable consideration." Noting that Fraser's method of construction had saved the country £800,000, the Council "recommended an immediate additional grant of £10,000, and a final payment of £5,000 at the end of further five years of service." Although approved by then–Secretary Gathorne Hardy, the Treasury refused any further payment four times; in April of 1880 it relented, but agreed only to the final payment.[58]

The changing attitudes of the various Secretaries of War towards patents and rewards only exacerbated Fraser's case. In 1867, then–Secretary General Peel remarked that he did "not think it would be politic to lay down as a rule that officers of the Department should not be rewarded for any inventions." Such a rule, Peel felt, "would lead to your losing the services of some of your cleverest men, who would not consider the *pleasure* of inventing a sufficient reward." Cardwell, however, "considered it to be the duty of Officers employed in the Manufacturing Departments to suggest any improvements which may occur to them ... [without claiming] a reward for such improvements as their *right*." Finally, in 1872 the War Office prohibited any "officer or other person ... employed in the manufacturing or experimental departments" from obtaining or holding "any Letters Patent for articles needed for the use of the Government." Apparently this applied only to military officers and managerial civilian employees, as a foreman in the Royal Laboratory, Mr. T. Jackson, received a patent in 1875 for a machine that wrapped the paper patch around Martini-Henry bullets.[59]

Although in many ways dysfunctional, the military-industrial complex then growing in Victorian Britain could operate well. Once the *Thunderer* accident forced British military authorities to re-evaluate their chosen style of ordnance, Armstrong's company rapidly stepped up to offer remedies. In addition, the long history of military technical intelligence started by the OSC kept Arsenal authorities abreast of foreign developments, allowing it to react quickly in the face of new developments. This included the adoption of the Gatling and the crash development of a new field gun based on the nearly forgotten 1875 plan. It also included a radically new piece of naval ordnance: the Whitehead self-propelled torpedo, brought into the country for demonstration in 1870. The weapon's potential led to Britain's purchase of the license and right of manufacture the next year. By 1880, Woolwich technicians had materially increased both the speed and range of the "fish torpedo," and had begun testing a variety of methods for guidance.[60]

Despite such success, the fatal explosion on board the *Thunderer* led many Britons to question the condition of the nation's military technology, and the system which developed it. The questioners included one of the system's very architects: Adye, promoted to the post of Surveyor-General of Ordnance in 1880. Adye came to his new office with an understanding of the strengths and weaknesses of the system from his five years as Director of Artillery. He also brought a newfound appreciation for the rapid pace of change in military hardware then underway, a pace that would not let up any time soon—and one that Britain needed a better mechanism for coping with.

An "Epoch of Change and Improvement"?

The *Thunderer* accident drew considerable public attention to the state of British ordnance in 1879, and illustrated a disturbing fact: Great Britain, Europe's leading industrial nation, had fallen behind the rest of the Continent in ordnance. The long experiment with separate technical committees had failed; to stay current the country needed a full-time committee dedicated to weapons development. Reconstructed in 1881, the new Ordnance Committee added this needed second tier to the War Office's mechanism for technology evaluation. The Director of Artillery and his Experimental Branch sifted out the practical from the unworkable, and handed the former to the new committee for testing and implementation. Most questions related to new ordnance came from the War Office itself, but the public's continued efforts to bring forth new ideas made the screening function, which the older OSC lacked, an important part of the process. Although weaponry had advanced beyond where the average civilian or soldier could suggest a useful change without extensive technical education, hopeful inventors continued to try, especially as newspapers spread information about new and potentially useful weapons. If chemically unstable compounds, such as early forms of dynamite, couldn't be fired from guns, why not use giant crossbows or compressed-air cannon? Why couldn't infantrymen, such as those slaughtered by the Zulu at Isandlwana, use portable iron shields for defense? These questions and more were among the hundreds that came before the Ordnance Committee over the next several years. On the whole, the process worked; although rifled muzzle-loading artillery remained in service for some years—Victorian governments being nothing if not frugal—by the end of the decade both the army and Royal Navy were taking delivery of modernized breech-loading guns of much greater range and power.

In addition, the *Abstracts of Proceedings* show the ripple effect that even a small change in military stores could have in a far-flung empire. With the changeover from black powder to cordite—a new form of propellant that emitted no smoke, yet resulted in much higher velocities—came questions in both small-arms and ordnance. Would guns sighted for black powder have the same aim point when using cordite-based charges? Would barrel life be the same? Would fuzes perform differently using the two types of propellant? How would cordite react to storage conditions ranging from extreme cold to excessive heat and humidity? Such questions occupied a considerable amount of the Committee's time in determining future directions for the nation's weapons systems.

In the larger scope of history, however, the *Thunderer* accident serves as a bookend to two decades of highly active change in British military administration as well as weaponry. Driven by public concern regarding combat performance abroad and the need to secure India against a covetous Russian empire, in 1886 the Conservative Salisbury government launched commission after committee to examine army administration from all angles. Such investigations included questions regarding the "warlike stores" deployed by the British military, especially—and perhaps more importantly to British politicians—the value received for the money spent. Were the millions voted annually buying the best available weaponry? Who designed the fighting men's tools, manufactured them, inspected and assured their usefulness, and delivered them into the hands of the brave lads defending British interests in far-off places? Armed with results of these investigations, Salisbury's second Secretary of War, Edward Stanhope, tried to clean up the mire that still pervaded British military administration, but his effort stopped short of a complete purge. Although separating mixed military and civilian responsibilities in a clearer manner, one of the more potent ingredients of the muddle not only remained in place but was strengthened by Stanhope's reorganizations: the post of Commander-in-Chief, held by the increasingly reactionary Duke of Cambridge. Still responsible to the Secretary of War, Cambridge would be given direct control of the military functions of the War Office, reinforcing his position as the highest military authority in the nation. This gave him considerable influence over the civilian politicians he supposedly answered to. In addition, the duel between military and civilian authorities over war *matériel* production would sharpen in 1888 when the Treasury Department assumed control of the Royal Arsenal factories. Altogether, the Stanhope reforms merely postponed the drastic overhaul that British military administration required.

Reconstituting the Ordnance Select Committee

Efforts raised in Parliament to bring back the OSC show that the idea retained the support of both Liberal and Conservative politicians. Charles Hanbury-Tracey, a Liberal representing the Montgomery borough district, rose in the House of Commons to make an unsuccessful call for its return in 1875. The *Thunderer* accident, however, lent considerable urgency to the state of the nation's ordnance, and the question of resurrecting the OSC came up again in February of 1879. In a Commons debate over Maj. John Nolan's resolution for a "careful examination" of foreign systems of ordnance, Conservative MP Sir John Hay replied that "he desired to see the [OSC] re-established" on a permanent basis, but with more frequent rotation of members than during its original existence. "Instituting such [a] permanent Committee," Hay argued, "would give confidence and convey an assurance to the officers of both Services that the result of an impartial scientific investigation would be adopted." Hanbury-Tracey, by then Lord Sudeley, restated his desire for a return of the OSC in the House of Lords debate over the *Thunderer* accident the next month. "I am told that the Admiralty propose to reappoint the Ordnance Select Committee," he said, "and, indeed, after the occurrence of this calamity, I think it is absolutely necessary that it should be reappointed." He hoped that unlike what the earlier OSC became, however, any new committee "will be a judicial ... and not an inventors' one; and that if any officer on that Committee became an inventor, he should at once retire from it." Lord Elphinstone replied that Government had indeed decided to bring back a permanent committee, to a "general expression of approval" among the Lords. Cardwell, also having been promoted to the peerage, responded with neither approval nor argument, but instead capped the debate with the "hope that it will be a Committee composed of persons in whom the country will have unbounded confidence."[1]

Despite the announcement in the House of Lords, it took a change of government to see something like the OSC come back to life. Conservative Lord Cecil, then the Surveyor-General of Ordnance, stated before the Commons on 22 April 1879 that the proposed committee would "consist of four Artillery officers, including one who shall represent the India Office, two Naval officers, and one Engineer officer," but that "the names [were] not yet decided upon." Occupied by the ongoing war in Afghanistan, the War Office took no further action in the matter; while it dithered, however, the country prepared for general elections. In a series of speeches in Midlothian, Scotland, Gladstone lambasted the Disraeli government for its willingness to use force in the expansion of the empire at the cost of millions of pounds and a high tax rate. "Beaconsfieldism," as the press called it, tangled up the country in South Africa and again in Afghanistan, which Gladstone labeled "a war as frivolous as ever was waged in the history of man." The voting public agreed, and the Liberals recaptured the government in April of 1880. Gladstone replaced Disraeli as Prime Minister; Hugh Childers replaced Frederick Stanley as Secretary of State for War, and Sir John Adye replaced Cecil as Surveyor-General of Ordnance.[2]

In October of 1880, Adye and Campbell (now the Director of Artillery and Stores), marshaled their arguments for recreating an ordnance oversight committee. In a minute to Adye dated 2 October, Campbell wrote that "the subject of changes in our Ordnance, Carriages, &c, is exciting much controversy." The reappointment of an ordnance committee had to be considered, he continued, "especially bearing in mind that every Foreign nation of any importance had a standing Committee to consider such subjects." Rather than the current system of diverse committees answering to one man, "the Public perhaps would feel more confidence in decisions arrived at on the recommendations of a recognized Committee appointed expressly for the purpose of advising on such subjects." Adye agreed, and passed Campbell's minute along with his own memo to the War Office on 25 October. In it, Adye remarked that the pace of change in ordnance had been such that "even now we do not appear to have arrived at finality" in the size and power of artillery. "It is not only ... Ordnance alone that has required constant study and experiment," he continued. "Every article of military armament and equipment has ... undergone consideration" in an "epoch of change and improvement." Having spent five years in the office, Adye also felt the lack of a supervisory committee meant that "the Director of Artillery is not only overworked but too much responsibility is laid on his shoulders." The Director had "not only to advise on the introduction of improvements, but to supervise their manufacture, and the distribution of Reserves for the Army and Navy all over the world."[3]

Adye therefore recommended "that a permanent Ordnance Committee be re-established, and ... if properly composed, the Public Service will be greatly benefited." He proposed naming a Royal Artillery general as president, with an engineer, two artillery, and two naval officers as permanent members; one of the latter would be vice president. He also suggested one or two civil engineers, in the manner of the original OSC as envisioned by Panmure in 1855. Campbell suggested that an infantry or cavalry officer be included, but Adye did not carry that recommendation forward. The *Times*, in reporting on the creation of the Ordnance Committee on 25 November 1880, also noted that officers heading the Arsenal manufacturing departments would not be members. "This is entirely satisfactory," the paper said, as the Woolwich-designed gun that failed aboard the *Thunderer* "is on its trial, and those responsible for that system cannot properly sit among those who are to pass judgment upon it." Adye did, however, make specific suggestions as to pay scales for permanent members and special duty pay for associate or temporary members, "all to receive the usual traveling allowances." Adye also envisioned a more restricted role for the Committee. Instead of "being vested with power to deal with all the multifarious subjects of Armament and Army Equipment," he suggested its scope be limited to "Ordnance, their Ammunition[,] Carriages and equipments and inventions connected therewith." Separate committees would still consider questions related to small arms and engineer equipment, and temporary ones could be appointed as necessary, or specialists might be attached to the permanent Committee if required. Decisions regarding what subjects or proposals to be considered would still rest with the Director of Artillery "who will of course consult the Military Authorities and get the sanction of the Secretary of State [for experiments] in the usual way."[4]

Two hurdles had to be cleared before a new committee could be established: Cambridge and the Lords Commissioners of the Treasury. The Duke, who had favored the dissolution of the OSC in 1868, "strongly object[ed] to the re-establishment of [it] on its original basis"—meaning a broad-scoped committee of invention rather than a narrow one designed for evaluation. He approved Adye's plan, but only under the proviso that "it is distinctly understood that [the Committee] confines itself to the consideration" of "inventions and the conduct of experiments connected with Artillery." The Lords Commissioners were even more reluctant. In a 21 January 1881 reply to the War Office, they clearly stated their "unwillingness ... to concur in the revival of a Committee, which was abolished ... chiefly on the score of its expensiveness." In reply, both the Secretary of State for War and the Board of Admiralty emphasized "the absolute necessity of keeping pace with the rapid development of warlike inventions, which is so striking a feature of the present time." This persuaded the Lords "not to withhold their general sanction" to the recreation of the Committee.[5]

Adye issued the order forming the new Ordnance Committee (OC) on 11 March 1881, and passed to it the formal rules as received from the War Office.[6] The "General Instructions for the Guidance of the Ordnance Committee" charged the new body with "considering and reporting upon such questions as may be referred to them" by the Secretary of State. Such questions related to "improvements in ... ordnance and machine guns; including the method of construction" of the guns, equipment, ammunition, range finders "and other instruments required for the efficient working of ordnance" as well as "questions connected with gunpowder and explosives generally." Secretary of State Childers added the "Ordnance consulting officer for India" as an *ex officio* member, and stipulated that both civilians "be members of the Institution of Civil Engineers." Unlike the OSC, the new Committee would strictly be one of evaluation; the rules expressly stated that "no new subject will be entertained ... and no experiments will be undertaken by them without express authority from the War Office." In addition, the committee members were specifically prohibited from taking out patents on any article or improvement "in any way connected with their duties." The Director of Artillery and Stores remained the contact between the War Office and the

Committee, responsible for handing down instructions and receiving its reports as directed by the Secretary of State. The War Office also required the continued compilation of quarterly abstracts of Committee proceedings, as well as separate extracts that "omit details of private inventions and confidential information partaking of a controversial character." Finally, Childers directed the President to "make an annual report to the War Office ... stating briefly the inquiries in which the Committee have been engaged, and the general progress of artillery science." This last rule formalized the Committee's role in the gathering of technical intelligence from abroad, something that the Director of Artillery's office had continued after the end of the OSC.[7]

At the end of March, Adye gave the President of the OC, Gen. Sir Collingwood Dickson, the new committee's marching orders. All of the "special committees" whose work related to the topics of ordnance were directed to wrap up their business on the 31st, with "the final reports ... submitted to [the OC] as soon as printed." "The subjects to which the Committee should direct their early attention," wrote Adye, centered on "the new breech-loading guns" of all types, the carriages and platforms required for both land and sea service, and "the pattern of projectiles and powder, descriptions of cartridges, &c." Adye reinforced this with a second minute on 8 April. "The first consideration should be given to the future types of ordnance," he wrote, and "the Committee [is] to proceed without delay with the necessary experiments" on the several sizes of breech-loading guns and types of carriages passed to them by the Committee on Ordnance. The OC's first year of existence therefore, promised to be busy, and within weeks its original membership expanded with the addition of three associate members.[8]

From the "Best-Managed Expedition" to Disaster in Khartoum

While the Director of Artillery and the Ordnance Committee wrestled with the development of new ordnance for Britain, the nation's military remained engaged across the globe. Despite his election-year vitriol against "Beaconsfieldism," Gladstone could not keep the nation out of imperial entanglements, especially in Africa. In 1882 Britain involved itself in what historian Correlli Barnett arguably termed "the first purely imperialist British military expedition": the invasion of Egypt. Britain had developed a considerable financial stake in that country, beginning with Disraeli's purchase of the Egyptian government's shares in the Suez Canal in the previous decade. When Egyptian nationalists threatened revolution, Gladstone sent a British task force to support the Egyptian government in Alexandria. After an anti-foreign riot in that city killed or injured over a hundred Europeans, including the

British consul, British Admiral F. Beauchamp Seymour requested—and received—permission to intervene.⁹

Early in the morning of 11 July, Seymour's ships took up positions opposite the forts outside the port. On board HMS *Invincible*, the *Standard*'s correspondent reported the next day that the ship "dropped anchor at a distance of thirteen hundred yards from the shore, and prepared for a fight in Nelson fashion of hammer-and-tongs, broadside on." At 0700 hours HMS *Alexandra* "open[ed] the ball by firing one gun," to which Egyptian gunners responded by loading their own weapons. Taking their action as a signal that the Egyptians intended to fight, Seymour signaled the fleet to open fire. "The roar of their heavy guns, the ceaseless rattle of their Gatlings and Nordenfelt machines, and the rush of the rockets ... made up a deep and continuous din impossible to describe," the *Standard* reported, but "the Egyptian gunners fought their guns exceedingly well, sticking to them until the forts were mere crumbling ruins." By noon Egyptian fire ceased; an hour later, a dozen British volunteers went ashore to destroy what guns had not been disabled. British shelling continued until early evening, "in order to complete the dismantlement of the forts." Nationalist forces withdrew inland, leaving Alexandria to the tender mercies of Egyptian mobs. Three days of riot and arson finally forced Seymour to land troops on the 14th to restore order.¹⁰

Support for the operation came from several factions in the British Parliament. Radicals believed Colonel Ahmed Arabi Bey, commander of the nationalist forces, wanted to establish a military dictatorship in Egypt; Liberals felt the unrest posed a financial and security threat to British interests. Under pressure from both, the Gladstone government dispatched an expedition under the command of Lt. Gen. Garnet Wolseley to deal with the Egyptian nationalists once and for all. The 24,000-man force began landing at Alexandria in early August, and by 13 September the British were in position to strike. After a several-hours-long night march—a difficult exercise even in peacetime—Wolseley's forces smashed the Arab nationalists at their main encampment at Ter-el-Kebir. The victory capped what Wolseley himself later considered "the best-managed expedition in British military history."¹¹ It also marked the beginning of several decades of British involvement in Egypt.

Unfortunately for the Empire, such a swift and victorious campaign would not be repeated two years later. The effective takeover of the Egyptian government meant that London inherited an ongoing revolution in Egyptian-controlled Sudan, led by Mohammed Ahmed, a religious leader and self-proclaimed "Mahdi," or prophet. In November of 1883, Mahdist forces ambushed and annihilated an Egyptian army of nearly eleven thousand led by William Hicks, a retired British army officer in the employ of the Egyptian government. Concerned by the growing scope of the revolt, Evelyn Baring, the British consul-general and effective ruler of Egypt, approved the dispatch of Charles "Chinese" Gordon to supervise evacuation of the remaining Egyptian troops and civilians from Khartoum. Gordon unwisely elected to hold the city, which Mahdist forces surrounded in May of 1884. Gordon was a popular figure back home in Britain, and the press soon clamored for a military expedition to rescue him. Pressured by the papers, members of his own cabinet, and even the Queen, Gladstone finally relented and ordered Wolseley and the army back to Cairo in July. The expedition fought its way up the Nile and across open desert, only to arrive before Khartoum two days too late to save Gordon and the city.

A war scare with Russia followed closely on the heels of the very public death of Gordon, which represented a huge reversal for the Liberals. Victory in 1882, the *Pall Mall Gazette* reported on 13 September, had "clearly established that the GLADSTONE Administration is not cowardly or weak, and that when the interests of the country are assailed it has the courage to defend them." The death of Gordon and fall of Khartoum, however, showed what Conservative leader Robert Gascoyne-Cecil (Lord Salisbury) had long argued at "countless meetings, in parliamentary speeches, and in letters—that the Liberals could not be trusted with the stewardship of the Empire." The defeat also forced Gladstone to recall Wolseley and abandon the Sudan for the time being, which gravely weakened his government. Gladstone resigned in early June 1885; there followed a rapid flip-flopping of cabinets between the two political parties, until general elections held in 1886 put the Conservatives—and Salisbury—firmly in power for the next six years.[12]

The Ordnance Committee in Operation

As Britain's troops were engaged along the Nile in the early 1880s, the Director of Artillery and the Ordnance Committee remained engaged in modernizing the nation's weaponry. The flow of investigations remained somewhat similar to that of the previous decade; all proposals received by the War Office and passed to the Director of Artillery still had to be screened by the Experimental Branch before going before the Ordnance Committee. This two-step process solved one of the principal complaints of the older OSC: that too much of their time had been spent examining impractical, unworkable, and occasionally absurd suggestions. As with the decade before, the Experimental Branch checked for prior inventions, sounded the relevant heads of the manufacturing departments, and determined if there might be any merit in the idea. For the rare proposals that came before the Committee, such as H.J. Barrett's "steel wheels for field artillery and service wagons," the OC communicated with the inventor, worked up an experimental program, and reported the results.[13] Occasionally, however, the Director validated his rejection by asking the OC for its official opinion, such as with a plan for a "breech-closing apparatus for a quick-firing gun" patented and submitted to the War Office by W. E. Corrigall in 1882. As the invention could apply to both ordnance and small arms, the Experimental Branch passed it for comment to the Superintendents of the Royal Gun Factory and the Royal Small Arms Factory. Neither recommended Corrigall's design for trial. Before the creation of the OC, Campbell could have simply passed the project to the Surveyor-General for approval of his dismissal. Now, he forwarded the proposal for formal report to the OC, which "concur[red] with [the] Superintendents" that Corrigall's plan "is much too weak for the purpose for which it is designed."[14] On its face, the report seems like a rubber-stamping of the Superintendents' previous decisions; having the proposal judged by a larger committee, however, gave Campbell a more defensible position if the inventor questioned the rejection later.

An Armstrong 30-pdr naval "quick-firing" gun on display at the 1887 Royal Jubilee Exhibition held in Newcastle, England. The powder charge and projectile were fixed together in one cartridge, and the gun platform had hydro-pneumatic recoil-absorbing buffers. Both are common components of modern artillery (W.H. Maw and J. Dredge, eds., *Engineering, An Illustrated Weekly Journal*, Vol. XVIV, July–Dec. 1887, 122).

Corrigall's plan was one among dozens of unsolicited proposals still received by the War Office every year. Although the rejection rate remained high, hopeful individuals brought forward their inventions, suggestions, or claims for reward to the War Office at an average of 180 per year through 1889, a rate slightly higher than the years in between the OSC and the OC. The peak occurred in 1885, the last year of the 1st Mahdist War, the opening of the 3rd Burma War, and the Russian incursion into Afghanistan. Submissions remained high for the next four years, in part because of ongoing campaigns. J. Spyker, in proposing shields for field guns and machine guns, argued that such an invention was "a necessity, as shown by the results of the Boer war" of 1881. A Mr. Copeman left a model at the War Office of a transport cart with a rather complex wheel design, to get better traction in the sands of Egypt. J. C. Mertz also wrote in to suggest using a special powder discovered by "a friend of his" that caused blindness. By firing shells filled with the powder at Dervish troops, Mertz claimed, "the popular belief in the pretended divine power of the Mahdi might be successfully shaken."[15]

Other factors also induced inventors to come forward. Specific military interests, such as the War Office's 21 May 1888 advertisement in the *Morning Post* seeking examples of range finders for infantry use, generated thirty-seven submissions that year alone.[16] Inventors also sought to take advantage of changing technology. Dynamite, more powerful in its explosive effects than black powder, had obvious military applications, and despite being proven early after its 1867 patent to be too sensitive for use in explosive shells, Britons still approached the War Office promoting its use in such a role. Mr. A. Houston, for example, forwarded the results of an 1885 homemade experiment in which he "fired ... an Enfield rifle with regulation powder charge and 2 oz. dynamite as projectile ... at a ¾-inch wooden board, distant 60 yards." Exploding on impact, the projectile made a nine-inch hole in the target and shook houses "within a radius of 1,000 yards." The DA's office dismissed his "findings" as having "no bearing upon the possible firing of dynamite from guns, which, it has been amply demonstrated, is simply impossible with any chance of safety to the gun."[17] One can only imagine how popular Houston was as a neighbor.

The war in the Sudan also seemed like an excellent opportunity to try out new weaponry, such as Hiram Maxim's recently invented recoil-operated machine gun. Captain A. L. Patton wrote Maj. Gen. Henry Alderson, Director of Artillery in 1885, with the offer that Patton "should go to the Soudan, taking with him a limited number of Maxim guns and his own trained men to work them." This provoked a bit of a crisis; Col. Henry Arbuthnot, the Superintendent of the RSAF-Enfield, felt that putting civilians behind guns to be "against all the recognized rules of civilized warfare." He also wondered how Patton could procure "a number of guns on special carriages ready to start within 30 days" while "Her Majesty's Government has been for some months anxiously awaiting a gun ... for trial, which they had been led to believe would have been submitted long ago." Arbuthnot tersely suggested "that it is time that some definite understanding was arrived at with the Maxim Gun Company"; if they could furnish Patton with completed weapons, they had better get one before the Ordnance Committee. The company's manager replied that they had only agreed to lend Patton their early model of machine guns "conditional on his offer being accepted," and that they had been unwilling to "submit for trial a gun inferior to their latest pattern." They promised to have their improved gun available "to try at Enfield during the ensuing week."[18]

Despite all of the outside proposals, the vast majority of the work of the OC involved materials designed and manufactured at either the Royal Arsenal or the growing number of private arms-related industries. A solicitation for a new 6-pounder "quick-firing" gun, for example, showed that by 1882 Ordnance was willing to do business with whoever could supply the best weapon. Designs were solicited from Armstrong, Gardner, Hotchkiss, Nordenfelt, Whitworth, and Vavasseur; Campbell even extended the deadline to allow the American firm of Pratt & Whitney to submit a proposal.[19] Elswick Ordnance, now part of Armstrong, Mitchell & Co., remained chief among the British arms companies and worked closely with the Committee in perfecting new breech-loading ordnance. The degree of cooperation between the two is reflected in an 1884 suggestion by the company that "considerable advantage would be obtained by an interchange of [ballistic data] ... obtained from the experiments carried on from time to time by the Committee and by themselves." In return, Armstrong would send "full accounts of any trials they make of a similar nature ... [including] any results obtained by foreign Governments which may come within their cognisance, either directly or indirectly." In one of his last acts as Director of Artillery, Campbell forwarded the suggestion to the Committee with the recommendation that such a data-sharing program "would be most advantageous to the Service," to which the OC readily agreed.[20]

As with the earlier OSC, subject-specific sub-committees often assisted the Ordnance Committee in its work, as in the case of the design of a new light 12-pounder breech-loading gun intended for both field and horse artillery. Although the gun's design had been settled by 1884, the question of the carriage remained open. The OC thought the carriage designed by Elswick Ordnance "approximated more nearly ... the Service type of field carriage," but also felt that one designed by the Royal Carriage Department "offered great promise for future development." In April of that year, then, the question was handed off to a special committee chaired by Col. A. H. W. Williams of the Royal Horse Artillery for comparative trials. Ultimately, the special com-

HRH The Prince of Wales firing the last shots at Wimbledon out of the Maxim gun, Aug. 1888. The Prince is seated on the gun carriage; behind him, in top hat, is its American inventor, Hiram Maxim (Royal Collection Trust / © Her Majesty Queen Elizabeth II, 2018).

mittee selected the Elswick pattern with a modified brake; although judged too heavy for horse artillery, the gun entered service with Royal Artillery field batteries in 1886.[21]

Although experiments with guns, ammunition and explosives always carried some degree of risk, facilities at both Woolwich and Shoeburyness had advanced to the point that serious injuries rarely occurred, even to errant livestock. The illusion of safety came to a catastrophic end, however, with the accidental detonation of an artillery shell at Shoeburyness on 26 February 1885. During the course of testing a new "delayed action" fuze designed by Col. Francis Lyon, then the Superintendent of the Royal Laboratory, a six-inch shell exploded after having the fuze screwed into its base. According to witnesses, the experiment "was not considered a particularly dangerous one, [and] no special precautions were taken." Gunner Allen, who had just put the fuze in place and still stood over the shell, "was literally blown to pieces" according to the *Times* report on 28 February. Five others died of their injuries soon after, including Lyon, Col. W.A. Fox-Strangways (Commandant of the School of Gunnery), and Capt. J.M. Goold-Adams, Lyon's assistant superintendent and a member of the Experimental Branch. Several other individuals

A Gatling Model 1883 as exhibited by Armstrong, Mitchell & Co. in 1887, shown on a special field carriage that allowed it to be fired on the move. Atop the ten-barreled weapon is a 104-round Accles drum magazine, which proved very problematic (Maw and Dredge, 165; see also Joseph Berk, *The Gatling Gun: 19th Century Machine Gun to 21st Century Vulcan* [Boulder, CO: Paladin Press, 1991], 25).

An Armstrong 25-pounder "Elephant" breech-loader also shown at the 1887 Royal Jubilee Exhibition. The gun, designed to be broken down into three pieces, could be carried by elephants (Maw and Dredge, 115, 122).

were injured, including one officer posted three hundred yards away "rendered insensible" by a fragment of the shell, according to the *Standard* of the 27th.

In addition to the unfortunate deaths, the accident also points out the degree of amateurish "tinkering" still involved in the development of deadly devices. Goold-Adams had submitted a proposal for a base fuze in 1881, but after three years effort neither he nor Lyon could produce a working example. An 1884 comparison found both designs "very liable to premature action, and when this did not take place the time of burning was very irregular." The Ordnance Committee therefore "recommend[ed] that no further action be at present taken with respect to base time fuzes"; Lyon and Goold-Adams clearly disregarded the Committee's decision. In addition, an "apparatus for testing fuzes by jolting or shaking," developed by Lt. Col. Freeth of the Royal Artillery, had been approved by the OSC in 1867, and almost certainly had been improved upon in the intervening years. Knowledge of what procedures Lyon used to test his fuze beforehand, if any, went with him to the grave; regardless, Brig. Gen. William Reilly, then the Director of Artillery, issued a comprehensive set of new regulations regarding "the Conduct of Experiments with Ordnance Material" on 4 July 1885. In addition to laying down basic safety rules regarding the testing of ordnance and fuzes, the new regulations expanded the requirements for any experiments with explosives. A detailed program had to be prepared beforehand by either the OC "or other officials for whom the experiments are to be made," and given to the relevant official placed in charge of the experiment. That officer would make all necessary safety arrangements "such as shelters, mechanical appliances for firing from a distance, signalling and guard" beforehand. If any part of the program could not be safely carried out, that officer had authority to suspend the experiment and "refer the matter to the Director of Artillery." Such regulations were an important step in the professionalization of British weapons development.[22]

"Not a Sound Gun in the Service"

The War Office immediately handed over to the new Ordnance Committee a number of important questions, including the consideration of what material new British ordnance should be constructed of. Given the failure of the *Thunderer* gun, a better understanding of the workings of cannon when fired, and the development of new slower-burning powders, the future pointed to steel rather than wrought iron. After a year's worth of consideration the OC concurred, based in part on the experience of both France and Germany "who profess themselves thoroughly satisfied with cast steel." When asked his opinion, Col. Eardley Maitland, then Superintendent of the Royal

Gun Factory, agreed: "the time has now arrived when steel should be more largely used" for both the center tube and breech-piece, and the use of the material in outer coils "cautiously extended." This decision was reinforced by the report of a special committee composed of Armstrong, Maitland, "and any other persons that the [OC] may feel disposed to examine" on the entire question of gun construction. Within a month, the special sub-committee reported that "the superiority of steel over wrought-iron is so marked that ... [the latter] should be abandoned," and all new ordnance "made wholly of steel."[23] Such a decision soon led to a very public discussion of just *who* should manufacture these new weapons, a question of prime importance for the nation's steel producers in the South Yorkshire city of Sheffield.

Long known for its manufacture of steel cutlery, Sheffield by the 1880s boasted the factories of the nation's leading steel producers, including Henry Bessemer, John Brown, J. F. Firth & Sons, Cammell & Co., and Vickers, Sons & Co. Many had long done business with the War Department, supplying specialty steel products, artillery shells, and armor plate; Brown and Vickers had both tried to interest the Royal Artillery in the use of steel for ordnance but to no avail.[24] Bessemer himself had in 1859 convinced Col. Eardley-Wilmot, then Superintendent of the Royal Gun Factory, to try his patent manufacturing process to produce steel for heavy guns. Shortly afterward, however, the keys to the Factory were handed over to Armstrong, who had both a mandate to produce his breech-loading cannon and a preference for tried-and-true wrought iron.[25] The Arsenal's early flirtation with steel production therefore ended quickly, and the long shadow of Armstrong coupled with Parliament's preference for cheap ordnance meant wrought iron remained the chief component of gun construction until the accident aboard the *Thunderer*.

The 1882 decision to abandon wrought iron in favor of cast steel should have been welcomed by private industry, but any celebrations were dampened by the equally long shadow of the Royal Arsenal itself. Intent on remaining the primary source of ordnance, the Arsenal broke ground for its own steel plant in 1884, at a cost of £1,850.[26] Concerned about such a threat to the trade, Stuart Rendel, Liberal MP for Montgomeryshire and the London manager for Armstrong, began a campaign to keep Woolwich out of the steel business. In a letter to Henry Brand, then Surveyor-General of Ordnance, Rendel argued that Woolwich would prejudicially inspect and pass its own steel over that obtained from the trade, as it seemed to do with ordnance. He also argued that the Arsenal could not successfully undertake such a complex operation as steel making "with nothing more than an Artillery Officer to guide them."[27]

The question of steel for ordnance was part of a larger question over the privatization of weapons manufacture in general, pushed for by both sides of the political spectrum. In the House of Commons on 2 December 1884,

Conservative MP and former First Lord of the Admiralty William H. Smith pointed out that a "very interesting Report" from a U.S. commission on ordnance construction in Europe showed that the French had firmly embraced the idea of private manufacture. Prior to 1870, "it was the custom ... to confide all matters relating to cannon to the Artillery-Corps of the Army and Navy; aid from private sources was neither sought nor offered." After the war, however, the new French government thought it "desirable to encourage private industries, so that a spirit of emulation might be excited by competition, and a channel afforded through which new ideas and inventions might reach the national works." French companies were turning out dozens of heavy guns, and had taken orders from the French navy for hundreds more; England, by comparison, labored to produce just a handful. "The fact is that France, owing to her prudence, foresight, and energy, is some years ahead of us in the construction and manufacture of guns," Smith charged. Regarding steel itself, Smith asked "whether the Government will take the steps which are necessary to secure ... a supply of steel and material necessary for the production of steel guns?" Rather than rely on Woolwich, Smith suggested that "if the Government held out to the trade the prospect of a profitable business, they would certainly get the article they need."[28]

Brand agreed that the country needed to rely more on private industry; the major stumbling block to such participation, he pointed out, had not been the nation's production capabilities, but the Arsenal itself.[29] After the 1882 decision to use steel exclusively for building guns, Brand explained, acceptance tests of contract-supplied steel performed at Woolwich resulted in "a great many rejections" and an assumption that "the 'trade' in Sheffield could not supply steel ingots of the size and quality required." Such an assumption, based on what might have been a deliberate ploy to shut out the trade, allowed the Royal Gun Factory to justify pursuit of its own steel plant. Alarmed at the rejection rate, however, Campbell took a different view. He visited with producers throughout the UK and France to determine "what reasonable modification in the test would admit of the English trade producing steel that would be passed by the War Office Inspectors." Based on Campbell's findings, Brand reported that "the Ordnance Committee ... recommended a revised specification, and some further modifications were subsequently suggested by the manufacturers, which had within the last few days been adopted." This circular cooperative effort between the OC and private manufactures paid off, as Brand stated that "the position now was that the steel trade was both willing and able to meet the requirements of the War Office with regard to steel forgings."[30]

Hartington, Gladstone's Secretary of State for War, and Northbrook (now the First Lord of the Admiralty), also agreed that the War Office needed to rely on private industry for its steel needs. In the same debate, Brand noted that Hartington thought the manufacture of heavy steel ingots at Woolwich "would be mischievous, and ought not to be adopted except under the stress of the most imperative necessity." That same day, Northbrook claimed before the House of Lords that although £100,000 had been approved "for increasing the plant for the manufacture of the new guns at Woolwich ... it was not intended ... to set up the manufacture of steel there." Hartington, Northbrook stated, "had thought it better to go to the trade, and to encourage the great manufacturers of steel."[31] Edward Carbutt, a Liberal MP for Monmouth and former mayor of Leeds, took up the call for privatization. In a letter to the *Pall Mall Gazette* printed on 6 January 1885, Carbutt charged that "at the present moment we have not one single large steel breechloading gun in position." Deliberately taking Brand's comments of 2 December out of context, Carbutt claimed that Brand put the blame for the lack of guns on the Sheffield steel trade's inability to meet the War Office's needs. "If the trade could not ... whose fault would it be but the Government's, who will not encourage their own manufacturers?" Carbutt asked. The answer, however, lay with the Arsenal's own "mismanagement ... due to their not being conducted on commercial principles." Instead of a military head, Carbutt felt that a single person, "a man of great engineering knowledge and experience," should be appointed to head the Royal Arsenal on a permanent basis, rather than the five-year rotation then in practice. Such a post would "be worthy of the best talents in the kingdom." In addition, the Admiralty itself should be allowed "to order their guns either from private manufacturers or at Woolwich." Such measures would "obtain such competition as would give use the best gun with the least expenditure."

On 13 March 1885, Carbutt joined William Anderson and several other speakers at the Royal United Services Institute (RUSI) to present a lecture "on the capabilities of private firms to manufacture heavy ordnance for Her Majesty's service." Head of the engineering firm Easton and Anderson, Anderson had displayed considerable technical skill in his adaptation of a new hydraulic gun mount to double-gun turrets for Russia and Britain. As reported by the *Times* the next day, Anderson opened the lecture by outlining the changes in artillery that had occurred over the three decades since the Crimean War, and emphasized that current weaponry required a great deal of specialized skill and machinery. Only Whitworth and Armstrong's firms had such capability, but "they could only be brought to work ... for the national service in a time of emergency at an immense cost—at a time, too, when the works would be too late to make good disaster." The design of big guns "had been left practically in the hands of a Government department administered with great, indeed, with ruinous parsimony." After Anderson "resumed his seat amid great cheering," Carbutt then led off the post-lecture discussion. He stated that "the working classes were convinced that the country should be fully prepared to meet an enemy, and instanced the fact that the public were pressing the Government to increase the Navy." He also "spoke against the Government manufacturing all the war material," and that "the present system of gun manufacture in this country was wrong." Using Krupp as an example, he noted that the German firm "was manufacturing the largest guns for Russia, and was enlarging his plant, while at home a pattern of gun had not yet been decided on."

Carbutt followed up the RUSI discussion almost immediately with further debate in the House of Commons. On 16 March, he stated that "he was certain that the 2,000,000 voters who had been enfranchised" by the Third Reform Act the year before "would not protest against any reasonable expenditure of money for the preservation of the honour of the Empire." Yet the country remained in possession of faulty ordnance, such as a new 12-inch breech-loader designed to fire a 400 lb. charge of powder, but for safety reasons was limited to one over a hundred pounds lighter. Carbutt noted that "it did seem strange that we should be the leading nation in the manufacture of steel, and in the application of the inventions of Bessemer and Siemens, and yet that we should be 15 or 20 years behind other nations in adopting steel guns." Again, the question had support from both political parties, in particular from Sir John Hay, who had served in the Admiralty under Disraeli. Hay stated that Carbutt "had done a great service in bringing forward the question of guns." He also charged that "the guns of this country ... were in a most deplorable condition; and if war was to break out they would find themselves almost disarmed, and with the necessity of spending millions of money on a system not yet determined upon."[32]

Brand then rose to reassure both Carbutt and Hay that the Gladstone government was aware of the ordnance issues and were taking active steps to resolve them. Regarding steel, he stated that "the manufacturers at Sheffield and Newcastle were satisfied with the assurances which the Government had given," and "within a few weeks" several other companies besides Whitworth and Armstrong's "would be able to supply the Government with heavy forgings." In addition, a special committee "consisting of members of the Ordnance Committee and of gentlemen of very great experience outside the Department" had lately been appointed by Hartington to examine the current designs of heavy British ordnance. "Speaking generally," Brand claimed, "with the exception of some slight alterations for strengthening guns, the Committee approved of the present system of gun construction."[33]

The *Times* followed up on the debate regarding steel for ordnance with an article reviewing "Sheffield Trade for 1885" on 5 January 1886. The paper noted that Cammell, Brown, Firth, and Vickers had all "increase[d] their capacity for producing immense castings, chiefly for military material." In particular, Vickers had installed at their River Don Works "the largest forging press that has ever been made. It is capable of treating ingots for guns ... [of] any size required," with a crane able to lift 150 tons. The upgrades had come as a direct result of the public discussion over Sheffield's ability to supply the needs of the War Department. Vickers itself contended that although "they had made forgings 40 per cent heavier than the heaviest which had so far been required by Woolwich Arsenal ... [they had] decided still further on increasing their powers of production." Still, the *Times* noted that "the progress of steel making by the Government at Woolwich is regarded [in Sheffield] very jealously." Despite Northbrook's reassurance in the House of Lords, the Arsenal had pressed forward with construction of its own steel plant. The £100,000 earmarked in 1884 had not gone towards improvement of existing works, but instead been used to build a forge large enough to cast ingots for guns up to 6-inch in barrel diameter. The ruse proved both simple and effective, and by 1886 the Arsenal had "repaired" its forge to over double its original capacity, from 6 to 15 tons. Clearly, Woolwich authorities intended to maintain the Arsenal's position as gun maker for the Crown in spite of the wishes of some politicians, and perhaps with the complicity of the War Office. It would be at least two more years before any additional private ordnance makers joined Elswick in challenging the near-monopoly held by the Royal Gun Factory.[34]

Several weeks after the *Times* article, accidents occurred on board two of England's newest ironclads that again shook the nation's confidence in its heavy guns. In May, one of the 12-inch 43-ton Woolwich guns mentioned by Carbutt in his RUSI speech burst several inches from the muzzle aboard HMS *Collingwood*, when fired with just over a half-charge of 220 pounds of powder. This was followed shortly by reports from HMS *Ajax* of the failure of both forward 12-inch 38-ton guns during target practice. After firing just one round each, *St. James's Gazette* reported on 17 July, "there was such a discharge of refuse powder and gas from the axial vent that the men had to be ordered out of the turret." On examination, both guns were found to have cracks in their internal barrel tubes. Such accidents unleashed a hail of criticism against what Robert H. Armit, editor of the *Admiralty and Horse Guards Gazette*, dubbed the "Great Gun Ring" at the Royal Gun Factory. Armit not only broke the story about the *Ajax*, but claimed in a letter to the *Times* on 16 July that such accidents led to the "deplorable result that England has at this moment no artillery ... wherewith to defend her interests and her honour at home or abroad." He further accused "certain members of the [OC] and of the Ordnance Department" of being shareholders in Elswick Ordnance "which, in conjunction with Woolwich, has designed" the faulty guns. The charge had some degree of truth; Frederick Abel, for example, held £1,500 of shares in Elswick. Both Armstrong and Andrew Noble had also sat on a special committee that investigated several instances of burst guns, most of RGF design but including two by their firm. The guns aboard the *Collingwood*, and a similar one which later burst on board HMS *Colossus*, were designed and manufactured solely by Woolwich, however, despite active lobbying for its own designs by Armstrong's company. Still, Armit's cry that Britain had "not a sound gun in the service" was serious enough on its own, and pressure began to build for a Parliamentary investigation into the matter.[35]

"Guilty of Inefficiency and Ignorance"

The protestations of Carbutt and Armit against the Woolwich system combined with reports from abroad to raise serious questions regarding not just naval guns, but British military equipment and administration in general. The fleet at Alexandria fired over three thousand shells at the Egyptian forts, but due to faulty fuzes many did not detonate. After the battle, a clean-up crew found an 8-inch shell fired by HMS *Penelope* "lying harmless in a magazine containing over four hundred tons of powder." Wolseley's forces in Egypt and the Sudan returned home with reports of jammed machine guns, bent bayonets, and rifles rendered useless by stuck Boxer cartridges. The army faced considerable internal problems as well. Several factors, such as a high turnover rate caused by new short-service options and a lack of an effective recruiting program, combined to limit the pool of trained soldiers for overseas campaigning. The 1882 expedition had to draw heavily from the new reserve force, created by Cardwell in event of an invasion of England, not international expeditions. Considerable friction also existed between Wolseley, Adjutant-General of the army, and Cambridge, its commander-in-chief and cousin to the Queen. Wolseley, who saw much in the army that needed reform, clashed repeatedly and often publicly with the "pipeclay prejudices" against change held by the Duke.[36]

In July of 1886, Salisbury returned as prime minister after the short-lived third Gladstone government went down in defeat during the general election. His first Secretary of State for War, William H. Smith, took serious the charges regarding the failure of British armaments, and in September of 1886 appointed Sir James Stephen to head a special "Ordnance Inquiry Commission." Charged with examining "the system under which the patterns of warlike stores are adopted," the commission's royal warrant also directed it to investigate complaints and to determine "the persons, if any, responsible for any defects which you may find." Originally limited to recent issues, the commission expanded its scope to include charges of "systematic fraud and corruption" that dated to 1858, on the grounds that "the administration of the Ordnance Department has ever since been conducted more or less under the influence of that fraud."[37]

After a number of interviews with aggrieved inventors and others, including Armit, the Stephen Commission ultimately found that "the charges of corruption ... are false and unfounded, and that nearly all ... are either wholly untrue or distorted versions of innocent facts." "The charge of inefficiency," however, "both generally and in a variety of particular instances" could certainly be proved, and started at the top with the Secretary of State's office. The powers ceded to it over the preceding years were "so great that no single person can be expected to exercise them efficiently." As a political office, tenure could be fleeting, as witnessed by three different appointees in the politically turbulent year of 1886. In addition, every Secretary had a "presumable deficiency in [the] special knowledge" regarding the construction of weapons, as did the Surveyor-General of Ordnance, an office which by 1883 had devolved into a political appointment as well. This meant that both men were "practically in the hands of their subordinates," such as the Director of Artillery and Stores, "and this destroys all real responsibility and all effective superintendence."[38]

The Commission also had much to say about the dysfunctional small arms development system in Britain, through its review of the failed Enfield-Martini rifle program. Competition between Britain and Russia in their "Great Game" for dominance in Central Asia led to comparisons of the weapons fielded by both nations, particularly their infantry rifles. Much to the chagrin of British military leaders, the nearly off-the-shelf Berdan rifle adopted by the Russians proved more accurate than the committee-designed Martini-Henry at ranges under a thousand yards. "A certain number of soldiers thought that our rifle ought to be superior in every way to any foreign rifle," the Commission recounted, and in January of 1881 then-Secretary of War Hugh Childers appointed a "large committee" to design the nation's replacement for the Martini-Henry. Childers hobbled the committee, however, by ordering the retention of the Martini action, in part because Cambridge "decided that we had had great experience with [it], it had gone through campaigns satisfactorily all over the world, and there was nothing distinctly against it." Gen. Phillip Smith also supposed the decision was done "to secure the introduction of an arm which could not be turned into a magazine rifle" because "in those days the authorities"—meaning, again, the Duke, without identifying him by name—"were very much averse to anything like magazine rifles." Repeating the Fletcher committees' mistake of building a composite arm, the 1881 Rifle Committee married the Martini action to a smaller-diameter barrel with a pattern of rifling insisted on by Arbuthnot under the dubious claim that it was "the way the French do the rifling, and that it has its advantages." Two years into the existence of the Rifle Committee, the War Office formed a sub-committee, chaired by Gen. Smith, to examine magazine rifles; in 1884, the two committees were merged under Smith's oversight, and sat until March of 1886. By September, a thousand rifles were finally in the hands of troops for more extensive trials. That same month, the War Office formed a third committee, again directed by Smith, tasked with reporting on the trials but also to consider further the issue of magazine rifles.[39]

The turnover of committees meant that the design of the Enfield-Martini lurched along spasmodically and consumed an inordinate amount of time, instead of progressing at a smooth and more rapid pace. In addition, rather than "a pair of harmonious bodies constructing the thing," the Stephen Commission found that the first Rifle Committee spent three years designing an imperfect weapon, after which Smith's committee spent three more years trying "to diminish the evils which the first body had introduced." "The history of these ... committees," the Commission felt, "does little credit to the principle of constructive committees." In the meantime, advances in weapons and ammunition design pointed towards a much different future for military small arms. While England dithered about with the Enfield-Martini, Remington began marketing a box-magazine rifle designed by James P. Lee across the globe; China purchased 15,000 weapons in 1884, two years before the first batch of Enfield-Martini weapons were ready for troop trials. The next year Remington offered to supply England with 10,000 rifles along with five million rounds of ammunition. Echoing Lefroy's 1870 decision, Cambridge myopically rejected the offer, as he "[did] not consider that we need adopt the magazine rifle till other nations do."[40]

The United States was not the only country rapidly surpassing the desultory British efforts to develop its next generation infantry rifle. In Europe, Ferdinand Mannlicher of Austria perfected his clip-fed magazine rifle, adopted by the Austro-Hungarian Empire in 1886 and a principle eventually used by every rifle system into World War II. Switzerland's Maj. Eduard Rubin developed lighter and much smaller diameter metal-jacketed bullets beginning in 1880, and in 1885 a French chemist perfected what would become known as "Poudre B"—the first true smokeless powder. These two important changes would greatly increase the striking power of infantry weapons while allowing the soldier to carry much more ammunition. Such advances made the single-shot Enfield-Martini a technological dead end, something that Edward Stanhope, who took over the War Office in January of 1887, may have appreciated. In July he ordered the abandonment of the project and the conversion of any existing weapons to chamber the Martini-Henry cartridge as a stop-gap measure pending the introduction of a magazine rifle. Two years later—a crash development effort given its previous history—England adopted its first small-bore magazine rifle, the .303" Lee-Metford. The new rifle combined the Lee bolt-action box magazine with William Metford's rifling design. Originally adopted as the "Magazine Rifle Mk. I," this was changed to "Magazine Rifle, Lee-Metford" on 8 April 1891, to recognize the

The action of the Lee box magazine rifle (Norton, 168).

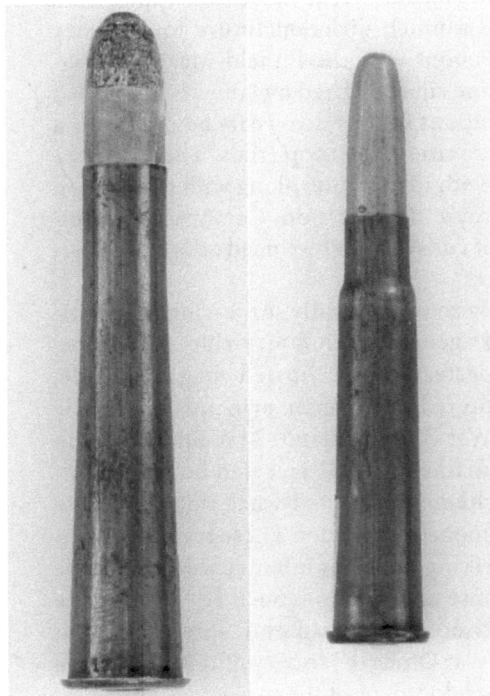

Cartridges for the .40" Enfield-Martini (left) and .303" Lee-Enfield. Though smaller and using a solid-drawn brass case, the Enfield-Martini did not differ materially from the .45" Martini-Henry, and still used a heavy, paper-patched lead bullet (Enfield-Martini photograph courtesy Woodin Laboratory).

contribution of the inventors. Metford had a long history of assisting British military firearms efforts, helping design the bullet used in the Pattern 1853 Enfield and also pioneering a pattern of explosive bullet adopted in 1861. Like so many other inventors, though, Metford had to fight for recompense over the government's use of his rifling design, finally being awarded £6,500 in September of 1891—a month before his death.[41]

In addition to the Enfield-Martini fiasco, the Commission also investigated the failure of the Pattern 1882 general-purpose cavalry sword, designed to replace several different forms of swords then in service. Tests of the new blade put emphasis on "the conveniences or inconveniences of the sword as an article to be worn," the Commission found, but "no one seems to have thought of testing their efficiency as weapons." When used as such, "they were found to be disgracefully deficient and quite unfit for their purpose." An emergency contract for 30,000 swords went to the German firm of Weyersberg in Solingen, Westphalia—a major embarrassment for England, since "the manufacture of swords is a perfectly simple matter, and has been well understood for many centuries." "There can hardly be a graver reflection on a system of military administration," the Commission wrote, "than that it makes no provision for ascertaining distinctly, and under the responsibility of properly qualified officers, the efficiency and adaptation to its purposes of all the arms issued to soldiers."[42]

One of the chief flaws of the entire system, the Commission felt, "originated in the inadequacy of the means provided for considering the numerous questions" related to small arms and other military stores. The Ordnance Committee, "the only permanent consultative body attached to the Ordnance Department," was by design "confined to questions connected with artillery." As the failures of the Enfield-Martini and Pattern 1882 cavalry sword showed, the development of small arms involved "considerations of as delicate and technical a nature as any which are involved in the construction of artillery." Without a central supervising body, such considerations were left in the hands of special committees "open to great objections, and ... surrounded by difficulties." The committees had "no continuity, they involve no official responsibility, they are often unpaid, and sit only when it suits their convenience." In addition, "they are liable to be dissolved, reconstituted, or superseded at a moment's notice," all of which plagued the development of the Enfield-Martini. A committee "with real knowledge and authority" to deal with all manners of warlike stores, the Commission felt, "would hardly have sanctioned" the imperfect cavalry sword, nor "have taken six years to arrive at a conclusion about a rifle."[43]

Rather than expand the Ordnance Committee's purview to meet that of the defunct Ordnance Select Committee, however, the Stephen Commission suggested a much broader restructuring of the whole system of ordnance administration. Critical to this would be the establishment of some form of army or ordnance council to settle basic questions such as the size and abilities of regular, reserve, and volunteer forces the nation required. "The provision of stores ... can hardly be determined unless there is an understanding as to the number of armed bodies for which provision is to be made," the Commission felt. Answering such questions meant "it would be possible to lay down in a clear intelligible way the amount and the nature of the stores which ought to be forthcoming at any moment, [as well as] the means by which and the proportions in which those stores should be increased in case of emergency." Such a council would also report the current state of stores, decide upon the technological direction of future weapons programs, and most importantly make their findings public. Although the latter carried the danger of providing information to potential enemies, "foreign countries already know all that they care to know about our warlike stores," as much as Britain knew about everyone else's. Such a danger would be outweighed, they felt, by the guidance such publication would give to "intelligent parliamentary discussion ... and public opinion, and give a strong security to the public in general that their money was being intelligently applied to the purposes for which it was intended."[44]

The Commission also recommended the resurrection of the post of Master-General of Ordnance. Unlike that abolished three decades earlier, the revised office would be limited to management of the military stores and manufacturing departments; command of the Royal Artillery would remain with the Commander-in-Chief. In addition, the holder of the new post "should be a soldier of the highest eminence" rather than a political appointment that the Surveyor-General of Ordnance office had devolved into. The new Master-General would submit annually "a statement of what he regards as necessary for his department," but the Secretary of State for War would retain responsibility for submitting army budgets to Parliament. In addition, the Commission felt that the Master-General should be assisted by a council responsible for advice on technical questions and evaluation of inventions, periodic inspection of stores, and investigations of any form of complaints.[45] By now, the older Ordnance Council only assembled as necessary to consider issues with inventors; clearly, the Commission felt that a permanent body with an expanded scope was required.

Once the Commission released its report in early May 1887, the press attacked. On the 18th, the *Derby Daily Telegraph* noted that the Stephen Commission had "placed a very liberal interpretation upon the precise letter of their instructions," and expanded its scope to examine the whole of British army administration. "It is clear," the *Lancashire Evening Post* wrote on the 24th, that the Commission "are of opinion that our whole War Office system is bad." The head of the Secretary of State for War held "either a co-ordinate or a supreme control" over several different functions, "any one of which is sufficient to occupy the whole time of a first-class administrator with special training and abilities. This, as is notorious, the [Secretary] does not usually possess." In particular, the *Post* emphasized that the Surveyor-General of Ordnance's post had turned into a civilian patronage position. "Out of seven gentlemen who have held the office in the course of sixteen years," the paper wrote, "three were never soldiers at all, others were mere subalterns and regimental officers." The paper went on to say that the office had originally been intended for "an officer of the same character" as those that held the Master-General of Ordnance prior to the Crimean War, most notably the Duke of Wellington. "The concerns of the Empire," the *Post* acerbically concluded, "have been too engrossing for our statesmen to take note of trifles of this kind. The Commission have acquitted the Ordnance Department of corruption, and practically found it guilty of inefficiency and ignorance."

"The Work ... Has Altogether Outgrown the System": Stanhope's Reorganization of 1887

The Stephen Commission was not the only body investigating ordnance matters. Just before the Gladstone government fell in July of 1886, then Secretary of State for War Henry Campbell-Bannerman formed a committee chaired by the Earl of Morley (Albert Edmund Parker) to "inquire into the organization and administration of the Manufacturing Departments of the Army." The same year also saw the launch of a commission chaired by Sir Matthew Ridley, directed "to inquire into the Establishments of the different Offices of State at Home and Abroad." Ridley's committee spent its first year examining "the two great spending departments, the War Office and Admiralty ... both of which have recently been the subject of much public criticism and discussion." Finally, in May of 1887 Lord Randolph Churchill and his "Select Committee on Army and Navy Estimates" began taking evidence on how both branches made their annual pleas for funds from Parliament. This brought the count of ongoing committees studying the British military to four, a surprising number considering Salisbury's lack of interest in military affairs.[46] It did, however, make good press for the Conservatives to be seen thoroughly examining the supposedly deteriorated state of nation's defenses left by the Liberals. Unfortunately, none of the committees took a whole-subject approach to their studies of the country's still-jumbled military administration system.

As the reports from the various committees were issued, the press made their details available to the public. The first release of evidence from Churchill's committee came out just a few days ahead of Morley's report; taken together, their findings caused the *Lancashire Evening Post* to write on 1 August 1887 that "the War Office has been in a very bad way of late." Both committees "tell the same tale of bad administration, want of control, and something like deliberate juggling in accounts," the paper continued. "The worst revelations ... belong to Lord Randolph's branch of inquiry.... The most serious of them all is the proof that Parliamentary control over the Estimates is a mere figment." Ultimately, the paper charged, responsibility for this financial confusion lay with the Secretary of State's office. "It is [this] official, sitting crowned, sceptered, and throned, whom the two Commissions present to our eyes, and whom honest men of both parties must try and topple from his seat."

Such an extreme measure did not get much support, but soon Stanhope had read enough committee reports to understand the confused state of military and civilian control. In the House of Commons debate over army estimates on 8 September, he unveiled his plan to dissolve the quagmire, prefaced with an explanation of what he saw to be a principal weakness put in place by Cardwell's reform efforts. Stanhope stated that all the subordinate departments under the Surveyor-General of Ordnance (SGO) "labour at present under grave disadvantages," including instability of the post itself and the five-year tenures of his principal assistants. In addition, although the officer held "absolute financial responsibility" for his departments, the Surveyor-General had "no permanent financial adviser with whose assistance he could alone exercise adequate supervision." Such failings, combined with the tremendous pace of change in military technology, meant that Stanhope felt that "the work [of the SGO's office] has altogether outgrown the system established a few years ago."[47]

Stanhope proposed three major principles for his reorganization of the War Office. First, the Military Department of the War Office would take over "administration of all the executive duties of the Army ... [and] to fix upon each military head of a [subordinate] Department full responsibility for that branch of the Service which he controls." Second, Stanhope intended to "separate altogether inspection of manufactured articles from [their] actual manufacture" through the formation of inspection departments at Woolwich and Enfield.[48] Finally, control of the Financial Department would be extended "to all the branches of the War Office." Such changes meant the elimination of the "false" position of the Surveyor-General, but also entailed a considerable alteration in the office of the Director of Artillery, the work for which "is absolutely beyond the power of any one man ... to cope with." In addition, the Director frequently found himself "divorced from the observation of [Stanhope's] military advisers and it might actually happen that even large changes might take place in the armaments of the country almost without their knowledge." Control of the manufacturing departments therefore passed from the Director of Artillery to a new Director-General of Ordnance Factories, under the supervision of the Finance Department of the War Office. The Director of Artillery himself would answer to the Commander-in-Chief, and would hold onto the duties of "approval of designs" as well as inspection of warlike stores, to be "assisted by a representative of the Admiralty" for materials required by the Navy.[49] This extended the influence that Cambridge already held over the nation's small arms to ordnance *matériel* as well, although unlike the former there is little evidence that the Duke interfered in artillery development.

Approved by an Order-in-Council on 21 February 1888, Stanhope's reorganization cleanly divided the entire War Office between its civilian and military functions, and finally eliminated the amorphous Ordnance Department as a separate, high-level department. As noted by historian Edward Spiers, this "established the control of the Commander-in-Chief over supply and operations, so imparting a degree of co-ordination to the military system hitherto lacking." Although he still answered to the Secretary, the 69-year-

A light 7-pdr mountain RML gun made by Armstrong. Weighing 400 pounds, the gun itself broke down into two mule-carried pieces. Four other mules would carry the carriage, ammunition, etc. "Excellent service has been rendered" by the gun "in India, Afghanistan, and Egypt," according to the *Engineering* magazine of 1887 (Maw and Dredge, 354, 358).

old Cambridge now held ultimate responsibility for both active and volunteer forces. It also made a man whom Wolseley once scoffed knew "as much of modern warfare ... as my top-boot does" the principal military adviser to the Secretary of State for War. For assistance, the Duke could turn to his principal military subordinates—the Adjutant-General, Quartermaster-General, Director of Artillery, and Inspector-General of Fortifications—for advice; the Secretary, on the other hand, could not consult with these officers except on an informal basis. Instead of a smoothly-operating military department, however, Stanhope's changes centralized too much power in the hands of the Commander-in-Chief. Without a proper staff department, the Duke's office became a communications bottleneck and a serious constriction on the responsibility of subordinate officers.[50]

Stanhope's reorganization of the War Office is important as much for what it did *not* do, as well as what it accomplished. It ignored the Stephen Commission's recommendation for a directing council on army requirements, as well as the resurrection of the post of MGO. As a result, the Commission's concerns regarding the limited scope of the Ordnance Committee were also overlooked, and British military technology remained the product of a disparate committee system. Rather than appoint an "Inspector-General of Warlike Stores" to head a unified inspection department, the reorganization split inspection duties between separate offices. One, headed by the Assistant Director of Artillery, handled the ordnance factories and inspection work at Woolwich; Enfield in turn had its own under the new post of "Chief Inspector of Small Arms." The split made sense, given the distance between the two facilities, but effectively created separate entities under the nominal responsibility of the Director of Artillery. Finally, placing the manufacturing departments under the control of the Finance Department opened the possibility of interference by a bureaucrat "who of course had no intimate knowledge of the technical requirements of the Service," something that Cambridge foresaw great problems with. In a later minute to Stanhope, the Duke worried that the army would have no voice in the operation the Ordnance Factories, and accurately predicted the eventual failure of this portion of Stanhope's plan.[51]

In addition, the reorganization exacerbated tensions over spending, as principal military officials such as Cambridge and Wolseley held politicians responsible for the inadequate state of the army. The latter had well-known views regarding what he saw as British military weaknesses; Wolseley had argued since 1885 that the French could land an army unopposed on the English coast, a position backed up by an April 1888 memorandum written by his Assistant Adjutant-General, Col. John Adargh. In such an invasion, Ardagh claimed, heavy French naval guns could lay down such a barrage of shrapnel that "the operation of disembarkation can hardly be interfered with." Until the release of the memo, Wolseley had only made his fears known in private conversations, but at a London dinner held on 23 April he publicly and acerbically blamed British politicians for the reason "all the nations of Europe ... with the one exception of England [are] armed to the teeth." "What do we see when any new administration comes into office," he asked? "It is the same with all parties. The first thing is the endeavor made by the Minister ... to obtain some clap-trap reputation by cutting down the expenses of the army and navy." If he does so, that minister then "plumes himself on the victory ... and as he chuckles over this success he says, 'Say what a good boy am I!'"[52]

The London *Daily Telegraph* followed Wolseley's widely-publicized speech with an alarmist article entitled "in large letters, England in Danger Our Army without Arms, Worst Guns in the World" on 11 May and which Viscount Charles Hardinge brought before the House of Lords that evening. Hardinge quoted the article as saying that, from "the highest military authority ... the subjoined facts are indisputable.... Owing to the deplorable neglect of Parliament ... we are wholly unprepared for war, if not, indeed, at the mercy of any European enemy."[53] Hardinge then mentioned some of the "indisputable" facts pointed out by the *Telegraph*, including "the worst [artillery] served out to any army of the present day," and a new magazine rifle yet to be distributed to a single regiment. "The guns served out to the Volunteers are obsolete," the article charged; "the armaments of the forts are obsolete; the piles of shot and shell at Woolwich are for the most part obsolete." Directing his questions to Cambridge, Hardinge asked if there was any foundation for the allegations raised by the *Telegraph*. The Duke dodged, first humorously claiming that until seeing that article he had believed himself to be the "the highest Military Authority." He then tacitly agreed, stating that "the circumstances are such that these questions are well worthy of the fullest and most anxious consideration" by Government. Salisbury, on the other hand, pointed out that despite what the *Telegraph* claimed both his and previous governments passed increases in both men and money available to the army. Salisbury also rebuked Wolseley and other "distinguished authorities upon military affairs [for] making statements against the Government under which they serve ... in a place where they cannot be answered," such as at the London dinner party. If Wolseley, a member of the House of Lords, "thinks his duty forces him to make such statements as these, let him come down here and make them."[54]

Such a public censure led many to expect Wolseley's resignation. Instead, the general appeared before the House of Lords on 14 May to both explain himself, and—to the relief of Salisbury—apologize. Wolseley denied "most emphatically that I have ever said one word that could be in any way construed into an attack" on Salisbury's government. Reading from a letter sent to Stanhope after the dinner speech, Wolseley insisted that he had "attributed our [military] shortcomings to the vicious system of Party Government, and not to any particular individual on one side of the House or the other. My reference to Ministers was to Ministers in the abstract." In a conciliatory gesture, Wolseley wound up his speech by "hop[ing] the Secretary of State for War and every Member of the Government will understand that I deeply regret that the words I made use of in that speech ... could by any possibility be considered as reflecting in any way upon any Member of Her Majesty's Administration." Salisbury accepted Wolseley's disavowal of any direct attack on himself or his cabinet, and "hope[d] he will not take this incident too seriously, for I should regard his leaving the Public Service as the greatest blow that could fall upon our military administration." The *Pall Mall Gazette*, however, reported on 15 May that Wolseley had "stuck to his guns like a gallant general" and reiterated his belief in the deficiencies of England's defenses. With a weakened Navy and an army dispersed "all over the world ... our military forces are not organized or equipped as they should be to guarantee even the safety of" London itself.[55]

Alive to the issues raised by Wolseley and other officers and concerned himself about the defense of the Empire, Salisbury already had plans to form yet another study, but this time of the whole of military administration for both the army and navy. On 7 June 1888, royal warrant directed the commission, chaired by Hartington, "to inquire into the Civil and Professional Administration of the Naval and Military Departments, and the relation of those Departments to each other and the Treasury."[56] Such a mandate limited the focus of the Commission to a very high-level examination of the entirety of British military administration, and precluded it from further investigating

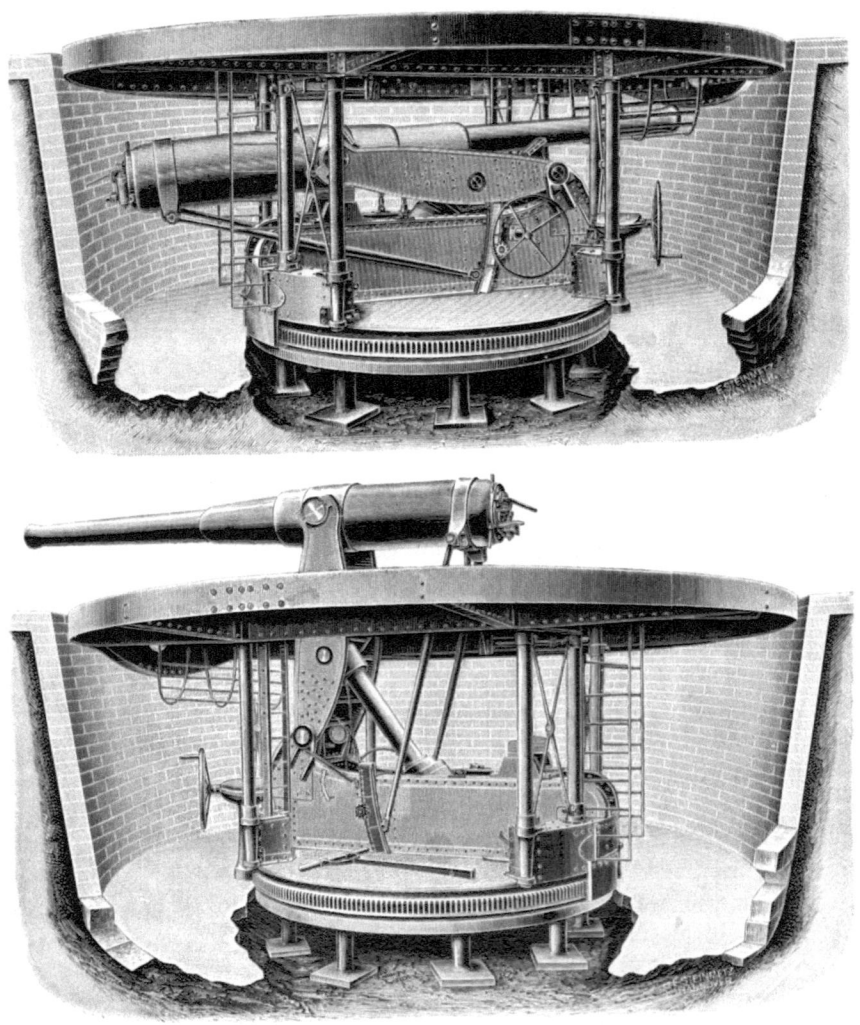

The Moncrieff hydro-pneumatic gun platform, as exhibited by Armstrong, Mitchell & Co. at the 1887 Royal Jubilee Exhibition (Maw and Dredge, 17).

any hardware or organizational issues raised by the Stephen Commission, or the concerns voiced by Wolseley and alluded to by Cambridge.[57] Regardless, the new commission would have a significant long-term impact on the future of British military administration.

Even with the Hartington Commission under way, Stanhope felt confident enough to assure voters that his government had made "substantial progress" in strengthening British land defenses in a 1 November 1888 speech at North Islington, printed the next day by the *Times*. The reorganization at the War Office, the unification of the ordnance factories under a single head, and the establishment of the separate Inspection Departments figured prominently in his list of improvements. Passage of the Imperial Defence Act, he claimed, provided £3,000,000 for the defense of ports and coaling stations at home and abroad. Designs for new artillery had been finalized, with "fresh facilities ... being afforded for testing both guns and ammunition with greater convenience and rapidity." The business given to private industry had also increased, not only with established firms; Stanhope made the point that "for the first time, a large contract for guns had been placed with" Vickers, Sons & Co. of Sheffield, Britain's newest entry into the "gun trade." Trials of the .303 Lee-Metford magazine rifle had been completed, and "reports from various climates and under all conditions proved that it was a weapon admirably adapted to its purpose." With full-scale manufacture scheduled, "Government hoped ... to begin the issue to the army of a rifle which they confidently believed to be superior to that now manufactured by any foreign Government." In addition, "the manufacture of the 12-pounder artillery recently described by Lord Wolseley as the best field gun in Europe" had also been pushed forward, as well as "another most formidable weapon ... the machine gun." Such pronouncements were met with outbursts of cheering throughout Stanhope's speech. The proceedings were closed with "votes of confidence in her Majesty's Government and in Mr. [G. C. T.] Bartley," the MP that arranged the event.

Tweaking the Machinery of Ordnance Development

Although Stanhope's reform program did not directly affect the constitution of the Ordnance Committee, several changes were made to its operations and scope during this decade, beginning with records-keeping. Since the reconstruction of the Committee in 1881, two separate sets of minutes had been kept by the Director of Artillery's office, one related to proposals considered by the Director and one specific to the Committee's business. On 17 February, Director of Artillery Alderson noted that the dual-minute system "causes difficulty of reference without any corresponding advantage." Effective beginning the next quarter of the year, Alderson consolidated the minutes of his office with those of the OC.[58] From 1889 forward, only one set of the *Abstracts of Proceedings* were published per year, instead of two as in 1881 through 1888.

The greatest change came with the elimination of the Surveyor-General's office and the assignment of the Director of Artillery underneath the Commander-in-Chief's office, which required the issuance of new "General Instructions for the Guidance of the Ordnance Committee." Forwarded for review on 12 December 1888, these directed the Committee to answer to the Commander-in-Chief rather than to the Secretary of State for War as in 1881. There were, however, important changes in the details. Gunpowder and explosives were removed from the Committee's purview, having been handed over to a new "Committee on Explosives" earlier in the year. The OC, on the other hand, now had "direct responsibility for the designs for all guns for H.M. Service," including those obtained from the trade, "except in special cases in which their recommendations have been overruled." In addition, the instructions gave the Committee limited leeway in undertaking experiments; any estimated to cost more than £25 required the express authority of the Director of Artillery.[59]

1889 saw additional changes, especially after a 10 January complaint by the Admiralty against the "very serious delays which take place in the settlement of questions connected with naval ordnance." Such delays, for example, had left the "fuze question in an unsatisfactory state" and components of a new 6-inch breech-loading gun still undecided after two years. "The Admiralty would refer many more questions to the Committee," they went on, "but the delays and consequent inconvenience to the Service are so serious, that they have been compelled ... to make other arrangements." What "other arrangements" are unknown, but that year the Director of Naval Ordnance's office began keeping its own records of questions considered, an important step in the separation of army and naval ordnance matters. As regards the OC, the Admiralty recommended that "greater facilities should be given ... for carrying out their experiments," and that the stricture against direct communication by the Committee with department heads be lifted. Alderson, however, met the latter suggestion only half way by giving the Committee permission to contact the *chief inspectors*, and not the heads of the manufacturing departments. In addition, he did so only on the understanding that "information imparted ... be considered as emanating from [the inspectors] personally, and on their individual responsibility only." In February, the Committee itself complained of a "want of executive power to carry out experiments," and in the "great delay" in getting authority for "detail experiments" connected with larger investigations. The Committee suggested a money cap for such detail work, and a "free hand to carry out experiments without further reference, provided the sum allowed be not exceeded." After a meeting at the War Office "in order that a distinct understanding may be arrived at," Alderson approved the change.⁶⁰

While the Admiralty wrangled with the Director of Artillery over the operation of the OC, a significant change occurred in the control of the great manufacturing departments. Salisbury's first pick for the new post of Director-General of Ordnance Factories (DGOF) had been Maitland, who retired altogether from the Royal Artillery in mid-1889. Salisbury agreed with Wolseley that the post should go to the most suitable candidate, and appointed William Anderson—the same engineer who had protested the Woolwich system before the United Services Institute four years earlier—as the new Director-General effective 11 August. The *York Herald* noted on 18 July that "there will be a good deal of discontent among Army men" over handing control of factories producing military goods to a civilian, and indeed there already had been. Cambridge had "complained bitterly" to Stanhope over the assignment of control of the ordnance factories to the Financial Department in September of the previous year, as he felt that the army would have no say in their operation. With Anderson's appointment it seemed that loss of input would be complete. Both the *Times* and the military-oriented *Broad Arrow* supported the Duke, and published opinions against having a civilian "straight from a manufacturing firm" in charge of Ordnance factories and unfamiliar with the needs of the military. Still, Anderson held the post until his death in December of 1898, and put in place many of the centralization and accounting changes recommended by the Morley and Churchill Committees.⁶¹

"It Is Only Because the Country Itself Has Spoken"

On 31 December 1889, the *Western Daily Press* took stock of the British army's situation at the end of the year. "Stanhope has employed his time, or most of it, very usefully" in putting his reforms into place, the *Press* reported, "and he can at least console himself that the army is to-day generally more efficient than it was twelve months ago." The paper, however, stopped short of giving Stanhope full credit. "It is only because the country itself has spoken ... that so much has been recently done," it claimed. "If our armaments are of a more serviceable character than they were when guns were bursting and bayonets were bending, it is because popular pressure has been brought to bear on the Secretary of State." Although unfair to Stanhope, the paper was in some ways correct; the British public, kept informed by agitators such as Carbutt and Armit and with the aid of the press, put considerable pressure on Government to improve its military hardware. Such improvements were indeed considerable. In the space of nine years, the infantry went from a large-bore single-shot rifle to the small-bore, ten-shot Lee-Metford, equal if not better than weapons carried by Continental armies. Both the Royal Artillery and Navy were fully committed to modernized breech-loading guns, although rifled muzzle-loaders would remain in service for another decade. The monopoly that the Royal Gun Factory held on both ordnance design and manufacture had finally cracked, with orders being let to Elswick Ordnance, Joseph Whitworth and Co., and newcomers such as Hotchkiss of Paris and Maxim Nordenfelt Co.[62] Finally, new chemical-based propellants and explosives promised to increase the range, hitting power, and accuracy of both artillery and small arms, without the clouds of smoke that black powder produced. While all required more work to perfect, 1889 found Britain much better off in terms of military technology than a decade before.

The same could not be said of the underlying machinery that supported the military. Stanhope's reorganization, while it helped clarify the distinction between civilian and military authority, stopped short of the complete rebuild that the nation's military administration system needed. Some of the tensions produced by the Cardwell reforms remained, most notably the heavy weight that the Financial Department exerted through its excruciating examinations

A Hotchkiss 3-pdr with hydro-pneumatic recoil control, which inspired similar mechanisms for larger weapons. Also part of Armstrong's 1887 display at Newcastle, the guns—capable of firing 20 rounds a minute—served as close-defense weapons aboard Royal Navy ships (Maw and Dredge, 354, 358).

of army spending. In addition, the dissolution of the Surveyor-General's post removed a layer of professional advice on ordnance matters available to the Secretary's office. Stanhope, like so many of his predecessors, came into office generally ignorant of military issues; Cambridge's "massive authority build on long tenure and royal connections" therefore gave him considerable influence at the War Office. This most likely affected Stanhope's decision to centralize military control under the Commander-in-Chief's office, but the expanded responsibilities overwhelmed the aging Duke. Stanhope also ignored the Stephen Commission's call for a more systematic determination of the army's needs, and their suggestion for better oversight of weapons development efforts through a resurrected MGO post.[63]

Stanhope's piecemeal selection of committee recommendations illustrates a governmental habit that bedeviled British military reform efforts since the Crimean War. Dozens of Royal Commissions and Select Committees had been called into existence to study military administration, including at least a half-dozen during Stanhope's tenure. Yet despite thousands of man-hours of testimony and hundreds of pages of reports, recommendations from such committees were often brushed aside. This issue was not unique to the War Office; any reform committee, no matter how strongly constructed, could find its work ignored if the department under study proved uninterested in change.[64] Unlike other governmental departments, however, the War Office and Admiralty's decisions could mean the difference between life and death for men on the bleeding edge of the Empire. With the Hartington Commission still in action at the turn of the decade, what remained to be seen is whether Stanhope would listen to advice from yet another report on British military administration.

"New Measures Demand New Men"

The British army coasted into the last decade of Queen Victoria's reign confident of its ability to defend the Empire, having lost only two small expeditions since Waterloo: a disastrous foray into Afghanistan in 1838, and a short 1881 campaign in South Africa. In 1890 Britain enjoyed a rare year of peace, with only a small army in the field against holdouts in Burma. Military technology continued to advance after the stall of the 1870s, and the reconstructed Ordnance Committee seemed to be accomplishing what it had been appointed to do: shepherd the nation's military hardware into the modern era. When Victoria died in January of 1901, however, her Empire found itself again embroiled in a faraway war where British forces suffered serious setbacks; worse, on the whole, than what it suffered during that terrible winter of 1854. That could at least be blamed on Mother Nature and the monstrous gale that sank so much of the army's winter supplies. Now, however, the setbacks were directly due to the military actions of the Empire's opponents, what on 25 August 1900 the *Western Times* labeled a bunch of "dirty, innocent-looking old farmers" that cost the British some 2,700 casualties in the "Black Week" of December 1899. The nation's weapons were also to blame: artillery outranged by that of the enemy, high-explosive shells that failed to detonate properly, rifles that did not shoot straight. The question for Britons, then, was did the OC fail its task, or were there other, more systemic flaws in the country's army? The whole system of military administration, tinkered and tampered with since the Crimean War but never completely overhauled, put all of its faults on public display in the opening months of the war. Despite so many years of study, including the ongoing Hartington Commission, the "disastrous muddle" that mired Raglan's forces in 1854 threatened to claim more victims nearly fifty years later.

As it did after the shock of 1854, both the public and the British government recovered from the initial disasters to make good the deficiencies in its army and bring the conflict to a successful conclusion. Until the advent of home rule a few years later, South Africa would be colored red on the world map of the British Empire, but at the cost of thousands of lives and millions of pounds sterling. True to form, calls for post-war retrenchment by some members of Parliament began soon after the conclusion of hostilities. Other politicians, however, began to take a much longer view of imperial defense than before, especially the situation at the War Office. Not without considerable pain and missteps, the "disastrous muddle" would finally be cleared away, beginning with the elimination of the anachronistic post of Commander-in-Chief. Ultimately both the office of Master-General of Ordnance and the Ordnance Board—shades of the institutions that fell in 1855 but with narrower focus and responsibilities—would also be recreated. The Boer War, therefore, proved to be a critical trial run that helped prepare the Empire for the cataclysm of 1914.

The Ordnance Committee at the End of the Century

The OC in the last decade of the century continued to function much as it had on its reconstitution in 1881, but on a larger scale. If the physical sizes of the *Abstracts* are any indication, the Director of Artillery and the Committee were quite busy; the publication for 1890 is split into two volumes, totaling nearly 1,450 pages, excluding the index. The volumes for 1895 and 1896 are also split, at 1,064 and 753 pages respectively. Proposals for products and inventions continued to flow into the War Office, albeit at a slightly lower yearly average of 175 than in the decade before. Although eccentric ideas still appear in the *Abstracts*, such as T. Le Poidevin's suggestion of a "catapult for throwing shells," what came forward in this decade consisted mostly of suggestions for improvements of existing hardware, rather than the "visionary and speculative projects" that had plagued the OSC.[1]

Increasingly mixed in with solitary individuals were a growing number of companies seeking a market for their wares. Some tried to tempt the War Office with free trials; the Porter and Thomas Paint Company, for example, stated they would "supply free of charge any quantity" of paint for iron and steel structures, and J.B. Wheen & Sons offered to submit a cask of axle grease. Such tactics rarely worked; usually the company would be turned away with the reply that there were "no orders to give" for their products. Occasionally, however, samples did get noticed; an electrical "accumulator," or rechargeable battery, from the Epstein Electric Accumulator Company impressed the Inspector-General of Fortifications enough in 1893 for him to recommend "that the firm should be placed on the list of manufacturers, in case accumulators should be required." The Weldless Chain Company also sent in samples of their patented product, which William Anderson (as Director-General of Ordnance Factories) reported favorably on. As a result, then-Director of Artillery Lt. Gen. Robert Hay "inform[ed] the Company that orders will be given should chains of this description be required."[2]

Both Epstein and Weldless Chain are examples of the numerous companies formed to work specific patents, and the risks such ventures carried for their investors. Occasionally there were winners, such as the Morris Tube & Ammunition Co., which by the 1890s did brisk business with the War Office selling all manner of target practice equipment for field and naval ordnance. Most firms folded often as fast as they came together; Weldless, for example, received a "compulsory winding-up order" in 1896 for non-payment of debts.[3] Despite such risks, the entrepreneurial spirit of British businessmen is quite evident in the *Abstracts*: the Eclipse Patent Safety Horseshoe Syndicate, Elmore's Patent Copper Depositing Company, Mackie Patent Stopper Syndicate, and the Shellbend Folding Boat Company lined up with dozens of others in their attempts to secure a slice of the War Office budget. Having a patented article could also backfire. Although the Inspector-General of Stores judged that W. Kenyon and Sons' improved cotton rope was "stronger and would probably wear better" than that already in use, he warned the Committee it was "more expensive" and covered by a patent. Unwilling to deal with royalty issues, even for a better product, the Committee declined to purchase the rope.[4]

Until the mid-1880s, the realm of the inventor remained exclusively male, with the very occasional request by a widow or surviving daughter for financial consideration in light of their husband's or father's prior inventions or service.[5] In 1886, however, Mrs. Ellen Graddon put her patent for "improvements in the apparatus for working Ordnance" before the War Office for consideration.[6] Although Alderson declined Mrs. Graddon's invention, she remains the first of a very small number of women in the late nineteenth century to step before the War Office with their ideas. Mrs. A. Wardroper, who proposed a new form of water bottle for infantry use in 1891, had perhaps the best success; Alderson ordered twenty of her zinc water bottles for trial, but tests at Aldershot found them "more liable to damage, and ... [unable to] keep the water so cool as the Service bottle."[7] Miss Fanny Godfrey tried in 1893 with her "improvements relating to buttons," and in 1895 Mrs. J. Clarke suggested "[putting] steel in bullets, in order to allow surgeons in probing wounds to find out, by means of a magnet, where the bullet is." Again, neither proposal received more than a "thanks for playing" notice. Those women had represented themselves; in 1896, however, a Mrs. Ronalds became the first woman to act as agent for an inventor, when she brought drawings and specifications for Mr. A.W. Tooley's "combined nosebag and water bucket" before the War Office. For her troubles, she received a very polite note "for bringing the invention to notice, [but] the S. of S. is not prepared to take any further steps in regard thereto."[8] Although these women only play a very small role in the story of British ordnance development, such participation—in an era not often recognized for women's independence—emphasizes how alive the British inventive spirit was at the turn of the century.

"This System Cannot and Does Not Work Well"

Unlike the stability exhibited by the Ordnance Committee, British military administration in the 1890s experienced considerable turmoil once the Hartington Commission released its report on the "Internal Administration of the War Office" on 11 February 1890. In the opening paragraph, the Commission recognized that while War Office administration "has undergone far more changes than that of the Admiralty," the process of building the office had been slow, and the responsibility of the Secretary of State for War remained "less real than that of the First Lord of the Admiralty." In particular, Stanhope's reorganization put "an excessive centralisation of responsibility in the person of the Commander-in-Chief," the only military officer who answered directly to the Secretary. Such centralization weakened the positions of other department heads within the office; the Commission also felt that "the system cannot adequately provide for the consultative ... duties of the War Department ... a point to which we attach much importance." This resulted in the repeated creation of committees similar to what occurred after the dissolution of the OSC but writ large across the whole War Office. "This system cannot and does not work well," the Commission pointedly stated. "It is impossible that sound and well matured decisions can be arrived at." As Adye had found with the interim technical committees in the 1870s, the Commission noted that "it is inevitable that the work of these numerous committees sometimes overlaps, and that there is a want of touch between them."[9]

The recommended solution to this and other problems involved nothing less than a total rebuilding of the British system of army administration. In the Commission's view, three aspects of the War Office especially needed strengthening: the Secretary's ultimate responsibility to Parliament, the important distinction between consultative vs. administrative and executive advice, and having officers with clearly defined duties answerable directly to the Secretary. To these ends, the Commission made several recommendations, beginning with the formation of a "Naval and Military Council" to jointly consider budget estimates and national defense policy. It also recommended a permanent "War Office Council" whose principal function would be to ensure smooth cooperation between the various branches of the War Office "in all cases in which they are collectively concerned." Finally, it recommended the creation of a Chief of Staff's office, in line with similar offices in other major European powers. The new department would handle military operations planning, intelligence gathering, and advising the Secretary on any other matter related to preparing the army for combat. In addition, the Commission felt that passing all responsibility through the Commander-in-Chief, "even for such a matter as the defective design of a heavy gun," to be a level of centralization not found in any other Great Power army. They argued that the heads of subordinate departments—including the recently created Director-General of Ordnance Factories—should be made directly answerable to the Secretary of State.[10] Such changes would effectively eliminate the need for a Commander-in-Chief's post, which the Commission recognized as problematic given Cambridge's long tenure. With due deference, the Commission noted that George's long service had helped the current military administration system to function, despite its flaws. The Duke had, "with the greatest loyalty," worked with successive Secretaries and brought "a personal popularity with the Army in general which cannot fail to be of public advantage" (although that advantage was not spelled out). "It is clear," the Commission warned, "that no possible successor could enjoy a position and influence which years of service to the State are alone capable of establishing." Therefore, the Commission recommended that the elimination of the Duke's post should be delayed until "the occurrence of a vacancy in the office of Commander-in-Chief, or at any favourable opportunity."[11] Such an opportunity, however, proved to be a few years in the future.

The Hartington Commission had significant long-term impact on British military administration, but royal and political pressure kept Stanhope from implementing most of its recommendations. Both Cambridge and Wolseley opposed the creation of a Chief of Staff, except as an appendage of the Commander-in-Chief's office, which the Duke was firmly determined to retire from—eventually. Although she had no direct influence over the choice of the Duke's successor, Queen Victoria hoped that Prince Albert, her third son and the Duke of Connaught, would be tapped for the post. Stanhope did form the War Office Council in May of 1890, but like the Ordnance Council before it, the new body became something other than what the Commission recommended. Rather than a higher-level board with responsibility for its own decisions, the Council became just another tool to assist the Secretary, if and when he saw fit to consult it. As the *Cheltenham Looker-On* predicted on 12 July 1890, "no very great changes result[ed] from the Report of the Hartington Commission," at least in the immediate years after its release.[12]

An important structural change, meanwhile, occurred in the relations between the army, navy, and their supply of warlike stores with the 9 May

1891 establishment of a formal Naval Ordnance Department. Such a division had been made possible by the transfer to the annual votes on Naval estimates of all amounts requested for guns, ammunition, and other stores previously carried in the Army votes, which went into effect in 1887.[13] Although it took several months to effect the transfer, by October of 1891 the new department stood ready to handle the "provision, care, custody, and distribution of all ordnance stores required for use in the Navy." The Admiralty headquartered the new Department at Woolwich, which the *Standard* reported on 10 October as the "most suitable position ... as it is there in close touch with the Ordnance Factories, the Royal Navy being [their] best customer." Although this finally freed control of the physical supply of ordnance products from the army, design remained with the Ordnance Committee, under ultimate authority of the Director of Ordnance. Given the presence of naval officers on the Committee, and despite the Admiralty's complaints regarding its performance, the arrangement worked well enough to remain in force through the end of the century.

Also in 1891 came an attempt to split field artillery design off from the OC, despite the Hartington Commission's condemnation of the War Office predilection for forming committees. During development of a new 12-pounder field gun, in 1883 the Committee had recommended a powder charge that resulted in a high initial muzzle velocity of 1,700 feet per second. The combination of gun and carriage also came in over 3,600 pounds, above the generally recommended weight for horse-drawn artillery but acceptable for field guns. When questioned, the OC replied that higher velocity produced a flatter trajectory and better terminal effects for shrapnel shells, "now fully recognized as, *par excellence*, the projectile for light Field Artillery." The Committee "consider[ed] that the gain more than counterbalance[d] the practical difficulty of attaining it," but in the intervening years other artillerymen had doubts. Maj. Gen. C. E. Nairne, the Inspector-General of Artillery in India, reported on 25 October 1891 that "a feeling of mistrust in the power of the 12-pr B.L. Gun is springing up, based on an unsound re-action in favour of low velocity fire." Such feelings were echoed in complaints reported by Gen. Sir Redvers Buller, who had succeeded Wolseley as Adjutant-General in 1890. "The high initial velocity ... was by no means absolutely essential to effective shrapnel fire," Buller claimed, and "lower velocity guns in other armies give as good results." In addition, "every Battery Officer he had spoken to condemned" the carriage of the new gun, "and declared the recoil to be excessive, while every Horse Artillery Officer declared that the gun and carriage is so heavy as to be positively unserviceable." Directed by Cambridge to investigate the matter, Buller apparently received a suggestion by former Assistant Director of Artillery Lt. Gen. W. H. Goodenough that a separate "Artillery Committee" be appointed to consider questions related to field and horse artillery.

Buller passed the suggestion to Lt. Gen. Hay in December of 1891, along with instructions to "consider the whole subject as to how Inventions and New Equipments are now dealt with."[14]

In response, Hay emphasized "the difficulties ... experienced by the Director of Artillery, in not having a properly constituted Committee to whom to refer, previous to determining on any new invention of war." Regarding the 12-pounder, Hay felt that "precisely the same course as now recommended was adopted," in that design of the carriage had been referred to a special committee prior to adoption. "Experience gained by actual trial" led to subsequent modifications to the carriage, and Hay could "not see how any definite conclusions could be arrived at otherwise." Not only did Hay "consider it unfortunate that opinions on such an important point as ballistics should be suddenly changed," he felt that "an independent Artillery Committee would ... clash with the duties of the [OC], and would raise the question of [its] continuance." In the spirit of careful contemplation, however, Hay laid out a scenario where the OC still played an intermediary role in developing new equipment based on specifications from technical committees for field, siege or other types of artillery. "Whatever system may be adopted," Hay warned, "it must be remembered that careful experiments can alone ensure that any equipment recommended will meet the requirements of the service, and that experiments necessarily take time." Hay won his point, and the Ordnance Committee survived. Buller, in his reply to the Duke, stated he didn't want to "substitute any Artillery Committee for any function of the Ordnance Committee," although he felt that technical committees would help design "advance ... with more decided steps than we do at present."[15]

The Retirement of "Poor George"

Stanhope reigned as Secretary of State for War for five and a half years, longer than any of his predecessors since the post came into being in 1854. His term of office, however, ended with the fall of Salisbury's government following the general elections of 1892. On 18 August, Campbell-Bannerman, or "C-B", once again took up the office, having held it for a brief five months in 1886. Bannerman retained his post after Archibald Primrose (Lord Rosebery) took over from Gladstone in March of 1894. Bannerman had been a member of the Hartington Commission, although he dissented in their final recommendation regarding a Chief of Staff office and had little use for the War Council once in power. He did, however, wish to solidify civilian control over the military, and agreed with the Commission's recommendation to abolish the post of Commander-in-Chief. To that end, "C-B" developed a two-prong plan of attack. In 1894, his staff began work on a revised version of the Commission's proposals, centered on the creation of an Army Board. This new entity would be composed of the five principal military officers (the Adjutant-General, generally in charge of Army personnel policies, the Quartermaster-General, Director of Artillery, and Inspector-General of Fortifications) and presided over by the C-in-C. The Board would take over numerous duties from the latter and "discuss such questions as may be … referred to it by the Secretary of State." Given equal access to the Secretary, this essentially made the other four officers contemporaries, rather than subordinates, to the Duke and greatly diminished the power of his office.[16]

The second part of the plan involved engineering the "favourable opportunity" suggested by the Hartington Commission: the resignation of Cambridge. Considerable pressure came from both Bannerman and the press; in a 4 May 1895 letter to his cousin the Queen, the Duke complained "that there are serious attacks being made in some of the newspapers on the Authorities of the War Office and on myself in particular." By then, however, even the Queen had been convinced that "poor George" had to go. On the 19th, she wrote that "on the advice of my Ministers … I have arrived at the decision, that for your own sake as well as in the public interest, it is inexpedient that you should much longer retain" the office, and that "you should be relieved at the close of your Autumn duties."[17]

Bannerman announced the Duke's impending retirement to the House of Commons on 21 June 1895. He opened with a very glowing description of the personal qualities of the officer, and disputed that "he [was] an impediment in the way of all reform." Instead, Bannerman said that "of late years he has never shown himself unwilling to adopt such changes …

The Duke of Cambridge, late in his career (Royal Collection Trust / © Her Majesty Queen Elizabeth II, 2018).

likely to be of advantage to the Army." He even held up Cambridge's retirement as illustration "that he now makes way in order that certain changes may be introduced" into army administration. Bannerman then outlined the changes he proposed, starting with the retention of the office of Commander-in-Chief, but in a reduced capacity. In addition, he proposed elevating "the other heads of the Military Departments, who will each be directly responsible" to the Secretary and who will "constitute a deliberative council" as recommended by the Commission. "I firmly believe," Bannerman continued, that with a "less centralized and more elastic" system in place, "great advantage to the Army will ensue."[18]

Unfortunately for Bannerman, however, his triumph proved *very* short-lived. When the debate returned to the army vote under consideration, Conservative MP William St. John Broderick bushwhacked the Secretary with a charge that reserve stocks of small arms ammunition had fallen to dangerous levels during the Liberal administration. Four years earlier, he claimed, the country had gone through "two processes that were always dangerous in Army matters": a change not only in the size of cartridge used in its infantry rifle (from the .45" Martini-Henry to the .303" Lee-Metford) but also in the propellant, switching from black powder to cordite. The newness of cordite meant British manufacturers lacked experience with the material, and supplies were very unsure. Private industry—the only real source of immediate expansion in time of war—had struggled to bring enough capacity online to meet just the needs of peacetime ammunition requirements, never mind an emergency stockpile in case of war. "This was a serious state of things," Broderick claimed. "To have practically no reserve of [small arms] ammunition was the height of impolicy." As he could not move to increase the vote for war supplies, Broderick moved to reduce the salary of the Secretary by £100, a "snap vote" tactic used to open debate on a subject. Bannerman proved unable to defend his policies; the motion passed, 132 to 125, and Rosebery's government resigned the next day.[19]

In the general election that followed, both the Conservatives and their Liberal Unionist allies made significant gains. This brought Salisbury back as head of a Conservative-led coalition government, his third term as Prime Minister and the last man to serve Queen Victoria in that office. Salisbury tapped Henry Fitzmaurice (Lord Lansdowne) to lead the War Office, and Lansdowne spent the next two months planning how to take advantage of the Duke's removal as Commander-in-Chief. Essentially, Lansdowne copied Bannerman's idea for a new Army Board, but renamed the Director of Artillery post to that of Inspector-General of Ordnance (IGO). Lt. Gen. Sir Edwin Markham officially took the office, established by an Order-in-Council dated 21 November 1895, on 1 April the next year. His duties included inspection and supply of equipment and military stores, and "dealing with questions of armament, of patterns, of inventions and designs, and with the direction of the Ordnance Committee." He also provided whatever technical advice the Secretary of State required regarding ordnance, if any.[20]

The Army Board, along with the War Office Council, gave Lansdowne and his successors better consultative support, but "hardly transformed the War Office." The Council met very infrequently, and the Secretary ultimately made the final decision on any subjects referred to it. The Army Board met more often, but other than the preparation of the annual estimates could only consider such subjects as the Secretary forwarded to it. In addition, the generals disliked having to "face one another & argue out their ideas instead of attempting to push them through independently," presumably within their own spheres of influence. They also disliked that a civilian not only witnessed the sausage-making involved in preparing the annual estimates, but forced them to keep financial considerations in mind. Wolseley, who replaced the Duke as Commander-in-Chief, also resented the gelding of the post and that the other military department heads were essentially his equals, to the point of requiring any correspondence to the Secretary to go through his office.[21] This would at least keep Wolseley informed of what was going on within the army, even if he lacked direct control.

One final change that directly affected the Ordnance Department took place before the end of a turbulent decade for British military administration. Stanhope's changes had put control of the Arsenal under the Director-General of Ordnance Factories (DGOF), who answered to the War Office's Financial Secretary. The change had rankled the military in 1888, and remained a point of contention ever since. The issue came to the fore with the death of William Anderson in December. Lansdowne selected Lt. Gen. Sir Henry Brackenbury to fill the position, who despite a difficult personality came with a host of credentials. Brackenbury had spent the previous two and a half years as president of the Ordnance Committee, served as the last Director of Artillery prior to that office's abolition, and had served on the Hartington Commission as well. Brackenbury's consent to fill the DGOF position, however, came with a price: the removal of the post from under the Financial Secretary and its return to direct control by the military. As he later testified, he felt this change to be absolutely essential; if the DGOF "had to go with his hat in his hand to the Financial Secretary and ask that this, that, and the other thing might be done," the needs of the service in wartime might never be met. At his behest Lansdowne reorganized the military departments one more time, replacing the Inspector-General of Ordnance post with a resurrected "Director-General of Ordnance." The duties were similar to those of the Inspector-General, but the Order-in-Council issued on 7 March 1899 explicitly granted "direction of the Ordnance Committee and the Manufacturing Departments of the Army" to the new post. In addition, the Orders made the new Director-

General answerable to the Secretary of State rather than Treasury. The DGOF itself transformed into a new "Chief Superintendent of Ordnance Factories," which while remaining open to civilians now answered to the Director-General's office. The reorganization led to considerable improvement in the day-to-day operations—accounting, internal communications, inspection and so forth—of the factories. As regards the products themselves, the upcoming war in South Africa showed there was much left to be desired.[22]

The press, in particular the *Times*, welcomed the change. On 14 March 1899 the paper announced that "the latest Order in Council ... introduces an organic change of great importance," which undid "the gross mistake of 1888." Placement of the factories under the Financial Secretary "could not succeed.... Friction, confusion, and a great increase of unproductive expenditure naturally resulted, while political considerations tended to more and more assert themselves in the management of the national factories." Brackenbury, the paper claimed, "has a wide experience of administration, and there is no one better able to bring order out of chaos in the great Ordnance Department." Putting him in charge, the *Times* stated, meant that "a great anomaly and growing evils are abolished." The *Pall Mall Gazette* agreed. On 28 March, it wrote that Stanhope's placement of the ordnance factories under the Finance Department "was notorious, and on the face of it, inefficient, absurd, and ... probably quite unconstitutional." Such facts, however, "did not in the least interfere with the resolution of the War Office to create the system, and 'to run it' until the whole affairs of the Government factories had been got into an inextricable muddle." Even periodicals such as the *Cheltenham Looker-On* took notice. In its 18 March edition the weekly decried Stanhope's change as "simply a sample of the manner in which we, a great business people, manage our public departments, particularly the War Office ... the result has been extravagance, friction, and confusion."

The turbulence in War Office administration in the last decade of the nineteenth century matched the unsettled and increasingly solitary position of Britain on the international stage, a result of Salisbury's policy of "splendid isolation." A war scare with the United States erupted over a boundary dispute between British Guiana and Venezuela in 1895; that same year, tensions with Germany frayed over the Kaiser's support for Boer nationalists in South Africa, made worse by a botched raid on Johannesburg by pro–British forces. The Russians and the French, formal allies since 1894, had by 1897 built up their Eastern fleets to match the Royal Navy's power in the area, and Japan's rise as a regional force could not be ignored. Both Britain and France were marching across Africa, and required conferences between the two nations to avoid going to war over territorial disputes. Britain found its ranks of potential allies growing thin, while the list of possible opponents seemed only to grow—making the question of imperial defense, and therefore the quality of its weaponry, all the more important. It also made the failure to thoroughly address the "disastrous muddle" all the more damning.

From Omdurman to the "Black Week" of 1899

Although the *Abstracts* illustrate the tremendous effort involved in upgrading British weaponry, the success of such efforts could only be measured on the battlefield. In 1898, the overwhelming victory at Omdurman seemed a conclusive demonstration of that modernization effort. On 2 September, an 8,000-man British expeditionary force under Gen. (later Lord) Herbert Kitchener, bolstered by 17,000 Sudanese and Egyptian troops, stood against 60,000 Dervishes under the banner of *Khalifa* Abdullah, successor to *Mahdi* Mohammed Ahmed. Kitchener's army could only be attacked across an open plain with little cover; at dawn, the Dervish infantry began a series of uncoordinated charges in an attempt to rush the plain. "From early morning to noon," historians D.H. Cole and E.C. Priestly wrote, "the Anglo-Egyptian army maneuvered as if on parade, wheeling to meet the successive attacks from different directions." "To all intents and purposes," they continued, it was "a battle of a much earlier period, save that the weapons used were infinitely more effective." With repeating rifles, Maxim machine guns, and shrapnel shells, Kitchener's army made a literal hash of their Sudanese attackers. By the end, 10,800 Dervishes lay dead, with another 16,000 wounded and 4,000 prisoners, against forty-eight dead and less than four hundred wounded on the Anglo-Egyptian side. It was, in the words of war correspondent G. W. Steevens, "not a battle, but an execution."[23]

Omdurman represented a tremendous victory for the British method of colonial warfare, and many Britons expected a repeat performance the following year when the nation found itself again at war in South Africa. This time, however, their opponents were not poorly trained tribesmen armed with spears and muskets. After the bungled raid against Johannesburg in 1895, President Paul Kruger of the South African Republic invested in modern weaponry for his army and the Boer farmers that made up the country's militia. The French firm of Creusot sold the South Africans four 155mm heavy and six 75mm field guns, and Krupp supplied four 120mm howitzers and eight 75mm field pieces. Ironically, Vickers of Sheffield sold them twenty quick-firing 1-pounder guns, shortsightedly rejected for service in the British army in 1894.[24] In addition, Kruger purchased 37,000 magazine rifles from Mauser, the well-regarded German rifle company. Not only did the 7mm ammunition used in the Mauser have a higher velocity and longer range than the .303" Lee-Enfield, but the rifles themselves could be reloaded faster. The British soldier had to recharge his magazine one cartridge at a time; the

Mauser, on the other hand, used a five-round "stripper clip" that allowed the shooter to refill his magazine with one action. This small difference in military technology—ignored by British small arms committees for over fifteen years—proved to be a game-changer in upcoming battles in South Africa.[25]

Much as they had forty-five years earlier, a "huge, cheerful, patriotic crowd" saw off the advance guard of the expeditionary force bound for South Africa on 14 October 1899. At 47,000 men strong, it would be the biggest army dispatched abroad since end of the Napoleonic Wars, and nearly twice the size of the force that sailed with Raglan in 1854. On the surface, the two expeditionary forces were materially different. Raglan's red-coated, long-service infantrymen were equipped with smoke-belching single-shot weapons, while Sir Redver Buller's khaki-clad reservists carried smokeless repeaters. But there were unsettling similarities between 1854 and 1899. In both wars, the army found itself in the midst of a change in infantry weapons, Raglan's between smooth-bore and rifled musket, and Buller's between two different versions of the Lee magazine rifle. In addition, the army still borrowed heavy guns from the navy, as they had for nearly every war since the Crimea; in South Africa, the field artillery had nothing to counter the range

A 1-pdr quick-firing gun, captured by soldiers of the 1st New South Wales Mounted Rifles. Known as the "pom-pom gun" for its distinctive report when fired, the guns were ironically supplied to the Boers by the English firm of Vickers, Sons and Maxim (Australian War Museum).

of the "Long Toms," as the French 155s were nicknamed.[26] Critically, infantry tactics also remained unchanged; soldiers were still drilled rigorously in line-of-battle tactics, schooled to stand shoulder-to-shoulder, deliver unaimed fire in volleys, and close with the bayonet. Such tactics worked in the numerous colonial wars of the nineteenth century, where small numbers of highly disciplined soldiers regularly won against amateurs armed with inferior weapons. The Boer, unfortunately for many a British infantryman, would not prove to be the same type of foe. Hardy farmers with generations of experience fighting the Zulu and other hostile tribes, they knew the best tactics for the South African landscape. In addition, most were excellent horsemen and marksmen, especially with their new Mauser rifles. Organized along regional lines, the mounted Boer *commandos*, or militia units, could move fast and hit hard. Rather than risk decisive battles, Boer leaders preferred to ride off before their units became hopelessly entangled. When they did choose to defend, Kruger's artillery units proved adept at moving their guns where needed, and the *commando* leaders encouraged their men to dig in rather than stay out in the open. Trench warfare, mounted infantry, mobile artillery, and rapid-fire rifles were not what the British army had trained to fight.

Nor were British— nor its soldiers, politicians, the public—prepared for the debacles that followed Buller's landing at Cape Town on 31 October. The Boer invasions into Natal and Cape Colony bottled up the British units already on the ground; after several sharp actions, the Boers laid siege to the town of Ladysmith, and severed communications to and from the towns of Mafeking and Kimberly. The sieges forced Buller to split his army into three wings, all of which suffered defeat during the "Black Week" of 10–17 December. "In less than a week," historian Byron Farwell wrote, the "famed military might" of England had "gone down to defeat before the rifles of a collection of rustics from a pair of tenth-rate republics" at a cost of over 2,700 dead, wounded, or captured.[27] Among the losses were two batteries of 15-pounder field guns, which Col. C.J. Long stupidly led parade-ground fashion into the teeth of Boer Mausers at Colenso—a major embarrassment in an age when losing artillery still brought considerable shame on a commander. "Since the days of the Indian Mutiny," the *Times* wrote on 16 December, "the nation has not been confronted with so painful and anxious a situation."[28]

The state of the nation's military, however, was much more serious than the public knew. The same day as the disaster at Colenso, Brackenbury brought a "very strong representation in writing" before Wolseley: the nation's stock of "warlike stores" had been seriously depleted with the outfitting of Buller's army. "It had simply never occurred to anyone [at the War Office] that a war might mean more than a one-day event," historian Thomas Pakenham later wrote. Brackenbury painted a dire situation indeed: very few field guns remained in country, for example, and no reserve ammunition stocks existed. Even after borrowing from the Navy and from the Indian Government, Brackenbury could not meet Buller's demand for 5-inch howitzer shells, a situation that foreshadowed the "shell shortage" of World War I. Supplies of saddlery, cavalry sabers, tents and transport vehicles were also dangerously low, as was the nation's reserve of small arms ammunition. Brackenbury estimated that, of a stock of 172 million rounds, 66 million cartridges "or thereabouts" were of the Mark IV type. This cartridge used a hollow-nosed expanding bullet, adopted after experience in the Chitral campaign of 1895 showed that the original round-nosed bullet then used in the Mark II cartridge didn't always stop a determined opponent. The Mark IV, unfortunately, had a tendency to shoot its lead core out of the surrounding nickel jacket under conditions "of great heat and a dirty rifle," leaving a dangerous obstruction in the barrel. This meant that Ordnance had to scramble to find enough trustworthy cartridges, and at one point "we had actually got reduced in this country to two or three boxes of Mark II ammunition." Brackenbury asked that steps be taken and money provided "to enable the country to be put into a condition of safety, so that this could never occur again." Wolseley in turn passed the report to Lord Lansdowne, along with Brackenbury's threat of resignation if the situation did not get corrected.[29]

The unfortunate parallels with the Crimean War continued past Black Week. Additional British forces landed in the Cape Colony in January of 1900, and as they pushed inland logistics became increasingly problematic. Supplies could only be sent up from the coast by a single railway line, and once offloaded, could only be carried by cart at a great cost in animals. Inadequate maps and a lack of entrenching equipment contributed to the "acre of massacre" at Spion Kop on 23 January, which cost the British a further 1,500 casualties and again kept them from forcing the Tugela River. Undeterred, Buller tried again at Vaal Krantz, a ridge of small hills a few miles east of Spion Kop, on 5 February; poor knowledge of local terrain worked against him, as artillery could not be hauled up to the crest of the ridge to engage the Boers. After three days, thirty dead and three hundred more wounded, Buller called off the attempt.[30] Clearly, the tactics and training of the British army were not producing the results Buller needed, despite the incredible bravery and sacrifice of many of his officers and men.

The final tragic reminder of 1854 surfaced in February of 1900 as well: disease, in the form of typhoid fever. Bloemfontein, occupied in March, became the epicenter, and as in the Crimea the army hospital system broke down. William Burdett-Coutts, a Liberal Unionist MP and special correspondent for the *Times*, wrote scathingly on 29 June about the conditions of the sick and wounded in army hospitals, criticizing the rule- and form-obsessed medical officers and especially the lack of female nurses. To him, the example of Florence Nightingale had been completely ignored. "Where are the women?

Where are the nurses? A wretched hundred or two or three are here; while thousands—trained, skilled, willing, eager—are sitting at home wringing their hands!" he wrote. "All this for an antiquated tradition, an unnatural, blind, stupid prejudice of some fusty 'department,' which the War Office ought to have knocked on the head at the outset of the war, with the medical profession and public opinion at its back." Burdett-Coutts's rant could easily have covered the condition of the army—from its hospitals, to its supply, to its armament—throughout the entire theatre of war.

The Reaction to the "Black Week"

Unlike Aberdeen's government half a century before, Salisbury's government did not fall as a result of "Black Week"; he would remain prime minister for the duration of the war. But clearly, something had to change, and that began with the British commander-in-chief in South Africa. After the battle of Colenso, Buller feared that he could not reach Ladysmith in time to prevent its fall, and suggested to Lansdowne that the town might need to be "let go." Although only a temporary bout of pessimism—within a few days, Buller began planning for another attack on Spion Kop—it was enough to get him sacked as overall commander. On 18 December, Lansdowne tapped Field Marshall Sir Frederick Roberts to replace Buller. Roberts, or "Bobs" as he was known to his men, had seen considerable service in India, and had lobbied for command of the operation with his friend Lansdowne for some time.[31] Buller remained in charge of British forces in the Natal, however, and continued to seek a way to break through Gen. Louis Botha's forces on the Tugela.

Lansdowne also convened a new Small Arms Committee in January of 1900 to deal with a major problem discovered on the battlefield: the Lee-Enfield, the nation's newest infantry rifle, had proven to be incorrectly sighted. Reports from the field claimed the weapon consistently shot low and to the right of its aim point; tests showed as much as twenty inches to the right at 200 yards depending on the rifle's place of manufacture. Given the long combat ranges experienced in South Africa, this constituted a dreadful handicap. In addition, the older Lee-Metford rifles still carried by many units were rapidly wearing out. The root causes of the accuracy issues proved not only to be flawed rifle sights, but also flawed accuracy acceptance standards. British inspectors only tested ten percent of newly-made weapons for *consistent* shot grouping at 500 yards, but not *accurate* shooting. All the strikes had to occur within a certain distance of each other, but not necessarily around a specific point on the target. The standards could, and were, changed quickly, especially after a survey showed that several Continental powers tested *all* their rifles for accurate shooting. The problem with the sights, on the other hand, required several months to sort out, and an updated design would not be approved until October.³²

Lansdowne also brought Brackenbury's minute on the deplorable state of British military supplies and equipment before his Cabinet. It immediately did what Victorian governments seemed to do best: appoint a committee, in this case two, to study the issue, which they did with alacrity. One, headed by Sir Robert Grant (late Inspector-General of Fortifications), reported back on 26 February 1900; the other, headed by Sir Francis Mowatt (Permanent Secretary to the Treasury) delivered its findings on 31 March.³³ Both recommended a greatly increased expenditure to rebuild and maintain a "true war reserve" at predetermined levels, "not only of guns and ammunition, but of every conceivable category of war requirements." Although they asked for £11.5 million, in April Parliament approved £10.5 million to be spent over the course of the next three years. The sum also contained monies needed for "alterations in the Ordnance factories and modernisation of existing machinery," as well as storage facilities for war reserves. Parliament's vote for the funds came with an important caveat: yearly certification by the Army Council "that the reserve was intact."³⁴ Here was final recognition that the defense of the realm required longer-term planning than could be done through the annual estimates and the management-by-crisis approach that had plagued every military action since the Napoleonic Wars.

The Mowatt committee also echoed the previous Morley commission's recommendation that private industry be invited to supply the military further than it had. This would allow the trade to meet the sudden expansion in military needs in time of war, which it clearly could not do in 1899. Brackenbury's minute of 15 December, for example, noted that he needed to dispatch to Gen. Buller "about 3 millions weekly" of rifle ammunition, but that "the Ordnance factories and the trade together can only produce about 2½ millions weekly." To get private firms familiar with the production of war *matériel*, Mowatt's committee recommended they be given "a definite proportion of all orders, including the more delicate articles, such as fuzes, not hitherto entrusted to the trade." The ordnance factories "should have as their primary function the creation of a standard of workmanship, and the demonstration of the true cost of production."³⁵ Such a recommendation could not be put into practice immediately, but would guide relations between the Ordnance department and private industry well beyond the end of the war.

"Black Week" also made Wolseley, Buller and others realize that they would need many more men to subdue South Africa, and in particular a mobile fighting force to match the abilities of the mounted Boer *commandos*. Even before war had been declared, several volunteer units had offered their services, but were declined for active duty; some militia units had been called up in November, but only to release regulars for the front. The day after

Colenso, however, Buller cabled home with the suggestion that the War Office "raise eight thousand irregulars ... equipped as mounted infantry, [and] able to shoot as well as possible and ride decently." George Wyndham, an under-secretary at the War Office, saw this as an opportunity to turn the long-established volunteer cavalry, or "yeomanry," into something more than "a theatrical reminder of the Cavalry which fought in the Crimea and the Peninsular" wars. Lansdowne agreed, and on 20 December the *Dundee Courier* announced that Government had "decided to raise for service in South Africa a Mounted Infantry force, to be named 'The Imperial Yeomanry.'"[36] The response was overwhelming; Charles Cavendish (Lord Chesham), appointed a battalion commander in the new force, "was besieged" at his office "by officers eager to join him. When they were not in his room, they waited outside the door ... [or] parleyed with the official at the bottom of the stairs." It was not just officers clamoring to serve, however; the *Courier* noted "enthusiasm throughout the country" as "the militia, yeomanry, and volunteers are readily offering themselves for active service in South Africa and garrison duty at home." Ultimately, over 100,000 men volunteered to fight in the war, and such enthusiasm drew considerable attention to the state of the volunteer movement, its weaponry, and its future role in the defense of the realm.[37]

Change occurred on the ground in South Africa as well as at home. Failed attacks at Spion Kop and Vaal Kratz finally demonstrated to Buller that "the old three-act, one-day battle of the past had been killed stone-dead by the combination of the trench and the magazine rifle." Rather than a single frontal assault on a key piece of terrain, Buller now planned for an extended campaign in both miles and days to clear the Boers hill by hill, in what historian Thomas Pakenham termed "the painful prototype of modern warfare." Buller's infantry had learned the hard way about cover, concealment, and innovation under fire; now came time to unite such knowledge with a new way to use artillery. Long's destruction at the hands of Boer riflemen at Colenso had clearly demonstrated that old-style direct fire tactics were a thing of the past. Between Brackenbury's efforts and loans from the Navy, Buller had now had fifty guns arrayed against the Tugela, and he decided to use this overwhelming advantage to provide a screen for his infantry. The batteries would fire over the heads of the attacking troops, and walk their barrage forward as the men advanced, to keep the heads of the enemy down in their trenches. This new "creeping barrage" form of indirect fire would become a staple of offensive artillery tactics in modern warfare. On 14 February Buller launched his final assault, and his new tactics worked. Over the next two weeks, his army kept up the pressure, driving the Boers back across the Tugela and off the hills that overlooked Ladysmith. Finally, on 27 February, the enemy pulled out altogether; the next day, the first British relief column reached the city. After 118 days, the siege had finally been broken.[38]

At home, Brackenbury did his best to feed, clothe, and equip the rapidly growing army in South Africa. Unable to secure everything he needed from the trade, he had to turn to overseas suppliers for items such as horse shoes, saddles, and even mule shoes, since "nobody in this country at first seemed to be able to make [them]." Brackenbury also had grave concerns about the state of British field ordnance. Not only were the numbers in the reserve dwindling, but the Royal Artillery was being outfought; the Boer field guns firing explosive shell outranged the shrapnel fired by British 15-pounders by 2,000 yards. The Creusot and Krupp pieces were also true quick-firing guns whose hydro-pneumatic recoil mechanisms allowed them to be rapidly reloaded without repositioning. The British gun, on the other hand, relied on a large spade suspended from the carriage axle to reduce recoil, which kept the gun in position, but caused it to jump in place instead of roll backwards. The spade saved the time and effort required to get the gun back into position, which improved the reloading time, but the crew still had to re-aim after each shot.[39]

Rather than design a new gun from scratch, which Brackenbury knew could take years, he took the unprecedented step of purchasing eighteen batteries—108 guns with limbers, support wagons, and 54,000 rounds of ammunition—from the German firm of Rheinische Metallwaaren und Machinenfabrik, in Dusseldorf. Known as the "Ehrhardt" gun, after its designer, Heinrich Ehrhardt, the contract for the weapons had to be made in great secrecy. German public opinion sided very much with the Boers, especially after the Royal Navy boarded three German passenger ships inbound to South African ports in December of 1899 to search for war supplies. There was also international law to consider, so to avoid any breach-of-neutrality issues, the April 1900 contract arranged the deal as if between two private firms: Ehrhardt's, and a shell English "Chartered Company." By December, when the news finally leaked out, the guns were on hand, and a further contract for twelve more batteries had been signed. While Brackenbury retained the new quick-firing guns to augment the reserve stockpile at Woolwich rather than complicate logistics in South Africa, they gave the Royal Artillery a weapon "markedly in advance of that of any Great Power except France." The Ehrhardt guns also gave British ordnance officials important experience with a weapon most artillerymen agreed represented the future, but which until the war "financial considerations ... stood in the way of."[40]

The Ordnance Committee in the Boer War

When Brackenbury took up the post of Director-General of Ordnance, he also assumed overall direction of the Ordnance Committee, whose operations had essentially remained unchanged since its creation in 1881. The war, however, caused several modifications that would ultimately spell the end of the Committee. On 30 April 1900, Brackenbury notified the OC that "the Quarterly Abstracts of the Committee's Proceedings need not be any longer rendered." Instead, indexes for their actual minutes, which had been published since 1881, were to be prepared on a quarterly basis.[41] Since compilation and printing ran two years behind, 1897 represents the last published volume of the *Abstracts of Proceedings*. The delay may be part of the reason for Brackenbury's decision; given the speed of change in military technology, he may have felt that two-year-old compilations did not warrant the staff work involved. He may have also felt that an index to the *Proceedings* would be an effective substitute, while eliminating the work required for compilation. At the same time, however, it appears he also ceased recording proposals not specifically considered by the Committee. The *Proceedings* for 1898 and 1899 show 158 and 107 new items, respectively, and on par with 1896–1897; the 1900 *Proceedings*, however, list only forty-five new entries, and the numbers decrease from there.

The end of the *Abstracts* meant the end of forty years of the often colorful *record* of public participation in military technology, but not the end of *actual* participation. Given the high level of press coverage of the war in South Africa and the public's past history of sending suggestions to the War Office, there is no reason to suppose the habit ended simply because such proposals were no longer listed. Brackenbury himself ordered the Ordnance Committee to begin daily meetings (Sundays excepted) for the duration of the war on 12 February 1900, possibly to handle an expected influx of suggestions passed from the War Office. Past record is no guarantee of present interest, however, and by 1900 the British public had other outlets for its martial spirit, including the volunteers and Imperial Yeomanry. Weaponry had also changed to the point that the average gun enthusiast, civil engineer, or even professional soldier could not thoroughly understand the technology without considerable specialized knowledge. Regardless of the reason, the wave of suggestions that besieged the War Office during the Crimean War seems not to have repeated itself, and Brackenbury rescinded the daily-meeting order on 14 June 1900.[42]

The Ordnance Committee still had plenty to do, however, especially as reports of British weapons performance came back from the field. One of the biggest disappointments proved to be Britain's choice of explosive filler for artillery shells. "Lyddite," named for the town where experiments with the new explosive were performed, had been adopted in 1888; the *Evening Telegraph & Star* claimed on 7 November 1888 that the explosive could "blow humanity into atoms with more expedition than any of its predecessors." A form of picric acid, the explosive had been licensed by Elswick from its French inventor Mons. E. Turpin, who had tried to interest the War Office in his development as early as 1881. Very insensitive to shock, lyddite performed well in the large armor-piercing shells required by the Navy, but not in the smaller explosive shells used by field artillery. One in four fired in South Africa failed to fully detonate; instead, the shells often popped in a cloud of greenish-yellow smoke, which the Boers at first thought poisonous but which soon proved not to be. The most common side effect in such cases was violent coughing, although one young defender at Spion Kop "pitifully complained that the lyddite had turned his hair and skin as yellow as a canary." Captured shells tested in Pretoria led the Boer command to conclude "that the projectiles were about as harmless as those of the early part of the 18th century."[43]

In May of 1900 Lansdowne appointed a "Special Committee on Propellants and High Explosives" to investigate both the problems with lyddite and concerns regarding cordite. Chaired by John W. Strutt (Lord Rayleigh), a noted professor of natural philosophy at the Royal Institution of Great Britain, the two other named members included Sir Andrew Noble, former Royal Artillery officer and now director of Armstrong, Mitchell & Co., and Richard B. Haldane, the future Secretary of State for War. They were joined later by Sir William Crookes and Sir William Roberts-Austen, both noted chemists, and Capt. T. G. Tulloch of the Royal Artillery, the only military member and secretary of the committee. This latest iteration of the Explosives Committee had three charges: to determine the best form of smokeless powder for both artillery and small arms, to report any modifications necessary to either class of weapon to develop "the full powers of any propellant which may be proposed," and to try out other high explosives "with as much safety as lyddite, with greater certainty of detonation, and with greater explosive effect." The *Daily News*, which derisively claimed "the destruction of flies" as lyddite's principal use in South Africa, welcomed the new committee, as did the *Times*. The latter prophetically wrote on 17 October that "even if [it] is barren of results, it will be highly satisfactory to those who either make or use our service explosives to know that we have not been on the wrong track."[44] Ultimately, both cordite and lyddite remained in service with the British military into World War I; the new committee, however, represented the first time that a panel of civilian experts had control over a major weapons program in Britain. The relationship between civilian scientists and the military remained problematic, however, into the opening months of the Great War. Not until 1915—when it was clear that the war in Europe would not end anytime soon—did the War Office form a civilian-led advisory body to guide military research efforts.

The same month that Rayleigh's committee began to meet, British fortunes seemed to improve in South Africa. Roberts's forces broke the siege of Mafeking on 17 May; at the end of the month he captured Johannesburg, and five days later Pretoria. After a summer's hard fighting, the British had annexed both the Transvaal and the Orange Free State, and Roberts returned home to take over as Commander-in-Chief from an ailing Wolseley. Annexation, however, did not mean total control; sizable Boer forces were still at large and fighting when and where they could. Still, Salisbury felt confident enough in both the direction of the war and the patriotic fervor it generated to call for general elections in late September. The result was a landslide victory for Salisbury and his Conservative/Liberal Unionist coalition, the first time since 1865 that a sitting government had been voted back into power.[45]

In November, Salisbury promoted Lansdowne to Foreign Secretary, and appointed Broderick to the War Office, a reward for engineering Salisbury's accession to premiership with the "cordite vote" of 1895. Aware of the problems shown by British artillery in South Africa, Broderick constructed a series of special "gun committees" formed along the lines of General Hay's 1891 suggestion. These technical committees were charged with working out the desired characteristics of a particular type of ordnance; the Ordnance Committee then handled details of construction and ammunition. The first, the "Special Committee on Horse and Field Artillery Equipments," formed in January of 1901 under the chairmanship of Maj. Gen. Sir George Marshall, who had commanded the Royal Artillery units in South Africa. A "Field Howitzer Committee" took the question of that form of gun over from Marshall soon after its appointment; that same year saw the formation of committees on machine guns and 1-pounder "pom-pom" guns, as the 37mm Vickers-Maxim came to be known. The next year the War Office also formed a "Heavy Battery Committee" to design its "guns of position" for coastal and fortification defense.[46]

Similar to the Fletcher small-arms committees of the 1860s, Marshall's "Equipments Committee" drew up a list of specifications, then invited private industry to submit their designs. Armstrong, Vickers, and the Royal Gun Factory (RGF) submitted several, and in 1902 specimen guns were examined and test-fired. In an echo of 1869 and the Martini-Henry rifle, the committee found no single weapon met all their requirements; rather than tweak the design themselves, however, they brought in representatives of the two firms to work with the RGF on a solution. The urgency of the program, coupled by the willingness of the three outfits to work together, meant that by 1903 four test batteries were ready, and in 1904 new quick-firing guns were approved for both horse and field artillery. A vast improvement on the older equipment, the 18-pound field gun could fire twenty rounds a minute, as opposed to three for the older 15-pounder, and with new longer-burning fuzes could deliver its shrapnel three thousand yards further.[47] The speed and success of the program was unprecedented; both gun designs saw wide use in World War I, and variants of the 18-pounder served the Royal Artillery into World War II.

Broderick also wasted little time trying to mop up the muddle that still pervaded the War Office, but in this regard was much less successful. On 17 December 1900, he drafted Clinton E. Dawkins to chair yet another committee to study the organization of the department, but with special emphasis on the financial business conducted by the office. In addition, he drew up a "radical and comprehensive scheme" to reorganize the army into six permanent corps "complete and fully equipped, and in every way ready to take the field ... practically at a moment's notice" according to the 16 March 1901 edition of the *Whitstable Times*. The plan, presented before Parliament the day before, ran into much resistance, and was still under debate when the Dawkins Committee delivered its report on 9 May 1901. It listed nineteen "important recommendations involving large changes" in both the Office and the existing military districts of the country. These included the simplification of regulations and the replacement of many of the civilian clerks with "carefully selected" soldiers or officers. The Committee also repeated the Hartington Commission's calls for greater decentralization and a permanent "War Office Board" to "control and supervise the business of the War Office as a whole." Broderick renamed the older War Office Council as the new War Office Board in October, and gave it and the Army Board power to originate topics, not just consider what the Secretary passed to them. Broderick's army corps plan, which foundered on a perceived need to increase the size—and hence the expense—of the army, overshadowed his attempts to put more of the Dawkins Committee recommendations into action.[48]

While Sir Marshall and his committee wrestled with the issue of field artillery, the war in South Africa ground on, with peace finally being signed on 31 May 1902. Technically, the British won; Kruger's South African Republic became part of the British Empire, and except for a force of about 25,000 men, the "Khakis" began their journey homeward. In truth, the war had cost the Empire much: twenty-two thousand dead, nearly a hundred thousand sick or wounded, at a cost of over £200 million. The latter included three million to pay off the debts of the former South African Republic, and another two in aid to help Boer farmers rebuild.[49] The greatest casualty, however, was the illusion of imperial security; the army that marched in 1899 clearly was not prepared to defend the empire, much less fight successfully in a modern European-style war.

With the peace in place, Salisbury resigned on 11 July due to in part to failing health, but also because of the impending coronation of Edward VII, whom Salisbury did not get along with. The premiership passed to Arthur James Balfour, First Lord of the Treasury and leader of the House of Commons. Serious questions still existed regarding the war, however, and in September Balfour's government formed the "Royal Commission on the War in South Africa" to study its preparations for and conduct in the conflict.

Chaired by Victor Alexander (Lord Elgin), the Commission heard evidence from 114 witnesses over fifty-five days of meetings, and issued their report on 9 July 1903. It clearly documented that the "disastrous muddle" that mired the nation's military efforts in 1854 had yet to be dissolved. Once the report went public, the press pounced; the *Times*, for example, printed a long letter from former Prime Minister Rosebery on 22 September that excoriated the government's policies. "We are not, outside our Fleet, in possession of the *minimum* of national security," Rosebery wrote. "With that report in their hands, foreign statesmen may commit the mistake of holding Great Britain cheap."[50]

The Esher Reports and Haldane Reforms

Fortunately for the country, no "foreign statesmen" made such a mistake, but the report clearly signaled that reforms were needed in the War Office. It also came shortly before a series of Cabinet resignations over tariff reform, and Balfour therefore decided to reshuffle his government in October of 1903. Broderick, tainted by the failure of his own scheme to reorganize the army, was bundled off to the India Office, and both Balfour and the King invited Reginald Baliol Brett (Lord Esher) to take Broderick's place. Esher had been a member of the Elgin Commission and therefore familiar with its findings, but he refused the office. Instead, he felt he could better effect change from the outside, and pitched the idea of yet *another* commission to draw up the needed reforms. As "chairman of such a body," Esher felt he "could take the War Office administration right through, from top to bottom, and ... make it a first-class business machine." Both Balfour and the King agreed, and appointed Esher head of a new "War Office Reconstitution Committee" in late 1903.[51]

The Esher Committee took as its model the Hartington Commission suggestions of 1890. If that previous commission "had not been ignored," the new Committee claimed, "the country would have been saved the loss of many thousands of lives, and of many millions of pounds, subsequently sacrificed in the South African War." Esher and his fellow committee members, Admiral John Fisher and Sir George Clarke, belonged to the "blue water school" of imperial defense, which made the Royal Navy the primary shield of the Empire. The army certainly needed to be an effective tool prepared for war, rather than managed for peace as it had in years past, and modernized along the lines of potential foreign adversaries. It also needed to be efficient, however, especially in its use of funds. "What would be the good of a British army as big as that of Germany," Fisher once asked, "if the navy were insufficient to keep command of the sea?" Among the goals of the Committee, therefore, were not only "the imperative need for harmonizing naval and military policy in the broadest sense," but also the reduction of army estimates from the current £52 million by nearly half. Such a goal was in keeping with the classic British tradition of retrenchment after war, although the Committee did intend to increase the share of defense spending given to the Navy.[52]

The Esher Committee delivered its recommendations in three parts between January and March of 1904, and Balfour acted quickly to put the changes into action. At the top stood a permanent, inter-departmental "Committee of Imperial Defence" which united both naval and army policy and directed both the War Office and Admiralty. In the War Office itself, Balfour finally eliminated the Commander-in-Chief's position; it gave way to a General Staff office, in line with that used by the German Army for overall planning and budget-calculation. Balfour also abolished the post of Inspector-General of Fortifications and reunited "the entire technical work of the Artillery and Engineers" under a recreated Master-General of Ordnance. Under him came a resurrected Director of Artillery, who in turn had full control of the ordnance factories as well as the Ordnance, Explosives, and Small Arms Committees. Such a move finally eliminated the vestigial control the Financial Secretary still had over the manufacturing departments, and made development of infantry weapons a direct responsibility of Ordnance once again.[53]

In the long run, the changes made by Balfour were necessary modernizations, and laid the groundwork for the future of both the army and the War Office. Between Broderick's failed restructure program and the "clean sweep" of the War Office, however, the British army in 1904 suffered extensively from demoralization and dishevelment. "New measures demand new men," the Committee had reasoned, "and we ... attach special importance to the immediate appointment of Military Members ... not likely to be embarrassed by the traditions of a system which is to be radically changed." All of the heads of the military departments, from Roberts to Brackenbury, suddenly found themselves on the retired list, as did many of their subordinates. The memory of the recent war had also receded to the point that fiscal retrenchment threatened to undo all the hardware modernizations proposed by the Marshall Committee. In the annual debate on army estimates before the House of Commons, for example, Bannerman complained vociferously about the cost of not only the army forces that remained in South Africa, but the upgrades to artillery hardware. The new 18-pounder, he argued, "does not involve any charge this year, because all the guns of the new pattern are to be sent to India, and paid for by India. But what will it be in subsequent years? Will there not be a large expenditure on this account?" He continued: "The cost of the whole Army has been allowed so to increase that the burden has become absolutely insufferable. I do not think I should find much disagreement if I said that at the present time the country is sick of war—sick of what I have called a policy of conquest and adventure. This scale of military expenditure cannot be maintained."[54] Such a pronouncement reflected less of a pacifistic streak on the part of Bannerman, but more of a political wish to redirect financial resources.

Bannerman misjudged the mood of the country, however. The British press, although distracted by the Russo-Japanese War, had noticed the delay in the gun modernization program, and on 15 December 1904 the *Times* published "one of those special articles which cannot be ignored." "Our Horse and Field Artillery," the paper wrote, were still equipped with weapons whose design "dated back to somewhere near the period of the Russo-Turkish war" of 1877. "Unless it wishes to risk disasters like that which befell Colonel Long's guns at Colenso," the paper continued, the army needed mobile, quick-firing guns to support the infantry through tactics such as Buller's "creeping barrage." Although the Arsenal stood ready to construct the new 18-pounder, the rearmament program remained unfunded. Had action been taken immediately, the *Times* remarked, "manufacture might have been begun in the spring of this year, and we should be well on our way towards proper artillery equipment." The *Dover Express* echoed the *Times* complaint, in a much shorter but more strident article. The Treasury's "extraordinary action," the paper charged on the 16th, meant the guns of the army remained "absolutely outclassed by the weapons of every other European country." The *Express* cried, "The voice of England must immediately condemn this foolish and wicked policy, for the Artillery is to the Army what the heart is to the body—its very life!" Such accusations were taken seriously enough that the very next day, the War Office released notice of "orders ... about to be issued ... for the expenditure of two and a half millions sterling" to re-equip "the Royal Horse and Royal Field Artillery at home and abroad."[55]

Balfour also misjudged the mood of the country, and resigned on 5 December without dissolving Parliament. He expected the Conservatives to win the election that must necessarily follow, but guessed wrong; instead, the King invited Campbell-Bannerman to construct a minority government, and the Liberals along with their Labour allies made significant gains in the 1906 election. Bannerman, in turn, appointed Richard Haldane as Secretary of State for War, a move that proved well for the British army over the next several years. Both subscribed to the same "blue water" opinion regarding the defense of the Empire, and over the rest of his tenure as head of the War Office, Haldane succeeded where Broderick and his successor H.O. Arnold-Foster could not. Haldane's program of reforms effectively created the Expeditionary Force that Britain would send to France in 1914. Over the next six-and-a-half years, he reduced the size and cost of the standing army and rebuilt

The British illustrated magazine *Punch* criticized the delay in rearming the Royal Artillery with this 1904 cartoon ("Our Gunless Army." *Punch, or the London Charivari*, Vol. CXXVII, July–December 1904, 353).

the nation's pool of reserves by reverting to the original terms of service established by Cardwell so many years before. Haldane also extended the control of the Imperial General Staff to the entire army, and transitioned the yeomanry, volunteers, and militia into a Territorial Army capable of both home defense and reinforcement of any expeditionary force abroad.[56]

The End of the Ordnance Committee

The changes that Haldane put into place included the elimination of the separate committees that oversaw British weapons technology. The Esher

Committee had noted the War Office's habit of assembling committees "whenever any question arises requiring special consideration." It recommended paring down several of the permanent bodies and formation of new ones only in "exceptional" cases, and "never ... as a means of evading responsibility."[57] Although such action reduced the number of committees, it did not break the War Office's penchant for forming them; 1905 saw the creation of a new "Mountain Gun Committee," which made the number of technical committees working with the Ordnance Committee inconvenient. The following year, therefore, the War Office and the Admiralty made their first joint attempt at reworking the entire system of ordnance design. The Explosives Committee became the "Ordnance Research Board," which had the president and vice-president of the Ordnance Committee in those same roles, plus a naval and army officer, also from the OC. The arrangement, however, merely increased the duties of men already heavily involved in ordnance work and soon proved unsatisfactory.

In October of 1907 the Director of Naval Ordnance (DNO), Rear Adm. J. R. Jellicoe, and the Master-General of Ordnance (MGO), Maj. Gen. C. F. Hadden, drew up a plan for a unified "Ordnance Board" to take the place of both the OC and the Research Board. The new body would consist of a naval and military officer, alternately, as President and Vice President. Military members would also include two naval officers and two army officers, and the Director-General of Ordnance for India. It also included the superintendent of the recently formed Research Department at Woolwich, created in April by the combination of several ongoing research bodies at Woolwich. Unlike the OC, civilian members would include a chemist and engineer from the Research Department who "would devote their *whole* time to the work of the Ordnance Board," rather than on an as-needed basis. The new Board also had direct communication with the Admiralty, something that all the previous ordnance committees had lacked. In addition, the Ordnance Board was specifically tasked with research, "with a view to increasing [British] knowledge on all ordnance matters"; design, manufacture and supply issues would hence forth be handled by the DNO or MGO offices. To assist the Master-General with such questions, the five technical committees were swept together into a single "Royal Artillery Committee" composed of the army officer members of the new Board and regimental officers from the Royal Horse, Field, and Garrison Artillery branches.[58] The new Ordnance Board took over the duties of the Ordnance Committee on 1 January 1908, and the Committee's final volume of proceedings closed a fifty-year record of public involvement in British weapons development.

Despite the cost in men and treasure, Royal Artillery historian John E. Headlam pointed out that the Second Boer War began "just when our old guns were wearing out." If the Royal Artillery had re-equipped before the war, it would have done so with a gun "little better in principle than those in the service.... It would not have been a true quick-firer, and it would have been a hard task to persuade any Government to re-arm again before 1914." There is much truth to the statement, and not just for artillery. Combat experience in the South African veld led the Small Arms Committee of 1900 to redesign the Lee-Enfield, and their work produced a shortened, simplified, charger-fed weapon in just two years. French infantry, on the other hand, remained principally armed with a magazine rifle reloaded one cartridge at a time into World War I.[59]

The war also caused British politicians to address the persistent problems in its military administration. The Esher Committee reforms ended "the struggle for supremacy between the civil and military authorities," the root cause of the "disastrous muddle" that had plagued the British army throughout the Victorian era. Haldane's subsequent reforms and the changes made to British weaponry by the various committees involved gave the nation a modernized volunteer army, properly equipped for war in Europe. The Expeditionary Force sent to France in 1914 would be "in every respect ... the best trained, best organized, and best equipped British Army which ever went forth to war"—yet woefully small in comparison to the huge conscript armies fielded by the Continental European powers.[60]

Conclusion
"A Projectile to Be Fired by the Royal Navy"

The sixty years that separate 1854 and 1914 represented a period of incredible change for military forces all over the world. Within the thirteen-year lifespan of the OSC alone, every single weapon that had served European armies in good stead for over a hundred and fifty years had been replaced, with the exception of the lance and sabre. Continued advances saw the constraints on warfare that had existed for centuries—bad weather, slow communications, muscle-powered transportation, and short range of combat—reduced or eliminated. Humanity, to paraphrase a recent Hollywood blockbuster, had prepared itself for a higher form of war.[1]

The tremendous advances in military technology this period ushered in are validated by their longevity. As the flintlock musket had for decades before, many weapons systems pioneered in the Victorian era persist on the modern battlefield. Despite experiments with new propellants and self-consuming ammunition, metallic-cased ammunition with nitrocellulose-based smokeless powder and percussion primers remain the norm for small arms across the world. Bolt-action rifles served admirably through both World Wars, until finally supplanted by automatic weapons in the 1950s. Even then, that rifle continued to serve as a frontline weapon in many armies until the late 20th century, and remains a popular choice for specialized military purposes. The recoil-operated machine gun, invented in 1883 by Hiram Maxim, remains a critical piece of technology. Although Maxim guns have long passed into the hands of collectors and museums, John Browning's 1921 follow-on design is still in service across the globe. The .50-caliber M2HB heavy machine gun, affectionately known as "Ma Deuce" to generations of American servicemen, is the oldest weapon in U.S. service and shows no sign of being retired. Gatling's rotary-barrel design for machine guns is also still in use, although now electrically powered and capable of spitting projectiles out at fearsome rates. The seven-barrel 30mm GAU-8A Avenger cannon forms the primary weapon of the Fairchild Republic A-10 Thunderbolt II ground-attack plane, known popularly as the "Warthog." Quick-loading, fixed-ammunition artillery is also still widely used, albeit with various refinements since its late-nineteenth-century introduction. Boxer's idea of coiling metal for cartridge cases—reinvented and scaled up—remained in use for the U.S. 105mm howitzer as late as Operation Desert Storm. Finally, the principle of the salvo rocket launcher that Hale tried unsuccessfully to interest British ordnance officials in on a number of occasions is still very much a part of modern arsenals today.

There are, of course, a number of mixed-use technologies that proved critical to military success before World War I, such as the railroad, telegraph, and new forms of medicine to name just a few. The year 1914 would also see many more "civilian" technologies harnessed and refined for military use, such as the automobile, telephone, and that most amazing bit of hardware of the age, the airplane. If anything, the military revolution that began in the mid–nineteenth century would be accelerated by the Great War, reignited by World War II, and shows no signs of abating any time soon. Although we seem to have plateaued in some regards—the current U.S. battle rifle, the M4, is a variant of the Armalite M16 introduced nearly fifty years ago—advances in other areas are producing weapons that were the stuff of science fiction only a generation ago.

Unlike the other major powers of the age, however, Britain emerged from the Victorian era with one major warfare constraint still in place: the political will of the nation accepted neither the spending nor the manpower levels required to field an army adequate to fight a major European war. Financial restraints remained an important factor throughout the nineteenth century, and echoed into the twentieth, as British politicians consistently refused to authorize the funds necessary to effectively defend the expanding Empire. Through choice, adroit diplomacy, and occasionally sheer luck, the nation steered clear of any major engagements against capable opponents between 1856 and 1899; when it finally did go to war, the tenacity and ability of Kruger's farmer-soldiers caught the nation by surprise. In the post–Boer War era, however, the desire to reduce taxation gave way to building social welfare programs, such as the 1908 old-age pension plan.[2] To fund such schemes while keeping the budget more-or-less in balance meant that reductions had to come from somewhere. Historically, these came from—and would continue to come from—defense spending. The other half of the political will issue expressed itself in how the army found its manpower. British parties consistently refused to tackle the thorny issue of conscription, which meant the country remained dependent on an all-volunteer army. Well-trained and adequately armed, expandable in times of war through reserves and an active volunteer component, British land forces still remained microscopic compared to the mass-conscription armies of its Continental counterparts. Not until the emergency of the Great War—and the destruction of the British Expeditionary Force (BEF) sent to assist France—did Parliament finally implement a draft.

In many ways, therefore, the military revolution that Britain underwent was incomplete; having constructed "a projectile to be fired by the Royal Navy," the nation found itself materially and mentally unprepared to launch that projectile more than once at any given foe.[3] When the war on the Western Front switched from one of movement to one of position, the BEF—which had successfully fought the Germans to a standstill in its sector—found itself exhausted. The battles of 1914 cost that army dearly: 89,000 trained men and officers who could not be easily replaced. While it rebuilt, British command shored up its lines in France with what units could be scrounged up at home, and both regular and colonial troops brought from overseas. As with the Second Boer War, the nation rediscovered that overreliance on the Royal Arsenal factories meant that industry lacked the ability to produce war supplies. Throttled by overly cautious attention to spending demanded by Parliament, the Ordnance Department could not rapidly ramp up production, repeating the situation of 1854. Private firms lacked both the familiarity with and the machinery required to simply make enough artillery shells, resulting in a critical battlefield shortage in 1915. It would take another year to train and equip an army on the scale needed to effectively fight on the Western Front. Once it did, however, Britain fielded "the largest, most complicated and most comprehensive single organization ever evolved by the ... nation."[4]

Such unpreparedness reached all levels of the country's forces on both land and sea, and included its system of weapons development. Although the "disastrous muddle" that plagued military administration throughout the Victorian era had finally been dissolved, change only occurred at the top levels of the War Office. Ordnance development into the Edwardian era continued to suffer from its own internal disorder, witnessed by the parade of commissions and the mind-numbing redefinitions of the chief ordnance positions. The root causes of these remaining problems were themselves deep, and recognized over the years by both politicians and the British press. An 1871 editorial in the *Quarterly Review*, for example, skewered politicians of the "blue water school" three decades before that term came into common usage. Champions of the Royal Navy as the nation's best means of preventing invasion, the author noted, "encouraged otherwise responsible statesmen to disregard the Army in peacetime, to reduce its establishments, to deprive it of weapons, to ill-treat its officers and neglect its men."[5] Brought about in part by the long shadow cast by Victorian financial principles, such retrenchment and redirection occurred again after the conclusion of the Boer War—and would take place yet again with the end of the Great War.

Regardless of the revolution's completeness, the *Abstracts of Proceedings*—interesting on their own for the great parade of colorful and occasionally eccentric characters—clearly show a public concerned for and trying to improve the defenses of the empire in the late Victorian era. Also clear is that British weapons development attracted considerable talent from within and outside of the Empire. Some of that skill and ingenuity remained accessible for long periods of time; Boxer spent thirty years in the Royal Artillery, much of it improving the nation's ordnance, and Armstrong did not pass on until 1900. And, while Boxer died leaving an estate valued at nearly £40,000, not much of this talent saw reward; most individuals went away from their meeting with the various ordnance committees empty-handed. Even in cases where proposals were adopted, inventors were occasionally ill-used by the War Office or Treasury Department. Jacob Snider, whose action had been selected for converting Pattern 1853 Enfields in 1865, died essentially penniless the next year, leaving it to his widow and eldest son to fight for his promised money.[6]

Much work remains to be done in the socio-technical history of British weapons development. Several collections came to light too late to be included in this study, such as the records of the Director of Naval Ordnance and the Research Department at Woolwich. In addition, MacCleod and Andrews mention the "hundreds of devices and suggestions ... from enthusiastic British inventors" submitted to the Admiralty since the beginning of World War I.[7] Given the history of such individuals over the course of the nineteenth century, this is both not surprising and reason to suspect the same occurred at the War Office. If details of such submissions survived the Battle of Britain, then cataloging them will shine additional light on how inventive the British public really was in this era. Regardless, the *Abstracts* contain a rich source of information on the military revolution in England in the Victorian era, and a very useful starting point for studying the changes the revolution brought about.

Chapter Notes

Preface

1. "The Great Gun Question (From the Times.)," *The Birmingham Daily Gazette*, 03 Sep 1863, 7.
2. John Sweetman, *War and Administration: The Significance of the Crimean War for the British Army* (Edinburgh: Scottish Academic Press, 1984); Roy M. MacLeod and E. Kay Andrews, "Scientific Advice in the War at Sea 1915–1917: The Board of Invention and Research," *Journal of Contemporary History* 6, no. 2 (1971): 3–40; Michael Pattison, "Scientists, Inventors and the Military in Britain, 1915–19: The Munitions Inventions Department," *Social Studies of Science* 13, no. 4 (1983): 521–68; Guy Hartcup, *The War of Invention: Scientific Developments, 1914–18* (London: Brassey's Defence Publishers, 1988).
3. I regret to say that both passed away in 2018.

Introduction

1. Orlando Figes, *The Crimean War: A History* (New York: Metropolitan Books, 2010), 147; Oliver MacDonagh, "The Nineteenth-Century Revolution in Government: A Reappraisal," *The Historical Journal* 1, No. 1 (1958), 52–67; Hampden Gordon, *The War Office* (London: Putnam, 1935), 81.
2. Michael Roberts, "The Military Revolution, 1560–1660" and Geoffrey Parker, "The 'Military Revolution, 1560–1660'—A Myth?" in *The Military Revolution Debate: Readings on the Military Transformation of Early Modern Europe*, ed. Clifford J. Rogers (Boulder, CO: Westview Press, 1995), 20, 37; James J. Farley, *Making Arms in the Machine Age: Philadelphia's Frankford Arsenal, 1816–1870* (University Park, PA: Pennsylvania State University Press, 1994), xii; William P. Tatum, "Challenging the New Military History: The Case of Eighteenth-Century British Army Studies," *History Compass* 5, no. 1 (2007): 72–84; John Whiteclay Chambers, "Conference Review Essay: The New Military History: Myth and Reality," *The Journal of Military History* 55, no. 3 (1991): 395–406; Clifford J. Rogers, "The Military Revolution in History" in *The Military Revolution Debate*, 3.
3. Geoffrey Parker, "In Defense of the Military Revolution" in *The Military Revolution Debate*, 337, and *The Military Revolution: Military Innovation and the Rise of the West, 1500–1800* (Cambridge: Cambridge University Press, 1996); Jeremy Black, *A Military Revolution? Military Change and European Society: 1550–1800* (Hampshire: Macmillan, 1991), ix—96.
4. Examples include, in chronological order: William Hardy McNeill, *The Pursuit of Power: Technology, Armed Force, and Society since A.D. 1000* (Chicago: University of Chicago Press, 1982); Jeremy Black, *War and the World: Military Power and the Fate of Continents, 1450–2000* (New Haven, CT: Yale University Press, 1998); Wawro, *Warfare and Society in Europe, 1792–1914*; MacGregor Knox and Williamson Murray, *The Dynamics of Military Revolution, 1300–2050* (Cambridge: Cambridge University Press, 2001); Max Boot, *War Made New: Weapons, Warriors, and the Making of the Modern World* (New York: Gotham Books, 2006); Antulio Joseph Echevarria, *Imagining Future War: The West's Technological Revo-*

lution and Visions of Wars to Come, 1880–1914 (Westport, CT: Praeger, 2007).

5. David Avrom Bell, *The First Total War: Napoleon's Europe and the Birth of Warfare as We Know It* (Boston: Houghton Mifflin, 2007), 7.

6. Dupuy, 156–167; Figes, 178–181; Hew Strachan, *Wellington's Legacy: The Reform of the British Army, 1830–54* (Manchester: Manchester University Press, 1984), 262–270.

7. In addition to *Wellington's Legacy*, see also "The Early Victorian Army and the Nineteenth-Century Revolution in Government" in *The English Historical Review* 95, no. 377 (1980), 782–809 and *From Waterloo to Balaclava: Tactics, Technology, and the British Army, 1815–1854* (Cambridge: Cambridge University Press, 1985).

8. Correlli Barnett, *Britain and Her Army, 1509–1970: a Military, Political, and Social Survey* (New York: W. Morrow, 1970), 272–273, 346. John Sweetman has also argued the same position in *War and Administration*.

9. Hans Speier, "Historical Development of Public Opinion," *American Journal of Sociology* 55, no. 4 (1950): 376.

10. Barnett, 260.

11. Owen Wheeler, *The War Office, Past and Present* (London: Methuen & Co., 1914); Gordon, endflap; Sweetman, 59–76; Hogg, *The Royal Arsenal*, 670.

12. Examples include Gwyn Harries-Jenkins, *The Army in Victorian Society* (London; University of Toronto Press, 1977); Edward M. Spiers, *The Army and Society, 1815–1914* (London: Longman, 1980) and *The Late Victorian Army, 1868–1902* (Manchester: Manchester University Press, 1992); Byron Farwell, *Mr. Kipling's Army* (New York: W.W. Norton & Company, 1981).

13. Two examples are Howard Bailes, "Technology and Imperialism: A Case Study of the Victorian Army in Africa," *Victorian Studies* 24, no. 1 (1980): 83–104; and Ian F. W. Beckett, "Victorians at War—War, Technology and Change," *Journal of the Society for Army Historical Research* 81, no. 328 (2003): 330–38. David Headrick has devoted much work to technology and imperialism; see "The Tools of Imperialism: Technology and the Expansion of European Colonial Empires in the Nineteenth Century," *The Journal of Modern History* 51, no. 2 (1979): 231–63; *The Tools of Empire: Technology and European Imperialism in the Nineteenth Century* (New York: Oxford University Press, 1981) and *The Tentacles of Progress: Technology Transfer in the Age of Imperialism, 1850–1940* (New York: Oxford University Press, 1988).

14. Melvin Kranzberg and Carroll W. Pursell, "The Importance of Technology in Human Affairs" in *Technology in Western Civilization*, edited by Kranzberg and Pursell (New York: Oxford University Press, 1967), 3–11.

15. Merritt Roe Smith, *Harpers Ferry Armory and the New Technology: The Challenge of Change* (Ithaca, NY: Cornell University Press, 1977); John Ellis, *The Social History of the Machine Gun* (London: Purnell Book Services, 1975); Dennis E. Showalter, *Railroads and Rifles: Soldiers, Technology, and the Unification of Germany* (Hamden, CT: Archon Books, 1975). Barton C. Hacker wrote a very useful survey regarding military technology history, see "Military Technology and World History: A Reconnaissance," *The History Teacher* 30, no. 4 (1997): 461–87.

16. The term is borrowed from Günter Ropohl's article, "Philosophy of Socio-Technical Systems," *Society for Philosophy and Technology*, Vol. 4 no. 3, Spring 1999, http://scholar.lib.vt.edu/ejournals/SPT/v4_n3html/ROPOHL.html. Ropohl identifies a *socio-technical system* as a "concept ... established to stress the reciprocal interrelationship between humans and machines and to foster the program of shaping both the technical and the social conditions of work, in such a way that efficiency and humanity would not contradict each other any longer."

17. Marshall J. Bastable, "From Breechloaders to Monster Guns: Sir William Armstrong and the Invention of Modern Artillery, 1854–1880," *Technology and Culture* 33, no. 2 (1992): 215. How militaries handle technological change has been the subject of numerous academic studies, but for the most part such studies concentrate on 20th-century weapons, especially post–World War II. For a summary of the field, see Adam Grissom, "The Future of Military Innovation Studies," *Journal of Strategic Studies* 29, no. 5 (2006): 905–34. For a broader historical scope, see Jeremy Black, "Military Organisations and Military Change in Historical Perspective," *The Journal of Military History* 62, no. 4 (1998): 871–92.

Theo Farrell explored a number of factors that influence military innovation that, while again based on recent history, can be used to build a model for Victorian Britain; see "The Dynamics of British Military Transformation," *International Affairs* 84, no. 4 (2008): 777–807.

18. Marshall J. Bastable, *Arms and the State: Sir William Armstrong and the Remaking of British Naval Power, 1854–1914* (Aldershot, Hants, UK: Ashgate, 2004), 5; Geoffrey Best, "The Militarization of European Society, 1870–1914" in *The Militarization of the Western World*, edited by John R. Gillis (New Brunswick, CT: Rutgers University Press, 1989), 13–19.

19. David Edgerton, *Warfare State: Britain, 1920–1970* (Cambridge: Cambridge University Press, 2006), 1.

20. Stephen Van Dulken, *British Patents of Invention, 1617–1977: A Guide for Researchers* (London: The British Library, 1999), 3–4.

21. James H. Lewis, "The Development of the Royal Small Arms Factory (Enfield Lock) and Its Influence upon Mass Production Technology and Product Design C. 1820–C. 1880" (PhD, Middlesex University, 1996), 66; David O. Pam, *The Royal Small Arms Factory, Enfield and Its Workers* (Enfield: D. Pam, 1998). BSA later diversified very successfully into motorcycle manufacture, and most of its chroniclers concentrate on this aspect of the company rather than on its small arms history. See Donovan M. Ward, *The Other Battle: Being a History of the Birmingham Small Arms Co. Ltd.* (York: B. Johnson, 1946) and Owen Wright, *BSA: The Complete Story* (Ramsbury, Marlborough, Wiltshire, UK: Crowood Press, 1992).

22. Tim Putnam and Daniel Weinbren, "The Royal Small Arms Factory and Industrial Enfield, 1855–1914," *London Journal* 21, no. 1 (1996): 46–63.

23. Ron Arnold, "How the EPA's empire-building got in the way of its science," *Washington Examiner*, 01 Jul 2014, http://washingtonexaminer.com/how-the-epas-empire-building-got-in-the-way-of-its-science/article/2550395.

24. Hogg, *The Royal Arsenal*, 1289–1292.

25. "Report of the Board for Selecting a Breech-System for the Muskets and Carbines of the Military Service," in *Ordnance Memoranda No. 15* (Washington: Ordnance Department, United States Army, 1873), 7–8. In fairness, other major European countries held the same attitudes towards weapons development as the British, the exception being Russia. Recognizing that his country lacked the technical expertise to produce its own rifles, the Tsar turned to Colt in the U.S. for assistance. Russian arsenal officials worked closely with Col. Hiram Berdan in the design of its new small-bore breech-loader, and ordered the first 30,000 from the Colt factory. It also placed orders with BSA, but the Russian inspector at that factory reported a "shocking percentage of defects in the parts" made there because of a lingering reliance on manual finishing. See Joseph Bradley, *Guns for the Tsar: American Technology and the Small Arms Industry in Nineteenth-Century Russia* (DeKalb, IL: Northern Illinois University Press, 1990), 154–155, and George A. Hoyem, *The History and Development of Small Arms Ammunition, Vol. 2: Centerfire: Primitive, and Martial Long Arms* (Tacoma: Armory Publications, 1982), 190.

26. Geoffrey Wawro, *The Franco-Prussian War: The German Conquest of France in 1870–1871* (Cambridge: Cambridge University Press, 2005), 58.

27. Sir Charles Petrie, "An Eccentric at the Horse Guards: 'The Royal George 1819–1904,' by Giles St. Aubyn," *Illustrated London News*, 09 Nov 1963, 769.

28. HCPP, "Report of the War Office (Reconstitution) Committee, Part I," 1904 (Cd. 1932), 3.

29. H.C.G. Matthew, "Disraeli, Gladstone, and the Politics of Mid-Victorian Budgets," *Historical Journal* 22, no. 3 (1979): 615–44; Ian St. John. *Gladstone and the Logic of Victorian Politics* (London: Anthem Press, 2010), 100–102. See also Angus B. Hawkins, "A Forgotten Crisis: Gladstone and the Politics of Finance during the 1850s," *Victorian Studies* 26 (Spring 1983): 287–321; Graham Goodlad, "From Peelite Technocrat to People's William," *Modern History Review* 16, no. 1 (2004): 17–20.

30. TNA, SUPP 6/4: "Abstracts of Proceedings and Reports of the Ordnance Select Committee for the year 1862" (hereafter referred to by year only), 343; Best, 14; Boot, 167.

31. Barnett, 330–340; 346; 359–367; Spiers 1980, 284.

32. Barnett, 373.

"Pregnant with Disastrous Muddle"

1. Barnett, 166. This practice continued with the "Army Discipline and Regulation Act" which replaced the Mutiny Act in 1879; see HCPP, "A Bill to Bring into Force the Army Discipline and Regulation Act, 1879, and for Other Purposes"; 1878 (248).
2. Barnett, 238, 260.
3. HCPP, "Abstract of return of the number of parliamentary electors in Great Britain and Ireland, according to the registrations of 1848 and 1849, and 1849 and 1850," 1850 (345); John A. Phillips and Charles Wetherell, "The Great Reform Act of 1832 and the Political Modernization of England," *The American Historical Review* 100, no. 2 (1995): 411–36.
4. "The Opening of the Session," *Blackwood's Edinburgh Magazine* Vol. 65 (1849, 357–82), 361.
5. Gordon, 40–50; Barnett, 19, 282; A. Forbes, *A History of the Army Ordnance Services* (London: Medici Society, 1929), 259; Strachan, *Wellington's Legacy*, 9.
6. Gordon 40–46; Barnett, 239. It is important to note the difference between titles of "Secretary of State for War" and "Secretary-at-War." The former were cabinet members and formed the highest rank of political office in Britain, short of the Prime Minister. Secretaries, such as the Secretary-at-War, ranked below Secretaries of State but were not necessarily subordinate to them. Answering directly to Parliament, the Secretary-at-War before Crimea "stood and acted still more than before as a *de facto* Secretary of State" (Gordon, 40).
7. Gordon, 40–42, 50; Forbes, 259; Barnett, 238–239.
8. Gordon, 50; E.L. Woodward, *The Age of Reform: 1815–1870* (Oxford: Clarendon Press, 1962), 269; Strachan, *Wellington's Legacy*, 9. Curiously, expedition commanders in the field lacked of any clear chain of communication and responsibility back to London; between the War of 1812 and the Crimean War, the issue never came up.
9. Hogg, *The Royal Arsenal*, 27; Strachan, *Wellington's Legacy*, 232; Forbes Vol. I, 190; TNA, SUPP 6/7: 1865, 388; "A Village Encamped," *Bath Chronicle and Weekly Gazette*, 28 Aug. 1849, 2; George Raudzens, *The British Ordnance Department and Canada's Canals, 1815–1855* (Waterloo, Ont.: Wilfrid Laurier University Press, 1979), 16.
10. Hogg, *The Royal Arsenal*, 1036–1038; Norman Skentelbery, *Arrows to Atom Bombs: A History of the Ordnance Board* (London: Norman Skentelbery, 1975), 12.
11. Skentelbery, 13–17; Hogg, *The Royal Arsenal*, 1046–1051; Raudzens, 13.
12. TNA, WO 47/2354, "Board of Ordnance Minutes, March 1853," Minute No. C/3611, 5 Mar 1853. Strachan noted that in 1848, over 32,000 items came to the Board for decisions (Strachan, *Wellington's Legacy*, 235).
13. Hogg, *The Royal Arsenal*, 177–185, 222; Lt. G. E. Grover, RE, FSA, "Historical Notes on the Royal Arsenal at Woolwich" in *Minutes of proceedings of the Royal Artillery Institute* VI (1870: 231–47), 246; *Survey of London* Vol. 48: Woolwich, ed. Peter Guillery (New Haven, CT: Yale University Press, 2012), 350.
14. *Survey of London*, 164; Hogg, *The Royal Arsenal*, 246–247, 492, 664, 675, 507–509, 521.
15. Whitworth Porter, *History of the Corps of Royal Engineers* Vol. 2 (London: Longmans, Green, 1889), 182.
16. Purchase had been allowed of two officer ranks at the company level (Adjutant and Quartermaster) until 1783; see Capt. Francis Duncan, *History of the Royal Regiment of Artillery*, Vol. II (London: J. Murray, 1873), 25.
17. Pam, 15–29; Lewis, 12. The Crown purchased a former armor plate mill at Lewisham in 1805 to manufacture musket barrels. Despite the installation of steam power in 1807, that factory proved unsatisfactory, leading to its relocation to Enfield Lock.
18. De Witt Bailey, and Douglas A. Nie, *English Gunmakers: The Birmingham and Provincial Gun Trade in the 18th and 19th Century* (London: Arms and Armour Press, 1978), 17; "Gun Trades," Birmingham Gun Museum, 2010–2012, http://www.birminghamgunmuseum.com/Gun_Trades.php. Few of these workers were organized into formal companies; of the 113 entries under "gun makers" in the 1850 Birmingham postal directory, less than twenty were entries identifiable as non-individuals. Of those, T. & S. Phillips is listed as gun maker "to the Board of Ordnance" and J. Scott & Co. as

"military." See *Post Office Directory of Birmingham, Staffordshire & Worcestershire, 1850* (London: W. Kelly & Co., 1850), 610–611.

19. "State of Trade. Birmingham, March 6," *Morning Post*, 08 Mar 1852, 8.

20. HCPP, "Report of the Committee Appointed to Inquire into the Organization and Administration of the Manufacturing Departments of the Army," 1837 (C.5116), xiv–xv; *Supplement to the Synopsis of Reports and Experiments of the Ordnance Select Committee: Shrapnel Shells* (London, for HM Stationery Office, 1858), 6; "Art. X: Report of the Commissioners Appointed to Inquire into the Practicability and Expediency of Consolidating the Different Departments Connected with the Administration of the Army, 1837," *The Monthly Review. II: from May to August Inclusive* (1838), 269.

21. HCPP, "Report of Commissioners on Promotion in the Army," 1854 (1802), 18; Charles J. B. Riddell, *Remarks on the Organization of the British Royal Artillery* (London: W. Clowes & Sons, 1852), 31–32; Hogg, *The Royal Arsenal*, 1433.

22. James Nasmyth and Samuel Smiles, *James Nasmyth Engineer; an Autobiography* (London: J. Murray, 1883), 317–319; Hogg, *The Royal Arsenal*, 671, 681, 703.

23. *Survey of London*, 164; John Grant, *A Guide to Woolwich* (Woolwich, 1841), 3; Harries-Jenkins, 5; Spiers, *The Army and Society*, 76–81, 92; Scott Hughes Myerly, "'The Eye Must Entrap the Mind': Army Spectacle and Paradigm in Nineteenth-Century Britain," *Journal of Social History* 26, no. 1 (1992): 105–31; 108–109, 114.

24. *Survey of London*, 155, 353–355; Hogg, 637–639.

25. "Appalling Accident at the Royal Arsenal, Woolwich," *York Herald*, 20 Sep 1845, 7.

26. "RLL" to the Master General of Ordnance, 13 Nov 1841, TNA, WO 44/620, File 15. The inventor declined to give his name, stating that it would "add no weight to a recommendation" of his plan.

27. "Obituary: Captain Warner," *The Gentleman's Magazine and Historical Review*, May 1854, 549–51.

28. "The Long Range," *The Examiner*, 03 Aug 1844, 1; HCPP, "Mr. Warner's Invention," 1847 (302); TNA, WO 44/627, File 397.

29. TNA, WO 44/620, File 1; TNA, SUPP 6/1, "Correspondence respecting the reorganisation of the Ordnance Select Committee," 5–7.

30. TNA, SUPP 6/1, "Correspondence," 5–6; TNA, WO 44/620, File 15.

31. TNA, SUPP 6/1, "Correspondence," 6–7.

32. TNA, WO 44/621, File 81.

33. John Norton, *A List of Captain Norton's Projectiles, and His Other Naval and Military Inventions: With Original Correspondence* (Gravesend: Caddel, 1860), 11–12.

34. "To the Editor of the Standard," *Standard*, 21 Jun. 1843, 3; "Concussion Shells," *Standard*, 12 Jul. 1843, 1.

35. "The Norton Shell," *Berkshire Chronicle*, 27 Apr. 1844, 4.

36. J. Southby, "Correspondence: New Rocket Signals," *The United Service Journal and Naval and Military Magazine*, Part 1 (1832): 390–91; TNA, WO 44/628, File 411.

37. "Electric Gun," *Littell's Living Age* Vol. 6 (1845): 168; "Mr. Beningfield's 'Electric Gun,'" *The Mechanics' Magazine, Museum, Register, Journal, and Gazette* Vol. XLIII, 5 July–27 Dec. (1845): 16.; "The Electric Gun," *Kentish Gazette*, 13 Jan. 1846, 1; TNA, WO 44/620, File 41.

38. TNA, WO 32/7126, "Copies of Minutes relating to the appointment of the Ordnance Committee 1880," 7; HC Deb 27 Jul 1855 vol 139 cc1458–9; TNA, SUPP 6/1, "Correspondence," 6. These counts are based on a survey of existing proposal files in WO 44/620 through WO 44/636. Files related to Armstrong's gun, Hale rocket and Minié rifle are not present in the collection, and later OSC records acknowledge others to be missing; the actual number of proposals, therefore, may be considerably higher.

39. Sir John Adye, *Recollections of a Military Life* (New York: Macmillan and Co., 1895), 290.

40. TNA, SUPP 6/1, "Correspondence," 22–23; William Greener, "The Invention of the Minie Rifle," *Newcastle Journal*, 27 Dec 1856, 6.

41. Hogg, *The Royal Arsenal*, 1433; "Deaths," *The New Annual Register* (1832): 70.

42. Southby, op. cit.

43. Sinclair, 243–244.

44. Spiers, *The Army and Society*, 91.

45. Strachan, *Wellington's Legacy*, 234; K. Theodore Hoppen, *The Mid-Victorian Generation, 1846–1886* (Oxford: Oxford University Press, 1998), 175; H.W.L. Hime, *History*

of the Royal Regiment of Artillery, 1815–1853 (London: Longmans, Green, and Co., 1908), 17; Barnett, 278–279; Brian Farwell, *Queen Victoria's Little Wars* (New York: Norton, 1985), 1; Peter Hopkirk, *The Great Game: The Struggle for Empire in Central Asia* (New York: Kodansha International, 1992), 1–8.

46. "Army Estimates," *Bradford Observer*, 17 Aug. 1837, 6; HC Deb 05 Apr 1837 vol 37 cc778–95.

47. "Trophies in the Tower," *Leicestershire Mercury*, 04 Dec. 1841, 4. The original article could not be located.

48. David Nicholls, "The Manchester Peace Conference of 1853," http://www.hssr.mmu.ac.uk/mcrh/files/2013/01/mrhr_05i_nicholls.pdf, 13–14.

49. "An Absurdity," *Westmorland Gazette*, 04 Feb 1854, 3.

50. HCPP, "Second Report from the Select Committee on the Public Income and Expenditure of the United Kingdom. Ordnance Estimates," 1828 (420), 10–12; Skentelbery, 16–17.

51. HCPP, "Report of the Commissioners Appointed to Inquire into the Practicability and Expediency of Consolidating the Different Departments Connected with the Civil Administration of the Army"; 1837 (78), Appendix B.

52. "Art. X," *The Monthly Review*, 267–269.

53. HCPP, 1837 (78), 8–11; HC Deb 17 Jul 1854 vol 135 cc317–42; Gordon, 45; Hoppen, 175.

"The War Will Not Last a Month"

1. Andrew D. Lambert, *The Crimean War: British Grand Strategy, 1853–56* (Manchester: Manchester University Press, 1990), 22; "Russia & Turkey—Peace or War," *Newcastle Guardian and Tyne Mercury*, 15 Oct 1853, 5.

2. "The Massacre at Sinope—Destruction of the British Vessel Howard," *Lloyd's Weekly Newspaper*, 08 Jan 1854, 7; "The Massacre at Sinope Investigated," *Stirling Observer*, 05 Jan 1854, 4.

3. Lawrence Sondhaus, *Naval Warfare, 1815–1914* (London: Routledge, 2012), 22–23; James Phinney Baxter, *The Introduction of the Ironclad Warship* (Hamden, CT: Archon Books, 1968), 18–25; Jeff Kinard, *Artillery: An Illustrated History of Its Impact* (Santa Barbara, Calif.: ABC-CLIO, 2007), 235–236; Walter Millis, *Arms and Men: A Study in American Military History* (New York: Putnam, 1956), 88–89.

4. Baxter, 69; Wawro, *Warfare and Society*, 53–54; Royle 93–94. The first actual use of shell-against-ship came in an obscure engagement between the Texian and Mexican navies during the latter's blockade of Campeche in 1843. On 30 April, the Mexican *Guadalupe*—an ironclad side-wheel steamship rejected for service in the Royal Navy—fired several *Paixhans* shells at the Texian 24-gun wooden-hulled sloop *Austin*. Fortunately for the Texians, only one shell hit the *Austin*, and caused only minor damage. See Mark N. Lardas, "For Your Information: The First Iron Warship," *Strategy & Tactics*, Jul-Aug. 2016, 68–71.

5. Figes, 142–143.

6. Baxter, 36–39.

7. Royle, 112–119.

8. Royle, 115, 127; "Bombardment of Odessa (from the Times)," *Dublin Evening Mail*, 12 May 1854, 2.

9. *Dublin Evening Mail*, op. cit.; "Iron-Clad Ships of War," *Blackwood's Edinburgh Magazine*. American Edition, Vol. LI, Jul-Dec (1860), 618.

10. Howard Douglas, *A Treatise on Naval Gunnery* (London: John Murray, 1860), 310; Frederick Myatt, *British Sieges of the Peninsular War* (Staplehurst, Kent: Spellmount, 1995), 20; William Laird Clowes, *The Royal Navy: A History from the Earliest Times to the Present* Vol. VI (London: S. Low, Marston and Co., 1901), 400–401. Douglas considered the use of hot shot aboard ships "exceptional" because of the risks. "There is already so much danger of fire in all ships" by incendiary devices, he wrote, "that it were better not to add another element to those perils."

11. *Dublin Evening Mail*, op. cit.

12. Clowes, *ibid.*; "Iron-Clad Ships of War," 617.

13. Blackmore, 44–45.

14. J. N. George, *English Guns and Rifles: Being an Account of the Development, Design, and Range of English Sporting Rifles and Shotguns* (Plantersville, SC: Small-Arms Technical Publishing Company, 1947), 247–249.

15. George, 258–259; Oliver F. G. Hogg,

Artillery: Its Origin, Heyday, and Decline (Hamden, CT: Archon Books, 1970), 202.

16. Col. Frances Macerone, "Rifle Cartridges, with Observations on Rifle Practice," *Colburn's United Service Magazine, and Naval and Military Journal*, 1831 Part 2 (1832): 513–21; George, 301.

17. Harding, Vol. III, 274.

18. Hoyem, Vol. 1, 31; Wawro, *Warfare and Society*, 83; Arthur B. Hawes, *Rifle Ammunition; Being Notes on the Manufactures Connected Therewith, as Conducted in the Royal Arsenal, Woolwich* (London: W.O. Mitchell, 1859), 2.

19. John Walter, *The Rifle Story: An Illustrated History from 1756 to the Present Day* (London: Greenhill Books, 2006), 48.

20. Strachan, *From Waterloo to Balaclava*, 38–40; Wawro, *Warfare and Society*, 83.

21. Charles J. Napier, *A Letter on the Defence of England by Corps of Volunteers and Militia* (London: Edward Moxon, 1852), 11, 24; William Cooke Stafford, *History of the Volunteer Movement, 1858–1863, and of the War with Russia, 1854–1856* (London: The London Printing and Publishing Co. Ltd., 1865), xx.

22. Sir Herbert Maxwell, *The Life of Wellington* Vol. II (Boston: Little, Brown and Co., 1899), 136; G. R. and Mary E. Gleig, *Personal Reminiscences of the First Duke of Wellington* (New York: Scribner, 1904), 308; Strachan, *From Waterloo to Balaclava*, 41; Peter Smithurst, "The Pattern 1853 Rifled Musket—Genesis," *Arms & Armour* 4, No. 2 (2007), 127.

23. Strachan, *From Waterloo to Balaclava*, 40–41.

24. Blackmore, 231–232; Smithurst, 140; Strachan, *From Waterloo to Balaclava*, 40–46.

25. Strachan, *From Waterloo to Balaclava*, 50–53.

26. Royle, 181; Strachan, *From Waterloo to Balaclava*, 40.

27. Royle, 220–227.

28. Figes, 235–236.

29. Somerset John Gough Calthorpe, *Letters from Head-Quarters; or, the Realities of the War in the Crimea, by an Officer on the Staff*, Vol. II (London: J. Murray, 1858), 445–449.

30. Figes, 235–236; Douglas, 581; Royle, 264.

31. Adye, 284; Alexander William Kinglake, *The Invasion of the Crimea* Vol. III (London: W. Blackwood and Sons, 1868), 313, 295–296.

32. Strachan, *From Waterloo to Balaclava*, 129; Porter, 427; Kinglake, 307–308.; Lambert and Badsey, 95–99.

33. Figes, 238; Lambert and Badsey, 96; Kinglake, 350–352.

34. Calthorpe, Vol. II, 111; Joseph J. Mathews, *Reporting the Wars* (Minneapolis: University of Minnesota Press, 1957), 64; "Siege of Sebastopol (from the Morning Herald)," *Standard*, 07 Nov 1854, 4.

35. "Iron-Clad Ships of War," *Blackwood's Edinburgh Magazine*. American Edition, Vol. LI, Jul-Dec (1860), 618; Figes, 239–240.

36. Hogg 1970, 186.

37. Hogg, *The Royal Arsenal*, 1400–1401, 187; Hime, 243.

38. Col. Julian R. J. Jocelyn, *The History of the Royal Artillery (Crimean Period)* (London: J. Murray, 1911), 70–71.

39. W. R. Barlow, *Treatise on Ammunition* (London: H.M.S.O., 1874), 37; A. F. Lendy, *Treatise on Fortification, or, Lectures Delivered to Officers Reading for the Staff* (London: W. Mitchell, 1862), 16.

40. *A Visit to Sebastopol a Week after Its Fall* (London: Smith, Elder and Co., 1856), 43

41. Antony Preston and John Major, *Send a Gunboat: The Victorian Navy and Supremacy at Sea, 1854–1904* (London: Conway, 2007), 20.

42. Figes, 240; Lambert and Badsey, 98; Calthorpe, Vol. II, 446–447.

43. Anthony L. Dawson, Paul L. Dawson, and Stephen Summerfield, *Napoleonic Artillery* (Ramsbury UK, Crowood, 2007), 248.

44. Gen. Cavalié Mercer, *Journal of the Waterloo Campaign Kept Throughout the Campaign of 1815* (New York: Da Capo Press, 1995), 164; Dawson et al., 247–249.

45. Hogg 1970, 179–180; Sinclair, 244.

46. "How Shrapnel Is Made and Used: Colonel Shrapnel of the British Army Invented This Hail of Death, So Important in the Present War—First Used in 1804," *New York Times*, May 30, 1915.

47. H.W.L. Hime, *Gunpowder and Ammunition, Their Origin and Progress* (London: Longmans, Green, 1904), 242–243; Charles Henry Owen, *The Principles and Practice of Modern Artillery*, Second ed. (London: J.

Murray, 1873) 123–125; A. Marshall, "The Invention and Development of the Shrapnel Shell," *The Field Artillery Journal* Vol. X (1920), 12–16; Strachan, *From Waterloo to Balaclava*, 117; Hogg, *The Royal Arsenal*, 1400–01.

48. HCPP, "Report from the Select Committee on Ordnance," 1863 (487), 104; TNA, SUPP 6/1: 1858, 133; W. Edmund M. Reilly, *An Account of the Artillery Operations Conducted by the Royal Artillery and Royal Naval Brigade before Sebastopol in 1854 and 1855* (London: HMSO, 1859), 208–221; Nick Lipscombe, "Shrapnel's Shell—a Force Multiplier," in *'...a damned nice thing ... the nearest run thing you ever saw in your life...': A Peninsular and Waterloo Anthology*, edited by Andrew Cormack (London: Society for Army Historical Research, 2015), 133–50.

"More Powerful Than the Charge of Cavalry"

1. Barnett, 260; William Howard Russell et al. *The Crimean War: As Seen by Those Who Reported It* (Baton Rouge: Louisiana State University Press, 2009), 101.
2. Figes, 302–303, 354–355.
3. Kingsley Martin, *The Triumph of Lord Palmerston* (New York: Dial Press, 1924), 185.
4. Royle, 113, 135–137; Hogg, *The Royal Arsenal*, 743; Forbes, 260–261.
5. HCPP, "Fifth Report from the Select Committee on the Army before Sebastopol," 1855 (318), 5; HC Deb 17 Jul 1854 vol 135 cc317–42.
6. HCPP, 1855 (318), 5.
7. E. M. Boxer, *Colonel Boxer and the War Department* (London: P.S. King, 1870), 40–41; HCPP, "Fourth Report from the Select Committee on the Army Before Sebastopol," 1855 (247), 117, 130.
8. Hogg, *The Royal Arsenal*, 1266; Jocelyn, 78–79.
9. Hogg, *The Royal Arsenal*, 745–746, 781–782; Boxer, 41.
10. Lionel Alexander Ritchie, "Anderson, Sir John (1814–1886)," *ODNB*, 2004, http://dx.doi.org/10.1093/ref:odnb/46572; HCPP, 1855 (247), 121.
11. Jocelyn, 79; HCPP, 1855 (247), 128–131.
12. Boxer, 41; HCPP, 1855 (247), 128–131, 139–141.
13. HCPP, 1855 (247), 142.
14. Hogg, *The Royal Arsenal*, 743. The other people that made up the WO staff included several clerks, a librarian, office keeper, and three porters; see HCPP, "An Estimate of the Sum Required to Pay the Salaries and Other Expenses in the Department of Her Majesty's Secretary of State for War, from 12 June 1854 to 31 March 1855," 1854 (359).
15. HL Deb, 12 Dec 1854 Vol 136 cc1–91; "The Conduct of the War," *Blackwood's Edinburgh Magazine*. 77, no. 381 (January 1855), 12.
16. Figes, 292.
17. TNA, SUPP 6/1, "Correspondence respecting the re-organisation of the Ordnance Select Committee," 1.
18. TNA, SUPP 6/1, "Correspondence," 1, 6; TNA, WO 44/630, File 529.
19. TNA, SUPP 6/1, "Correspondence," 1–2.
20. TNA, SUPP 6/1, "Correspondence," 11–12.
21. Tony Hill, *Guns and Gunners at Shoeburyness* (Buckingham: Baron, 1999), 11–16; TNA, SUPP 6/1, "Correspondence," 11.
22. HC Deb 29 Jan 1855 Vol 136 cc1121–233; John Arthur Roebuck, *Life and Letters of John Arthur Roebuck*, ed. Robert Eadon Leader (London: E. Arnold, 1897), 260.
23. David Steele, "Temple, Henry John, third Viscount Palmerston (1784–1865)," *ODNB*, May 2009, http://www.oxforddnb.com/view/article/27112.
24. Hogg, *The Royal Arsenal*, 1087–90.
25. TNA, WO 33/2B: "Memoranda on the Office of Ordnance," 01 May 1855, 12–14; "Present and Future Arrangements," 02 May 1855, 2.
26. TNA, SUPP 6/1, "Correspondence," 13–14.
27. HCPP, "Second Report from the Select Committee on the Army Before Sebastopol," 1855 (156).
28. TNA, WO 33/2B, 02 May 1855, 1–2. While not naming either, this probably referred to Hastings and Monsell.
29. TNA, WO 33/2B, 02 May 1855, 2.
30. Hogg, *The Royal Arsenal*, 1087–1088; HCPP, "Report from the Select Committee on Military Organization," 1860 (441), vi; HCPP, "Copy of an Order of the Queen's Most Excellent Majesty in Council (Passed on the 6th Day of June 1855), Regulating the

Establishments of the Civil Departments of the Army," 1855 (307).
31. Sweetman, 74–75; Hogg, *The Royal Arsenal*, 1087.
32. TNA, SUPP 6/1, "Correspondence," 11.
33. TNA, SUPP 6/1, "Correspondence," 15.
34. "The Balaklava Railway," *Westmoreland Gazette*, 19 May 1855, 2; Figes, 355–356, 364; HCPP, 1855 (318), 22; Royle, 397–398.
35. Norman Rich, *Why the Crimean War? A Cautionary Tale* (Hanover, NH: University Press of New England, 1985), 128; Alan Palmer, *The Banner of Battle: The Story of the Crimean War* (New York: St. Martin's, 1987), 208; Royle, 404; Jocelyn, 411.
36. Royle, 412–414, 473–475.

"Steering Among the Designs of Rival Inventors"

1. Vaclav Smil (*Creating the Twentieth Century: Technical Innovations of 1867–1914 and Their Lasting Impact* (Oxford: Oxford University Press, 2005), 13.
2. TNA, SUPP 6/1, "Correspondence," 15, 20–21. The four bound volumes are WO 44/637–40, "Board of Ordnance Letters: Inventions, 1855"; the records for 1856 appear to have been lost.
3. TNA, SUPP 6/1, "Correspondence," 26–27.
4. TNA, SUPP 6/1, "Correspondence," 27.
5. TNA, SUPP 6/1: 1858, 27.
6. TNA, SUPP 6/1, "Correspondence," 43–44.
7. HCCP, "Report from the Select Committee on Military Organization," 1860 (441), 69. The reorganization of the OSC included the dissolution of the special Royal Engineer committee. In 1862, a new subcommittee of RE officers "more conveniently placed than the [OSC] came together at Chatham to investigate pontoons for cross-river bridges. In 1866, its scope expanded to "consider questions of Military Engineering, on which ... the S. of State for war should be specially informed," which effectively resurrected the committee of 1857. See Porter Vol. II, 204–207.
8. TNA, SUPP 6/7: 1865, 615; SUPP 6/8: 1868 (Q1), xx; TNA, SUPP 6/21: 1872, 172.
9. TNA, SUPP 6/1, "Correspondence," 30–33; SUPP 6/1: 1859, 90.
10. TNA, SUPP 6/1: 1859, 223; 1857, 76; 1859, 101.
11. TNA, TNA, SUPP 6/4: 1862, 460; SUPP 6/6: 1864, 735; SUPP 6/4: 1862, 191.
12. TNA, SUPP 6/1: 1859, 219–220.
13. TNA, SUPP 6/1: 1859, 148–150; SUPP 6/2: 1860, 45–46, 290–292.
14. TNA, SUPP 6/7: 1865, 921–922; SUPP 6/4: 1862, 410.
15. TNA, SUPP 6/1: 1858, 163; SUPP 6/1: 1859, 88; SUPP 6/3: 1861, 343.
16. TNA, SUPP 6/2: 1860, 76.
17. TNA, SUPP 6/1, "Correspondence," 31; SUPP 6/1: 1859, 12–13.
18. TNA, SUPP 6/5: 1863, 85.
19. TNA, SUPP 6/1: 1857, 41; 1858, 99; 1859, 20; SUPP 6/2: 1860, 590–591.
20. David Moore and Geoffrey Salter, *Mallet's Great Mortars* (Fareham, UK: David Moore, 1996), 2, 4–9; TNA, SUPP 6/1: 1858, 99. Both mortars still survive, one at Ft. Nelson, the other at Woolwich.
21. TNA, SUPP 6/4: 1862, 439–440.
22. Bastable, *Arms and the State*, 100–101; "Rifled Ordnance in England and France," *Blackwood's Edinburgh Magazine*, 119, no. 244 (April 1864), 496. The OSC already had some patterns of Krupp guns in trial; the War Office therefore declined the offer, as it considered "that the guns already supplied are sufficient to test both the material and the method of breech-loading advocated by Mr. Krupp." See TNA, SUPP 6/4: 1862, 535–6.
23. Unfortunately, the *Leeds Intelligencer* reported the same day, a French sergeant-major in the presentation party broke his leg while unloading an ammunition box for the piece. Her Majesty "gave orders that every necessary attention be paid" to the soldier, and "expressed a desire" to see him before he returned to France.
24. TNA, SUPP 6/8: 1866, 604.
25. TNA, SUPP 6/3: 1861, 324.
26. John Kane and William Harrison Askwith, *List of Officers of the Royal Regiment of Artillery from the Year 1716 to the Year 1899* (London: Royal Artillery Institution, 1900), 59; TNA, SUPP 6/1, "Correspondence," 23–24, 32; SUPP 6/1: 1857, 50–51 and 1858, 12–13. Addison's "valuable invention" is unknown, coming before the compilation of OSC records.
27. HCPP, "Revised Army Estimates of

Effective and Non-Effective Services, for 1858–59," 1857 (206), 114; "Army Estimates of Effective and Non-Effective Services, for 1857–58," 1857 (33), 114 (hereafter "Army Estimates"); "Army Estimates," 1863 (40), 64; "Army Estimates," 1863 (40), 64; "Army Estimates," 1868 (47), 77–78.

28. TNA, SUPP 6/10: 1868, 670–671, 883; HCPP 1867 (74), and HCPP 1868 (47).

29. TNA, SUPP 6/1, "Correspondence," 32; SUPP 6/7: 1865, 226; SUPP 6/4: 1862, 356.

30. TNA, SUPP 6/9: 1867, 382, 980.

31. TNA, SUPP 6/9: 1867, 382, 980; SUPP 6/2: 1861, 531; SUPP 6/4: 1862, 137.

32. William Greener, *Gunnery in 1858* (London: Smith, Elder and Co., 1858), iv–v.

33. TNA, WO 33/9, "History of Sir W. G. Armstrong's Introduction of his Gun," 1–5.

34. Frederick C. Schneid, *The Second War of Italian Unification 1859–61* (Oxford, UK: Osprey Publishing, 2012), 26; Jennings C. Wise, *The Long Arm of Lee* (New York: Oxford University Press, 1959), 30; "Rifled Ordnance in England and France," *Blackwood's Edinburgh Magazine*, 491–499; J. H. Stocqueler, *A Familiar History of the British Army, from the Earliest Restoration in 1660 to the Present Time* (London: E. Stanford, 1871), 287.

35. TNA, WO 33/9, 33.

36. Because of the method of transcription of the minutes of the OSC, it is difficult to know for certain how many proposals came directly from Armstrong, or from him as representative of Elswick Ordnance or the Royal Gun Foundry; the same holds true for superintendents of the manufacturing departments, who may have been passing forward ideas from subordinates. In at least one case, however, that of a fuze designed by Mr. W. Pettman, Boxer was careful to forward the design and clearly indicated it had been invented by Pettman, "a leading foreman of" the Royal Laboratory. See TNA, SUPP 6/2: 1860, 214.

37. Bastable, *Arms and the State*, 93; HC Deb 03 Mar 1864, vol. 173, cc 1430–31.

38. Bastable, *Arms and the State*, 59, 95–96; HCPP 1863 (487), v.

39. Bastable, *Arms and the State*, 72–80; TNA, WO 33/21A, "History of the Palliser System of Converting Cast-Iron Smooth-Bored Guns into Rifled Muzzle-Loading Guns," 6–26.

40. Steven Roberts, "Captain Alexander Blakely RA: 'Original Inventor of Improvements in Cannon and the Greatest Artillerist of the Age,'" 2012, 3–5, 47; Alexander L. Holley, *A Treatise on Ordnance and Armor* (New York: D. Van Nostrand, 1865), 36–47. Joseph Whitworth, *Miscellaneous Papers on Mechanical Subjects. Guns and Steel* (London: Longmans, Green, Reader, & Dyer, 1873), ii; Bastable, *Arms and the State*, 76–80. The first entry for Blakely in OSC records is dated 12 Feb 1857; the entry notes that "a hoop on a 68-pounder gun ... fractured during experiment" (TNA, SUPP 6/1: 1857, 4).

41. TNA, SUPP 6/5: 1863, 109; HCPP, "Report of the Special Armstrong and Whitworth Committee (Vol. I)" 1866 (3605), iii–xliv; Capt. F. S. Stoney, "A Brief Historical Sketch of Our Rifled Ordnance, from 1858 to 1868," *Minutes of Proceedings of the Royal Artillery Institution.* Vol. VI (Woolwich: Royal Artillery Institution, 1870), 105; J. B. A. Bailey, *Field Artillery and Firepower* (Annapolis, Md.: Naval Institute Press, 2004), 189.

42. On 25 November 1868 the *Pall Mall Gazette* complained that "the most convenient and economical manner" of changing back to muzzle-loading guns "would be not to carry them into effect at all," and the returns for 1868 on serviceable rifled guns show no muzzle-loaders for field artillery in use (HCPP, "Returns of the Present Number of Serviceable Rifled Guns and Carriages &C," 1868 (415), 3; see also "Breechloading Heavy Guns," *Times*, 16 Jan 1871, 4.

43. TNA, SUPP 6/8: 1866, 44; SUPP 6/9: 1867, 896.

44. Hogg, *The Royal Arsenal*, 518; Frank H. Winter, *The First Golden Age of Rocketry* (Washington: Smithsonian Institution Press, 1990), 20–28, 58–59; WO 44/621 #76.

45. Winter, 180–182.

46. Winter, 182, 202–204.

47. Hale declared bankruptcy in 1849 ("Bankrupts," *North Devon Journal*, 8 Nov 1849, 8), but had it annulled the next year ("Bankrupts," *Gloucester Journal*, 16 Mar 1850, 4).

48. Winter, 182–184; "The Late Government Seizure of War Rockets," *Standard*, 29 Apr 1853, 1.

49. "The Gunpowder Plot," *Exeter Flying Post*, 05 May 1853, 7; "Mr. Hale's Rocket Manufactory," *Newcastle Guardian and Tyne Mercury*, 25 Jun 1853, 6; TNA, WO 44/627, File 354; Winter, 184–189.

50. TNA, SUPP 6/3: 1861, 578; SUPP 6/4: 1862, 453; SUPP 6/5: 1863, 316.
51. TNA, SUPP 6/5: 1863, 477–478; SUPP 6/7: 1865, 497, 733.
52. A. W. F. Taylorson, "The Manufacture and Proof of Firearms," in Hugh B. C. Pollard and Claude Blair, *Pollard's History of Firearms* (New York: Macmillan, 1983), 472.
53. Greener 1858, 335–337; TNA, SUPP 6/1: 1859, 50. Richards had a considerable reputation for quality sporting firearms in this era. How he brought his weapons before the War Office is unknown; the first entry in the *Abstracts* states that a member of the Small Arms Committee had made some trials, and that "Mr. Richards has been requested to furnish a rifle and ammunition." Information on the Westley Richards arms may be found in Subjects 1645 and 1739 of the *Abstracts* for 1859 through 1864. See William W. Greener, *The Gun and Its Development* (London: Cassell and Company, Ltd, 1910), 128–129, and Hoyem Vol. 1, 72–75. The firm is still in business; unfortunately, a 2 May 2012 email from Simon D. Clode stated that company records on their military arms were "very few."
54. TNA, SUPP 6/3: 1861, 776; SUPP 6/5: 1863, 327.
55. HCPP, "Copy of Report of the Committee upon Breech Loaders for the Army," 1864 (578). Burton had also assisted in the outfitting of the RSAF Enfield; see "Harpers Ferry National Park: James H. Burton," https://www.nps.gov/hafe/learn/history culture/james-h-burton.htm.
56. TNA, SUPP 6/6: 1864, 531–532; SUPP 6/1: 1859, 109; SUPP 6/6: 1864, 532. Britain was not alone in this approach; the United States, without funds to re-arm after the Civil War, elected to convert its million-weapon supply of muzzle-loading rifles, and France did the same thing to provide its reserve forces with a breech-loader beginning in 1867; see Hoyem, Vol. 2, 33, 132.
57. "Breech-Loaders for the Army—from the Times," *Birmingham Journal*, 27 Aug 1864, 7.
58. TNA, SUPP 6/6: 1864, 523, 714–716.
59. HCPP, "Copy of the Report of the Ordnance Select Committee on the Trials at Woolwich of Enfield Rifles Converted to Breech-Loaders," 1865 (462), 13; TNA, SUPP 6/7: 1865, 677–678, 894–895.
60. TNA, SUPP 6/6: 1864, 716; SUPP 6/7: 1865, 679, 901–90.

61. "Gunpowder for Great Guns," *Standard*, 16 April 1870, 2; TNA, SUPP 6/6: 1862, 457–458, and SUPP 6/7: 1863, 4; Charles Dupin, *View of the History and Actual State of the Military Force of Great Britain* (London: J. Murray, 1822), 249–265; W. N. Glascock, *The Naval Service: or, Officer's Manual for Every Grade in His Majesty's Ships* (London: Saunders and Otley, 1836), 49.
62. Stephen Vincent Benét, *Electro-Ballistic Machines and the Schultz' Chronoscope* (New York: D. Van Nostrand, 1871), 5–7; TNA, SUPP 6/1: 1857, 95–96; 1858, 18, 53, 150; SUPP 6/2: 1860, 33.
63. HCPP, "Report of a Committee on the Admission of University Candidates to the Scientific Corps," 1874 (C.935), iii; TNA, SUPP 6/3: 1861, 589–590.
64. Hogg, *The Royal Arsenal*, 135–136; E. A. B. Hodgetts, ed. *The Rise and Progress of the British Explosives Industry* (London: Whittaker, 1909), 326; TNA, SUPP 6/8: 1866, 799–800.
65. Based on searches performed 8 December 2017.
66. George H. Daw, *The Central-Fire Cartridge Before the Law Courts, the Government, and the Public* (London: George H. Daw, 1867); Westley Richards, *Loading at Breech, and Loading at Muzzle, for Military Weapons* (London: William Ridgway, 1863), vi.
67. Tennent, v; Patrick Barry, *Shoeburyness and the Guns: A Philosophical Discourse.* (London: S. Low, Son, and Marston, 1865), 112–113, 127. The *Standard* noted in a 14 April 1864 article that "the War Office has been exceedingly indulgent to Mr. Whitworth to an extent that is very creditable to Lord De Grey; and to an extent that is known to very few." To assist Whitworth in the development of explosive and shrapnel shells, De Grey "ordered that the whole of the Royal Laboratory resources" be made available, including Boxer, "certainly one of the ablest scientific servants of the Crown." There is no evidence that there were any commercial dealings between the two.
68. Joseph Whitworth, *The Report of the Armstrong & Whitworth Committee, with a Letter Thereon to Earl De Grey, and Appendices* (Manchester: J. Thomson & Son, 1866), iv.
69. TNA, SUPP 6/1: 1857, 81; SUPP 6/7: 1865, 731–733.
70. "Business of the Committee," TNA, SUPP 6/10: 1868, 961.

"A New Era of Great Guns"

1. David G. Chandler, "The Expedition to Abyssinia, 1867-8," in *Queen Victoria's Little Wars*, 151-152; John A. R. Marriott, *England since Waterloo* (London: Methuen, 1957), 306-307.
2. TNA, SUPP 6/10: Abstracts 1868, 961; HCPP, "Observations by Colonel Jervois, C.B., R.E., on the Report of the Special Committee on the Iron Shields Supplied for Malta and Gibraltar," 1867 (4003).
3. TNA, WO 32/7126, "Copy of Minutes relating to the appointment of the Ordnance Committee 1880," 2; RAL, "General Index to the Abstracts of Proceedings of the Department of the Director of Artillery for the Year 1870," ii; TNA, WO 32/7125, "Cost of the Ordnance Select Committee (abolished in 1868), as compared with the present system of Experimental Branch and Special Committees," 1880.
4. TNA, SUPP 6/48, "Proceedings of the Ordnance Council, 1868-1871," "Ordnance Council," 1-2. The *Ordnance Council* should not be confused with the later *Ordnance Committee* or *Ordnance Board*; the Victorians were, unfortunately, not very imaginative in their committee naming practices.
5. HCPP, "Reports of a Committee Appointed to Inquire into the Arrangements in Force for the Conduct of Business in the Army Departments," 1870 (C.54), 8.
6. HCPP, "A Bill for Making Further Provision Relating to the Management of Certain Departments of the War Office," 1870 (30); see also Spiers, 6-8.
7. HCPP 1870 (C.54), 71; TNA, SUPP 6/10: 1870, 280. Adye later wrote that Cardwell, whom he had never met before, "unexpectedly offered the appointment" (Adye, 243).
8. Adye, 249; Kane and Askwith, 52; TNA, SUPP 6/10: 1870, 280.
9. Beeler, 78; TNA, SUPP 6/10: 1870, 329-330, 412. For the composition as initially proposed, see "Ordnance Council," 1-2. The members that actually sat in Council meetings varied by topic and existence of the post.
10. TNA, SUPP 6/23: 1874, 246.
11. TNA, SUPP 6/23: 1874, 103; SUPP 6/19: 1870, 411.
12. TNA, SUPP 6/19: 1870, 284, 344; SUPP 6/20: 1871, 410.
13. TNA, SUPP 6/19: 1870, 407; SUPP 6/24: 1875, 262; HCPP, "Copy of Reports and Correspondence Explanatory of Item C (Rewards to Inventors) in Vote 15 of the Army Estimates for 1870-71," 1870 (266), 5; TNA, SUPP 6/26: 1877, 201.
14. TNA, SUPP 6/19: 1870, 389, 555; SUPP 6/21: 1872, 73, 305; SUPP 6/22: 1873, 93.
15. TNA, SUPP 6/23: 1874, 196; SUPP 6/28: 1879, 367; SUPP 6/20: 1871, 91.
16. TNA, SUPP 6/23: 1874, 110.
17. TNA, SUPP 6/23: 1874, 110; SUPP 6/20: 1871, 399.
18. TNA, SUPP 6/19: 1870, 281-282; "Winding-up Notice," *Western Daily Press*, 19 Jan 1876, 3.
19. TNA, SUPP 6/19: 1870, 280.
20. TNA, SUPP 5/889, "Reports of Breech-Loading Arms by a Special Sub-Committee of the Ordnance Select Committee, 1868," 2-3.
21. TNA, SUPP 5/889, 3, 13.
22. TNA, SUPP 5/889, 14, 32-34, 57.
23. TNA, SUPP 5/890, "Reports of a Special Committee on Breech-Loading Rifles," i-xxv.
24. TNA, SUPP 5/890, xxv; Charles B. Norton, *American Breech-Loading Small Arms* (New York: F.W. Christern, 1872), 83.
25. TNA, SUPP 6/48, "Proceedings of a Committee held at the War Office on the 23rd March, 1869," 5-6.
26. B. A. Temple, *The Boxer Cartridge in the British Service* (Wynnum Central, Australia: B.A. Temple, 1977), 61-63. Eley received British Pat. No. 166, Jan. 1869 for his design.
27. TNA, SUPP 5/892, "Reports of Special Committee on Martini-Henry Breech-Loading Rifles," 6; SUPP 6/48, "Proceedings of a Committee assembled at the War Office, on Thursday, the 30th March, 1871"; B. A. Temple and Ian D. Skennerton. *A Treatise on the British Military Martini: The Martini-Henry, 1869-C.1900* (Burbank, Australia: B. A. Temple, 1983), 85.
28. HC Deb Vol 205 cc1872-910, 28 Apr 1871; "The Martini-Henry at Wimbledon," *Western Times*, 24 Jul 1871, 4; HC Deb vol 208 cc216-7, 25 Jul 1871.
29. "Royal Small Arms Factory," *Standard*, 15 May 1872, 2; Pam, 77; HCPP, "Return of the Annual Accounts of the Several Manufacturing Establishments under the War Office, for the Year 1871-72," 1873 (111), 115.
30. TNA, SUPP 5/893, "Conferences on Martini-Henry Rifles," 3-8.

31. TNA, SUPP 5/893, 16- 40. For a summary of reports of cartridge jamming, see TNA, WO 33/44, "Abstracts of the Proceedings of the Department of the Director of Artillery, 1885," (hereafter "AP-DDA"), 283–284. No other European army adopted the composite cartridge on the scale that Britain did. The French licensed the Boxer case for converted muzzle-loaders, and Belgium adopted a wrapped-foil design for its infantry arm, but replaced it with solid-drawn cases by 1876. See Hoyem Vol. 2, 131–132 (France) and 152–158 (Belgium).

32. Temple and Skennerton, 111–116; Hoyem Vol. 2, 190; Bradley, 108–113; TNA, SUPP 6/19: 1870, 138–139.

33. David Stone, *"First Reich": Inside the German Army During the War with France 1870-71* (London: Brassey's, 2002), 127.

34. Kinard, 227; Wawro, *The Franco-Prussian War*, 58; "Dr. Russell on the Battlefield of Sedan," *Western Daily Press*, 07 Sep 1870, 3.

35. "Last Week's Battles," *Cork Examiner*, 09 Sep 1870, 3.

36. Wawro, *The Franco-Prussian War*, 296–299.

37. "The Magazines," op. cit.; I. F. Clarke, *The Tale of the Next Great War, 1871-1914* (Syracuse, N.Y.: Syracuse University Press, 1995), 14–15; "Literary, Scientific, and Artistic Notes," *Bucks Herald*, 19 Aug 1871, 3; "The Battle of Dorking," *Morning Post*, 02 Jan 1872, 6.

38. TNA, SUPP 6/19: 1870, 280.

39. Stone, *First Reich*, 291; Wawro, *The Franco-Prussian War*, 53; Ellis, 63–64; TNA, SUPP 6/9: 1867, 591. *Mitrailleuse* literally means "grapeshot shooter" in French, although since the invention of the weapon the word has also come to mean "machine gun."

40. Stone, *First Reich*, 52–53; Wawro, *The Franco-Prussian War*, 53, 99; Ellis, 64.

41. TNA, SUPP 6/19: 1870, 511, 565–566.

42. TNA, SUPP 6/19: 1870, 416–426.

43. TNA, SUPP 6/19: 1870, 163–164; SUPP 6/20: 1871, 124; Peter Labbett, *British Small Arms Ammunition, 1864-1938: Other Than .303 Inch Calibre* (London: P. Labbett, 1993), 67–77.

44. TNA, SUPP 6/19: 1870, 545–553; SUPP 6/20: 1871, 32, 121; SUPP 6/21: 1872, 157–158.

45. Hogg, *The Royal Arsenal*, 1963, 904–905; TNA, SUPP 6/27: 1878, 72–73.

46. TNA, SUPP 6/21: 1872, 304–305.

47. Eric Dorn Brose, *The Kaiser's Army: The Politics of Military Technology in Germany During the Machine Age, 1870-1918* (Oxford: Oxford University Press, 2004), 31; TNA, SUPP 6/28: 1879, 548–550.

48. HC Deb 05 Apr 1875 vol 223 cc303-19; see also Beeler, 74–75.

49. HC Deb 22 Jun 1875 vol 225 cc317-50; TNA, SUPP 6/24: 1875, 368.

50. HCPP, "Report of the Committee Appointed to Inquire into the Cause of the Bursting of One of the 38-Ton Guns in the Turret of H.M.S. 'Thunderer,' 13th February 1879," 1879 (C.2248), 16; TNA, SUPP 6/28: 1879, 390–393, 584–585; SUPP 6/29: 1880, 10–13.

51. "Reported Purchase of the Turkish Ironclads by the English Government," *Western Daily Press*, 12 Feb 1878, 8; TNA, SUPP 6/28: 1879, 393, 584–589.

52. TNA, SUPP 6/28: 1879, 548–550.

53. The *Abstracts* for 1895 shows some of the last questions related to heavy RML ordnance, including the monster 17.72-inch gun emplaced at Malta; see TNA, SUPP 6/95: 1897, xix. Presumably they were all retired between then and 1900, when the *Minutes of Proceedings* resumed.

54. Two years later, this decision baffled Cambridge. He could not believe that any rifle "can be considered safe in the hands of the troops, unless a half-cock can be introduced"—a physical impossibility, since the weapon had no external hammer as had every previous British military small arm. He had to be reminded of this and then he signed off on the change. See TNA, SUPP 5/893, 61.

55. TNA, SUPP 6/29: 1880, 280.

56. Brian R. Mitchell and Phyllis Deane, *Abstract of British Historical Statistics* (Cambridge, UK: University Press, 1962), 396–398; TNA, SUPP 6/28: 1879, 393, 317.

57. TNA, SUPP 6/10: 1868, 591; SUPP 6/17: 1869, 35; SUPP 6/48, "No. 2: Mr. Parson's Case"; HCPP, "Copy of Papers Relating to the Dismissal of Colonel Boxer from the Office of Superintendent of the Royal Laboratory," 1870 (60).

58. TNA, SUPP 6/749, "Ordnance Council: Abstracts of Proceedings, 1–202," 15.

59. TNA, SUPP 6/49, "Proceedings of the Ordnance Council, 183; SUPP 6/21: 1872, 318; SUPP 6/749, 28.

60. Charles W. Sleeman, *Torpedoes and*

Torpedo Warfare (Portsmouth: Griffin, 1889), 177.

An "Epoch of Change and Improvement"?

1. HC Deb 22 Jun 1875 vol 225 cc317–50; HC Deb 27 Feb 1879 vol 243 cc1861–72; HL Deb 17 Mar 1879 Vol 244 cc999–1018.

2. HC Deb 22 Apr 1879 vol. 245 c837; David Brooks, "Gladstone and Midlothian: The Background to the First Campaign," *The Scottish Historical Review* 64, no. 177 (1985): 42–67; 61. Disraeli had been granted the title of Lord Beaconsfield in 1876.

3. TNA, WO 32/7156, "Copies of Minutes relating to the appointment of the Ordnance Committee 1880," 1–6.

4. TNA, WO 32/7156, 5–12.

5. TNA, WO 32/7156, 13; Skentelbery, 282.

6. RAL, "Abstracts of the Proceedings of the Ordnance Committee, 1881," 69. To differentiate between the *Abstracts* issued by the Ordnance Committee and the Director of Artillery in this era, the abbreviations "AP-OC" and "AP-DDA" will hereafter be used.

7. HCPP, "Copy of the Instructions Given to the Ordnance Committee by the Secretary of State for War," 1881 (161), 1–3; HCPP, 1881 (161).

8. RAL, AP-OC 1881, 70–72.

9. Barnett, 319; R. C. K. Ensor, *England, 1870–1914* (Oxford: Clarendon Press, 1936), 77–79; M. J. Williams, "The Egyptian Campaign of 1882," in *Victorian Military Campaigns*, ed. Brian Bond (New York: Praeger, 1967), 242–247; Juan R. I. Cole, "Of Crowds and Empires: Afro-Asian Riots and European Expansion, 1857–1882," *Comparative Studies in Society & History* 31, no. 1 (1989): 106–33.

10. Michael Barthorp, *War on the Nile* (Poole, Dorset: Blandford Press, 1984), 35.

11. Ensor, 79; Williams, 242.

12. Andrew Roberts, *Salisbury: Victorian Titan* (London: Weidenfeld & Nicolson, 1999), 309; Ensor, 86–99.

13. TNA, SUPP 6/79: AP-OC 1883, 162, 371, 557; SUPP 6/80: AP-OC 1884, 158, 527, 724.

14. TNA, WO 33/39: AP-DDA 1882, 277.

15. TNA, WO 33/44: AP-DDA 1885: 243, 135; AP-DDA 1884, 185.

16. TNA, SUPP 6/84: AP-OC 1888, 703–709.

17. TNA, WO 33/44: AP-DDA 1885, 114.

18. TNA, WO 33/44: AP-DDA 1885, 265.

19. TNA, WO 33/39: AP-OC 1882, 284–286. "Quick-firing" guns of this era used "fixed" ammunition in which the projectile and charge formed one piece, after the style of small-arms ammunition. They still lacked any mechanism for controlling recoil.

20. TNA, WO 33/44: AP-OC 1884, 195. Armstrong's firm had merged with Charles Mitchell's ship-building company in 1882.

21. TNA, SUPP 6/88: AP-OC 1891, 1231–1232.

22. TNA, WO 33/44: AP-OC 1884, 152–153; SUPP 6/9: 1867, 635; TNA, WO 33/44: AP-OC 1885, 445–446.

23. RAL, AP-OC 1881, 280–281, and AP-OC 1882, 423.

24. See Subj. 2458.2, TNA, *Abstracts* 1864–66, and Subj. 1788, TNA, *Abstracts* 1859–63.

25. Bastable, *Arms and the State*, 173.

26. HCPP, "Army Estimates" 1884 (75), 63. This is the only direct reference to a "steel foundry" in any of the Estimates through 1887–88.

27. Bastable, *Arms and the State*, 182.

28. HC Deb 02 Dec 1884 vol 294 cc468–471.

29. This was not the first time that a difference of opinion regarding metal testing had arisen between the Royal Arsenal and private industry. Kenneth Pryke ("The Woolwich Arsenal and Acadian Mines," *Scientia Canadensis* 34, no. 1 (2011): 25–50) detailed the struggles that the Acadian Charcoal Iron Company experienced trying to demonstrate the acceptability of its Nova Scotia ore for ordnance. Ultimately, mechanical and chemical analysis of the finished pig iron yielded differing results; the former suggested the iron would work, the latter reported too many flaws in its composition. This led to the Arsenal's rejection of the ore as unsuitable. Pryke's article illustrates the very complex nature of metal testing and the differences of opinion that even noted experts in metallurgy had.

30. HC Deb 02 Dec 1884 vol 294 cc491–492.

31. HC Deb 02 Dec 1884 vol 294 cc491–492.; HL Deb 02 Dec 1884 vol 294 cc428–430.

32. HC Deb 16 Mar 1885 vol 295 cc1285–92.

33. HC Deb 16 Mar 1885 vol 295 cc1298–99. Brand's dismissal of the changes as "slight alterations" is open to interpretation. The committee examined all sizes of heavy naval guns from 4- through 16.25-inch, and made recommendation for changes to some—but not all—the designs; see HCPP, "Recommendations of the Ordnance Committee (with Special Associated Members), as to the Construction of Ordnance," 1885 (C.4508).

34. Bastable, *Arms and the State*, 182–183; "Return Showing the Number, Description, Name of Designer, Place of Manufacture, and Approximate Cost of the Various Rifled Iron and Steel Guns Supplied by the War Department to the Naval and Land Service During Each of the Years 1859–60 to 1885–86," HCPP, 1887 (109).

35. HCPP, 1887 (C.5062), lviii, and 141–142; "Ordnance Committee Reports 400–457, 1885," TNA, SUPP 6/99, "Ordnance Committee—Report 429, with Appendices and Plates—Construction of Ordnance; 30th April 1885"; Beeler, 79–81.

36. Harold John Hanham, *The Nineteenth-Century Constitution 1815–1914* (London: Cambridge U.P., 1969), 357; Caspar F. Goodrich, *Report of the British Naval and Military Operations in Egypt, 1882* (Washington: Govt. Print. Off., 1885), 37, 67; Williams, 250; Farwell, *Queen Victoria's Little Wars*, 255.

37. HCPP, 1887 (C.5062), iii–vi; see also Spiers, *The Late Victorian Army*, 40–42.

38. HCPP, 1887 (C.5062), cv.

39. HCPP, 1887 (C.5062), xxii–xxiii, 231, 382; B. A. Temple and Ian D. Skennerton, *A Treatise on the British Military Martini: The .40 & .303 Martinis, 1880–1920* (Burbank, Queensland: B.A. Temple, 1989), 349–369.

40. HCPP, 1887 (C.5062), xxii–xxiii; Roy M. Marcot, *The History of Remington Firearms* (Guilford, CT: Lyons Press, 2005), 59–60; TNA, WO 33/44: AP-DDA 1885, 323.

41. Hoyem Vol. 2, 178, 182–185; Melvin M. Johnson, and Charles T. Haven, *Ammunition; Its History, Development and Use, 1600 to 1943 -.22 BB Cap to 20 mm. Shell* (New York: W. Morrow, 1943), 54; Temple and Skennerton 1989, 369; TNA, SUPP 6/3; 1861, 691; Ian D. Skennerton, *The Lee-Enfield: A Century of Lee-Metford & Lee-Enfield Rifles & Carbines* (Labrador, Queensland: Ian D. Skennerton, 2007), 15–16, 61–66.

42. HCPP, 1887 (C.5062), xxiv–xxv.

43. HCPP, 1887 (C.5062), xx, xxv.

44. HCPP, 1887 (C.5062), xxxvii–xxxviii.

45. HCPP, 1887 (C.5062), civ–cv.

46. HCPP, "First Report of the Royal Commission Appointed to Inquire into the Civil Establishments of the Different Offices of State at Home and Abroad," 1887 (C.5226), xxv; Rodgers, 496.

47. HC Deb 08 Sep 1887 vol 320 cc1708–68.

48. The distance between Woolwich and Enfield made separate departments a logical choice; see Hogg, *The Royal Arsenal*, 859.

49. HC Deb 08 Sep 1887 vol 320 cc1708–68.

50. Spiers, *The Late Victorian Army*, 44; Williams, 253; Spiers, *ibid.*, 45.

51. Hogg, *The Royal Arsenal*, 859–860.

52. Spiers, *The Late Victorian Army*, 46; Roberts, 495; "Plain Words by Lord Wolseley," *Gloucester Citizen*, 25 Apr 1888, 3. Roberts noted the date as 27 April, but the *Citizen* reported the speech as being given the Monday before publication, making it the 23rd. Ardagh's memo was dated the 17th, just a few days before the dinner speech. See TNA, CAB 37/21/6, "Defence of England: Mobilization of the Regular and Auxiliary Forces for Home Defence."

53. The *Telegraph's* source remains unknown; the "highest military authority" may have been Wolseley himself.

54. HL Deb 11 May 1888 vol 326 cc1–7.

55. HL Deb 14 May 1888 vol 326 cc91–110.

56. HCPP, "Preliminary and Further Reports (with Appendices) of the Royal Commissioners Appointed to Enquire into the Civil and Professional Administration of the Naval and Military Departments and the Relation of Those Departments to Each Other and to the Treasury," 1890 (C.5979), iii.

57. Spiers, *The Late Victorian Army*, 46.

58. TNA, SUPP 6/84: AP-OC 1888, 271–272.

59. TNA, SUPP 6/84, AP-OC 1888, 1250; Hogg, *The Royal Arsenal*, 1436; Skentelbery, 284–289.

60. TNA, ADM 256/21-44; SUPP 6/85: AP-OC 1889, 372–373.

61. Hogg, *The Royal Arsenal*, 860; C. Orde Browne, "Our Ordnance Factories," *The Naval Annual* (1896): 167–74; 167. Anderson pushed hard to centralize the administration of the Royal Arsenal. Among his

changes included the establishment of a central headquarters at Woolwich for both communications and accounting, and the creation of a Central Stores Branch to take the place of the individual efforts of the manufacturing departments. In 1890, as a result of the investigation of the Churchill Committee, "the whole method of factory accounting was overhauled and centralized" under Anderson's supervision, a process that continued into 1891 (see Hogg, *The Royal Arsenal*, 871–879, 1108). An 1895 article in *Carrier's Magazine* noted that, in addition to "arranging many of the departments, [and] in improving the systems of accounts and cost-keeping," Anderson had supervised "the introduction of many new manufactures" for cordite, the production of wire-cored artillery pieces, cast- and forged-steel projectiles, and quick-firing ammunition cases. See "Dr. William Anderson: Director-General of the British Royal Ordnance Factories," *Carriers Magazine: Engineering Illustrated*, Vol. VIII (May–Oct 1895), 457–458.

62. Whitworth received its first contract for 6-inch breech-loading guns in 1887, although its founder did not live to see the results of so long a labor. See HCPP, "Army and Navy Guns," 1889 (95).

63. Ian F. W. Beckett, "Edward Stanhope at the War Office, 1887–92," *Journal of Strategic Studies* 5, no. 2 (1982), 280, 286.

64. John Ehrman, *Cabinet Government and War, 1890–1940* (Cambridge, UK: University Press, 1958), 7. Ehrman noted that prior to 1880, "no fewer than seventeen Royal Commissions, eighteen Select Committee, nineteen Committees of officers inside the War Office, and thirty-five Committees of Military Officers had considered matters of policy affecting the army."

"New Measures Demand New Men"

1. TNA, SUPP 6/6: AP-OSC 1864, 733.
2. TNA, SUPP 6/90: AP-OC 1893, 809–810, 1056.
3. "Chancery of Lancashire," *Manchester Courier and Lancashire General Advertiser*, 28 Jul 1896, 3. The company made another go of things later, as the *Shields Daily Gazette* reported on 26 May 1900 that new works had been established in Newcastle-on-Tyne, "and the Company hope to produced their first steel weldless chain within the next two months."
4. TNA, SUPP 6/90: AP-OC 1893, 809; SUPP 6/90: AP-OC 1893, 494; SUPP 6/89: AP-OC 1892, 648; SUPP 6/143, Q1–2 1898, Min. 45318; SUPP 6/136, 01 Oct 1894, Minute 37,533.
5. An example of such a case: in 1865, the widow of Lt. A. H. Bell appealed for some form of reward for his work on a "Hydroscope, or instrument for determining the distance of an object at sea from an elevated battery." The OSC thought her appeal to be "a very proper case for a gratuity of £50," in view of the expenses Lt. Bell might have incurred "in maturing his instrument, and the credit justly due to him for its introduction." See TNA, SUPP 6/7: AP-OSC 1865, 147.
6. TNA, WO 33/47: AP-DDA 1886, 303.
7. TNA, SUPP 6/88: AP-OC 1891, 314.
8. TNA, SUPP 6/90: AP-OC 1893, 239; SUPP 6/91: AP-OC Q1–2 1895, 254; SUPP 6/93: AP-OC 1896 Q1–2, 377.
9. HCPP, 1890 (C.5979), xix, xxii.
10. HCPP, 1890 (C.5979), viii, xxvii; xxii–xxiii; see also Spiers, *The Late Victorian Army*, 46–47.
11. HCPP, 1890 (C.5979), xxii.
12. Spiers, *The Late Victorian Army*, 47–48.
13. *The Orders in Council for the Regulation of the Naval Service*. Vol. VI: 7th February 1888 to 26th November 1892 (London: HMSO, 1893), 127–129. Such a split had been under consideration for decades; evidence presented to an 1886 "Inter-Departmental Committee" appointed to study the division included memoranda dating to 1833. See TNA, WO 33/47, "Naval Armaments: Papers and Correspondence relating to the Question of Responsibility for provision of Money, Custody of Stores, &c.," 11.
14. TNA, SUPP 6/88: AP-OC 1891, 1230; WO 32/7156, "Question of appointment on Artillery Committee in addition to Ordnance Committee. Introduction of 12 PR B.L. gun."
15. TNA, WO 32/7156, Minute of Gen. Hay, 16 Dec 1891; Minute of Gen. Buller, 22 Dec 1891.
16. HC Deb 31 Aug 1895 vol. 36 cc1379–414; Spiers, *The Late Victorian Army*, 48–49.

17. Willoughby Verner and Erasmus Darwin Parker, *The Military Life of H.R.H. George, Duke of Cambridge.* Vol. II: 1871–1904 (London: J. Murray, 1905), 395–396; Elizabeth Longford, *Queen Victoria: Born to Succeed* (New York: Harper & Row, 1964), 533. See also Spiers, *The Late Victorian Army*, 49.

18. HC Deb 21 Jun 1895 vol. 34 cc1673–713.

19. "Orders of the Day: Army Estimates, 1895–6." See also Spiers, *The Late Victorian Army*, 49, and Wheeler, 247.

20. HCPP, "War Office. Orders in Council Defining the Duties of the Principal Officers Charged with the Administration of the Army," 1899 (113). 4. See also "The Army Reorganisation," *The Star*, 29 Aug 1895.

21. Spiers, *The Late Victorian Army*, 50–52.

22. HC Deb 25 Mar 1898 vol 55 cc929–1035; Maj. Gen. Sir Charles E. Callwell and Maj. Gen. Sir John E. W. Headlam. *The History of the Royal Artillery from the Indian Mutiny to the Great War*, Vol. 1: 1860–1899 (Woolwich: Royal Artillery Institution, 1931), 211; HCPP, "Royal Commission on the War in South Africa (Volume I)," 1904 (Cd. 1790) 72; HCPP, 1899 (113), 6.

23. Maj. D. H. Cole and Maj. Edgar C. Priestley. *An Outline of British Military History, 1660–1936* (London: Sifton, Praed & Co., 1936), 236–240; Farwell, *Queen Victoria's Little Wars*, 335–337.

24. The gun had been brought before the OC in 1892, and recommended for further tests in 1893; Lt. Gen. Hay ruled on 10 Jan 1894 that he "does not consider that this gun is required for Land Service" (TNA, SUPP 6/135, "Proceedings of the Ordnance Committee, Q1–2 1894, Minute 35,327; SUPP 6/89: AP-OC 1892, 850, 1157, and SUPP 6/90: AP-OC 1893, 454, 702, 976).

25. Thomas Pakenham, *The Boer War* (New York: Random House, 1979), 35.

26. Pakenham, 111–114; Major D.D. Hall, "The Naval Guns in Natal 1899–1902," *Military History Journal*, Vol 4 No. 3, Jun 1978; The South African Military History Society, http://samilitaryhistory.org/vol043dh.html.

27. Raymond Sibbald, *The Boer War: The War Correspondents* (Johannesburg: J. Ball, 1993), 40; Byron Farwell, *The Great Anglo-Boer War* (New York: Harper & Row, 1976), 142.

28. Sibbald, 74; Pakenham, 234–250.

29. Pakenham, 261. HCPP, 1904 (Cd. 1789), 73–75, 278–280.

30. Pakenham, 298–307, 361; Julian Symons, *Buller's Campaign* (London: Cresset Press, 1963), 257.

31. Pakenham, 249, 253–256.

32. Skennerton, 93; HCPP, "Report of His Majesty's Commissioners Appointed to Inquire into the Military Preparations and Other Matters Connected with the War in South Africa," 1904 (Cd. 1789), 94; Reynolds, 55–63.

33. HCPP, "Royal Commission on the War in South Africa (Volume II)," 1904 (Cd. 1791), 518. Mowatt's committee studied the general state of reserve equipment, while Grant's "expert committee" considered the question of "movable armaments," presumably field and horse artillery; see HCPP, "Summary of the Recommendations of the Interdepartmental Committee, 1900, on the Reserves of Guns, Stores, &C., Required for the Army," 1904 (Cd. 1908). Lansdowne's testimony regarding their appointment does not explain the need for two committees, nor their different scopes. In addition, the first volume mentions only Mowatt's committee in its index of "Commissions and Committees referred to in Evidence; see HCPP, 1904 (Cd. 1789), 289.

34. HCPP, 1904 (Cd. 1790), 75; John E. W. Headlam, *The History of the Royal Artillery from the Indian Mutiny to the Great War*. Vol. II: 1899–1914 (Woolwich: Royal Artillery Institution, 1937), 13.

35. Headlam, 12–13; HCPP, 1904 (Cd. 1789), 279.

36. I. F. W. Beckett, *The Amateur Military Tradition: 1558–1945* (Manchester: Manchester University Press, 1991), 200; Pakenham, 263.

37. Stephen M. Miller, *Volunteers on the Veld* (Norman: University of Oklahoma Press, 2007), 9.

38. Pakenham, 363–384.

39. HCPP, 1904 (Cd. 1790), 73–74; John P. Wisser, *The Second Boer War, 1899–1900* (Kansas City: Hudson-Kimberly, 1901), 254; Headlam, 14–15; Michael Davitt, *The Boer Fight for Freedom* (New York: Funk & Wagnalls, 1902), 67–68.

40. Headlam, 16; Pakenham, 264.

41. TNA, SUPP 6/147, "Proceedings of the Ordnance Committee, 1900: January to June," Minute 49,364.

42. TNA, SUPP 6/147, Minutes 48,744 and 49,498.

43. TNA, WO 33/38, AP-DDA 1881, 232;

WO 33/41, AP-DDA 1883, 89; SUPP 6/30, AP-DDA 1887, 10; "Military News," *York Herald*, 24 Oct 1888, 5; "Some Lessons from the War," *Sheffield Independent*, 03 May 1900, 5; "Boers and Lyddite," *Dundee Evening Post*, 13 Feb 1900, 2.
44. TNA, SUPP 6/147, Minute 49,307; "Explosive Committee and Lyddite." *Cheltenham Chronicle*, 19 May 1900, 2.
45. Pakenham, 617; David G. Chandler and I. F. W. Beckett, *The Oxford Illustrated History of the British Army* (Oxford; Oxford University Press, 1994), 204; Roberts, 775–779.
46. Roberts, 785; Headlam 85–86; TNA, WO 32/9029, "Report of Special Committees on Automatic Q.F. Gun (Pom-pom) and Machine Guns," and WO 33/137, "Report of Special Committees on: (i) 1-pr. automatic QF gun (Pom Pom) (ii) Machine guns."
47. Headlam, 72–76; "The Rearmament of the Artillery," *Times*, 15 Dec 1904, 7.
48. HCPP, "Report of the Committee Appointed to Enquire into War Office Organisation," 1901 (Cd.580), 23–24; Wheeler, 259–261; 1904 (Cd. 1789), 142; Barnett, 356.
49. Chandler and Beckett, 204–205; Pakenham, 607–608.
50. Roberts, 796–816; Robin Harris, *The Conservatives: A History* (London: Bantam, 2011), 227–229; HCPP, 1904 (Cd. 1789), 3.
51. Peter Fraser, *Lord Esher: A Political Biography* (Barnesly, South Yorkshire: Pen & Sword Politics 2013), 92–93; Chandler and Beckett, 205.
52. HCPP, "Report of the War Office (Reconstitution) Committee. (Part III)," 1904 (Cd. 2002). 1; Fraser, *ibid*.
53. HCPP, 1904 (Cd. 2002), 12–15; Chandler and Beckett, 205.
54. HCPP, "Report of the War Office (Reconstitution) Committee, Part I," 1904 (Cd. 1932). 10; HC Deb 09 Mar 1904 vol 131 cc599–652.

55. Headlam, 77; "The Artillery—Its Re-Armament," *Exeter and Plymouth Gazette*, 17 Dec 1904, 6; "Field Artillery- Extraordinary Action of the Treasury," *Dover Express*, 16 December 1904, 2.
56. Edward M. Spiers, *Haldane, an Army Reformer* (Edinburgh: Edinburgh University Press, 1980), 62–4, 95, 116, 143; Chandler and Beckett, 207.
57. HCPP, 1904 (Cd. 2002), 20.
58. Hogg, *The Royal Arsenal*, 1440; TNA, DEFA 15/3, "History of Research Department, Woolwich, 1900–1919"; Skentelbery, 29, 290–295; Headlam, 86.
59. Headlam, 87; Garry James, "The 1886/93 Lebel," *American Rifleman*, October 2014, 67–70.
60. Gordon, 81; Spiers, *The Army and Society*, 284.

"A Projectile to Be Fired by the Royal Navy"

1. *The Avengers*. DVD. Directed by Joss Whedon. Los Angeles: Marvel Studios, 2012.
2. Searle, 367.
3. Jehiel Keeler Hoyt and Kate Louise Roberts, *Hoyt's New Cyclopedia of Practical Quotations* (London: Funk & Wagnalls, 1940), 847.
4. Barnett, 377–392.
5. Sir Charles Petrie, "An Eccentric at the Horse Guards: 'The Royal George 1819–1904,' by Giles St. Aubyn," *The Illustrated London News*, 09 Nov 1963, 769.
6. TNA, SUPP 6/48, "Proceedings of the Ordnance Council," 269–275; "Jacob Snider papers 1840–1873," *The New York Public Library Archives & Manuscripts*, 2017, http://archives.nypl.org/mss/2801.
7. MacCleod and Andrews, 6–7.

Bibliography

Primary Sources

National Archives, Kew, UK

DEFA 15/3, "History of Research Department, Woolwich, 1900–1919"
SUPP 5/42–43, "Book of Photolithographs made in the Laboratory of drawings of shells and cartridges"
SUPP 5/119, "Report of Select Committee on Ordnance and Minutes of Evidence, 1862
SUPP 5/889, "Reports of Breech-Loading Arms by a Special Sub-Committee of the Ordnance Select Committee, 1868"
SUPP 5/890, "Reports of a Special Committee on Breech-Loading Rifles"
SUPP 5/892, "Reports of Special Committee on Martini-Henry Breech-Loading Rifles"
SUPP 5/893, "Conferences on Martini-Henry Rifles"
SUPP 6/1–10, "Abstracts of Proceedings of the Ordnance Select Committee," 1855–1868
SUPP 6/17, "Abstracts of Proceedings of the Director-General of Ordnance, 1869"
SUPP 6/19–29, "Abstracts of Proceedings of the Department of the Director of Artillery," 1870–1880
SUPP 6/48–51, "Proceedings of the Ordnance Council," 1868–1904
SUPP 6/79–95, "Abstracts of Proceedings of the Ordnance Committee," 1883–1897
SUPP 6/116–162, "Proceedings of the Ordnance Committee," 1881–1907
SUPP 6/749, "Ordnance Council: Abstracts of Proceedings, 1864–1899"
WO 32/6283, "Reports on system under which patterns of warlike stores are adopted and stores obtained and passed, 1887–1888"
WO 32/7120, "Inception of Council of Ordnance to replace Ordnance Select Committee on arms, armanents and experiments"
WO 32/7121, "Composition of Council of Ordnance"
WO 32/7125, "Re-institution of an Ordnance Select Committee. Minutes by Director of Artillery and Stores and Surveyor General"
WO 32/7126, "Question of appointment on Artillery Committee in addition to Ordnance Committee"
WO 32/7133, "Question of best principle of rifling for small arms: Recommendations of Ordnance Select Committee Enfield rifle compared to other patterns, 1863"
WO 32/9029, "Report of Special Committees on Automatic Q.F. Gun (Pom-pom) and Machine Guns"
WO 33/2B, "Memoranda on the Office of Ordnance"
WO 33/2B, "Past and Present Arrangements"
WO 33/9, "History of Sir W. G. Armstrong's Introduction of his Gun, with Reports of Experiments, &c."
WO 33/21A, "History of the Palliser System of Converting Cast-Iron Smooth-Bored Guns into Rifled Muzzle-Loading Guns"

WO 33/37–47, "Abstracts of Proceedings of the Department of the Director of Artillery," 1881–1886
WO 33/137, "Report of Special Committees on: (i) 1-pr. automatic QF gun (Pom Pom) (ii) Machine guns"
WO 44/620–636, "Board of Ordnance Letters: Inventions"
WO 47/2354, "Board of Ordnance Minutes, March 1853"

Library of the Royal Armouries Museum, Leeds

"Abstracts of Proceedings of the Ordnance Committee," 1881–1882
"Annual Reports of the Ordnance Committee," 1881–1889
"Breech-loading small arms, 1859–1867"
"Experimental investigations into rifled cannon, 1858"
"General Index to the Abstracts of Proceedings of the Department of the Director of Artillery"
"Index to the Abstracts of Proceedings of the Ordnance Committee, 1869–1883"

House of Commons Parliamentary Papers

> The following is a partial list of the most important documents retrieved from http://parlipapers.chadwyck.co.uk/marketing/index.jsp.

"Appendix to the Third Report from the Select Committee on Army and Navy Estimates," 1887 (232) (232-I).
"Army (Machine Guns). Copy of Report of the Result of Recent Experiments with Machine Guns at Shoeburyness," 1881 (223).
"Army (Ordnance Committee). Copy of the Instructions Given to the Ordnance Committee by the Secretary of State for War," 1881 (161).
"Army Civil Departments. Copy of an Order of the Queen's Most Excellent Majesty in Council (Passed on the 6th Day of June 1855), Regulating the Establishments of the Civil Departments of the Army," 1855 (307).
"Army Discipline and Regulation (Commencement). A Bill to Bring into Force the Army Discipline and Regulation Act, 1879, and for Other Purposes," 1878 (248).
"Army. Summary of the Recommendations of the Interdepartmental Committee, 1900, on the Reserves of Guns, Stores, &C., Required for the Army; Showing Also to What Extent These Recommendations Have Been Carried Out," 1904 (Cd. 908).
"Artillery Officers (Woolwich). Copy of the Correspondence Relative to the Reconstruction of the Select Committee of Artillery Officers and Others at Woolwich, Including the General Order of the 30th Day of March Last, Appointing Some Additional Members, and a List of the Days of Meeting to the Present Time," 1854 (277).
"Committee on War Office Organisation. Report of the Committee Appointed to Enquire into War Office Organisation," 1901 (Cd.580).
"Enfield Rifles. Copy of the Report of the Ordnance Select Committee on the Trials at Woolwich of Enfield Rifles Converted to Breech-Loaders," 1865 (462).
"Fifth Report from the Select Committee on Army and Navy Estimates; Together with the Proceedings of the Committee and Minutes of Evidence," 1887 (259) (259-I) (259-II).
"Fifth Report from the Select Committee on the Army Before Sebastopol; with the Proceedings of the Committee, and an Appendix," 1855 (318, 318-I).
"First Report from the Select Committee on Army and Navy Estimates; Together with the Proceedings of the Committee, and Minutes of Evidence," 1887 (216) (216-I).
"First Report from the Select Committee on Army and Ordnance Expenditure," 1849 (277).
"First Report from the Select Committee on the Army Before Sebastopol; with the Proceedings of the Committee," 1855 (86).
"First Report of the Royal Commission Appointed to Inquire into the Civil Establishments

of the Different Offices of State at Home and Abroad, with Minutes of Evidence, Appendix, &C," 1887 (C.5226).
"Fourth Report and Special Report from the Select Committee on Army and Navy Estimates; Together with the Proceedings of the Committee, and Minutes of Evidence," 1887 (239).
"Fourth Report from the Select Committee on the Army Before Sebastopol; with the Minutes of Evidence, and Appendix," 1855 (247).
"Fourth Report of the Royal Commission Appointed to Inquire into the Civil Establishments of the Different Offices of State at Home and Abroad," 1890 (C.6172).
"Index to Second Report from the Select Committee on Army and Ordnance Expenditure. (Ordnance Expenditure.)," 1849 (499, 499-II).
"Mr. Warner's Invention. An Account of Public Money Placed at the Disposal of the Officers Appointed by Her Majesty's Government to Report Upon the Trials to Be Made of Mr. Warner's Invention Called "Long Range," to Enable Him to Exhibit Its Powers; &C,." 1847 (302).
"Parliamentary Electors. Abstract of Return of the Number of Parliamentary Electors in Great Britain and Ireland, According to the Registrations of 1848 and 1849, and 1849 and 1850," 1850 (345).
"Preliminary and Further Reports (with Appendices) of the Royal Commissioners Appointed to Enquire into the Civil and Professional Administration of the Naval and Military Departments and the Relation of Those Departments to Each Other and to the Treasury," 1890 (C.5979).
"Report by the Special Committee on Ordnance. Subject: Experiments with a 12-Inch R.M.L. Gun Returned from H.M.S. Thunderer," 1880 (C.2722).
"Report from the Select Committee on Army and Ordnance Expenditure; with the Proceedings of the Committee," 1851 (564).
"Report from the Select Committee on Commissariat and Transport Services (Egyptian Campaign); Together with the Proceedings of the Committee, Minutes of Evidence, and Appendix," 1884 (285).
"Report from the Select Committee on Explosive Substances; Together with the Proceedings of the Committee, Minutes of Evidence, and Appendix," 1874 (243).
"Report from the Select Committee on Military Organization; Together with the Proceedings of the Committee, Minutes of Evidence, and Appendix," 1860 (441).
"Report from the Select Committee on Ordnance; Together with the Proceedings of the Committee, Minutes of Evidence, Appendix, and Index," 1862 (448).
"Report from the Select Committee on Royal Gun Factories; Together with the Proceedings of the Committee, Minutes of Evidence, and Appendix," 1867 (459).
"Report from the Select Committee on Small Arms; Together with the Proceedings of the Committee, Minutes of Evidence, and Appendix," 1854 (236).
"Report of a Committee on the Admission of University Candidates to the Scientific Corps; with Minutes of Evidence, &C," 1874 (C.935).
"Report of Commissioners on Promotion in the Army; with an Appendix," 1854 (1802).
"Report of Committee on Cutlasses and Cutlass Sword Bayonets Supplied to the Royal Navy. Together with War Office Minutes on the Subject. February 15th to March 17th, 1887," 1887 (C.5014, C.5014-I).
"Report of His Majesty's Commissioners Appointed to Inquire into the Military Preparations and Other Matters Connected with the War in South Africa," 1904 (Cd. 1789).
"Report of the Commissioners Appointed to Inquire into the Organization of the Indian Army; Together with the Minutes of Evidence and Appendix," 1859 (2515).
"Report of the Commissioners Appointed to Inquire into the Practicability and Expediency of Consolidating the Different Departments Connected with the Civil Administration of the Army," 1837 (78).
"Report of the Committee Appointed by the Secretary of State for War to Consider the Terms and Conditions of Service in the Army," 1892 (C.6582).
"Report of the Committee Appointed to Inquire into the Cause of the Bursting of One of the

Bibliography

38-Ton Guns in the Turret of H.M.S. 'Thunderer,' 13th February 1879," 1879 (C.2248, C.2248-I).

"Report of the Committee Appointed to Inquire into the Organization and Administration of the Manufacturing Departments of the Army; with Minutes of Evidence, Appendix, and Index," 1887 (C.5116).

"Report of the Committee on the Machinery of the United States of America," 1854 (0.11).

"Report of the Committee on the Organization of the Royal Artillery, with Minutes of Evidence and Appendices. 27th April, 1888," 1888 (C.5491).

"Report of the Royal Commission Appointed to Inquire into the System under Which Patterns of Warlike Stores Are Adopted and the Stores Obtained and Passed for Her Majesty's Service," 1887 (C.5062).

"Report of the Special Committee on M.L. V. B.L. Field Guns," 1871 (C.283).

"Report of the War Office (Reconstitution) Committee. (Part II.)," 1904 (Cd. 1968).

"Report of the War Office (Reconstitution) Committee. (Part III.)," 1904 (Cd. 2002).

"Report on the Navy Estimates, from the Select Committee on Navy, Army, and Ordnance Estimates; Together with Minutes of Evidence, and Appendix," 1847 (555) (555-II).

"Reports of a Committee Appointed to Inquire into the Arrangements in Force for the Conduct of Business in the Army Departments," 1870 (C.54).

"Royal Commission on the War in South Africa. Appendices to the Minutes of Evidence Taken before the Royal Commission on the War in South Africa," 1904 (Cd. 1792).

"Royal Commission on the War in South Africa. Minutes of Evidence Taken before the Royal Commission on the War in South Africa. (Volume I.)," 1904 (Cd. 1790).

"Royal Commission on the War in South Africa. Minutes of Evidence Taken before the Royal Commission on the War in South Africa. (Volume II.)," 1904 (Cd. 1791).

"The Royal Commission on War Stores in South Africa. Report of the Royal Commission on War Stores in South Africa, Together with Appendices," 1906 (Cd. 3127).

"The Royal Commission on War Stores in South Africa. Vol. I. Minutes of Evidence Taken before the Royal Commission on War Stores in South Africa," 1906 (Cd. 3128).

"The Royal Commission on War Stores in South Africa. Vol. II. Minutes of Evidence Taken on Behalf of the Royal Commission on War Stores in South Africa, by the Special Commissioner in South Africa," 1906 (Cd. 3129).

"The Royal Commission on War Stores in South Africa. Vol. III. Report, with Appendices, of Messrs. Annan, Kirby, Dexter & Co., Chartered Accountants," 1906 (Cd. 3130).

"The Royal Commission on War Stores in South Africa. Volume IV. Reports on South African Contractors with Appendices by Messrs. Deloitte, Dever, Griffiths, Annan & Co., Johannesburg," 1906 (Cd. 3131).

"Second Report from the Select Committee on Army and Navy Estimates; Together with the Proceedings of the Committee, and Minutes of Evidence," 1887 (223) (223-I).

"Second Report from the Select Committee on the Army Before Sebastopol; with the Minutes of Evidence, and Appendix," 1855 (156).

"Second Report of the Royal Commission Appointed to Inquire into the Civil Establishments of the Different Offices of State at Home and Abroad, with Minutes of Evidence, Appendix, &C," 1888 (C.5545).

"Summary of the Speech of the Secretary of State for War with Regard to the Re-Organization of the Army," 1904 (Cd. 1907).

"Third Report from the Select Committee on Army and Navy Estimates; Together with the Proceedings of the Committee, and Minutes of Evidence," 1887 (232) (232-I).

"Third Report from the Select Committee on the Army Before Sebastopol; with the Minutes of Evidence, and Appendix," 1855 (218).

"Third Report of the Royal Commission Appointed to Inquire into the Civil Establishments of the Different Offices of State at Home and Abroad. Minutes of Evidence, with Summary," 1889 (C.5748).

"War Office (Reconstitution) Committee. Report of the War Office (Reconstitution) Committee, Part I," 1904 (Cd. 1932).

"Warlike Stores. Second Report of the Royal Commission Appointed to Inquire into the System under Which Patterns of Warlike Stores Are Adopted and the Stores Obtained and Passed for Her Majesty's Service: Together with an Appendix," 1888 (C.5413).

Newspapers

Articles from the *Times* retrieved online from *The Times Digital Archive 1785-2009*
Articles from most other newspapers retrieved online from *The British Newspaper Archive*

Secondary Sources

Books

Adye, John. *Recollections of a Military Life*. New York: Macmillan and Co., 1895.
Alder, Ken. *Engineering the Revolution: Arms and Enlightenment in France, 1763-1815*. Princeton, NJ: Princeton University Press, 1997.
Auerbach, Jeffrey A. *The Great Exhibition of 1851: A Nation on Display*. New Haven, CT: Yale University Press, 1999.
Auerbach, Jeffrey A., and Peter H. Hoffenberg, eds. *Britain, the Empire, and the World at the Great Exhibition of 1851*. Aldershot, UK: Ashgate, 2008.
Bailey, De Witt, and Douglas A. Nie. *English Gunmakers: The Birmingham and Provincial Gun Trade in the 18th and 19th Century*. London: Arms and Armour Press, 1978.
Bailey, J. B. A. *Field Artillery and Firepower*. Annapolis, MD: Naval Institute Press, 2004.
Barclay, Glen St. John. *The Empire Is Marching: A Study of the Military Effort of the British Empire 1800-1945*. London: Weidenfeld & Nicolson, 1976.
Barlow, W.R. *Treatise on Ammunition. Corrected up to December 1877*. London: H.M.S.O., 1874.
Barnett, Correlli. *Britain and Her Army, 1509-1970: A Military, Political, and Social Survey*. New York: W. Morrow, 1970.
Barry, Patrick. *Shoeburyness and the Guns: A Philosophical Discourse*. London: S. Low, Son, and Marston, 1865.
Barthorp, Michael. *War on the Nile*. Poole, Dorset: Blandford Press, 1984.
Bastable, Marshall J. *Arms and the State: Sir William Armstrong and the Remaking of British Naval Power, 1854-1914*. Aldershot, Hants, UK: Ashgate, 2004.
Baxter, James Phinney. *The Introduction of the Ironclad Warship*. Hamden, CT: Archon Books, 1968.
Beckett, I.F.W. *The Amateur Military Tradition: 1558-1945*. Manchester History of the British Army. Manchester: Manchester University Press, 1991.
Beeler, John. *Birth of the Battleship: British Capital Ship Design 1870-1881*. Annapolis, MD: Naval Institute Press, 2001.
Bell, David Avrom. *The First Total War: Napoleon's Europe and the Birth of Warfare as We Know It*. Boston: Houghton Mifflin Co., 2007.
Benét, Steven Vincent. *Electro-Ballistic Machines and the Schultz' Chronoscope*. New York: D. Van Nostrand, 1871.
Black, Jeremy. *The Age of Total War, 1860-1945*. Westport, CT: Praeger, 2006.
_____. *A Military Revolution? Military Change and European Society: 1550-1800*. Hampshire: Macmillan, 1991.
_____. *War and the World: Military Power and the Fate of Continents, 1450-2000*. New Haven, CT: Yale University Press, 1998.
Blackmore, Howard L. *British Military Firearms, 1650-1850*. London: Greenhill Books, 1994.
Bond, Brian, ed. *Victorian Military Campaigns*. New York: Praeger, 1967.
Boot, Max. *War Made New: Weapons, Warriors, and the Making of the Modern World*. New York: Gotham Books, 2006.

Boxer, E.M. *Colonel Boxer and the War Office*. London: P.S. King, 1870.
Bradley, Joseph. *Guns for the Tsar: American Technology and the Small Arms Industry in Nineteenth-Century Russia*. DeKalb: Northern Illinois University Press, 1990.
Brassey, Sir Thomas. *The British Navy: Its Strength, Resources, and Administration, Vol. II.* London: Longmans, Green, and Co., 1882.
Brock, W. H. *William Crookes (1832–1919) and the Commercialization of Science*. Aldershot, England: Ashgate, 2008.
Brose, Eric Dorn. *The Kaiser's Army: The Politics of Military Technology in Germany During the Machine Age, 1870–1918*. Oxford: Oxford University Press, 2004.
Cain, P.J., and A.G. Hopkins. *British Imperialism: Innovation and Expansion, 1688–1914*. London: Longman, 1993.
Callwell, Maj. Gen. Sir Charles E., and Maj. Gen. Sir John E. W. Headlam. *The History of the Royal Artillery from the Indian Mutiny to the Great War*. Vol. 1: 1860–1899, Woolwich: Royal Artillery Institution, 1931 (rep. Naval & Military Press, 2009).
Calthorpe, Somerset John Gough. *Letters from Head-Quarters; or, the Realities of the War in the Crimea, by an Officer on the Staff*. 2 vols. London: J. Murray, 1858.
Chandler, David G., and I. F. W. Beckett. *The Oxford Illustrated History of the British Army*. Oxford: Oxford University Press, 1994.
Clarke, Bob. *From Grub Street to Fleet Street: An Illustrated History of English Newspapers to 1899*. Aldershot, Hants, England: Ashgate, 2004.
Clarke, I. F. *The Tale of the Next Great War, 1871–1914: Fictions of Future Warfare and of Battles Still-to-Come*. Syracuse, NY: Syracuse University Press, 1995.
Clowes, William Laird. *The Royal Navy: A History from the Earliest Times to the Present* Vol. VI. London: S. Low, Marston and Co., 1901.
Coggins, Jack. *Arms and Equipment of the Civil War*. Garden City, NY: Doubleday, 1962.
Cole, Maj. D. H., and Maj. Edgar C. Priestley. *An Outline of British Military History, 1660–1936*. London: Sifton, Praed & Co., 1936.
Coles, Cowper Phipps Y. A. *Spithead Forts: Reply to the Royal Commissioners' Second Report on Our National Defences*. London: Mitchell's Military Library, 1861.
Congreve, Major-Gen. Sir William. *A Treatise on the General Principles, Powers and Facility of Application of the Congreve Rocket System, as Compared with Artillery*. London: Longman, Rees, Orme, Brown, and Green, 1827.
Davitt, Michael. *The Boer Fight for Freedom*. New York; London: Funk & Wagnalls, 1902.
Daw, George H. *The Central-Fire Cartridge before the Law Courts, the Government, and the Public: Showing Who Introduced the System into England, Who Has Improved It, Who Has Benefited by It, and Who Ought to Be Rewarded for It*. London: George H. Daw, 1867.
Dawson, Anthony L., Paul L. Dawson, and Stephen Summerfield, *Napoleonic Artillery*. Ramsbury UK: Crowood, 2007.
Douglas, Howard. *A Treatise on Naval Gunnery*. London: John Murray, 1860 (rep. La Vergne, TN: Kessinger Publishing, 2010).
Duncan, Francis. *History of the Royal Regiment of Artillery, Compiled from the Original Records*. London: J. Murray, 1873.
Dupin, François Pierre Charles. *View of the History and Actual State of the Military Force of Great Britain*. London: N.p., 1822.
Dupuy, Trevor N. *The Evolution of Weapons and Warfare*. Indianapolis, IN: Bobbs-Merrill, 1980.
Echevarria, Antulio Joseph. *Imagining Future War: The West's Technological Revolution and Visions of Wars to Come, 1880–1914*. Westport, CT: Praeger, 2007.
Edgerton, David. *Warfare State: Britain, 1920–1970*. Cambridge, UK: Cambridge University Press, 2006.
Ehrman, John. *Cabinet Government and War, 1890–1940*. Cambridge, UK: University Press, 1958.
Ellis, John. *The Social History of the Machine Gun*. London: Purnell Book Services, 1975.

Embree, Michael. *Bismarck's First War the Campaign of Schleswig and Jutland 1864*. Solihull: Helion, 2006.
Ensor, R. C. K. *England, 1870–1914*. Oxford History of England. Oxford: Clarendon Press, 1936.
Farley, James J. *Making Arms in the Machine Age: Philadelphia's Frankford Arsenal, 1816–1870*. University Park: Pennsylvania State University Press, 1994.
Farwell, Byron. *The Great Anglo-Boer War*. New York: Harper & Row, 1976.
———. *Mr. Kipling's Army*. New York: W.W. Norton & Company, 1981.
———, ed. *Queen Victoria's Little Wars*. New York: Norton, 1985.
Figes, Orlando. *The Crimean War: A History*. New York: Metropolitan Books, 2010.
Forbes, A. *A History of the Army Ordnance Services*. 2 vols London: Medici Society, 1929.
Fortescue, J. W. *A History of the British Army*. Vol. XI: 1815–1838, London: Macmillan and Co., 1930.
Fraser, Peter. *Lord Esher: A Political Biography*. Barnesly, South Yorkshire: Pen & Sword Politics, 2013.
George, J. N. *English Guns and Rifles: Being an Account of the Development, Design, and Range of English Sporting Rifles and Shotguns*. Plantersville, SC: Small-Arms Technical Publishing Company, 1947 (rep. Birmingham, AL: Paladium Press, 1999).
Glascock, W.N. *The Naval Service: Or, Officer's Manual for Every Grade in His Majesty's Ships*. London: Saunders and Otley, 1836.
Gleig, G. R., and Mary E. Gleig. *Personal Reminiscences of the First Duke of Wellington: With Sketches of Some of His Guests and Contemporaries*. New York: Scribner's, 1904.
Goodrich, Caspar F. *Report of the British Naval and Military Operations in Egypt, 1882*. Washington: Govt. Printing Office, 1885.
Gordon, Hampden. *The War Office*. London: Putnam, 1935.
Grampp, William D. *The Manchester School of Economics*. London: Oxford University Press, 1960.
Grant, John. *A Guide to Woolwich*. Woolwich: N.p., 1841.
Greener, William. *Gunnery in 1858: Being a Treatise on Rifles, Cannon, and Sporting Arms; Explaining the Principles of the Science of Gunnery, and Describing the Newest Improvements in Fire-Arms*. London: Smith, Elder and Co., 1858.
Greener, William W. *The Gun and Its Development*. London: Cassell and Company, Ltd., 1910 (rep. Fairfax, VA: National Rifle Association, 2002).
Grenville, J. A. S. *Lord Salisbury and Foreign Policy: The Close of the Nineteenth Century*. London: University of London, Athlone Press, 1964.
Guillery, Peter, ed. *Survey of London*, Vol. 48: Woolwich. New Haven, CT: Yale University Press, 2012.
Hamilton, Douglas T. *Shrapnel Shell Manufacture*. New York: The Industrial Press, 1915.
Hanham, H. J. *The Nineteenth-Century Constitution 1815–1914: Documents and Commentary*. London: Cambridge University Press, 1969.
Harding, C. W. *Eley Cartridges: A History of the Silversmiths and Ammunition Manufacturers*. Shrewsbury: Quiller, 2006.
Harding, David. F. *Smallarms of the East India Company, 1600–1856*. 4 vols. Vol. III: *Ammunition and Performance*. London: Foresight Books, 1997.
Harries-Jenkins, Gwyn. *The Army in Victorian Society*. Studies in Social History. London: Routledge & Keegan Paul, 1977.
Harris, Robin. *The Conservatives: A History*. London: Bantam, 2011.
Hartcup, Guy. *The War of Invention: Scientific Developments, 1914–18*. London: Brassey's Defence Publishers, 1988.
Hawes, Arthur Briscoe. *Rifle Ammunition; Being Notes on the Manufactures Connected Therewith, as Conducted in the Royal Arsenal, Woolwich*. London: W.O. Mitchell, 1859.
Headlam, John Emerson Wharton. *The History of the Royal Artillery from the Indian Mutiny to the Great War*. Vol. II: 1899–1914, Woolwich: Royal Artillery Institution, 1937.
Headrick, Daniel R. *The Tentacles of Progress: Technology Transfer in the Age of Imperialism, 1850–1940*. New York: Oxford University Press, 1988.

———. *The Tools of Empire: Technology and European Imperialism in the Nineteenth Century.* New York: Oxford University Press, 1981.
Hill, Tony. *Guns and Gunners at Shoeburyness.* Buckingham: Baron, 1999.
Hime, H. W. L. *Gunpowder and Ammunition, Their Origin and Progress.* New York: Longmans, Green, 1904.
———. *History of the Royal Regiment of Artillery, 1815–1853.* London: Longmans, Green, and Co., 1908.
Hodgetts, E. A. Brayley, and Tom Gregorie Tullock. *The Rise and Progress of the British Explosives Industry.* London: Whittaker, 1909.
Hogg, Oliver Frederick Gillilan. *Artillery: Its Origin, Heyday, and Decline.* Hamden, CT: Archon Books, 1970.
———. *The Royal Arsenal: Its Background, Origin, and Subsequent History.* London: Oxford University Press, 1963.
Holley, Alexander L. *A Treatise on Ordnance and Armor: Embracing Descriptions, Discussions, and Professional Opinions Concerning the Material, Fabrication, Requirements, Capabilities, and Endurance of European and American Guns for Naval, Sea-Coast, and Iron-Clad Warfare, and Their Rifling, Projectiles and Breech-Loading.* New York: D. Van Nostrand, 1865.
Hopkirk, Peter. *The Great Game: The Struggle for Empire in Central Asia.* New York: Kodansha International, 1992.
Hoppen, K. Theodore. *The Mid-Victorian Generation, 1846–1886.* The New Oxford History of England. Oxford: Oxford University Press, 1998.
Hounshell, David A. *From the American System to Mass Production, 1800–1932: The Development of Manufacturing Technology in the United States.* Baltimore, MD: Johns Hopkins University Press, 1984.
Hoyem, George A. *The History and Development of Small Arms Ammunition.* 4 vols. Vol. 1: *Martial Long Arms, Flintlock through Rimfire.* Tacoma: Armory Publications, 1981.
———. *The History and Development of Small Arms Ammunition.* Vol. 2: *Centerfire: Primitive, and Martial Long Arms.* Tacoma: Armory Publications, 1982.
Hoyt, Jehiel Keeler, and Kate Louise Roberts. *Hoyt's New Cyclopedia of Practical Quotations.* New York; London: Funk & Wagnalls Co., 1940
James, Harold. *Krupp: A History of the Legendary German Firm.* Princeton, NJ: Princeton University Press, 2012.
Jocelyn, Col. Julian R. J. *The History of the Royal Artillery (Crimean Period).* London: J. Murray, 1911.
Johnson, Melvin M., and Charles T. Haven, *Ammunition; Its History, Development and Use, 1600 to 1943—.22 BB Cap to 20 mm. Shell.* New York: W. Morrow, 1943.
Kane, John, and William Harrison Askwith. *List of Officers of the Royal Regiment of Artillery from the Year 1716 to the Year 1899.* London: Royal Artillery Institution, 1900.
Kennedy, Paul M. *The Rise and Fall of the Great Powers: Economic Change and Military Conflict from 1500 to 2000.* New York: Random House, 1987.
Kinard, Jeff. *Artillery: An Illustrated History of Its Impact.* Santa Barbara, CA: ABC-CLIO, 2007.
Kinglake, Alexander William. *The Invasion of the Crimea: Its Origin and an Account of Its Progress Down to the Death of Lord Raglan.* Vol. III. London: W. Blackwood and Sons, 1868.
Knox, MacGregor, and Williamson Murray. *The Dynamics of Military Revolution, 1300–2050.* Cambridge: Cambridge University Press, 2001.
Kochanski, Halik. *Sir Garnet Wolseley: Victorian Hero.* London: Hambledon Press, 1999.
Labbett, Peter. *British Small Arms Ammunition, 1864–1938: Other Than .303 Inch Calibre.* London: P. Labbett, 1993.
Lambert, Andrew, and Stephen Badsey. *The War Correspondents: The Crimean War.* Stroud, Gloucestershire: A. Sutton, 1994.
Lambert, Andrew D. *The Crimean War: British Grand Strategy, 1853–56.* Manchester: Manchester University Press, 1990.

Lendy, A. F. *Treatise on Fortification, or, Lectures Delivered to Officers Reading for the Staff.* London: W. Mitchell, 1862.
Longford, Elizabeth. *Queen Victoria: Born to Succeed.* New York: Harper & Row, 1964.
Macleod, John. *Military Memoir of the Late Lieutenant-General Sir John Macleod, G.C.H., Senior Colonel Commandant and Director General of Artillery.* London: Printed for R. and C. Byfield, 1834.
Marcot, Roy M. *The History of Remington Firearms: The History of One of the World's Most Famous Gun Makers.* Guilford, CT: Lyons Press, 2005.
Marriott, John Arthur Ransome. *England since Waterloo. A History of England.* Edited by Sir Charles Oman. London: Methuen, 1957.
Martin, Kingsley. *The Triumph of Lord Palmerston: A Study of Public Opinion in England before the Crimean War.* New York: Dial Press, 1924.
Mathews, Joseph J. *Reporting the Wars.* Minneapolis: University of Minnesota Press, 1957.
Mathias, Peter. *The First Industrial Nation: An Economic History of Britain, 1700–1914.* London: Methuen, 1983.
Maxwell, Herbert. *The Life of Wellington: The Restoration of the Martial Power of Great Britain.* Boston: Little, Brown and Co., 1899.
McConnell, David. *British Smooth-Bore Artillery: A Technological Study to Support Identification, Acquisition, Restoration, Reproduction, and Interpretation of Artillery at National Historic Parks in Canada.* Ottawa, Ont.: National Historic Parks and Sites, Environment Canada-Parks, 1988.
McNeill, William Hardy. *The Pursuit of Power: Technology, Armed Force, and Society since A.D. 1000.* Chicago: University of Chicago Press, 1982.
Mercer, Cavalié. *Journal of the Waterloo Campaign Kept Throughout the Campaign of 1815.* New York: Da Capo Press, 1995.
Miller, Stephen M. *Volunteers on the Veld: Britain's Citizen-Soldiers and the South African War, 1899–1902.* Norman: University of Oklahoma Press, 2007.
Millis, Walter. *Arms and Men: A Study in American Military History.* New York: Putnam, 1956.
Mitchell, Brian R., and Phyllis Deane. *Abstract of British Historical Statistics.* Cambridge: Cambridge University Press, 1962.
Moore, David, and Geoffrey Salter. *Mallet's Great Mortars.* Fareham, UK: Palmerston Forts Society, 1996.
Myatt, Frederick. *British Sieges of the Peninsular War.* Staplehurst, Kent: Spellmount, 1995.
Myszkowski, Eugene. *The Remington-Lee Rifle.* Latham, NY: Excalibur Publications, 1994.
Napier, Charles James. *A Letter on the Defence of England by Corps of Volunteers and Militia: Addressed to the Members of Parliament.* London: Edward Moxon, 1852.
Napier, William Francis Patrick. *History of the War in the Peninsula and in the South of France, from the Year 1807 to the Year 1814.* Oxford: Christy, 1836.
Nasmyth, James, and Samuel Smiles. *James Nasmyth Engineer; an Autobiography.* London: J. Murray, 1883.
The National Encyclopædia: A Dictionary of Universal Knowledge. London: W. Mackenzie, 1875.
Norton, Charles B. *American Breech-Loading Small Arms: A Description of Late Inventions, Including the Gatling Gun, and a Chapter on Cartridges.* F. W. Christern, 1872.
_____. *American Inventions and Improvements in Breech-Loading Small Arms, Heavy Ordnance, Machine Guns, Magazine Arms, Fixed Ammunition, Pistols, Projectiles, Explosives, and Other Munitions of War.* 2nd Ed. Boston: James R. Osgood and Company, 1882.
Norton, John. *A List of Captain Norton's Projectiles, and His Other Naval and Military Inventions: With Original Correspondence.* Gravesend: Caddel, 1860.
O'Connor, Damian P. *Between Peace and War: British Defence and the Royal United Services Institute 1831–2010.* London: Royal United Services Institute for Defence Studies, 2011.
Owen, Charles Henry. *The Principles and Practice of Modern Artillery: Including Artillery Material, Gunnery and Organization and Use of Artillery in Warfare.* Second ed. London: J. Murray, 1873.

Pakenham, Thomas. *The Boer War.* New York: Random House, 1979.
Palmer, Alan. *The Banner of Battle: The Story of the Crimean War.* New York: St. Martin's, 1987.
Pam, David O. *The Royal Small Arms Factory, Enfield and Its Workers.* Enfield: D. Pam, 1998.
Parker, Geoffrey. *The Military Revolution: Military Innovation and the Rise of the West, 1500–1800.* 2nd ed. Cambridge, UK; Cambridge University Press, 1996.
Patents for Inventions: Abridgments of Specifications. Class 119, Small-Arms. Period A.D. 1855–1930. 7 vols. London: British Patent Office, 1905 (rep. Oceanside, CA: Armory Publications, 1993).
Pollard, Hugh B.C., and Claude Blair. *Pollard's History of Firearms.* New York: Macmillan, 1983.
Porter, Whitworth. *History of the Corps of Royal Engineers.* Vol. II, London: Longmans, Green and Co., 1889.
Preston, Antony, and John Major. *Send a Gunboat: The Victorian Navy and Supremacy at Sea, 1854–1904.* London: Conway, 2007.
Ransford, Oliver. *The Battle of Majuba Hill: The First Boer War.* London: John Murray, 1970.
Raudzens, George. *The British Ordnance Department and Canada's Canals, 1815–1855.* Waterloo, Ontario: Wilfrid Laurier University Press, 1979.
Reilly, W. Edmund M. *An Account of the Artillery Operations Conducted by the Royal Artillery and Royal Naval Brigade before Sebastopol in 1854 and 1855.* London: HMSO, 1859.
Reynolds, E. G. B. *The Lee-Enfield Rifle.* London: Herbert Jenkins, 1960.
Rich, Norman. *Why the Crimean War? A Cautionary Tale.* Hanover, NH: University Press of New England, 1985.
Richards, Westley. *Loading at Breech and Loading at Muzzle, for Military Weapons: With a Few Remarks on the Simplest Mode of Keeping the Accounts of Government Manufacturing Departments.* N.p.: 1863.
Riddell, Charles James Buchanan. *Remarks on the Organization of the British Royal Artillery.* London: W. Clowes & Sons, 1852.
Roberts, Andrew. *Salisbury: Victorian Titan.* London: Weidenfeld & Nicolson, 1999.
Roebuck, John Arthur, and Robert Eadon Leader. *Life and Letters of John Arthur Roebuck. With Chapters of Autobiography.* London; New York: E. Arnold, 1897.
Rogers, Clifford J., ed. *The Military Revolution Debate: Readings on the Military Transformation of Early Modern Europe.* Boulder, CO: Westview Press, 1995.
Royle, Trevor. *Crimea: The Great Crimean War, 1854–1856.* New York: St. Martin's Press, 2000.
Russell, William Howard, et al. *The Crimean War: As Seen by Those Who Reported It.* Baton Rouge: Louisiana State University Press, 2009.
St. Aubyn, Giles. *The Royal George, 1819–1904; the Life of H.R.H. Prince George, Duke of Cambridge.* New York: Knopf, 1964.
St. John, Ian. *Gladstone and the Logic of Victorian Politics.* Anthem Perspectives in History. London: Anthem Press, 2010.
Schneid, Frederick C. *The Second War of Italian Unification 1859–61.* Essential Histories. Oxford, UK: Osprey Publishing, 2012.
Scott, Percy. *Fifty Years in the Royal Navy.* New York: George H. Doran Co., 1919.
Searle, G. R. *A New England? Peace and War, 1886–1918.* Oxford: Oxford University Press, 2004.
The Second Armada: A Chapter of Future History; Being a Reply to the German Conquest of England in 1875, and Battle of Dorking. London: Harrison and Sons, 1871.
Showalter, Dennis E. *Railroads and Rifles: Soldiers, Technology, and the Unification of Germany.* Hamden, CT: Archon Books, 1975.
Sibbald, Raymond. *The Boer War: The War Correspondents.* Johannesburg: J. Ball, 1993.
Sinclair, John. *Memoirs of the Life and Works of Sir John Sinclair, Bart.* Edinburgh1837.
Skennerton, Ian D. *The Lee-Enfield: A Century of Lee-Metford & Lee-Enfield Rifles & Carbines.* Labrador, Queensland: Ian D. Skennerton, 2007.

Skentelbery, Norman. *Arrows to Atom Bombs: A History of the Ordnance Board.* London: Norman Skentleberry, 1975.
Sleeman, Charles William. *Torpedoes and Torpedo Warfare: Containing a Complete and Concise Account of the Rise and Progress of Submarine Warfare.* Portsmouth: Griffin, 1889.
Smil, Vaclav. *Creating the Twentieth Century: Technical Innovations of 1867-1914 and Their Lasting Impact.* Oxford: Oxford University Press, 2005.
Smith, Merritt Roe. *Harpers Ferry Armory and the New Technology: The Challenge of Change.* Ithaca, NY: Cornell University Press, 1977.
Sondhaus, Lawrence. *Naval Warfare, 1815-1914.* London: Routledge, 2012.
Spiers, Edward M. *The Army and Society, 1815-1914.* London: Longman, 1980.
_____. *Haldane, an Army Reformer.* Edinburgh: Edinburgh University Press, 1980.
_____. *The Late Victorian Army, 1868-1902.* Manchester, UK: Manchester University Press, 1992.
Stafford, William Cooke. *History of England's Campaigns in India and China; and of the Indian Mutiny, 1857-1859. England's Battles by Sea and Land.* Vol. 3, London: The London Printing and Publishing Co. Ltd., 1865.
Stocqueler, J. H. *A Familiar History of the British Army, from the Earliest Restoration in 1660 to the Present Time.* London: E. Stanford, 1871.
Stone, Charles John. *What Happened After the Battle of Dorking: Reminiscences of a Volunteer; Being an Account of the Victory at Tunbridge Wells.* London: G. Routledge, 1871.
Stone, David. *"First Reich": Inside the German Army During the War with France 1870-71.* London: Brassey's, 2002.
Strachan, Hew. *From Waterloo to Balaclava: Tactics, Technology, and the British Army, 1815-1854.* Cambridge: Cambridge University Press, 1985.
_____. *Wellington's Legacy: The Reform of the British Army, 1830-54.* Manchester, UK: Manchester University Press, 1984.
Sumida, Jon Tetsuro. *In Defence of Naval Supremacy: Finance, Technology, and British Naval Policy, 1889-1914.* Boston: Unwin Hyman, 1989.
Sweetman, John. *War and Administration: The Significance of the Crimean War for the British Army.* Edinburgh: Scottish Academic Press, 1984.
Symons, Julian. *Buller's Campaign.* London: Cresset Press, 1963.
Tate, Thomas K. *From Under Iron Eyelids: The Biography of James Henry Burton, Armorer to Three Nations.* Bloomington, Ind.: AuthorHouse, 2005.
Temple, B. A. *The Boxer Cartridge in the British Service.* Wynnum Central, Australia: B.A. Temple, 1977.
Temple, B. A., and Ian D Skennerton. *A Treatise on the British Military Martini: The .40 & .303 Martinis, 1880-1920.* Burbank, Queensland: B.A. Temple, 1989.
_____. *A Treatise on the British Military Martini: The Martini-Henry, 1869-C.1900.* Burbank, Australia: B. A. Temple, 1983.
Tennent, James Emerson. *The Story of the Guns.* London: Longman, Green, Longman, Roberts, & Green, 1864.
Trebilcock, Clive. *The Vickers Brothers: Armaments and Enterprise, 1854-1914.* London: Europa, 1977.
Van Dulken, Stephen. *British Patents of Invention, 1617-1977: A Guide for Researchers.* London: The British Library, 1999.
Verner, Willoughby, and Erasmus Darwin Parker. *The Military Life of H.R.H. George, Duke of Cambridge.* Vol. II: 1871-1904, London: J. Murray, 1905.
Walter, John. *The Rifle Story: An Illustrated History from 1756 to the Present Day.* London: Greenhill Books, 2006.
Ward, Donovan M. *The Other Battle: Being a History of the Birmingham Small Arms Co. Ltd.* York: B. Johnson, 1946.
Wawro, Geoffrey. *The Franco-Prussian War: The German Conquest of France in 1870-1871.* Cambridge, UK: Cambridge University Press, 2005.
_____. *Warfare and Society in Europe, 1792-1914.* London: Routledge, 2000.

Wheeler, Owen. *The War Office, Past and Present*. London: Methuen & Co., 1914.
Whitworth, Joseph. *Miscellaneous Papers on Mechanical Subjects. Guns and Steel* London: Longmans, Green, Reader, & Dyer, 1873.
_____. *The Report of the Armstrong & Whitworth Committee with a Letter Thereon to Earl De Grey and Appendices*. Manchester: Thomson, 1866.
Williams, David. J. *The Birmingham Gun Trade*. Stroud, Gloucestershire, UK: Tempus, 2004.
Willing's (Late May's) British & Irish Press Guide and Advertiser's Directory and Handbook. London: James Willing, Jun., 1891.
Winter, Frank H. *The First Golden Age of Rocketry: Congreve and Hale Rockets of the Nineteenth Century*. Washington: Smithsonian Institution Press, 1990.
Wise, Jennings C. *The Long Arm of Lee: The History of the Artillery of the Army of Northern Virginia*. New York: Oxford University Press, 1959.
Wisser, John P. *The Second Boer War, 1899–1900*. Kansas City, Mo.: Hudson-Kimberly Pub. Co., 1901.
Woodward, Llewellyn. *The Age of Reform: 1815–1870*. Oxford History of England. Oxford: Clarendon Press, 1962.
Wright, Owen. *BSA: The Complete Story*. Ramsbury, Marlborough, Wiltshire, UK: Crowood Press, 1992.
Young, Henry Alfred. *The East India Company's Arsenals & Manufactories*. Oxford, UK: Clarendon Press, 1937. The Naval & Military Press Ltd, Uckfield, East Sussex, 2006.

Journal Articles and Book Sections

Arnold, Ron. "How the EPA's Empire-Building Got in the Way of Its Science." *Washington Examiner*, 01 Jul 2014, http://washingtonexaminer.com/how-the-epas-empire-building-got-in-the-way-of-its-science/article/2550395.
Bailes, Howard. "Technology and Imperialism: A Case Study of the Victorian Army in Africa." *Victorian Studies* 24, no. 1 (1980): 83–104.
Bastable, Marshall J. "From Breechloaders to Monster Guns: Sir William Armstrong and the Invention of Modern Artillery, 1854–1880." *Technology and Culture* 33, no. 2 (1992): 213–47.
Beckett, Ian F. W. "Edward Stanhope at the War Office, 1887–92." *Journal of Strategic Studies* 5, no. 2 (1982): 278–307.
_____. "Victorians at War—War, Technology and Change." *Journal of the Society for Army Historical Research* 81, no. 328 (2003): 330–38.
Best, Geoffrey. "The Militarization of European Society, 1870–1914." In *The Militarization of the Western World*, edited by John R. Gillis, 13–29. New Brunswick: Rutgers University Press, 1989.
Bilby, Joseph G. "Grenade!: The Little-Known Weapon of the Civil War." *America's Civil War*, 2007.
Black, Jeremy. "Military Organisations and Military Change in Historical Perspective." *The Journal of Military History* 62, no. 4 (1998): 871–92.
Brooks, David. "Gladstone and Midlothian: The Background to the First Campaign." *The Scottish Historical Review* 64, no. 177 (1985): 42–67.
Browne, C. Orde. "Our Ordnance Factories." *The Naval Annual* (1896): 167–74.
Chambers, John Whiteclay. "Conference Review Essay: The New Military History: Myth and Reality." *The Journal of Military History* 55, no. 3 (1991): 395–406.
Cole, Juan R. I. "Of Crowds and Empires: Afro-Asian Riots and European Expansion, 1857–1882." *Comparative Studies in Society & History* 31, no. 1 (1989): 106–33.
Dodsworth, Charles. "Low Moor Ironworks Bradford." *Industrial Archeology* 18, no. 2 (1971).
Farrell, Theo. "The Dynamics of British Military Transformation." *International Affairs (Royal Institute of International Affairs 1944-)* 84, no. 4 (2008): 777–807.
Goodlad, Graham. "From Peelite Technocrat to People's William." *Modern History Review* 16, no. 1 (2004): 17–20.

Gordon, Robert J. "Does the "New Economy" Measure up to the Great Inventions of the Past?." *The Journal of Economic Perspectives* 14, no. 4 (2000): 49–74.
Grissom, Adam. "The Future of Military Innovation Studies." *Journal of Strategic Studies* 29, no. 5 (2006/10/01 2006): 905–34.
Grover, Lt. G. E. "Historical Notes on the Royal Arsenal at Woolwich." *Minutes of Proceedings of the Royal Artillery Institute* VI (1870): 231–47.
"Gun Trades," *Birmingham Gun Museum*, 2010–2012, http://www.birminghamgunmuseum.com/Gun_Trades.php.
Hacker, Barton C. "Military Technology and World History: A Reconnaissance." *The History Teacher* 30, no. 4 (1997): 461–87.
Hall, Major D. D. "The Naval Guns in Natal 1899–1902." The South African Military History Society, http://samilitaryhistory.org/vol043dh.html.
"Harpers Ferry National Park: James H. Burton," https://www.nps.gov/hafe/learn/historyculture/james-h-burton.htm.
Hawkins, Angus B. "A Forgotten Crisis: Gladstone and the Politics of Finance During the 1850s." *Victorian Studies* 26 (Spring 1983): 287–321.
Headrick, Daniel R. "The Tools of Imperialism: Technology and the Expansion of European Colonial Empires in the Nineteenth Century." *The Journal of Modern History* 51, no. 2 (1979): 231–63.
"Jacob Snider papers 1840–1873," *The New York Public Library Archives & Manuscripts*, 2017, http://archives.nypl.org/mss/2801.
James, Garry. "The 1886/93 Lebel." *American Rifleman*, October 2014, 67–70.
Kranzberg, Melvin, and Carroll W. Pursell. "The Importance of Technology in Human Affairs," in *Technology in Western Civilization*, edited by Melvin Kranzberg and Carroll W. Pursell, 3–11. New York: Oxford University Press, 1967.
Lambert, Andrew. "Politics, Technology and Policy-Making, 1859–1865: Palmerston, Gladstone and the Management of the Ironclad Naval Race." *Northern Mariner / Le Marin du Nord* 8, no. 3 (1998): 9–38.
Lardas, Mark N. "For Your Information: The First Iron Warship." *Strategy & Tactics*, Jul–Aug 2016: 68–71.
Lipscombe, Nick. "Shrapnel's Shell—a Force Multiplier," in '*...a damned nice thing...the nearest run thing you ever saw in your life...': A Peninsular and Waterloo Anthology*, edited by Andrew Cormack. London: Society for Army Historical Research, 2015, 133–50.
MacDonagh, Oliver. "The Nineteenth-Century Revolution in Government: A Reappraisal." *The Historical Journal* 1, no. 1 (1958): 52–67.
MacLeod, Roy M., and E. Kay Andrews. "Scientific Advice in the War at Sea 1915–1917: The Board of Invention and Research." *Journal of Contemporary History* 6, no. 2 (1971 Apr 01), 3–40.
Marshall, A. "The Invention and Development of the Shrapnel Shell." *The Field Artillery Journal*. Vol. X (1920), 12–16.
Matthew, H. C. G. "Disraeli, Gladstone, and the Politics of Mid-Victorian Budgets." *Historical Journal* 22, no. 3 (1979): 615–44.
Maw, W. H. and J. Dredge, Ed. *Engineering, An Illustrated Weekly Journal*, Vol. XVIV, July—Dec 1887.
Myerly, Scott Hughes. "'The Eye Must Entrap the Mind': Army Spectacle and Paradigm in Nineteenth-Century Britain." *Journal of Social History* 26, no. 1 (1992): 105–31.
Nicholls, David. "The Manchester Peace Conference of 1853." http://www.hssr.mmu.ac.uk/mcrh/files/2013/01/mrhr_05i_nicholls.pdf.
Pattison, Michael. "Scientists, Inventors and the Military in Britain, 1915–19: The Munitions Inventions Department." *Social Studies of Science* 13, no. 4 (1983): 521–68.
Phillips, John A., and Charles Wetherell. "The Great Reform Act of 1832 and the Political Modernization of England." *The American Historical Review* 100, no. 2 (1995): 411–36.
Pryke, Kenneth. "The Woolwich Arsenal and Acadian Mines." *Scientia Canadensis* 34, no. 1 (2011): 25–50.

Putnam, Tim, and Daniel Weinbren. "The Royal Small Arms Factory and Industrial Enfield 1855–1914." *London Journal* 21, no. 1 (1996): 46–63.

Roberts, Steven. "Captain Alexander Blakely RA: 'Original Inventor of Improvements in Cannon and the Greatest Artillerist of the Age.'" 2012. https://www.scribd.com/doc/97550420/Captain-Alexander-Blakely-RA.

Ropohl, Günter. "Philosophy of Socio-Technical Systems" *Society for Philosophy and Technology*, http://scholar.lib.vt.edu/ejournals/SPT/v4_n3html/ROPOHL.html.

Roy, Kaushik. "Equipping Leviathan: Ordnance Factories of British India, 1859–1913." *War in History* 10, no. 4 (2003): 398.

Smithurst, Peter. "The Pattern 1853 Rifled Musket—Genesis." *Arms & Armour* 4, no. 2 (2007): 123–40.

Speier, Hans. "Historical Development of Public Opinion." *American Journal of Sociology* 55, no. 4 (1950): 376–88.

Stoney, Capt. F. S. "A Brief Historical Sketch of Our Rifled Ordnance, from 1858 to 1868." *Minutes of Proceedings of the Royal Artillery Institution*. Vol. VI (1870), 89–122.

Strachan, Hew. "The Early Victorian Army and the Nineteenth-Century Revolution in Government." *The English Historical Review* 95, no. 377 (1980): 782–809.

Tatum, William P. "Challenging the New Military History: The Case of Eighteenth-Century British Army Studies." *History Compass* 5, no. 1 (2007): 72–84.

Taylorson, A. W. F. "The Manufacture and Proof of Firearms," in Hugh B. C. Pollard and Claude Blair, *Pollard's History of Firearms*. New York: Macmillan, 1983.

Trebilcock, Clive. "Legends of the British Armament Industry 1890–1914: A Revision." *Journal of Contemporary History* 5, no. 4 (1970): 3.

Dissertations

Lewis, James H. "The Development of the Royal Small Arms Factory (Enfield Lock) and Its Influence upon Mass Production Technology and Product Design C1820-C1880." PhD, Middlesex University, 1996.

Scales, Robert Hinds, Jr. "Artillery in Small Wars: The Evolution of British Artillery Doctrine, 1860–1914." Ph.D., Duke University, 1976.

Waller, Michael L. "The Conservatism of the British Cavalry and Its Effect on the British Army of WW II." Ph.D., Drew University, 2009.

Index

Abbott, Charles 32–33
Abdullah, Khalifa 215
Abel, Frederick 16, 97, 128, 186
Aberdeen, Lord *see* Hamilton-Gordon, George (Lord Aberdeen)
Abney, Lt. W. de W. 142
Abstracts of Proceedings 8, 10, 12, 14, 16–17, 94–95, 105, 119, 129, 164–165, 168, 173, 200, 205–206, 215, 223, 236
Abyssinian Campaign of 1868 133, 186
accident: at private foundry 24; at Shoeburyness 100, 179–181; HMS *Thunderer see* HMS *Thunderer*; Woolwich RML guns 186–187
accumulator 205
Adargh, Col. John 196
Addison, Captain 104
Addison, H.R. 154
Adjutant-General 42, 187, 195, 196, 209, 211
Admiralty and Horse Guards Gazette 186
Adye, Gen. Sir John Miller 16, 37, 137–139, 141–142, 148, 151, 158–159, 167, 170–173, 207
Afghan War 153
Ahmed, Mohammed 174, 215
HMS *Ajax* 186
Albert, Duke of Connaught 208
Aldershot 206
Alderson, Maj. Gen. Henry 177, 199–201, 206
Alderson, Capt. H.I. 121
Alexander, Victor (Lord Elgin) 227
HMS *Alexandra* 174
Alexandria, shelling of 173–174, 187
Allen, Gunner 179
Alma, battle of 46, 51, 58
American Civil War 1, 18, 61, 66, 102, 113, 165
Anderson, John 75

Anderson, William 184, 213
Andrews, E. Kay 2, 236
Anglesey, Lord *see* Paget, Henry (Lord Anglesey)
Anstruther, Col. Philip 96, 98
Arabi Bey, Colonel Ahmed 174
Arbuthnot, Col. Henry 177–178, 188
Armalite 234
Armit, Robert H. 186–188, 201
armor 1, 48, 109, 113, 134, 159, 182, 224
Armstrong, Maj. Gen. J.W. 148
Armstrong, Sir William 10, 13–14, 102, 107–109, 111–114, 116, 119, 126–129, 133–134, 140, 151–152, 158–159, 161–163, 166–167, 176, 178, 180, 182, 184–187, 195, 198, 202, 224–225, 236
Armstrong, Mitchell & Co. 178, 180, 198, 224
Army Council 17, 220
Arnold-Foster, H.O. 229
Artillery Committee 209–210
Artillery Department 86
artillery: field 15, 24, 66–67, 114, 133, 140, 151, 156, 158–159, 164, 167, 177, 199, 209, 215, 217, 222, 225; quick-firing (or loading) 7, 17, 176, 178, 216, 222, 225, 229
Arundel, Duke of 55
Ashantee 139
Assistant Firemaster 74
Austro-Hungarian Empire 189

Balaklava 58, 71–72, 91
Balfour, Arthur James 226–229
ballistic pendulum 125–126
Baring, Evelyn 174
Baring, Thomas George (Lord Northbrook) 135–137, 142, 183–184, 186
Barnett, Correlli 8, 173
Barrett, H.J. 175
Barry, Patrick 129
Bartley, G.C.T. 199

269

270 Index

Barttelot, Sir Walter 147
bayonet 6, 25, 52, 89, 143, 187, 201, 217
Beaconsfieldism 170, 173
Behenna, Quarter-Master H. 97
Belfast 5
Belgium 154
Bell's Life 45, 70
Beningfield, Thomas 36
Berdan, Gen. Hiram 149
Bessemer, Henry 182, 185
Birmingham 13, 25, 55–57, 89, 120
Birmingham Daily Post 100
Birmingham Journal 26
Birmingham Small Arms Company (BSA) 13, 120
Black, J. (inventor) 154
Black, Jeremy (author) 5
black powder 5, 25, 60 149, 164, 169, 177, 202, 212
Black Week 204, 215, 217–220
Blackwood's Edinburgh Magazine 20, 22, 50–51, 60, 78, 108, 152
Blakely, Cap. Thomas A. 113–114
Blakely gun *see* Blakely, Cap. Thomas A.
Blakely Ordnance Company *see* Blakely, Cap. Thomas A.
Bloemfontein 218
blue water school 4
Board of Admiralty 48, 109, 172
Board of Ordnance 2, 8–10, 14, 20, 23, 26, 31–32, 34, 39, 41–43, 72–74, 76–77, 82, 87–89, 92, 101, 113, 116, 118, 138
Board of Trade 22, 135
Bolton, Lt. Francis 106
Botha, Gen. Louis 219
Boxer, Maj. Gen. Edward M. 16, 27, 34, 38, 62–64, 68–70, 74–77, 86, 96, 99–101, 105, 107, 111–112, 116–117, 120, 123–126, 128–129, 132, 141, 143–145, 149, 156, 166, 187, 234, 236
Boxer cartridge 2, 125, 143–144, 166, 187
Brackenbury, Lt. Gen. Sir Henry 213–214, 217–218, 220–223, 228
Brand, Henry 182–185
breech-loading 10, 122, 151, 168, 184
Brett, Reginald Baliol (Lord Esher) 227–229, 230, 232
Bright, John 41
British Expeditionary Force (BEF) (WW1) 235
Britten, Bashley 89–90
Broad Arrow 201
Broderick, William St. John 212, 225–229
Brown, John *see* John Brown & Co.
Brown Bess *see* Musket, Pattern 1842 ("Brown Bess")

Browning, John 233
Bryant, A. 156
Buller, Gen. Sir Redvers 209–210, 216–221, 229
Burdett-Coutts, William 218–219
Burgoyne, Sir John 58, 60, 96
Burma 177, 204
Burnley Advertiser 84
Burton, James H. 121
Butt, George 73
Byerley, B. 98

Calamita Bay 51
Callow, Edward 82
Calthorpe, Somerset 60
Cambridge, Duke of *see* George, Second Duke of Cambridge
Cammell & Co. 182, 185
Campbell, Sir Frederick A. 138, 140–141, 159, 163, 165–166, 171, 176, 178, 183
Campbell-Bannerman, Henry 193, 210, 229
canister 67, 108
cannon, compressed air 168
Cape Colony 217–218
Cape Town 217
Carbutt, Edward 184–187, 201
carcass 24, 56
Cardwell, Edward 16, 135–136, 147, 166–167, 170, 187, 194, 202, 230
carriage: gun 10, 12, 15, 22, 24, 26, 42, 59, 109, 130, 153–154, 156, 158, 164, 171–173, 178–180, 195, 209–210, 222; Moncrief disappearing 164, 198; mortar 100
carronade 12
cartridge 2–3, 24, 55–57, 99, 120, 123–125, 128, 140, 143–146, 156–157, 165–166, 173, 176, 187, 189–190, 212, 215, 218, 232, 234; Boxer-Henry 145, 147, 149, 156; Hayes's patent combustible 107
case shot *see* canister
catapult 205
Cator, Maj. Gen. William 33, 81–83, 86, 88, 95, 97
Cattell, Thomas 104
cavalry sword, Pattern 1882 190–191
Cavendish, Charles (Lord Chesham) 221
Cavendish, Spencer (Lord Hartington) 109, 183–184, 193, 199, 203–204, 207–211, 213, 226–227
Cecil, Lord Eustace 160, 170, 175
Chartered Company 222
Chassepôt *see* rifle, Chassepôt
Chatham, Lord Pitt, John (Lord Chatham)
Chelmsford Chronicle 79, 118

Index 271

Cheltenham Looker-On 208, 214
Chesney, Col. George 152–153
Chief Inspector of Small Arms 196
Chief of Staff, office of 208, 210
Childers, Hugh 16, 170, 172–173, 188
Chobham 28
Christian News 41
Christie, Samuel 33
Christophe, Louis 154
chronograph 158
chronoscope 127
Churchill, Lord Randolph 193, 201
Ciofti, A. 140
Clarke, Sir George 227
Clarke, Mrs. J. 206
Clerk of Deliveries 23, 42
Clerk of Ordnance 23, 37, 73, 87
Cobden, Richard 41
Colburn's United Service Magazine 30, 36, 53
Coldstream Guards 49
Cole, D.H. 215
Colenso 217, 219, 221, 229
HMS *Collingwood* 186–187
HMS *Colossus* 187
Comité d'Artillerie 108
Commander-in-Chief (C-in-C) 15–16, 21, 39, 42, 55, 85, 87, 136, 169, 192, 194–195, 200, 203, 205, 207–208, 210, 212–213, 219, 225, 228
commandos 217, 220
Commissariat Department 21
Committee of Imperial Defence 228
Committee on Explosives 164, 200
common shell 66
Congreve, Sir William, Jr. 116–118
Congreve, Maj. Gen. William, Sr. 28, 51, 116
Congreve rocket *see* rocket, Congreve
Copeman, Mr. 177
Copenhagen 116
cordite 169, 212, 224–225
Cork Examiner 35, 58
Corrigall, W.E. 176–177
creeping barrage 221, 229
Creusot gun 215, 222
Crimean War 6, 9–10, 12–16, 19–22, 27, 31, 37, 39, 42–44, 48, 57, 61, 71, 78, 93, 107, 115, 117, 119, 126, 132, 137, 149, 184, 192, 203–204, 218, 223
Crookes, Sir William 224
crossbow 168
crusher gauge 127
cycloidal field gun 140

Dacres, Gen. Sir Richard 62, 114–115
The Daily News 41, 79–82, 85, 97, 104, 119, 224

Daw, George H. 128, 144
Dawkins, Clinton E. 226
Dawkins Committee *see* Dawkins, Clinton E.
Denmark 103, 121, 140
Derby Daily Telegraph 192
Derby, Lord *see* Smith-Stanley, Edward (Lord Derby)
de Reyffe *mitrailleuse see mitrailleuse*
Dervish 177, 215
detonator 139
Deutsch, Carl 140
diaphragm shrapnel shell 66–69
Dickson, Col. Sir Alexander 42
Dickson, Gen. Sir Collingwood 173
Director-General of Artillery (DGA) 33, 82–83, 86
Director-General of Ordnance (DGO) 134, 136, 159, 213, 222
Director-General of Ordnance Factories (DGOF) 194, 201, 206, 208, 213–214
Director-General of Ordnance for India 231
Director of Artillery 16, 132
Director of Artillery and Stores 137–138, 171–172, 188
Director of Naval Ordnance (DNO) 138, 200, 231, 236
Director of Stores 105
Disraeli, Benjamin (Lord Benningfield) 134–135, 170, 173, 185
Donnithorne, Lt. E. 141
Dorking, Battle of 149, 152–153
Douglas, Lt. Gen. Robert 38
Dreyse, Johann Nicolaus von 55
Dreyse needle-gun 55, 120–121, 123, 125, 146, 150
Dublin Evening Mail 55, 65, 135
Dundee Advertiser 121
Dundee Courier 87, 221
dynamite 153, 168, 177

Eardley-Wilmot, Col. Frederick 81, 182
East India Company *see* Honorable East India Company
Easton and Anderson 164, 184
Eclipse Patent Safety Horseshoe Syndicate 206
Edgerton, David 11
Edmonds, Brig. Gen. J.E. 18
Egypt 149, 173–175, 177, 187, 195, 215
Ehrhardt, Heinrich 222
Ehrhardt gun 222
Eisenhower, Dwight D. 164
electro-ballistic apparatus *see* Navez, Capt. A.J.A.

Index

Eley, William T. 145
Eley Brothers (ammunition firm) 145, 157, 165–166
Elgin Commission *see* Alexander, Victor (Lord Elgin)
Elgin Courier 85
Ellis, John 10
Elmore's Patent Copper Depositing Company 206
Elphinstone, Lord 170
Elswick Ordnance Company 13, 102, 108, 113, 127, 133, 156, 163–165, 178–179, 186, 202, 223
Enfield (factory) *see* Royal Small Arms Factory (RSAF), Enfield
Enfield (rifle) *see* Rifled Musket, Pattern 1853
Enfield-Martini (rifle) 17, 188–191
Epstein Electric Accumulator Company 205–206
Equipments Committee 225
Esher Committee *see* Brett, Reginald Baliol (Lord Esher)
Evening Telegraph & Star 223
Examiner and London Review 151
HMS *Excellent* 35
Experimental Branch 132, 134–135, 138–142, 144, 153, 156, 168, 175–176, 179

Farrington, Lt. Gen. Sir Anthony 38
The Field 147
field gun *see* artillery, field
Field Howitzer Committee 225
Financial Department, War Office 194, 201–202
Firemaster 74
Fisher, Admiral John 227
Fitzmaurice, Henry (Lord Lansdowne) 212–213, 218–221, 224–225
Fletcher, Lt. Col. H.C. 143, 147
Fletcher, William 98
Fletcher Committee 143–145, 147, 188, 225
Forbes, Archibald 154
Forsyth, Rev. Alexander 52–53
47th Regiment 64
Fox-Strangways, Col. W.A. 179
France 4, 7–8, 14, 40, 43, 45, 47–49, 54, 103–104, 108–109, 122, 133, 146, 149, 152, 155, 158–159, 181, 183, 214, 222, 229, 232, 235
Fraser, R.S. 149, 158–159, 161, 166–167
Freeth, Lt. Col. 181
Friedrich, Crown Prince 144, 150
HMS *Furious* 49
fuze 35, 37–38, 70, 99–100, 108, 169, 179, 187, 200, 220, 225; common 61–62; Free-
burn 62; impact 62; Moorsom 62, 64; time 61–64, 67–68, 112, 141, 181

Gallwey, Lt. Col. T.L 121
Gardner 178
Gascoyne-Cecil, Robert (Lord Salisbury) 169, 175, 187, 193, 197, 201, 210, 212, 214, 219, 225–226
Gatling, Richard 156
Gatling gun *see* machine gun, Gatling
George, Second Duke of Cambridge 15–16, 109, 123, 134, 136, 139, 141, 165, 169, 172, 187–189, 194–197, 199, 201, 203, 208–209, 211–212
George III 20, 24, 29
Germany 7–8, 133, 152, 155, 159, 162, 181, 214, 227
Gibraltar 31, 50, 134
Gladstone, William Ewart 135, 147, 165, 170, 173–175, 183, 185, 187, 193, 210
La Glorie 109, 130
Goddard, Samuel 140
Godfrey, Miss Fanny 206
Goodenough, Lt. Gen. W.H. 209
Goold-Adams, Capt. J.M. 179, 181
Gordon, Charles "Chinese" 175
Gordon, Hampden 9
Gordon-Lennox, Charles (Duke of Richmond) 42
Graddon, Mrs. Ellen 206
Grant, Gen. James Hope 109
Grant, Sir Robert 220
Grantham Journal 137
grape shot 67, 100
Graves, J. Woodcock 98
Great Exhibition of 1851 4, 20, 45, 65
Great Game 40, 188
Great Gun Ring 186
Great Master of Ordnance 23
Greener, William 12, 38, 90, 107, 120
grenade 141; incendiary 139
Grey, Earl Charles 42
Grey, Sir George 73
Grey, Henry George (Lord Howick) 42
gun carriage *see* carriage, gun
gun pendulum 125
guncotton 153
gunpowder 24–25, 35, 41, 52, 55, 59, 61, 66–67, 71, 109, 119, 127–128, 130, 132, 153, 159, 172, 200

Hadden, Maj. Gen. C.F. 231
Haldane, Richard B. 17, 224, 227, 229–230, 232
Hale, William 117–120, 130
Hale rocket *see* rocket, Hale

Index

Hale's Rocket Co. 142
Hamilton, Sir W. 99
Hamilton-Gordon, George (Lord Aberdeen) 72–73, 77–78, 84–85, 91, 135, 219
Hanbury-Tracey, Charles (Lord Sudeley) 169–170
Hardinge, Viscount Charles 196–197
Hardinge, Sir Henry 43, 56–57, 68, 85
Hardy, Gathorne 166, 217
Harries-Jenkins, Gwyn 28
Hartcup, Guy 2
Hartington, Lord *see* Cavendish, Spencer (Lord Hartington)
Hastings, Captain (RN) 35
Hastings, Sir William 73, 88
Haughton, Prof. Samuel 80
Hawes, Sir Benjamin 105
Hay, Sir John 170, 185
Hay, Lt. Gen. Robert 206, 210, 225
Hayes, Capt. J.M. *see* cartridge, Hayes's patent combustible
Headlam, John E. 231
heated shot 50–51
Heavy Battery Committee 225
Henry, Alexander 144–145
Herbert, Sir Sidney 73, 101
Hereford Journal 53
Hereford Times 77
Herts Guardian 77
Heyman, Lt. Col. 140–141
Hicks, William 174
Hime, Lt. Col. Henry 40
Hinton, Maj. F. 140
Hogg, Oliver F.G. 9, 38, 73–74
Hole, Guillaume 32
Home Office 20–21, 119
Honorable East India Company 22, 93
Horse Guards 16, 21, 43, 109, 133
Hotchkiss 178, 202
Houston, A. 177
Howick, Lord *see* Grey, Henry George (Lord Howick)
howitzer 24, 51, 60, 62, 66–67, 69, 103, 126, 215, 218, 225, 234
Hubbell, W.W. 98–100
Hughes, Lt. John 36
Hume, Joseph (MP) 22, 40–41
Hunter, Sergeant 99
Hutchinson, Maj. Gen. 122

Imperial Defence Act 199
Imperial General Staff 230
Imperial Yeomanry 221, 223
India 15, 22, 55, 137–138, 140, 151, 158, 169–170, 172, 195, 209, 218–219, 227–228, 231

Indian Mutiny of 1857 93, 107, 217
Industrial Revolution 1, 7, 11, 15, 17, 44, 70, 92–94
Inspector-General of Fortifications 96, 195, 205, 228
Inspector-General of Ordnance 211–213
Inspector of Artillery 24
Inspector of Machinery, Woolwich *see* Anderson, John
HMS *Invincible* 174
Isandlwana, battle of 168

Jackson, H.K. 98
Jackson, T. 167
J.B. Wheen & Sons 205
Jellicoe, Rear Adm. J.R. 231
J.F. Firth & Sons 182, 185
Jocelyn, Col. Julian 62, 75
John Brown & Co. 164, 182, 185
Joseph, I. 140
Joseph, J.A. 140
Joseph Whitworth and Co. 202

Kellow, John 106
Khartoum, Siege of 175
Kimberly, 217
Kitchener, Gen. Lord Herbert 215
Knapton, Colour-Sergeant G. 99
Knight-Storks, Maj. Gen. Sir Henry 142
Kossuth, Lajos 118
Kourgané Hill 58
Kruger, Paul 215, 217, 226, 234
Krupp 15, 103, 114, 116, 150, 153–154, 158–160, 162, 164, 185, 215, 222

Ladysmith, siege of 217, 219, 221
la Hitte rifling system 103, 108, 113, 150
Lancashire Evening Post 192–193
Lancaster, Charles W. 65, 80
Lancaster gun 63, 65–66, 70, 75, 79–80, 90, 93
Lansdowne, Lord *see* Henry Fitzmaurice (Lord Lansdowne)
Lee, James P. 189
Lee-Enfield rifle *see* magazine rifle, Lee-Enfield
Lee-Metford rifle *see* magazine rifle, Lee-Metford
Leeds Intelligencer 71
Leeds Times 31
Lefroy, Maj. Gen. John Henry 37–38, 81, 86, 130, 134, 149, 159, 189
Leicester Chronicle 58
Le Poidevin, T. 205
Lieutenant-General of Ordnance 23
Lipscombe, Nick 69

Liverpool Daily Post 93
Liverpool Mercury 93
Lloyd, Col. H.H. 140–141
Long, Col. C.J. 217, 221
Long Tom 217
Longridge, James 113
Lovell, George 25, 56
Low Moor Ironworks 74
Lushington, Capt. Stephen 66
lyddite 223–224
Lyon, Col. Francis 179, 181

MacCleod, Roy 2, 236
Maceroni, Col. Frances 53
machine gun 7, 15, 94, 154, 172, 187, 199, 225; Gatling 156–157, 167, 174, 180, 233; Maxim 17, 177–179, 202, 215–216, 225, 233; Nordenfelt 174
Macintosh, J. 140
Mackie Patent Stopper Syndicate 206
Macleod, Sir John 38
Mafeking 217, 224
magazine rifle 17, 188–190, 199, 215–216, 221, 232; Lee-Enfield 190, 215, 219, 232; Lee-Metford 189, 199, 202, 212, 219; Mauser 215–217
Mahdi *see* Ahmed, Mohammed
Mahdist War 177
Maitland, Col. Eardley 181–182, 201
Malakov Tower 60, 66, 92
Mallet, Robert 101, 107
Mallet mortar *see* Mallet, Robert
Manchester Evening News 150
Manchester Ordnance Company 129
Manchester Times 40
Mannlicher, Ferdinand 189
Manufacturing Departments, Royal Arsenal 11, 13, 25–26, 85, 98, 100, 129–103, 137, 139, 164, 167, 171, 175, 192–194, 196, 200–201, 213, 228
Markham, Lt. Gen. Sir Edwin 212
Marshall, Maj. Gen. Sir George 225–226, 228
Martin, J. 130
Martini, Friedrich von 144–145
Martini-Henry *see* Rifle, Martini-Henry
Master-General of Ordnance (MGO) 21, 49, 192, 195, 203, 205, 228, 231
Master of Ordnance 23
Maule, Fox (Lord Panmure) 76–77, 81, 85–88, 90, 95–97, 104, 108, 126, 171
Maule, Lauderdale 73, 76
Maxim, Sir Hiram 177–179, 233
Maxim Gun Company 178
Maxwell, Sir Herbert 56
The Mechanics' Magazine 30

Melville, Alexander 82
Merbury, Nicholas 23
Mercer, Gen. Cavalié 67
Mertz, J.C. 177
Metford, William 189–190
Metropolitan Police 22
Military Department, War Office 194, 198, 212–213, 228
military-industrial complex 12, 164–165, 167
Millar gun *see* shell gun, Millar
Millis, Walter 47
Millward, Col. T.W. 139, 142
Minié, Capt. Claude-Etienne 54–55
Minié rifle, Pattern 1851 *see* Rifled Musket, Pattern 1851
Mitchell, Col. John 54
mitrailleuse 153–156
Mokyr, Joel 93
Moncrieff 164, 198
monkey press 118
Monsell, William 37, 73–74, 76–77, 89
Mont Storm, William 121–123
Montigny, Joseph 154, 156
Moorsom, Lt. William 62
Morley Commission *see* Parker, Albert Edmund (Earl of Morley)
Morning Chronicle 49
Morning Herald 60
Morning Post 30, 50, 55, 57, 91, 133–134, 151–152, 177
Morris Tube & Ammunition Co. 206
mortar (artillery) 33, 46, 58, 60, 62, 69, 101, 107
Mountain Gun Committee 231
Mowatt, Sir Francis 220
Musket, Pattern 1842 ("Brown Bess") 31, 52, 54, 56–57, 87, 152
Mutiny Act 19, 21
muzzle velocity 125, 209
Myerly, Scott Hughes 28

Nairne, Maj. Gen. C.E. 209
Nakhimov, Vice-Admiral Pavel 46–47
Napier, Sir Charles 55–57
Napier, Gen. Sir Robert 133
Napoleon III 3, 103, 152
Napoleonic Wars 5–6, 12, 20, 31, 40, 44, 46, 49, 55, 66, 68–69, 72, 216, 220
Nasmyth, James 27
National Rifle Association (UK) 147
Naval and Military Council 207
Naval Director of Artillery 88
Naval Ordnance Department 209
Navez, Capt. A.J.A. 126
Needham, Joseph 154

Index

Needle-fire rifle *see* Dreyse needle-gun
Newcastle, city of 176, 185, 202
Newcastle, Duke of *see* Pelham-Clinton, Henry (Duke of Newcastle)
Newcastle Journal 90
Nightingale, Florence 72, 78, 218
nitrocellulose 153, 233
Noble, Sir Andrew 127, 186, 224
Noble, Capt. William H. 126, 134–135
Nolan, Maj. John 170
Nolan, Capt. Philip 160
Northbrook, Lord *see* Baring, Thomas George (Lord Northbrook)
Northern Whig 103
Norton, Capt. John 34–36

Odessa, bombardment of 46, 49–51, 61, 119
Omdurman, battle of 215
Orange Free State 225
Order-in-Council 194, 212–213
Ordnance Committee (OC) 17, 168, 171–173, 175, 178, 181, 183, 185, 191, 195, 199–200, 204, 207, 209–210, 213, 222–223, 225, 231
Ordnance Council 132, 136, 138, 145, 147–148, 166, 192, 208
Ordnance Department 9, 21–23, 31–32, 39, 41–42, 53, 74, 81, 85–86, 88, 104, 186–187, 191–192, 194, 209, 213–214, 220, 235
Ordnance Inquiry Commission *see* Stephen Commission
Ordnance Research Board 231
Ordnance Select Committee (OSC) 4, 10, 72, 81, 86, 92–93, 95, 116, 128–129, 131, 170, 191
Osborne, Ralph 147
Ottoman Empire 4

Paget, Henry (Lord Anglesey) 56, 118
Paixhans, Col. Henri-Joseph 46–48, 58
Paixhans gun *see* Paixhans, Col. Henri-Joseph
Pakenham, Thomas 217, 221
Pakington, Sir John 105, 131–137, 166
Pall Mall Gazette 133–134, 136, 150–152, 156, 175, 184, 197, 214
Palliser, Sir William 111–112, 116, 166
Palliser gun *see* Palliser, Sir William
Palmerston, Lord Temple, Henry John (Lord Palmerston)
Panmure, Lord *see* Maule, Fox (Lord Panmure)
parachute flare 38
Parker, Albert Edmund (Earl of Morley) 193, 201, 220

Parker, Geoffrey 5
Parliament 6–7, 14, 19–22, 27–28, 31, 37, 39–42, 44, 70, 78, 85, 104–105, 116, 128, 135–136, 147, 159, 163, 165–166, 169, 174, 182, 192–193, 196, 205, 207, 220, 226, 229, 235
Parsons, Perceval M. 166
Pattison, Michael 2
Patton, Captain A.L. 177–178
Peabody, Henry O. 145
Peel, Maj. Gen. Jonathan 97, 107, 143–144, 167
Pelham-Clinton, Henry (Duke of Newcastle) 32, 37, 73–74, 77–79, 81–86, 88, 90–91, 97
HMS *Penelope* 187
percussion lock 52–53
Phipps, Edmund 23
picric acid 223
Pitt, John (Lord Chatham) 24, 53
Playfair, Dr. Lyon 33
Plumstead Marsh 38, 84
pom-pom gun 216, 225
Porter and Thomas Paint Company 205
Poudre B 189
Pratt & Whitney 178
Preston Chronicle 66
Priestly, E.C. 215
Primrose, Archibald (Lord Rosebery) 210, 212, 227
Prince, sinking of 71
Principal Storekeeper 23, 73
Providence Tool Company 145
Prussia 15–16, 55, 103, 114, 121–122, 125, 140, 146, 149–152, 154–155, 158
Punch 152, 230
Putnam, Tim 13

Quarterly Review 235
Quartermaster-General 195, 211
Queen Victoria 78, 87, 204, 208, 212

Raglan, Lord *see* FitzRoy James Henry Somerset (Lord Raglan)
Ramsden, Sir J. 95
range finder 172, 177
Reform Act 7, 16, 20, 185
Reilly, Brig. Gen. William 181
Remington Arms Co. 145, 149, 189
Rendel, Stuart 182
Research Department, Woolwich 231, 236
Resolute, sinking of 71
HMS *Retribution* 47
Rheinische Metallwaaren und Maschinenfabrik 222
Richards, Westley 121, 128

Index

Ridley, Sir Matthew 193
rifle: Berdan 188; Chassepôt 125, 145–146, 150; Martini-Henry 143–151, 156–157, 165, 167, 188–190, 212, 225
Rifle Committee (1881) 188–189
rifle stopper, Bolton *see* Bolton, Lt. Francis
Rifled Musket, Pattern 1851 55, 57
Rifled Musket, Pattern 1853 56–57, 69, 106, 113, 120–125, 130, 143, 177, 190, 236
rifled muzzle-loader (gun) 102–103, 111–115, 133, 152, 158–159, 164, 168, 195, 202
RML gun *see* rifled muzzle-loader (gun)
Roberts, Field Marshall Sir Frederick 219, 224–225, 228
Roberts, Michael 5
Roberts-Austen, Sir William 224
Robins, Benjamin 125
Robinson, George F.S. (Earl de Grey and Ripon) 121–122, 124, 129
rocket: Congreve 24, 50–51, 74, 117–118, 130; Hale 116–120, 130, 142, 165, 234
Rodman gun 103–104
Roebuck, John Arthur 84–86, 91
Roebuck Committee *see* Roebuck, John A.
Rogers, Clifford 5
Ronalds, Mrs. 206
Rosebury, Lord *see* Primrose, Archibald (Lord Rosebery)
Ross, Lt. Gen. Sir Hew 73, 76, 81, 86, 88
Rotunda *see* Royal Military Repository
round shot 66–67
Royal Armoury Mills, Enfield 25, 56
Royal Arsenal 9, 11–13, 18, 20, 22, 26–27, 30, 33, 37, 74, 82, 97, 103, 118–119, 136–137, 159, 164, 169, 178, 182, 184, 235
Royal Artillery 16, 19, 24, 26–27, 38, 40, 42, 57–58
Royal Artillery Committee 231
Royal Artillery Institution 81
Royal Brass Foundry (RBF) 24, 27, 108
Royal Carriage Department (RCD) 24, 27, 106, 178
Royal Commission on the War in South Africa *see* Alexander, Victor (Lord Elgin)
Royal Cornwall Gazette 100, 125
Royal Dockyards 24
Royal Engineers 24–25, 60, 96, 141–142, 152
Royal Gun Factory (RGF) 104, 108, 138, 141, 158–159, 176, 182–183, 186, 202, 225
Royal Horse Artillery 38, 114, 164, 178
Royal Jubilee Exhibition 176, 180, 198
Royal Laboratory 24, 69–70, 74, 76, 86, 99, 116, 118–120, 139, 142, 157, 167, 179
Royal Military Academy 21, 25, 33, 74, 82, 97, 127
Royal Military Repository 25, 28–30
Royal Navy 1–2, 20, 22, 24, 36–37, 50, 57, 60, 65, 97, 133, 138, 152, 158, 160, 168, 202, 209, 214, 222, 227, 233, 235
Royal Patriotic Fund 72, 79, 81
Royal Powder Mills, Waltham Abbey 25
Royal Small Arms Factory (RSAF), Enfield 13, 89, 120, 124, 145, 148, 176–177
Royal United Services Institute (RUSI) 184–186
Royle, Trevor 92
Rubin, Maj. Eduard 189
Russell, Lord John 73, 85
Russell, William 60, 66, 71, 77–78, 150–151
Russia 4, 6, 20, 37, 40, 44–47, 49–51, 58–61, 63, 66, 69–70, 77–79, 88, 91–93, 103, 113–114, 119, 149, 154, 159–160, 163–164, 169, 175, 177, 184–185, 188, 214
Russo-Japanese War 229

St. George, Maj. Gen. Sir John 124
St. James's Gazette 186
Salisbury, Lord *see* Gascoyne-Cecil Robert (Lord Salisbury)
Saxe-Weimar, Prince of 27
Schleswig-Holstein 121
School of Musketry 57
Scientific Corp 24
Scutari 72, 78
Sebastopol *see* Sevastopol
Second Boer War 1, 8, 14–15, 231, 235
Secretary-at-War 21, 73, 85
Secretary of Experiments 139–140
Secretary of State for War 1, 16, 32, 43, 73, 76, 83, 85, 99, 105–107, 109, 135, 170, 172, 183, 187, 192–193, 195, 197, 200, 207, 210, 224, 229
Secretary of State for War and Colonies 21, 73
Sedan, battle of the 150–152
Sedgwick, Lt. W. 141
segment shell 108
Select Committee of Artillery Officers 32, 72, 81–83, 89
Select Committee on Army and Navy Estimates 193
Sevastopol 46, 58–60, 62–63, 69–71, 77–80, 91–93, 96, 107
Seymour, Admiral F. Beauchamp 174
Sheffield Daily Telegraph 122
shell gun 46–48, 51, 62, 158; Millar 58–59; Paixhans *see* Paixhans, Col. Henri-Joseph
Shellbend Folding Boat Company 206

Shoeburyness 34, 65, 79, 84, 100, 117, 126, 129, 179
Shot furnace, Addison's see Addison, Captain
Showalter, Dennis 10
Shrapnel, Henry 39, 67–68
shrapnel shell 24, 38, 66, 68–69, 74–75, 99, 111, 140, 209, 215
Simpson, Maj. Gen. Sir James 91
Sinope, bombardment of 46–48, 51, 61
Slade, Adolphus 47
Small Arms Committee 55–56, 100, 105, 122, 219, 228, 232
Smith, Merritt Roe 10
Smith, Gen. Phillip 188–189
Smith, T. 140
Smith, William H. 183, 187
Smith-Stanley, Edward (Lord Derby) 78, 84
smokeless powder 7, 153, 189, 224, 233
snap vote 212
Snider, Jacob 123–125, 128, 130, 143–147
Snider rifle see Snider, Jacob
Solferino, battle of 108
Somerset, FitzRoy James Henry (Lord Raglan) 19, 42–43, 49, 58, 60, 72–73, 77, 88, 91, 119, 204, 214
South African Republic 215, 226
Southby, Joseph 36, 38
Soyer, Chef Alexis 72
Special Committee on Horse and Field Artillery Equipments 225
Special Committee on Mitrailleurs 156
Special Committee on Ordnance 166
Special Committee on Propellants and High Explosives 224
Special Committee on Shell Guns 158
Special Committee on the Construction of Ordnance 162
Speier, Hans 7
Spencer, Earl 100
Spencer repeating rifle 121, 123
spherical case shot 67–69; see also "shrapnel shell"
Spiers, Edward 9, 18, 194
Spion Kop 218–219, 221, 224
Spyker, J. 177
Standard 22, 27, 35, 39, 54, 129–130, 135, 146–147, 162, 174, 181, 209
Stanhope, Edward 169, 189, 193–197, 199, 201–203, 207–208, 210, 213–214
Stanley, Frederick 170
The Star 139
Steevens, G.W. 215
Stephen, Sir James 187
Stephen Commission 187–189, 191–193, 195, 199, 203

Sterling Observer 47
Stocqueler, J.H. 108
Strachan, Hew 6
Strutt, John W. (Lord Rayleigh) 224
Sublime Porte 47
Sudan 17, 149, 174–175, 177, 187, 215
Sudeley, Lord see Hanbury-Tracey, Charles (Lord Sudeley)
Suez Canal 173
superintendent 96, 98–99, 108–109, 116, 138–139, 148, 159, 176–177, 179, 181–182, 214, 231
Surveyor-General of Ordnance (SGO) 23, 32, 73, 76, 136–137, 142, 167, 170, 176, 182, 188, 192, 194, 200, 203
Sussex Advertiser 71
Sweetman, John 1, 9
Switzerland 189
Sylvester, Prof. James Joseph 96

Taif 47
Temple, Henry John (Lord Palmerston) 42, 72, 85, 101, 105, 119, 135
Tennent, Sir James Emerson 128
Ter-el-Kebir, battle of 174
HMS *Terrible* 50
Territorial Army 230
Thomas, Lynall 100
HMS *Thunderer* 17, 133, 162–164, 167–171, 181–182
HMS *Tiger* 51
Times 1, 35, 49–50, 60, 66, 71–72, 77–78, 85, 88–89, 101, 107–109, 120–122, 128, 133, 147, 150–152, 171, 179, 184–186, 199, 201, 214, 217–218, 224, 227, 229
Tooley, A.W. 206
torpedo 130, 152–153, 167
Tower of London 31, 40, 52, 54
Transvaal 225
Tugela River 218–219, 221
Tulloch, Capt. T.G. 224
Turpin, Mons. E. 223

United Service Gazette 88, 148
United Service Magazine see *Colburn's United Service Magazine*

Vaal Krantz 218
Vandeleur, Maj. Arthur 104
Vane, Charles William (Marquess of Londonderry) 43
Varna 49, 73, 119
Vauban 50
Vauban, Marquis de 80
Vavasseur and Co. 178
Vickers, Sons & Co. 164, 182, 185–186, 199, 215–216, 225

HMS *Victory* 2
Villiers, George 48
Vimeira, battle of 68
Vivian, Sir Richard 27

W. Kenyon and Sons 206
Walker, Col. Beauchamp 121
Waltham Abbey *see* Royal Powder Mills, Waltham Abbey
War Department *see* War Office
War Office 1, 8–9, 11, 13–17, 31, 40, 73–74, 81–82, 84, 86, 88, 90, 92, 94–95, 97, 99–101, 103–109, 111, 113–114, 119–123, 126, 128–129, 132–136, 138–144, 147–148, 151, 153–154, 157, 164–173, 175–177, 181–184, 186, 188–189, 192–195, 199, 201, 203, 205–209, 211–214, 217, 219, 221, 223–229, 231, 235–236
War Office Act, 1870 136
War Office Board 226
War Office Council 207–208, 213, 226
War Office Reconstitution Committee *see* Brett, Reginald Baliol (Lord Esher)
War Secretary *see* Secretary of State for War
Wardroper, Mrs. A. 206
Warner, Samuel Alfred 31–32
HSM *Warrior* 2
Warry, Armourer-Sergeant 141
water bottle 206
Waterloo, battle of 4, 6, 23, 44, 49, 67, 91, 116, 204
Watson, R.J. 139
Wawro, Geoffrey 154

Weinbren, Daniel 13
Weldless Chain Company 206
Wellington, Duke of 19, 23, 28, 36, 39, 42–45, 56, 192
West Kent Guardian 43
Western Daily Press 164, 201
Weyersberg 191
Wheatstone, Prof. Sir Charles 96, 126
Wheeler, Capt. Owen 9
Whitstable Times 226
Whitworth, Joseph 89–90, 113, 115–116, 128–129, 134, 138, 162, 178, 184–185, 202
Williams, Col. A.H.W. 178
Wimbledon 28, 147, 179
windage 61–62, 79
Wolseley, Sir Garnet 174–175, 187, 195–197, 199, 201, 208–209, 213, 217–218, 220, 225
Woodford, Gen. Sir J.G. 98
Woods, Nicholas 60, 66
Woolwich 9, 13, 21, 23–29, 35, 37, 39, 59, 75, 80–82, 97, 101, 103, 108, 117, 126–127, 134, 138, 140, 158–160, 162, 164, 167, 179, 182–184, 186–187, 194, 196–197, 201, 209, 222, 231, 236
Woolwich Infant 159, 162
Worcester Journal 45, 77
Wyndham, George 221

York Herald 201
Yorkshire Gazette 41, 118
Yturriaga, Col. M. 102

Zulu War 153